Fargo
™
THIS IS A TRUE STORY

NOAH HAWLEY

GRAND CENTRAL PUBLISHING

New York Boston

Cover design by Nick Misani

Grand Central Publishing
Hachette Book Group
1290 Avenue of the Americas, New York, NY 10104
grandcentralpublishing.com
twitter.com/grandcentralpub

First edition: October 2019

Grand Central Publishing is a division of Hachette Book Group, Inc. The Grand Central Publishing name and logo is a trademark of Hachette Book Group, Inc.

The publisher is not responsible for websites (or their content) that are not owned by the publisher.

The Hachette Speakers Bureau provides a wide range of authors for speaking events. To findoutmore,goto www.hachettespeakersbureau.com or call (866) 376-6591.

All photos by Chris Large except photos on the following pages by Dana Gonzales: 2, 87, 149, 205, 249, 257, 263, 277, 286, 298, 411, 426, 427

Print book interior design by Ashley Prine, Tandem Books

Library of Congress Cataloging-in-Publication Data

Name: Hawley, Noah, author.
Title: Fargo : this is a true story / Noah Hawley.
Description: First edition. | New York : Grand Central Publishing, 2019.
Identifiers:LCCN2019000523 | ISBN9781538731307(paperoverboard) | ISBN 9781538731314 (ebook)
Subjects: LCSH: Fargo (Television program)
Classification:LCCPN1992.77.F315H392019 | DDC791.45/72—dc23
LC record available at https://lccn.loc.gov/2019000523

ISBNs: 978-1-5387-3130-7 (hardcover); 978-1-5387-3131-4 (ebook)

Printed in China

Imago

10 9 8 7 6 5 4 3 2 1

For Joel and Ethan.

Those are some giant shoulders.

CONTENTS

FX Orders Its First Limited Series—*Fargo*

Novelist/Writer Noah Hawley Adapted the Series for Television from the Award-Winning and Acclaimed Feature Film of the Same Title—Noah Hawley, Joel and Ethan Coen, and Warren Littlefield to Serve as Executive Producers—FX Productions and MGM Television to Produce Ten Episodes—Production Begins This Fall and the Series Is Slated to Premiere in Spring of 2014

NEW YORK (March 28, 2013)—FX has ordered its first limited series, *Fargo*, from MGM Television. The series is adapted by novelist/writer Noah Hawley from the award-winning film of the same title. Warren Littlefield and Joel and Ethan Coen will serve as Executive Producers on the series, it was announced today by John Landgraf, President and General Manager, FX Networks.

FX's *Fargo*, a ten-episode limited series inspired by the film, will follow an all-new "true crime" story. The series will follow a new case and new characters, all entrenched in the trademark humor, murder, and "Minnesota nice" that has made the film an enduring classic.

"For years, people have tried to adapt this Academy Award®–winning gem into a TV series with no success," said Landgraf. "I have always loved *Fargo* and I was skeptical about this as a series, but Noah Hawley's script made me a believer. This script is so good and so true to the tone of the original movie."

"MGM Television is thrilled to be producing a fresh and exciting re-envisioning of *Fargo* for FX's television audience. With the stellar creative team lead [*sic*] by Noah Hawley, Joel and Ethan Coen, and Warren Littlefield, we are re-imagining one of the most iconic titles from MGM's rich film library," said Roma Khanna, President of Television and Digital, MGM. "FX is the perfect partner for the series and we look forward to working with them on our shared vision of captivating audiences within the unique world of *Fargo*."

Written by Noah Hawley (*The Unusuals, My Generation*) and executive produced by Hawley, Joel and Ethan Coen (*True Grit, A Serious Man, No Country for Old Men*), and Warren Littlefield (*The Unusuals*), *Fargo* is produced by MGM Television and FX Productions. MGM Television will be the lead studio and will handle worldwide distribution of the series outside of the U.S. and Canada.

Fargo, released in 1996, was nominated for seven Academy Awards® and won for Best Original Screenplay for Joel and Ethan Coen and Best Actress for Frances McDormand. It was named as one of the 100 Greatest American Movies by the American Film Institute. A wildly unique blend of comedy, drama and thriller, the film starred Frances McDormand as a pregnant Minnesota police chief pursuing two bumbling criminals hired by a car salesman to kidnap his wife.

FARGO

The Original Pitch Document

by Noah Hawley

for

Littlefield Company

MGM

F X

THE CHALLENGE

To create a TV version of *Fargo* without Marge, or any of the characters from the film. Can we create a parallel version, maintaining the same elements—similar characters, structure, tone, theme—without simply xeroxing the movie? Without making the MARGE GUNDERSON show?

The answer is yes. But before I tell you how, I want to make three points.

FIRST: So the movie is called *Fargo*, but most of it actually takes place in Minnesota. That's because *Fargo*, for the Coens, is more than just a place. It's a state of mind. A metaphor for the edge of the world. The place where the sedate innocence of unremarkable American life collides with the lawless frontier. Mall food and frozen tundra. Pee Wee hockey games on thin ice.

But it's more than that. *Fargo* is the people we long to be (simple, kind, neighborly) versus the people we fear the most (hardened, vicious, unfeeling).

That said, most of the people who commit crimes in *Fargo* are harmless in a modern sense. They have relatable problems that they try to solve with crime. Their mistakes are human mistakes. Like BILL MACY, a buttoned-down man in the middle of a financial crisis who makes a colossal error, who thinks he can control a situation he is completely clueless about. A man who enters the Wild Frontier without realizing he's left his own safe world behind.

But even within the Frontier there are gradations of evil. There is STEVE BUSCEMI, a bad man, petty, violent, but ultimately human. A criminal. And then there is PETER STORMARE, who is a monster. A being of pure evil—ultimately unknowable.

This is a recurring idea with the Coens—Look at NIC CAGE in *Raising Arizona* versus the LONE BIKER OF THE APOCALYPSE. Look at JOSH BROLIN in *No Country for Old Men* versus ANTON CHIGURH. There are hard men, criminals, and then there are demons.

And while Police Chiefs MARGE GUNDERSON from *Fargo* and TOMMY LEE JONES from *No Country for Old Men* have plenty of experience dealing with bad men like Buscemi, they have no idea how to handle a monster. He's the devil, and his very existence threatens the foundation of everything they believe.

Because innocence can't survive in a world of demons. There's a reason the majority of the violence in the movie happens outside Marge's field of vision. Because even brave, honest Marge would become jaded and hard if she spent too long working the kinds of cases that the movie explores.

That's an important idea, and I'll come back to it in a minute.

The SECOND point I want to make is that the movie isn't a detective story. It's not a whodunit about a cop solving a mystery. It's a crime story that focuses on all the players equally—BILL MACY, STEVE BUSCEMI, FRANCES MCDORMAND—a crime story where the truth of what happened, and who did what, is clear from the beginning. Watch it again. Marge is really only in a third of the film. You don't see her until thirty minutes in. We remember her as the star, but she's an element that's been exaggerated by our memories. *Fargo* is not her story. It's the story of what happened. The truth.

Which brings me to my THIRD point: truth. The movie starts with the following text:

> THIS IS A TRUE STORY. The events depicted in this film took place in Minnesota in 1987. At the request of the survivors, the names have been changed. Out of respect for the dead, the rest has been told exactly as it occurred.

Which is, of course, a lie. The movie isn't true. It's an invention. The Coens say it's true because it gives them license to tell a story that unfolds in a different way than traditionally scripted crime. To explore the objective, truth-is-stranger-than-fiction feel that makes the movie so unique and powerful.

But what it really is, is a fable. An allegory. A morality play, where the idiosyncrasies of the script make it feel true—a botched kidnapping that ends with a dead state trooper, a woman in a hood running through the snow, a late night phone call from an old high school classmate who turns out to be crazy.

Which means that for us, truth—that hindsight-is-20/20, messy reality of unexpected detours and details—is critical to making this show as good as the movie.

Which means the wrong way to make a television show out of *Fargo* is to turn it into *Columbo* or *Picket Fences*. An honest, lovable cop battling a dark tide week after week. That's the network television version. But this is FX. We need to aim higher.

Plus, as I mentioned before, the kinds of cases we'll explore in *Fargo* become toxic over time. Marge (or her surrogate) might survive physically, but the qualities we love about her, her common sense, her unspoiled heart, would be lost.

So what are we left with? Cop shows always have a hero, a detective, and their satellites. Family, coroners, judges, prosecutors. And every week the hero solves cases.

But remember, *Fargo*, the movie, isn't a cop show. It's a crime story, an allegory about what happens when a civilized man puts on his mukluks and tromps out into the wilderness. It's a dark, 3-D look at the mess he makes and the demon he brings back.

Over the course of multiple seasons, what we are building, you see, is a portrait of Middle America. The best of us versus the worst of us. The goodness of simple, commonsense people, versus the evil of the lawless frontier.

Yes, we have problems. But look who's solving them.

Thanks for listening.

Noah

Fargo

SEASON 1

THIS IS A TRUE STORY

2014 EMMY® AWARDS

Outstanding Miniseries

Colin Bucksey—Outstanding Directing for a Miniseries, Movie, or Dramatic Special ("Buridan's Ass")

2014 EMMY® NOMINATION HIGHLIGHTS

Martin Freeman—Outstanding Lead Actor in a Miniseries or Movie

Billy Bob Thornton—Outstanding Lead Actor in a Miniseries or Movie

Colin Hanks—Outstanding Supporting Actor in a Miniseries or Movie

Allison Tolman—Outstanding Supporting Actress in a Miniseries or Movie

Adam Bernstein—Outstanding Directing for a Miniseries, Movie, or Dramatic Special ("The Crocodile's Dilemma")

Noah Hawley—Outstanding Writing for a Miniseries, Movie, or Dramatic Special ("The Crocodile's Dilemma")

2015 GOLDEN GLOBE AWARDS

Best Limited Series or Motion Picture Made for Television

Billy Bob Thornton—Best Performance by an Actor in a Limited Series or Motion Picture Made for Television

2015 GOLDEN GLOBE NOMINATIONS

Martin Freeman—Best Performance by an Actor in a Limited Series or Motion Picture Made for Television

Allison Tolman—Best Performance by an Actress in a Limited Series or Motion Picture Made for Television

Colin Hanks—Best Performance by an Actor in a Supporting Role in a Limited Series or Motion Picture Made for Television

in CONVERSATION with DANA GONZALES *(Director of Photography, S 1–3)*

NOAH: I learned pretty quickly [that] you can't ask Joel and Ethan, "How do you make a Coen brothers movie?" But I knew from enough research that they had a camera approach that they saw as much more documentary. The camera is never part of the story—it's faithfully recording what's going on. I think we stuck to that mostly in the first season.

DANA: For season 1, I like to think that the storytelling evolved a little differently from the first two episodes to three through ten. We were finding something you, John [Cameron, executive producer], and I were happy with. "How do we tell this ten-hour story a little differently, still serving the Coen brothers?" I think that's what happened, and I think that seasons 2 and 3 were evolutions of that.

Episode 1

The Crocodile's Dilemma

The following text fades in over black:

This is a true story. The events depicted took place in Minnesota in 2006. At the request of the survivors, the names have been changed. Out of respect for the dead, the rest has been told exactly as it occurred.

FLARE TO WHITE:

EXT. TWO-LANE HIGHWAY. RURAL MINNESOTA—DUSK

The white becomes snowfall, a blizzard. Through it we can make out a two-lane road. A car emerges from the snow—rust-spotted—coming towards us.

CUT TO:

INT. CAR (TRAVELING)—NIGHT

LORNE MALVO, age unknown, birth place unknown, sits behind the wheel, his breath white with frost. If he minds he doesn't show it. He reaches over, turns off the radio.

There's an OLD BLACK BRIEFCASE on the seat next to him. We become aware of THUMPING coming from inside the trunk. As if someone is in there who doesn't want to be. Malvo ignores it.

A DEER

appears in the road ahead of him. Malvo turns too late, HITS it. The CAR SKIDS off the road, ROLLS twice before coming to rest on its wheels.

Beat. The TRUNK swings open. A MAN emerges from the trunk wearing only underwear. He is stunned from the crash, but sound enough of mind to know this is his chance. As we watch he LOPES off through waist-deep snow, making for the tree line.

Beat. The driver's door opens. Slowly, Malvo climbs out. His head is bleeding where it hit the steering wheel, and it's clear he bruised or broke some ribs. He stands unsteadily in the snow, getting his bearings.

ANGLE ON THE OTHER MAN

loping off through the snow. Malvo could catch him if he tried, but he makes no attempt. Instead he walks into the center of the road where the deer lies on its side, struggling to get up. Three of its four legs are broken, but still it fights for life. Malvo stands over the wounded animal, looking down.

      CLOSE UP ON THE DEER

its eyes wild, blood bubbles foaming from its nose and mouth, mortally wounded.

      CLOSE UP ON MALVO

studying its eyes. What does he see in there?

We begin to hear <u>a strange throbbing, churning sound</u>, half animal, half machine.

      CUT TO:

      A WASHING MACHINE

Working hard, chugging, lurching, unbalanced. The noise we heard is coming from here. We are in . . .

INT. BASEMENT. LESTER'S HOUSE. BEMIDJI, MINNESOTA—DAY

As we watch the washer struggle, we RISE UP through the ceiling into . . .

INT. KITCHEN. LESTER'S HOUSE. BEMIDJI, MINNESOTA—DAY

LESTER NYGAARD, 40, home for lunch, sits at the kitchen table.
Lester is the kind of guy who apologizes when you step on his
foot. His wife, PEARL, 39, is heating up a can of soup at the
stove. We get the sense she has been talking nonstop since
Lester walked in the door.

                    PEARL
     — Saturday. I said we'd bring a Jell-O salad, but Kitty said
     meatloaf, so —

The surging, churning sound is louder now, coming from under
the floor. Nygaard listens to it, both fascinated and slightly
disturbed.

                    PEARL (CONT'D)
                 (exasperated)
     Hon?

                    LESTER
                 (snaps out of it)
     What's that, hon?

Pearl brings the pot over, ladles tomato soup into his bowl.

                    PEARL
                 (exasperated)
     I said it's Gordo's birthday Saturday. We're supposed ta be
     at your brother's at four. With meatloaf.

                    LESTER
                 (beat, listening)
     It sounds different today, don't ya think? Angry.

                    PEARL
     I'm washing towels. That's the towel sound.

She sits. They eat.

                    PEARL (CONT'D)
     Kitty says they just got one of those fancy European all
     in ones. Says it washes and dries. One machine. Can you
     believe that?

                    LESTER
     I bet that set them back a penny.

                    PEARL
     He can afford it, your brother. Kitty said he just got a big
     promotion. After only working there a year.

We can tell his brother is a touchy subject for Lester.

PEARL (CONT'D)
Kitty said they got one of those new surround-sound systems
too.
                    (Lester eats)
Guess I married the wrong Nygaard. That's what I said. We
had a good laugh.

                    LESTER
It's just slow now. At the shop.

                    PEARL
Oh, hon. That's what you always say. Slow.

Beat. They eat. Lester wipes his mouth, stands.

                    LESTER
Well, better get back to it.

                    PEARL
You make your own wins. That's what Kitty said Chazz told
her. Salesmen make their own wins. You gotta try harder,
hon. Smile, for Pete sake. Maybe wear a nicer tie.

                    LESTER
                    (looks down)
You gave me this tie.

                         PEARL
          Well, if you were a better salesman, I'da bought you a
          nicer tie.

The sound of the washing machine takes on a new urgency.

                         PEARL (CONT'D)
          At least take a look. I keep thinking maybe it's the
          settings. Kitty said Chazz fixes things around the house
          all the time. Says he took the toaster apart over the
          weekend. Good as new now. Browns to beat the band.

Lester's jaw is tight. He opens the door to the basement.

               CUT TO:

INT. BASEMENT. LESTER'S HOUSE—DAY

Lester stands at the bottom of the stairs. The washing machine
is acting like a caged animal, roaring and bucking. Lester
stares at it, hypnotized. We get the sense he's looking at his
own trapped heart.

               CUT TO:

INT. BO MUNK INSURANCE SHOP. BEMIDJI, MINNESOTA—DAY

Lester Nygaard sits across from a YOUNG COUPLE.

                         LESTER
          So, that's — like I said, there's two kinds of policies you
          should be thinking about. You got your Whole Life and your
          Whole Life Plus. Which is — has all the benefits of Whole
          Life — plus a heck of a lot more.

                         YOUNG MAN
          We just came in to get Charline on my health care.

                         YOUNG WOMAN
          On account of I'm having a baby.

                         YOUNG MAN
          Ya. A boy we're hoping.

                         YOUNG WOMAN
          Or a little girl. I'd just about hug the pants off a little
          girl.

                         LESTER
          Oh ya? Even more reason to — all the more —

He digs through his desk, pulls out a brochure.

                    LESTER (CONT'D)
— because, I mean, what happens if you have an accident at
your job?

                    YOUNG MAN
I work at the library.

                    LESTER
Well, what if you're in a car crash and you go out the
windshield? Or say you're on a ladder cleaning out the
gutters and fall off the darn thing and break your neck.
These things happen every day. People fall asleep smoking in
bed and burn ta death. What I'm saying is the morgue is full
of guys thought they didn't need life insurance.

The young couple stares at him, horrified.

                    LESTER (CONT'D)
                    (losing steam)
— for peace of mind, I'm saying. To know that your little
boy —

                    YOUNG MAN
Or girl.

                    LESTER
Right. Or little girl is taken care of.

                    YOUNG WOMAN
                    (beat, creeped out)
We're supposed to be at my mom's by four.

                    YOUNG MAN
Ya, so we're gonna —

They stand, head for the door.

                    LESTER
Oh. Okay, well — at least let me give you a brochure. Or I
got these nifty pens. Look at that. Black and red ink. You
just click the — Okay, well, come on back if you —

The couple exits. Nygaard sits for a moment.

                    LESTER (CONT'D)
Well, heck.

     CUT TO:

EXT. APPLIANCE SHOP. BEMIDJI, MINNESOTA—DAY

Lester stands outside the store, staring in through the plate
glass window at a brand-new washer-dryer set. He's wearing a
puffy orange coat and a wool hat with ear flaps.

SAM HESS, 40, approaches with his TWIN SONS, MICKEY and MOE,
15. Hess is a big guy, intimidating. His boys look like two
identical blocking sleds.

                    MOE
          Dad said I could get pie for lunch.

                    MICKEY
                (snickers)
          Ya. Hair pie.

Sam WACKS Mickey in the back of the head. Moe cracks up.
Oblivious, Lester stares at the washer-dryer. Walking by, Hess
recognizes him.

                    SAM HESS
                (stopping)
          Will ya look at that.

                    MICKEY
          What is it, Dad?

                    MOE
          Ya, Dad. What is it?

Lester turns, sees Hess. It takes a moment for him to recognize
him, but when he does he looks nervous.

                    LESTER
          Oh, hey there, Sam.

                    SAM HESS
          That, boys, is a black man.

                    MICKEY
          He don't look black, Dad.

                    MOE
          Ya, Dad. He don't look black. More like a big pumpkin.

                    MICKEY
                (grinning)
          Ya, a stupid big pumpkin.

Hess smiles at Lester, like a shark.

                    SAM HESS
          Lester *Niggered*.

                    LESTER
          Come on now, Sam. It's — well, it's Nygaard. Same as in high
          school.

                    MICKEY
You went to high school with the black man, Dad?

                    MOE
Ya, Dad, did you —

                    SAM HESS
Shut up. How you been, Lester?

                    LESTER
Oh ya. Real good.

                    SAM HESS
Ya, me too. Truckin company's doin super. Got rigs all over
the Great Lakes. Just bought a summerhouse up Bear Island.
It's pretty sweet.
                    (to his sons)
Hey, you remember I told you the story of the boy I put in
the oil drum and rolled onto the highway?

                    MICKEY
Is that him, Dad?

                    MOE
Ya, Dad. Is that him?

                    SAM HESS
Oh you betcha. Good old Lester pencil dick. Say, Lester.
What was the name of that girl you went with in high school?
The curvy one?

                    LESTER
Pearl.

                    SAM HESS
Ya, Pearl. What a rack on that girl.

                    MOE
                    (to Mickey)
Dad's saying she had big titties.

                    MICKEY
I know what rack means, ya fairy.

Hess smacks both boys in the back of the head.

                    MICKEY (CONT'D)
Ow.

                    MOE
Ya, Dad. Ow.

SAM HESS
(to Lester)
You know she gave me a tug once. Homecoming, senior year.
Had these nice fat hands. Real soft. Let me feel up her tits
while she did it.

LESTER
We're married now. Going on eighteen years.

Sam is taken off guard by this. The kids crack up.

MICKEY
Oh, Dad. That's embarrassing.

MOE
Ya, Dad. Super embarrassing.

Hess's eyes narrow. His face is burning and he doesn't like the
feeling.

SAM HESS
Eighteen years, huh? That's something.
(beat)
Never knew what she saw in you, really.

LESTER
Oh, well —

SAM HESS
I mean, help me out. Is it your stupid pencil dick or your
little rat face?

Lester can tell he's in danger.

LESTER
Ya. Well. I should get back to it.

But Hess won't let him go.

SAM HESS
(to his sons)
Did I ever tell you how I used to beat this little guy up in
high school?

Sam manages to get in front of Lester.

SAM HESS (CONT'D)
I'd write my name on my fist in Sharpie fore I punched him,
so everyone would know who did it.

MICKEY
That's a good one, Dad.

                              MOE
          Ya, Dad. A real good one.

Hess lifts his fist, shows Lester.

                            SAM HESS
          Remember?

                            LESTER
          Ha. Ya. That was — a long time ago.

Slowly, Hess moves his fist right in front of Lester's face,
enjoying his fear. Lester stands there, humiliated, not knowing
what to do. Hating his helplessness, his base cowardice.

Then Hess drops his fist and smiles to show it's all just a big
joke. Lester starts to relax. Then HESS FAKES A PUNCH. Lester
panics, turns, and RUNS FACE-FIRST into the PLATE GLASS WINDOW of
the appliance store—CRACK! He falls to the ground, lies on his
back.

                            MICKEY
          Jeez, Dad. His face is pretty messed up.

                              MOE
          Ya, Dad. It's real messed up.

              CLOSE UP OF LESTER'S FACE

as he lies there, his nose broken and bleeding, staring up at
the sky. Beat. We PULL OUT and discover we are now in . . .

INT. WAITING ROOM. HOSPITAL. BEMIDJI, MN—DAY

Lester, now sitting, lifts an ice pack to his nose. He is on a
bench in the emergency room. And just as we realize this, we
see that sitting next to him is LORNE MALVO, a nasty bruise and
cut on his forehead from the car crash. The briefcase is at his
feet.

Lester lowers the ice pack. Beat.

                            LESTER
          What a day.
                       (to a passing nurse)
          Excuse me, miss. Do ya think — will it be much longer? This
          thing hurts like the dickens.

                         SUE ROUNDTREE
          We'll call your name.

                            LESTER
          Ya, but I been here an hour already.

SUE ROUNDTREE
We'll call your name.

She walks away. Lester opens a soda, tries to drink, but it hurts too much. He puts the soda down.

MALVO
Could I have a sip?

Lester turns. Malvo is looking at him.

LESTER
Heck, take the whole can. I can't drink the darn thing without a straw.

He hands Malvo the soda. Malvo tips it back and drains it. Lester tries not to stare at Malvo's head injury.

MALVO
Obliged.
                    (puts down the can)
What happened to your nose?

LESTER
Oh, well. That was just — a misunderstanding.

MALVO
Is that you misunderstanding the other fella, or him misunderstanding you?

                           LESTER
Pardon?

                           MALVO
Who misunderstood whom?

                           LESTER
No. What I'm saying is — it's not good to dwell on these
things.

                           MALVO
Why?

                           LESTER
Pardon?

                           MALVO
Why is it not good to dwell on things? Especially things
that put you in the hospital.

Beat. Lester doesn't know what to say. Malvo watches him.

                           LESTER
It was — I was outnumbered if you wanna know the truth.
Three to one. Big guys too. Well, one of them. The other two
were just kids. But big fer their age.
                    (beat, getting worked up)
Ya know — if I was any kind of man — I'da shown that Sam
what's what.

                           MALVO
Sam?

                           LESTER
Hess. He was a bully in high school and he's a bully now.

                           MALVO
So why didn't you?
                    (off Lester)
Show him what's what.

                           LESTER
Well, his, uh, he had his sons with him, and —

                           MALVO
So you let a man beat you in front of his children. To send
them a message.

                           LESTER
No. That's not —
                    (frustrated)
Heck. Just — heck.

                    MALVO
In my experience, you let a man break your nose, next time
he'll try to break your spine.

                    LESTER
Sam? No way. I mean, I don't think. It's just — I guess I
embarrassed him in front of his boys.

                    MALVO
You embarrassed him.

                    LESTER
By — he was telling me about a time when he and my wife —
see, they —
                    (gesturing)
— but he didn't know she was my wife, is the thing. And when
I told him —

                    MALVO
A man slept with your wife, and you're worried you
embarrassed <u>him</u>.

                    LESTER
Not slept with — they didn't — he said it was just — she has
soft hands, see? — and I —

                    MALVO
Mister, we're not friends. Maybe one day we will be. But
I gotta say, if that was me — in your position — I woulda
killed that man.

                    LESTER
Well, now. Hold on.

                    MALVO
You said he bullied you in high school?

                    LESTER
                    (reluctantly)
Four years. Gave me an ulcer.
                    (humiliated)
One time he put me in an oil barrel and rolled me in the
road.

                    MALVO
Seriously?
                    (Lester nods)
And now he tells you he had relations with your wife. Then
bullies you again in front of his children. Friend, this is
not a man who deserves to draw breath.

Beat. All the humiliation and pain Lester has suffered threatens
to bubble up.

                              LESTER
          Ya. Okay. But here's the thing —

                              MALVO
          No. That _is_ the thing.

                              LESTER
                              (beat)
          Well — heck — I mean, okay. Okay. But what am I supposed ta
          do?
                              (beat)
          Heck, you're so sure about it, maybe you should just kill
          him for me.

                              MALVO
                              (beat)
          Are you asking me to kill this man?

                              LESTER
          No. That was — I was joking.

The nurse walks up.

                           SUE ROUNDTREE
          Mr. Nygaard.

Lester looks at Malvo.

                              LESTER
          Ya, that's — just a second.
                              (to Malvo)
          We're just two fellas talking, right? Just blowing off
          steam?

Malvo studies him.

                           SUE ROUNDTREE
          Sir, it's real busy —

                              LESTER
          Ya, like I said — just a second.

                              MALVO
          Sam. Hess.

                              LESTER
          No. Now wait just a second — that's not —

                           SUE ROUNDTREE
          Sir!

But Lester is focused on Malvo, like a mouse hypnotized by a
snake.

MALVO
One word. Yes. Or no.

Lester looks at him, feeling a strange tickle down his spine.
All he has to do is say no, but he doesn't.

SUE ROUNDTREE
Sir, I'm gonna give your spot to —

LESTER
(stands)
Ya, I'm — I'm coming for Pete sake.

He shares one last moment of eye contact with Malvo, then grabs
his coat and hat, follows the nurse to an exam room. Malvo
watches him go.

CUT TO:

EXT. TWO-LANE HIGHWAY. BEMIDJI, MN—DAY

The site of Malvo's accident. The car is still there, its trunk
now closed. A POLICE CAR is parked nearby, lights flashing.
DEPUTY MOLLY SOLVERSON, 29, stands behind the wreck, kicking her
feet to stay warm.

A POLICE BRONCO pulls up. Police Chief VERN THURMAN (40s) gets
out. Molly comes over to greet him.

MOLLY
Cold enough for ya, Chief?

VERN
Supposed to get down to negative ten later.

MOLLY
Heard that. Don't much like the sound of *negative*.

VERN
(deadpan)
Thought I might strip down to my shorts. Work on my tan.
(nods)
So what's this here then?

Molly shows him the scene.

MOLLY
Chief, I arrived on the scene at thirteen hundred hours,
found this ninety-three New Yorker. Looks like she fled the
road and crashed the fence. I found a set of footprints
leading away from the car. Possible our driver, injured,
got confused, wandered into the woods. I was about to
investigate.

Vern circles the car, crouches at the front grille.

                         VERN
      Blood here. Hair too.

                         MOLLY
      Saw that. I was thinkin maybe a deer, but couldn't find the
      evidence.

Vern walks out into the road, looking for something. Fresh snow
covers everything. Vern does some mental calculations, picks a
spot, and kicks the snow away.

                         VERN
      Here it is.

Molly looks down, sees the under layer of snow is pink with
blood.

                         MOLLY
      Son of a gun.

Vern walks back to the car. The driver's door is open.

                         VERN
                      (leans in)
      Blood on the steering wheel. Driver coulda hit his head.

                         MOLLY
      Or her head.

Vern hears something, straightens. It comes again, louder.
THUMPING. From the trunk.

                         VERN
      You check the trunk?

                         MOLLY
      No, sir.

The thumping continues. Vern and Molly approach the trunk.

          ANGLE ON THE TRUNK

Something is inside, banging.

          VERN

thinks about opening it, the pros and cons.

                    MOLLY (CONT'D)
      Should I unholster my sidearm?

                              VERN
          Not unless you think there's a ninja inside.

He reaches down and pops the trunk. It swings open, revealing:

          THE DEER

Still alive, flailing weakly.

          VERN AND MOLLY

look at the deer.

                              MOLLY
          Huh.

Vern takes out his gun, puts the deer out of its misery. They
stand for a moment in silence, breath misty.

                              MOLLY (CONT'D)
                         (beat)
          So — wanna take a look at those footprints then?

                              VERN
          Sounds good.

          CUT TO:

EXT. WOODS. BEMIDJI, MINNESOTA—DAY

Vern and Molly trudge through the deep snow.

                              MOLLY
                         (beat, walking)
          How's Ida?

                              VERN
          Any day now.

                              MOLLY
          You got a name picked out?

                              VERN
          I can't even get that woman to decide what color to paint
          the nursery.

                              MOLLY
                         (beat, walking)
          Can't believe I missed that deer in the trunk.

                              VERN
          Don't take it hard. I been doin this a long time. Never
          checked for a deer in the trunk.
                         (beat)

Or any wildlife.

Molly sees something.

                    MOLLY
    Chief.

He looks where her flashlight is pointed. There, sitting in the
snow, is A MAN IN HIS UNDERWEAR, frozen to death.

                    VERN
                    (beat)
    Okay.

         CUT TO:

INT. THURMAN HOUSE. BEMIDJI, MINNESOTA—DAY

Vern comes home. He hangs his heavy coat on the wall.

                    VERN
    Hiya, hon.

                    IDA (O.S.)
    In the kitchen.

                    CUT TO:

INT. KITCHEN. THURMAN HOUSE—CONTINUOUS

Vern enters, kisses his wife. IDA (30s) is eight months
pregnant.

                         VERN
    Something smells good.

                         IDA
                  (touches her belly)
    Your boy wanted a hamburger.

                         VERN
    Sounds like my boy.

Vern goes into the . . .

          BEDROOM

Takes off his holster, locks his gun in the safe. Heading back
to the kitchen, Vern stops outside the BABY'S ROOM. All the
furniture—crib, changing table, etc.—has been pushed to the
center. We see a tarp, paint trays, and clean rollers on the
floor.

                    CUT TO:

INT. KITCHEN. THURMAN HOUSE—DAY

Vern and Ida eat dinner. Vern has a beer.

                         VERN
                        (beat)
          Molly found a wreck out on seventy-one. Looks like the
          driver tried ta head out on foot, but got lost, froze ta
          death in the woods.

                         IDA
          Oh my.

                         VERN
          Ya. Funny thing is, the fella was just wearing underpants.

                         IDA
          That so?

                         VERN
          Ya. No ID. Nothin. Couldn't find his clothes anywhere.

                         IDA
          Maybe he ate 'em.

Vern nods like that's a real possibility, then smiles. They eat
for a bit.

                         IDA (CONT'D)
          I was thinking maybe blue. For the nursery.

                         VERN
          Ya?

                         IDA
          Earlier. I was thinking maybe blue, but then I changed
          my mind.

                         VERN
          Blue's nice.

                         IDA
          Maybe green.

Vern nods. We can tell they've been having this conversation
for months.

                         VERN
          Green's possible.
                        (beat)
          Well, I'm ready to get painting. Soon as you decide.

                                    IDA
          You're a good man, Vern Thurman. My sister was crazy telling
          me not to marry you.

                                    VERN
                              (beat, chews)
          Your sister is crazy.

          They eat for a while in comfortable silence.

                    CUT TO:

          INT. HESS AND SONS TRUCKING. BEMIDJI, MINNESOTA—DAY

          A large garage housing a raised DISPATCH OFFICE. Through the
          office window we see Sam talking to MAX GOLD (40s). Gold is
          Sam's lawyer. TWO BIG GUYS sit with them.

          In the main garage there is a big rig parked along the far wall.
          The logo on the trailer reads NARCOL. Sam Hess's truck is parked
          next to it.

          Boxes of INFLATABLE WOMEN are stacked against the wall. Mickey
          and Moe have one of them open. Mickey is using a high-pressure
          air hose to fill up one of the women. She gets fatter and
          fatter, then explodes. They crack up.

                                    MOE
          Dad said we should take turns.

                                    MICKEY
          Dad told me he thinks you got a potato brain.

          Moe attacks him. They wrestle. Mickey gets Moe in a headlock.
          Lorne Malvo enters the garage, watches them.

                                    MALVO
          You're doing it wrong. You wanna press your forearm against
          the back of his neck, then grab your elbow with the other
          hand. Choke him right out.

          The two boys separate, unsettled.

                                    MICKEY
          Whatcha want, mister?

                                    MOE
          Ya, mister. Whatcha want?

                                    MALVO
          Sign outside says Hess and Sons.

          Malvo studies them, Tweedle Dum and Dumber.

                    MALVO (CONT'D)
    Which is the older boy?

                      MICKEY
    Me. Mickey. So that means I'm in charge when Dad's gone.

                       MOE
    Are not. Mom said —

                      MICKEY
    Mom's got nothing ta do with it, sister.

Upstairs, Sam sees his boys talking to Malvo, comes out of the
office.

                     SAM HESS
    Help you with something?

Malvo sizes him up, ignoring the hired muscle.

                      MALVO
    Sam Hess?

Hess and the two big guys come down the stairs. It's clear they
don't like strangers coming around, asking questions.

                     SAM HESS
    Who wants ta know?

Malvo checks to see if there's another guy behind him asking
questions.

                      MALVO
    Me.

He nods to the big rig.

                    MALVO (CONT'D)
    See you do work for Narcol. You know Romo?

                     SAM HESS
    You know Romo?

                      MALVO
                     (beat)
    Never heard of him.

Hess looks at his guys to see if they're hearing this.

                     SAM HESS
    Is he serious?

Hess closes on him.

                    SAM HESS (CONT'D)
Only two reasons to come to my shop, friend. Either you need
a truck. Or you drive a truck. You a truck driver?

Malvo is unintimidated.

                         MALVO
I was just talking to your boys. I think the younger one's a
little dim.

                       SAM HESS
What did you say?

                         MALVO
His IQ seems low, I'm saying. Have you had him tested?

The two heavies close around Malvo.

                        MICKEY
Hit him, Dad.

                          MOE
Ya, Dad. Hit him.

Max Gold clears his throat. Hess looks at him. Gold shakes his
head.

                       SAM HESS
I'm gonna restrain myself — on accounta you got an obvious
head injury — and not beat you ta death with a tire iron.
But I'm gonna ask you again. What the heck do ya want?

                         MALVO
Just wanted to get a look at you.

Malvo gives Sam a slow once-over.

                     MALVO (CONT'D)
Okay. That'll do it.

Malvo walks out. Off Hess: *What the fuck was that about?*

          CUT TO:

EXT. CHAZZ NYGAARD'S HOUSE. BEMIDJI, MINNESOTA—DAY

An expensive two-story home. Lester and Pearl stand on the
threshold with a meatloaf. Lester's broken nose is taped, his
eyes black.

                         PEARL
How does a grown man fall over his own feet?

                              LESTER
          It was ice. I slipped on ice.
                                   (feels his nose)
          We shoulda canceled.

                              PEARL
          Don't be a baby.

     Unhappy, Lester rings the bell. GORDO, 10, opens the door.

                              LESTER
                                   (animated)
          We're here.

     The boy SLAMS the door in their faces. Beat. Lester rings the
     bell again. KITTY NYGAARD, 32, opens the door. She's pretty,
     well appointed.

                              LESTER (CONT'D)
                                   (tries again)
          We're here.

                              KITTY
          Come on in. Chazz's working the ham.

                    CUT TO:

     INT. KITCHEN. CHAZZ NYGAARD'S HOUSE—DAY

     CHAZZ NYGAARD (30s) stands at the kitchen counter. It's clear he
     got all the looks and charm in the family. Lester holds a can of
     beer with a straw in it. Chazz massages honey into a ham with
     his bare hands.

     Behind them, Kitty and Pearl set the table. Gordo watches TV in
     the living room.

                              CHAZZ
          — took the whole team down to Duluth Tuesday. Big spread at
          the Marriot.

                              PEARL
          Ooh. I've always wanted ta stay there.

                              CHAZZ
          Ya. It's real sweet. King-sized bed. View of the lake. You
          name it. Boss took me out for dinner.

                              KITTY
          Just the two of them.

                              CHAZZ
          Steak big as a catcher's mitt. Said, Chazz, you're going
          places in this world.

                          KITTY
          Gave him a raise and a corner office.

                          PEARL
          Hear that, Lester? A corner office.

                          LESTER
          Ya. Real good.

                          PEARL
          And him your younger brother.

                          LESTER
          Ya. I said I heard.

                          KITTY
          Vice President Sales, Midwest Region.

Chazz massages the ham.

                          CHAZZ
          Bought the surround sound to celebrate. Pretty sweet, huh?

Lester sips beer through a straw, watches his brother work the
meat.

                          LESTER
          You may have ta marry that ham, you get any more familiar
          with it.

                          CHAZZ
          Saw it on Rachael Ray. She says massaging breaks the muscle
          down. Makes the meat juicier.

                          PEARL
          Lester never wants to try new things.

                          LESTER
          Now hold on — that's not —

                          KITTY
          Oh, we make Gordo try stuff all the time. Chazz says we
          hafta open his horizons.

                          CHAZZ
          Broaden his horizons. It's a big world, ya now. There's more
          to life than just Minnesota.

Lester sips gingerly from his can of beer.

                          CHAZZ (CONT'D)
          Took a real tumble, huh?

                              LESTER
          There's a spot over by the fire station. Always icy. Don't
          know what the heck I was thinkin.

Chazz washes his hands.

                              CHAZZ
                            (to Lester)
          Come out ta the garage. Help me get some more beer.

                    CUT TO:

INT. GARAGE. CHAZZ NYGAARD'S HOUSE—DAY

A sweet setup with tools hanging on the wall. A big, steel-jawed
BEAR TRAP is mounted in a prominent spot. Chazz opens a mini-
fridge, hands Lester a beer.

                              CHAZZ
          We took Gordo to a specialist last month. Think he might
          have the autism. Won't stop drawin on the walls. Also, Kitty
          found a mason jar in his closet. I guess he pees in it at
          night. What's that about? Hey. Wanna see something cool?

He goes over to a locked GUN CASE, types a CODE into the digital
keypad lock.

Lester comes over.

                    ANGLE ON THE GUN CASE

Inside are multiple RIFLES and SHOTGUNS.

                              LESTER
          Sweet.

                              CHAZZ
          Ya, not those.

Chazz KNEELS. There's a FALSE BOTTOM. He pries it loose.
Underneath is a <u>large automatic weapon</u>, gleaming and deadly.

                              LESTER
          Jeez. What is it?

                              CHAZZ
          That there is your M-249 SAW light machine gun. Sometimes
          referred to as "the piglet."

                              LESTER
          Are you allowed to — can you even have that?

CHAZZ

Is it legal? Technically no way. But I got a buddy works
supply over Camp Ripley. And heck, I'm an American. I pay my
taxes. Take a look. It's gas operated, air cooled. Shoots
seven hundred twenty-five rounds per minute.

He takes the machine gun out of the box, hefts it, then hands
it to Lester, who, unprepared for the weight, DROPS IT on the
concrete floor.

LESTER

Aw jeez.

Chazz bends down. The machine gun is clearly damaged.

LESTER (CONT'D)

You shoulda told me it was so heavy. Is it okay?

CHAZZ

No, Lester. It's not okay. You bent the darn —
(sighs)
Why are you such a G.D. screw-up?

LESTER

Hey, now —

CHAZZ

Ever since you were — And now Kitty said she talked to Pearl
last week. And she's had it. Your wife. Said yer acting just
plain weird. Mopin around. Said she caught you standing in
the bathroom with yer toothbrush in yer hand just looking
in the mirror. Said foam was comin outta yer mouth like a
rabid dog.

LESTER

That's — come on — that's not — how I may — or may not — be
feeling. And fer yer information I was — I hadn't had a lotta
sleep the night before. So the toothpaste — that was just —

CHAZZ

Did you really trip on the ice and break yer nose?

LESTER

Ya. Yes. I told ya. Outside the fire station. Ya know they
run the hoses and wash the trucks and the ground gets all
wet. Real slippery.

Chazz shakes his head.

CHAZZ

Guys at work. They talk about how they look up to their
brothers. Their older brothers.
(beat)
Sometimes I tell people you're dead.

                              LESTER
You —

                              CHAZZ
     I mean, heck, Lester. You're forty years old. When are you
     gonna get yer act together?

Beat. Lester stares at him, ire rising.

          CUT TO:

INT. CAR—NIGHT

Lester drives. Pearl sits next to him, fuming.

                              PEARL
     Yer own brother. You didn't have ta hit him. I mean,
     seriously. What is the matter with you?

Lester drives, jaw clenched. The world is pressing down.

          CUT TO:

EXT. RUNDLE REALTY. RENO, NEVADA—DAY

It's still light out west. We're in the parking lot of a
nondescript strip mall. Ahead of us is the entrance to RUNDLE
REALTY—a kind of low-level real estate clearing house. A RENO
TAXI lets out an OLDER COUPLE. Maybe we notice a tumbleweed at
rest against a parked car. We HEAR brokers making sales calls
from inside.

                         BROKER #1
                         (answering)
     Yes, hello, Mrs. Trask, it's Matt Wasakowski again, from
     Rundle Realty.

                         BROKER #2
     . . . that's right, Mr. Dykstra, a prime house in a prime
     neighborhood.

We DOLLY INSIDE to . . .

INT. RUNDLE REALTY. RENO, NEVADA—CONTINUOUS

. . . past the REALTORS at their desks making deals, past the
run-down bathroom, to a METAL SECURITY DOOR with a digital lock.

          DISSOLVE TO:

INT. BACK OFFICE. RUNDLE REALTY—CONTINUOUS

MR. RUNDLE stands looking at a MAP of the U.S. on the wall.
COLORED PINS lay out the location of certain assets all over the
country. Rundle is a crime broker, of sorts.

On the desk behind him are ten TELEPHONES. Each has a place name
typed on a card in front of it—Milwaukee, Boise, Cincinnati,
etc.

Rundle is on the phone marked FRESNO.

                    MR. RUNDLE
          . . . before the seventeenth. Do you need that to look like
     an accident, or —
                         (beat, listening)
     Well, figure it out and call me back.

He hangs up. The telephone marked ST. PAUL rings.

                    MR. RUNDLE (CONT'D)
                         (answering)
     Realty.

          INTERCUT WITH:

INT. CAR (TRAVELING). BEMIDJI, MN—NIGHT

Lorne Malvo drives in a newly stolen car, on his phone. We see
an SUV in front of him.

                    MALVO
     It's me.

                    MR. RUNDLE
     St. Paul, your call was expected yesterday.

                    MALVO
     I got delayed.

                    MR. RUNDLE
     Problems?

                    MALVO
     Car trouble. Fixed now.

                    MR. RUNDLE
     But you finished the assignment?

                    MALVO
     Of course.

                    MR. RUNDLE
     And when can they expect you in Duluth? The new client is
     anxious to begin.

                              MALVO
        Soon. I took a detour.

                            MR. RUNDLE
        And the nature of this detour.

The SUV ahead of Malvo pulls into the LUCKY PENNY, a strip club.
Malvo follows.

                              MALVO
        Personal. Shouldn't be more than a day or two.

                            MR. RUNDLE
        I'll let Duluth know.

Malvo hangs up. He watches <u>Sam Hess</u> get out of the SUV with his
two guys, walk to the front door.

        CUT TO:

INT. LUCKY PENNY—NIGHT

A dive bar with a stripper pole. Malvo sits at the bar, a drink
in front of him.

        ANGLE ON SAM HESS

He's chatting up one of the strippers, PAPRIKA. As Malvo
watches, she leads him into the back.

        CUT TO:

INT. BACK ROOM. THE LUCKY PENNY—NIGHT

Sam Hess is giving it to Paprika, who couldn't look more bored,
a cigarette dangling from her lips.

                            PAPRIKA
        Oh, yeah, big fella. Oh, yeah.

Hess works towards his big finish, huffing and puffing. Then
suddenly, he STOPS. BLOOD pours from his mouth. Hess falls on
top of Paprika, revealing: LORNE MALVO, who has just stuck a
KNIFE into the back of Hess's head. Hess blocks Paprika's view.

She opens her mouth to scream, but instead we hear:

SFX: A ringing telephone.

        CUT TO:

INT. BEDROOM. THURMAN HOUSE. BEMIDJI, MINNESOTA—NIGHT

Vern is sleeping next to his wife. The phone rings.

                              VERN
                        (answering)
Ya?
                        (beat, listening)
Aw jeez. Where?
                        (beat, listening)
Okay. Pick me up, huh?

He sits up, scratches. Ida is half awake.

                              IDA
Gotta go?

                              VERN
Homicide. Molly's coming ta get me. Go back to sleep, hon.

She throws her arm over him, sleepily.

                              IDA
Love ya.

                              VERN
Love ya too.

        CUT TO:

EXT. THURMAN HOUSE. BEMIDJI, MINNESOTA—NIGHT

Molly pulls up in her prowler. Vern comes out, climbs in. Molly
hands him a coffee.

                              VERN
Thanks.

Molly drives.

                              MOLLY
Ida sleeping?

                              VERN
Ya.

                              MOLLY
Bill's over at the Lucky Penny. Says it's a real mess.

                              VERN
Bar fight?

                              MOLLY
Nope. Ya know those back rooms they got for hanky-panky?
Well, sounds like a customer was givin it to one of the
girls. Got himself stabbed in the head.

                              VERN
          The girl stabbed him?

                              MOLLY
          Bill says no. Says it was an assassination type deal.

                              VERN
                         (thinks about that)
          Huh.

                    CUT TO:

INT. BACK ROOM. THE LUCKY PENNY-NIGHT

Sam Hess lies facedown on the bed, the knife still sticking out
of the back of his head. Vern and Molly stand by the bed looking
down at him.

                              MOLLY
          Whatcha want me to write for cause of death?

                              VERN
          Put self-explanatory.

DEPUTY BILL OSWALT stands in the doorway, unable to look.

                              VERN (CONT'D)
          You okay, Bill?

                         BILL OSWALT
          Oh, ya. Threw up a bit ago.

                         VERN
          Not in here, I hope.

                         BILL OSWALT
          Oh no. Went out to the parkin lot. Wife made spaghetti for
          dinner. Seemed a shame to barf it up. I'm okay now though,
          long as I don't look.

          Vern crouches, examines Hess's profile.

                         VERN
          Well, heck. That's Sam Hess.

                         MOLLY
          Hess that owns the trucking company?

                         VERN
          Ya. With the two boys, both dumb as a dog's foot.

          Molly looks around. A thought hits her.

                         MOLLY
          Hold on. Isn't Hess tied to that syndicate of fellas outta
          Fargo? Gun runners and such.

                         VERN
          So they say. Never seen the proof.

                         MOLLY
          Jeez. Ya think this was, like, an organized crime thing? A
          hit or the like?

                         VERN
                      (straightens)
          Don't know what I think yet. Except that I was warm in bed a
          half hour ago.

               CUT TO:

          INT. LEROY'S MOTOR INN. BEMIDJI, MINNESOTA—NIGHT

          The owner, a heavyset WOMAN, is yelling at a sullen TEEN. Malvo
          enters.

                         WOMAN
          How many times I gotta tell ya? You can't just take dirty
          sheets offa one bed and put 'em on another. It's unsanitary.

                         TEEN
          I shake 'em out first.

                         WOMAN
You don't have the sense God gave a clam, do you? Go shovel
the walk.

The sullen teen exits.

                         MALVO
I need a room.

                         WOMAN
Just you?

                         MALVO
Pardon?

                         WOMAN
Is it just for you? The room.

                         MALVO
What difference does that make?

                         WOMAN
Different rate for two. And if ya got pets — dog, cat —
that's an extra ten bucks.

                         MALVO
What about a fish?

                         WOMAN
Excuse me?

                         MALVO
Would a fish cost me ten dollars?

                         WOMAN
Well —

                         MALVO
Or say I kept spiders. Or mice. What if I had bacteria?

                         WOMAN
Sir, bacteria are not pets.

                         MALVO
Could be.

                         WOMAN
Sir, perhaps you'd be happier in a different motel.

                         MALVO
I just want to know the policy. I'm a student of
institutions.

                    WOMAN
                 (exasperated)
        Sir, do ya have a pet or not?

                    MALVO
        Nope. Just me.

            CUT TO:

EXT. LEROY'S MOTOR INN. BEMIDJI, MINNESOTA—NIGHT

Malvo approaches his room. The teen is shoveling snow nearby.

                    MALVO
        Why do you let her talk to you like that?

                    TEEN
        Aw, she's not that bad.

                    MALVO
        Son, she compared you to a clam.

The teen thinks about it. The woman is kind of a bitch.

                    TEEN
        Well, what should I do?

                    MALVO
        Guy insulted me once. I pissed in his gas tank. Car never
        drove straight again.

The teen smiles, puts down the shovel. He walks over to the
woman's car. Malvo lets himself into his room.

INT. MOTEL ROOM. BEMIDJI, MN—CONTINUOUS

Malvo goes to the phone, dials the front desk. He looks out
through the curtain. We can see the teen with his pants undone,
pissing into the gas tank.

                    WOMAN
        Leroy's Motor Inn.

                    MALVO
        Yeah, I'm looking out my window and there's a young fella
        urinating into the gas tank of a red Miata.

                    WOMAN
        Son of a —

Malvo hangs up, watches as the woman comes out of the office
with a shotgun. She YELLS at the teen, who panics and stumbles
away, his pants falling down.

Malvo closes the curtain.

                CUT TO:

INT. LOU'S COFFEE SHOP. BEMIDJI, MINNESOTA—DAY

A family place. Molly Solverson sits at a table, going over a
case file. LOU SOLVERSON (60) limps over with a pot of coffee.

                        LOU SOLVERSON
        Warm ya up, hon?

                        MOLLY
        Thanks, Dad.

                        LOU SOLVERSON
        Whatcha lookin at?

                        MOLLY
        Murder file.

                        LOU SOLVERSON
        Oh ya?

                        MOLLY
        Ya. Sam Hess got himself killed last night over the Lucky
        Penny.

                        LOU SOLVERSON
        Ya don't say.

                        MOLLY
        Ya. Knife in the head. But ya didn't hear that from me.

Vern Thurman comes in, sees Molly, comes over.

                        VERN
        Hey there, Molly. Lou.

                        LOU SOLVERSON
        Coffee? Eggs over medium.

                        VERN
        Won't say no. How's the leg?

                        LOU SOLVERSON
        Goes from my ass to the ground, same as the other. Thinking
        of doin some ice fishin this weekend.

                        VERN
        Sorry to hear it.

                        LOU SOLVERSON
        Interested?

                              VERN
        No. Only thing I ever caught fishin in winter was a cold.

Lou goes back behind the counter.

                              MOLLY
        Say, Chief. I been thinkin. That fella in the snow. With the
        underpants. Somethin odd about that.

                              VERN
        Yer sayin other than the fact he was just wearin panties.

                              MOLLY
        Ya. See, we know from the wreck that whoever was driving the
        vehicle cracked their head on the steering wheel. But the
        fella in the snow —

                              VERN
        No head injury.

                              MOLLY
        Right. So, ya see —

                              VERN
        That's some good police work there, Deputy.

                              MOLLY
                           (smiles)
        Thanks.

                              VERN
        But if he's not the driver — I guess we gotta ask — who is
        he?

                              MOLLY
        I ran his prints. Nothin. Plus, turns out the car was
        stolen.

                              VERN
        Oh ya?

                              MOLLY
        Ya. Over in Grand Forks. I called the local PD. Waiting for
        a call back.

                              VERN
                           (nods to Hess file)
        Any thoughts there?

                              MOLLY
        Not as such. The lady Hess was with didn't get a good look
        at the fella killed him on accounta all the blood in her
        eyes. But we're checkin the knife fer prints. Also Bill's
        goin around to the stores, see if the knife was maybe bought
        here in Bemidji.

Vern studies her.

                    VERN
     You'll make a good chief one day.

                    MOLLY
                 (surprised)
     Me? What about Bill? He's got seniority.

                    VERN
     Bill cleans his gun with bubble bath. No. It'll be you. If
     you want.

Off Molly: A lot to think about.

          CUT TO:

INT. HESS HOUSE. BEMIDJI, MINNESOTA—DAY

Mickey and Moe, still in sweats, sit on the sofa, looking bored.
Their mother, GINA HESS (30s) sits in a chair, wearing red.
She's not from around here. Max Gold, Hess's consigliere, is
there, drinking coffee.

                    MAX GOLD
     When you talk to the police just keep it simple. Thanks but
     no thanks in other words. I've already talked to Fargo and
     they want to deal with this themselves. They're sending
     guys.

                         GINA HESS
         Deal with what? He was in a whorehouse. I'm glad he's dead.

                         MICKEY
         Ma, don't talk like that.

                         MOE
         Ya, Ma. Don't talk like that.

Through the living room WINDOW we see Vern's prowler pull up.
Vern and Molly get out.

                         GINA HESS
         Makes me live in the North Pole and then he has the nerve to
         — I'm not kidding. I'm gonna sing at his funeral.

She breaks into tears, inconsolable. The men of Minnesota watch
her cry, mystified by her emotional range.

A MAID comes in.

                         MAID
         Mr. Mickey. You have a phone call.

Mickey and Moe stand together.

                         MICKEY
         She said me, doofus.

                         MOE
         Can't I come?

                         MICKEY
         No. Jeez. Stay here with Ma.

Mickey follows the maid into the . . .

         KITCHEN

He picks up the phone.

                         MICKEY
         Hello?

         INTERCUT WITH:

INT. MOTEL ROOM. BEMIDJI, MINNESOTA—SAME TIME

Lorne Malvo is shirtless, on the phone. We see a BIG, UGLY
BRUISE on his right side.

                         MALVO
         Mickey, it's Lewis Grossman. Your dad's estate attorney.
         First let me say how sorry I am for your loss.

                              MICKEY
Okay.

            ANGLE ON MALVO'S BRUISED SIDE

The skin is black and blue. As Malvo talks, he wraps his broken
ribs (from the car crash) with an ace bandage.

                              MALVO
Next thing is, I'm responsible for overseeing the dispersal
of your dad's vast estate.

                              MICKEY
                           (brightening)
You mean the money?

                              MALVO
Right. Money, real estate holdings, automobiles. And — well,
there's no delicate way to put this — the will is very
clear. Your dad decided to leave everything to your younger
brother, Moe.

                              MICKEY
Are you kidding?

                              MALVO
I know it's hard to hear. But the will is very specific.
Quote, I leave the entirety of my vast estate to my
second-born — and favorite — son, Moe. That's sweet. He
musta really loved that boy.

Malvo finishes wrapping his ribs.

                        MALVO (CONT'D)
Anyway, that's it. Again, sorry for your loss. If you have
any questions, please don't hesitate to call.

Malvo hangs up.

            CUT TO:

INT. LIVING ROOM. HESS HOUSE—DAY

Vern and Molly have come in while Mickey was on the phone. They
stand talking to Gina, Moe, and Max Gold.

                              VERN
Well, like I said, Mrs. Hess, we're checking some things
on our end. But anything you could tell us — about yer
husband's business, or —

MAX GOLD

Appreciate the visit, Chief. But Mrs. Hess had no kind of
involvement in Sam's business. Frankly, she's mystified. Her
husband being a pillar of the community and all. I mean,
heck, voted Bemidji Businessman of the Year, 1996 and '98.

Mickey comes back from the kitchen, looking stunned/pissed. He
stands in the doorway.

MOE
(mouths)

Who was it?

Mickey waves Moe over (*come outside and I'll tell ya*). The two
go to the front door.

VERN

Ya. Like I said, it's a puzzler. Course we both know some of
yer boys have had run-ins with the law over time — stolen
merchandise charges and the like.

MOLLY

And, ya know, the Staties had that case as to maybe your
outfit's got ties to a crime syndicate out of Fargo.

There is a HOCKEY STICK resting against the wall. Mickey GRABS
it on his way out.

MAX GOLD

You're gonna stand here — let me get this straight — stand
here and call the victim a criminal in front of his wife?
His kids?

Through the LIVING ROOM WINDOW we see Mickey and Moe walk out
into the front yard, Mickey holding the hockey stick.

VERN

Well now, no one's callin anyone a criminal.

Outside, MICKEY CLOBBERS MOE with the hockey stick. Moe
staggers. Mickey hits him again.

VERN (CONT'D)

Just tryin to figure out what happened.

Moe goes down. Mickey BEATS him mercilessly. Molly glances out
the window, sees Moe on the ground, taking a beating.

MOLLY

Chief! 217! 217!

She sprints for the door and out into the yard. We watch through
the window as she TACKLES Mickey.

                    CUT TO:

EXT. HESS HOUSE. BEMIDJI, MN—DAY

Mickey leans against the tailgate of Vern's truck, handcuffed,
hands behind him. Molly stands next to him. At the curb we can
see PARAMEDICS loading Moe on a gurney into an ambulance.

                         MOLLY
          I don't understand. Why would ya do a thing like that? And
          to yer own brother.

Mickey says nothing.

                    CUT TO:

INT. LESTER'S CAR. BEMIDJI, MINNESOTA—DAY

Lester is driving to work. As he passes the Leroy's Motor Inn,
he sees Lorne Malvo exit his room. Lester slows, watches Malvo
go into the ORIENTAL GRILLE next door.

                         LESTER
          What the heck?

                    CUT TO:

INT. BO MUNK INSURANCE SHOP. BEMIDJI, MINNESOTA—DAY

Lester Nygaard arrives for work. He takes off his puffy coat,
hangs it on the coat rack. His boss, BO MUNK (50s) comes over.

                         BO MUNK
          Heya, Lester.

                         LESTER
          Oh, hiya, Bo.

                         BO MUNK
          What happened to yer face there?

                         LESTER
          Ya know that spot near the fire station?

                         BO MUNK
          Where they wash the trucks?

                         LESTER
          Ya, slipped on the ice.

                         BO MUNK
          Ouch. Say, Lester. I needya ta pull the policy for Sam Hess.

                              LESTER
                              (beat)
For — who now?

                              BO MUNK
Sam Hess, owns the truck depot over on Winslow. You know.
Big fella. Well, he's dead.

The color goes out of Lester's face.

                              LESTER
Oh ya?

                              BO MUNK
Ya. Shame. That's a big policy.
                              (lowers his voice)
Murder, they're sayin. Stabbed ta death is what I heard.
                              (off Lester)
You okay there, Lester?

                              LESTER
Oh sure. I, uh — you know I went ta high school with him.

                              BO MUNK
Ya don't say. Well, anyway. I need ya ta pull the policy.
Gotta get on the phone with his wife later.

Bo walks away. Lester stands there, feeling both terror and a
peculiar elation.

     CUT TO:

INT. ORIENTAL GRILLE. BEMIDJI, MINNESOTA—DAY

Lorne Malvo sits at a formica table, finishing his meal. Lester
comes in, hat on, agitated. He sees Malvo, comes over.

                              LESTER
Did you — jeez.
                              (leans in)
Did you really kill him?
                              (almost can't say it)
Sam.

                              MALVO
Oh my God. Is Sam dead?
                              (off Lester)
How do you feel about that?

                              LESTER
I mean, of course. It's — ya know, tragic —

                              MALVO
Then why'd you kill him?

                         LESTER
                       (too loud)
      Now hold on a second.

Lester looks around, sits.

                         LESTER (CONT'D)
                       (quiet)
      I never —

                         MALVO
      You did actually. Remember? Yes or no.

                         LESTER
                       (hisses)
      I never said *yes*.

                         MALVO
      Well, you didn't say *no*.

Beat. Lester is tied up in knots.

                         LESTER
      Now, that's not — that won't — in a court a law — that
      won't —

                         MALVO
                       (dangerous)
      Who said anything about a court of law?

                         LESTER
      No. I just mean — Aw jeez. He had a wife. And those boys.

                         MALVO
      He put you in a barrel and rolled you in the road. Your
      problem is, you lived your whole life thinking there are
      rules. There aren't. We used to be gorillas. All we ever had
      was what we could take and defend. The truth is, you're more
      of a man today than you were yesterday.

                         LESTER
      How do ya figure?

                         MALVO
      It's a red tide, Lester. This life of ours. The shit they
      make us eat. Day after day — the boss, the wife, et cetera
      — wearin us down. If you don't stand up to it — show 'em
      you're still an ape deep down where it counts — you're just
      gonna get washed away.

Off Lester: this resonates.

```
            CUT TO:

INT. NURSE'S STATION. EMERGENCY ROOM. BEMIDJI, MN—DAY

Paramedics wheel Moe in on a gurney. Molly is with them. She
breaks away, approaches the nurse's station. SUE ROUNDTREE
(30s), the same nurse from earlier, is working.

                    SUE ROUNDTREE
        That the domestic?

Molly takes off her gloves and hat.


                    MOLLY
        Ya. Brother worked him over real good. Broken collarbone
        they're sayin. Maybe a concussion.


                    SUE ROUNDTREE
        Family.


                    MOLLY
        Ya.
                    (beat)
        Say, while I'm here — we found a car wreck out by Paine
        Lake yesterday morning. Blood on the steering wheel, but no
        driver. So I'm wondering — you see any head injuries in the
        last day or so, coulda been caused by those circumstances.


                    SUE ROUNDTREE
        There was this one fella.


                    MOLLY
        Oh ya?


                    SUE ROUNDTREE
        Ya. Looked like he banged his head real bad, but wouldn't
        give ID. So we couldn't treat him. Super intense though.
                    (remembers)

                    SUE ROUNDTREE (CONT'D)
        And, ya know, I think he was talkin ta this other fella.

                    MOLLY
        Other fella.

                    SUE ROUNDTREE
        Ya. Here for a broken nose. Looked like they were maybe
        havin an argument.

                    MOLLY
        Ya don't say.

Sue looks through her files.
```

                    SUE ROUNDTREE
Lester Nygaard. He was here around four in the p.m.

                    MOLLY
You remember what they were arguing about?

                    SUE ROUNDTREE
Well, ya know, it's funny, but I wanna say they were arguing
about that dead fella.

                    MOLLY
Who?

                    SUE ROUNDTREE
Hess.

                    MOLLY
                (that's interesting)
Really.

                    SUE ROUNDTREE
                (nodding)
Ya. Heard 'em say his name. Is that, like, a lead?

                    MOLLY
Oh ya.

Molly nods absently for a moment, thinking *jackpot*.

        CUT TO:

INT. BEMIDJI POLICE STATION, BEMIDJI, MN—DAY

Vern sits in his office, eating a brown bag lunch. We see his
NAME stenciled on the glass door. Deputy Bill Oswalt knocks.

                    BILL OSWALT
Phone call, Chief. It's the wife.

Vern picks up the phone.

                    VERN
Hey hon.

        INTERCUT WITH:

INT. THURMAN HOUSE. BEMIDJI, MINNESOTA—SAME TIME

Ida is in the kitchen.

                    IDA
White.

                    VERN
White what?

                    IDA
I decided. We're gonna paint the nursery white.

                    VERN
It's already white.

                    IDA
Well, I want to paint it again. The baby's room should have
a new coat, don't ya think?

                    VERN
I do. Any particular shade?

                    IDA
What do ya mean?

                    VERN
Well, ya got yer bright white, yer snow white.

                BILL OSWALT
                 (hasn't left)
Eggshell.

                    VERN
Right. There's eggshell.

                    IDA
Oh. I hadn't thoughta that.

Vern realizes he's opened a whole other can of worms.

                    VERN
     Tell ya what. Why don't I stop at the hardware, pick up some
     different shades and we'll figure it out tonight?

                    IDA
     We're havin a baby, Vern.

                    VERN
     That's true.

                    IDA
     No. I mean, it's finally sinkin in. We're gonna have a baby.

                    VERN
                 (beat, happy)
     I can't wait. See ya soon.

He hangs up.

          CUT TO:

EXT. HARDWARE STORE PARKING LOT. BEMIDJI, MINNESOTA—NIGHT

Vern puts two cans of paint into the backseat of his Bronco. His
radio buzzes.

                    MOLLY (O.S.)
     Come in, Chief.

Vern picks up the handset.

                    VERN
     This is Vern, go ahead.

          INTERCUT WITH:

INT. HOSPITAL. BEMIDJI, MN—SAME TIME

Molly stands in the hall.

                    MOLLY
     Chief, I'm over at the hospital. I was checkin on the Hess
     boy and —

                    VERN
     How is he?

                    MOLLY
     Broken collarbone, got his bell rung pretty good.

                    VERN
     That's a shame.

                              MOLLY
Ya. Hey, so I got ta talkin to Sue Roundtree, and I asked
her if they'd had any head injuries lately — ya know my
theory about the driver in that wreck — and Sue says they
did yesterday. A peculiar fella, she says. Real intense. And
here's where it gets interesting. Cause she says the fella
with the head injury was talkin to another fella. About Sam
Hess.

                              VERN
Oh yeah?

                              MOLLY
Yessir. Says the two was thick as thieves. So suddenly I'm
thinking, maybe these two cases, maybe they're connected,
huh?

                              VERN
                           (impressed)
Could be. She say who the other fella was?

                              MOLLY
                        (looks in her pad)
Lester Nygaard.

                              VERN
Really.

                              MOLLY
You know him.

                              VERN
Sure. I know Lester. Sells insurance over at Bo's shop.

                              MOLLY
Ya. I called over. They're closed. So I was gonna go by
Lester's place.

                              VERN
No. I know Lester. I'll do it. You call it a day. Good work.

        CUT TO:

INT. KITCHEN. LESTER'S HOUSE. BEMIDJI, MN—NIGHT

Pearl comes home, sees Lester's coat.

                              PEARL
Lester?

                          LESTER (O.S.)
                           (calling)
In the basement.

```
          CUT TO:

INT. BASEMENT. LESTER'S HOUSE. BEMIDJI, MINNESOTA—NIGHT

Pearl comes downstairs. Lester has his tool kit out. He's trying
to fix the washing machine.

                    PEARL
          Whatcha doin, hon?


                    LESTER
          Trying ta fix the darn thing. Looks like the motor mount
          broke.

                    PEARL
          Ya sure ya know what yer doin?

                    LESTER
          Seems pretty straightforward.

He puts the screwdriver down.

                    LESTER (CONT'D)
          Okay. Give that a try.

                    PEARL
          But there's nothing in it.
```

                         LESTER
          I'm sayin just fer a test.

Pearl turns the machine on. Beat. It fills with water, then the
agitator kicks in. A harsh shriek fills the air.

                    LESTER (CONT'D)
                      (panicked)
          Turn it off.

Pearl tries to turn it off. The shriek worsens. SMOKE starts
to pour out of the back of the washing machine. Lester finally
pulls the plug. The shriek fades slowly, as the engine cycles
down.

They stare at the now dead washing machine.

                    LESTER (CONT'D)
          Well —

                         PEARL
          You killed it.

                         LESTER
          I, uh —

                         PEARL
          You killed my washing machine.

                         LESTER
          It's — I was — ya know, the tide. I was standing up to the —
          I was bein a man.

                         PEARL
          But yer not a man, Lester. Yer not even half a man.

Lester stares at her, his nuts cut once again.

                    PEARL (CONT'D)
          Honestly. I don't know what got into me, marrying you. My
          mom said, don't do it, Pearl. She said, he's the kind of boy
          who loses all the time. And you know what those boys grow up
          ta be, don't ya? Losers.

             LESTER

looks at his tools.

          ANGLE ON A CLAW HAMMER

resting on top of the toolbox.

                         LESTER
          Take it back.

                              PEARL
         Or what? What are you gonna do? Ya can't even face me when
         we're having sex.

                              LESTER
         Well, hold on. It's you not facin me.

                              PEARL
         That's so I can picture a real man.

         This gets his goat.

                              LESTER
         You take that back.

                              PEARL
         Loser.

         Lester picks up the claw hammer. He walks towards Pearl.

                           PEARL (CONT'D)
         Oh, what are you gonna do, hit me? That's a laugh.

         The first blow catches her by surprise. A stunned beat, where
         Lester and we think that maybe no damage was done. Maybe he
         can just take it back. But then blood pours from her hairline

and down her face. And Lester, past the point of no return,
BEATS HER TO DEATH with the hammer. Each blow is a release.
Eventually, he stops. Stands there panting. Slowly the red haze
lifts. He looks down at his blood spattered clothes.

                         LESTER
          Aw jeez.

He is about to panic, when he looks up.

               CLOSE UP ON AN INSPIRATIONAL POSTER

taped to a bare concrete wall. On it a school of yellow fish all
face the same direction, except one. The poster reads *What if
you're right and they're wrong?*

                    LESTER

stares at it. As he does, <u>an idea hits him</u>. A brilliant,
dangerous plan. Could he really do it? As we watch, Lester
strips off his clothes, shoves them in a garbage bag.

Carefully, he slides the washing machine back against the wall,
and puts the toolbox back where he found it.

Over this we hear:

                    LESTER (O.S.) (CONT'D)
                      (pre-lap, distraught)
          Ya, it's me. I — you need ta — I need help.

               CUT TO:

INT. KITCHEN. LESTER'S HOUSE. BEMIDJI, MN—NIGHT

Lester, dressed in new clothing, stands with his back to us. We
<u>move towards him</u> as he practices for his phone call.

                         LESTER
          Ya, it's me. I can't talk long. She's — I did something —
                      (beat)
          Ya, it's — there's been an accident and I —

Beat. He picks up the phone, dials.

                         MALVO (O.S.)
                      (answers)
          Yes?

                         LESTER
                      (worked up)
          Ya, it's me — Lester — she's — my wife, she's — aw hell — I
          think I — she's in the basement, dead, and —

> MALVO (O.S.)
> How did you get this number?

> LESTER
> What? I was — I saw you this morning on my way ta — look,
> I'm freakin out here — I don't know what ta do.

> MALVO (O.S.)
> Lester, have you been a bad boy?

> LESTER
> Aw jeez. I just — the hammer, and I — can you come over?
> It's — I'm on Willow Creek Drive. Number six thirteen.

> MALVO (O.S.)
> (a long beat)
> Sure, Lester. I'll be right there.

Lester hangs up. Beat. He thinks about his next step.

> CUT TO:

INT. LIVING ROOM. LESTER'S HOUSE. BEMIDJI, MN—NIGHT

Lester pulls a chair over to the armoire. He climbs up, roots
around on top, pulls down a SHOTGUN. He finds some shells, loads
it. Malvo will be here soon and Lester plans to kill him and
frame him for his wife's murder.

> CUT TO:

INT. FRONT HALLWAY. LESTER'S HOUSE—NIGHT

Lester holds the gun in one hand. Practices opening the door
with the other, raising the gun. It's too clunky. Plus he needs
to lure Malvo inside the house before he shoots him.

> LESTER
> (practicing)
> What did you do? You killed her. You *killed* her.

Lester looks around. He decides to hide the shotgun against the
KITCHEN WALL, hidden from sight, just on the other side of the
doorway.

Maybe we notice the back kitchen door as he does this, over his
shoulder.

Looking around, Lester loses his nerve a little. But no. He has
a plan. This will work. He sets the shotgun in its hiding place,
looks around. Has he forgotten anything?

THERE IS A KNOCK ON THE FRONT DOOR.

Lester panics, tries to calm down.

                    LESTER (CONT'D)
                  (under his breath)
     You killed her. *You* killed her.

Lester goes to the front door, takes a deep breath, opens it.

VERN THURMAN stands outside.

                    VERN
     Evenin, Lester.

                    LESTER
                  (nervous)
     What — what do ya want?

                    VERN
     Well, I suppose first I'd like ta come in.

Lester looks behind him.

                    LESTER
     Uh, ya. Well — it's just — now's not a good —

                    VERN
     Just take a second.

Vern steps forward and Lester, by instinct, steps back. Now Vern
is in the house. He takes off his gloves and hat.

                    VERN (CONT'D)
     Supposed ta get down to negative ten tonight, I hear.

Lester is a mass of nerves. Vern steps towards the kitchen.

                    VERN (CONT'D)
     Pearl home?

Lester moves to block him, putting his back to the kitchen
doorway.

                    LESTER
     Uh — no — she's, uh — at my brother's.

                    VERN
     Okay then. How's the nose?

                    LESTER
     Huh? Oh, hurts.

                    VERN
     How'd that happen anyway?

                    LESTER
Slipped. Over at the fire station.

                    VERN
Ouch. Go to the hospital?

                    LESTER
Ya. They, uh, set it.

                    VERN
Talk to anyone while you were there?

                    LESTER
What do ya mean?

                    VERN
Well, the reason I'm here — not sure if ya heard — but Sam
Hess got killed last night over at the Lucky Penny. Nasty
business. And, well, I heard you were talkin to another
fella about Hess before he died. Over at the hospital.

                    LESTER
                    (pale)
No. I don't think —

                    VERN
What was his name again? The other fella?

Lester tries to decide what to say. Then the cuckoo clock chimes
from the living room. Eight o'clock. Lester jumps, startled.

                    VERN (CONT'D)
Ya okay there, Lester? Ya seem a bit jumpy.

                    LESTER
Ya, I'm, uh — it's just Pearl's gonna be home soon and —

Looking past Lester, Vern sees the basement door is open. He
notices something on the floor. A BLOODY FOOTPRINT. Alarmed,
Vern DRAWS HIS GUN.

                    VERN
Lester. Listen to me very carefully. I need ya to get down
on the ground.

                    LESTER
No. Wait. Just — listen to me — it's not what it —

                    VERN
Lester. On the ground. Now.

Gun on Lester, Vern backs towards the cellar door.

                              LESTER
          No. Now hold on. Hold on. Don't — there's nothin down there —

Vern glances down the basement stairs.

          ANGLE ON PEARL'S FEET

visible at the bottom of the stairs.

                         LESTER (CONT'D)
          — That's not — I didn't do nothin — I just got home. I just
          got home and —

          CLOSE UP ON VERN

trying to catch up to events. He keeps the gun on Lester,
reenters the front hall. Behind him we see LORNE MALVO STEP INTO
VIEW in the kitchen (He came in through the kitchen door). Vern
doesn't see Malvo, but Lester does. His face goes white as Malvo
walks calmly and quietly to the spot Lester hid the shotgun,
picks it up. Vern keeps his gun on Lester, keys his radio
handset.

                              VERN
          This is Chief Thurman. I'm at six one three Willow Creek
          Drive. Requesting —

A SHOTGUN BLAST catches VERN in the BACK, spins him around.
LORNE MALVO racks LESTER'S SHOTGUN. He FIRES AGAIN, the spray
catching Vern in the chest and throat. Vern falls.

                              MALVO
          Any more?

Lester is in shock, white as a sheet.

                          MALVO (CONT'D)
          Lester. Are there any more cops?

Lester shakes his head. Malvo kicks Vern's gun away, looks down.

          ANGLE ON VERN

eyes wild, like the deer in the opening. He is mortally wounded,
blood bubbles coming out of his mouth as he struggles for air.

          CLOSE UP ON MALVO

struck by the synchronicity of this. He studies the dying man's
eyes.

                          MALVO (CONT'D)
          What did you tell him?

                          LESTER
          Nothing — I, uh — he asked about Sam.

                          MALVO
          You got any more shells for this?

Lester shakes his head. Malvo lays the shotgun on the table.

                          MALVO (CONT'D)
          Where's the basement?

Lester points. Malvo enters the kitchen, goes down the stairs.

          ANGLE ON LESTER

He pulls two shotgun shells out of his pocket, eyes the shotgun.
How long to grab it and reload?

He reaches out his other hand, then realizes it's bleeding.
There's a <u>shotgun pellet</u> buried in the meat of his thumb.
Then Lester becomes aware that his injured hand is now lit by
flashing red and blue lights. Another police car has just pulled
up outside.

          CUT TO:

INT. MOLLY'S SQUAD CAR—SAME TIME

Pulling up to Lester's house, Molly sees Vern's prowler. She
CLIMBS OUT of the car, approaches the door.

          CUT TO:

INT. KITCHEN. LESTER'S HOUSE. BEMIDJI, MINNESOTA—SAME TIME

Lester hurries over to the basement door.

                         LESTER
        They're here. The police.

No response. Lester starts down the stairs into . . .

             THE BASEMENT

                         LESTER
        I said the police are here. What do we . . .

But <u>Malvo is gone</u>. Vanished like a ghost. Pearl lays alone on
the floor, a bloody mess.

Off Lester: trapped.

             CUT TO:

EXT. LESTER'S HOUSE. BEMIDJI, MINNESOTA—SAME TIME

Molly pounds on the door.

                         MOLLY
        Bemidji Police. Open up.

Nothing. She looks in the nearest window, sees Vern lying dead
on the hall floor.

                         MOLLY (CONT'D)
                         (upset)
        Oh. Oh.

She keys her handset.

                         MOLLY (CONT'D)
        Officer — officer down! Send help.

She pulls her weapon, starts kicking the front door.

             CUT TO:

INT. BASEMENT. LESTER'S HOUSE—SAME TIME

Nygaard hears the front door CRASH OPEN upstairs. He is trapped.
He looks around. No exit. Can he hide? No. They'll find him.
Then his eyes hit . . .

             THE INSPIRATIONAL POSTER

on the wall. Pearl's blood has speckled it.

LESTER

knowing he will be found at any moment, makes a decision. He
RUNS towards the wall, his head down. Crack. <u>He knocks himself
out</u>.

CUT TO:

INT. FRONT HALLWAY. LESTER'S HOUSE—SAME TIME

Molly kneels next to Vern, checks his pulse. But her mentor
and friend is dead. Struggling to stay professional, she
straightens, her gun up.

MOLLY
   Bemidji Police! If there's someone in the house, come out
   with yer hands up.

Nothing. Cautiously, Molly goes room to room, searching. We know
Malvo could still be in the house. Each blind corner and dark
space offers certain death. We can tell Molly is afraid, out of
her league, but she keeps her wits.

CUT TO:

INT. BASEMENT. LESTER'S HOUSE—NIGHT

Slowly, Molly comes down the stairs, gun drawn. She sees Pearl
and Lester, lying facedown. The basement looks like the scene of
a massacre. From upstairs she hears . . .

                    BILL OSWALT (O.S.)
Molly?

                         MOLLY
Down here!

Molly assesses the situation. Pearl is clearly dead. Molly
holsters her weapon, kneels next to Lester, takes his pulse.

                    MOLLY (CONT'D)
Husband's alive!

She looks up. There on the poster she sees A BLOODY HUMAN FACE
PRINT with what appears to be a HALO over it.

What if you're right and they're wrong?

Off Molly: what does it mean?

          CUT TO:

EXT. TWO-LANE HIGHWAY. DULUTH, MINNESOTA—NIGHT

The outskirts of town. A local police car is parked in a speed
trap.

          CUT TO:

INT. PATROL CAR—NIGHT

Deputy GUS GRIMLY (30s) sits behind the wheel, sipping a cup of
coffee. His walkie-talkie crackles.

                    GRETA GRIMLY (O.S.)
Dad. Come in, Dad. Over.

Gus picks up the walkie-talkie.

                    GUS GRIMLY
Dad here. Come back.

                    GRETA GRIMLY (O.S.)
Vikings up by thirteen. Over.

                    GUS GRIMLY
What happened? Over.

                    GRETA GRIMLY (O.S.)
Walsh kicked another field gold. Over.

                    GUS GRIMLY
Sweet. Did you brush your teeth? Over.

                    GRETA GRIMLY (O.S.)
Yes. Over.

                    GUS GRIMLY
Homework? Over.

                    GRETA GRIMLY (O.S.)
Did my math and science. Still have to do English. Over.

                    GUS GRIMLY
Okay, well. As soon as the game's over. Over.

A CAR SPEEDS PAST.

Gus hits his siren, pulls out onto the road. We stay with him as
he follows the speeding car, its taillights visible through the
front windshield.

The car in front of him pulls over. Gus pulls in behind it.
Beat. He writes down the license plate number, notes the time.
Then climbs out of the car.

EXT. TWO-LANE HIGHWAY. RURAL MINNESOTA—CONTINUOUS

Gus approaches the driver's side, flashlight out. The inside of
the car is dark, ominous. We can't see the driver.

Then the driver's side window rolls down. Now we see the driver
is Lorne Malvo.

                    MALVO
Evening, Officer.

                    GUS GRIMLY
License and registration, please.

                    MALVO
Well, we could do it that way. You ask me for my papers and
I tell you it's not my car. That I borrowed it. And see
where things go from there. We could do that. Or, you could
just get back in your car and drive away.

                    GUS GRIMLY
Why would I do that?

                    MALVO
Because some roads you shouldn't go down. Because maps used
to say *there be dragons here*. And now they don't. But that
don't mean the dragons aren't there.

From the prowler, we hear Gus's walkie-talkie.

                    GRETA GRIMLY (O.S.)
Dad. Come in, Dad. Over.

                    GUS GRIMLY
Step out of the car, please.

                    MALVO
How old's your kid?

Gus puts his hand on his revolver.

                    GUS GRIMLY
I said step out of the car.

                    GRETA GRIMLY (O.S.)
Dad. Come in, Dad. Over.

                    MALVO
Let me tell you what's going to happen . . .
                (reads his name tag)
Officer Grimly. I'm gonna roll up my window. And then I'm
gonna drive away. And you're gonna go home to your daughter.
And every few years you're gonna look at her face and know
that you're alive because you chose not to go down a certain
road on a certain night. Because you chose to walk into the
light, instead of into darkness. Do you understand?

                    GUS GRIMLY
Sir.

                    MALVO
I'm rolling up my window.

The window rolls up. Gus stands there, knowing he should
pull his gun. That he should order Malvo out of the car, but
something stops him. The feeling the rabbit gets in the presence
of the wolf.

So he stands there as Malvo's car pulls away.

                    GRETA GRIMLY (O.S.)
Dad. Come in, Dad. Over.

Gus walks back to the . . .

        PATROL CAR

climbs in, closes the door. Beat. He picks up the walkie-talkie.

                    GUS GRIMLY
Dad here. Over.

                    GRETA GRIMLY (O.S.)
Detroit just got a touchdown. Over.
                    (beat)
Dad? Are you there? Over.

Beat. Gus sits, shaken.

                    GUS GRIMLY
     I hear ya. We'll get 'em in the fourth. And hey, don't
     forget ta do yer English homework, okay? Love ya.

A long silence.

                    GRETA GRIMLY (O.S.)
     Ya didn't say over. Over.

                    GUS GRIMLY
                      (smiles)
     Over and out.

Beat. Gus sits in his warm car, while outside the temperature
drops. Then he picks up his note pad, examines Malvo's license
plate number.

          CUT TO:

EXT. LESTER'S HOUSE. BEMIDJI, MN-NIGHT

It's really snowing now. Every police car in town is there,
along with an ambulance. Patrolmen go in and out of the house.
Molly sits on a planter by the front door, in shock.

Inside the lobby we can see Vern's body covered with a blanket.
After a moment, Molly gets to her feet and walks down the
driveway.

She passes Vern's prowler. Something inside catches her eye.

          ANGLE ON TWO CANS OF HOUSE PAINT

in the backseat.

          MOLLY

stands looking in at them, and all they represent.

          CUT TO:

EXT. THURMAN HOUSE. BEMIDJI, MN-NIGHT

Molly's car pulls up. She gets out, grabs the paint cans, starts
for the house. There are responsibilities she will take on now,
unspoken promises that must be kept.

The front door opens. Ida comes out, pulling a coat on over
her housedress. She knows from Molly's face that the worst has
happened.

                    CUT TO:

INT. HOSPITAL ROOM. BEMIDJI, MN—DAY

Lester is in bed, unconscious. His head is bandaged. He looks
terrible. Outside, snow falls. He wakes up. Gets his bearings.
He is in the hospital. Not dead. Better still, he is not
handcuffed to the bed. There are no cops.

Could it be? Could he have gotten away with it? He lifts his
right hand to get some water.

                    ANGLE ON THE HAND

We see a RED BUMP. This is the spot where the shotgun pellet
caught him. It is UNTREATED, which means doctors missed the
pellet.

Off Lester: he may have caught a break.

                    CUT TO:

EXT. ICE. BEMIDJI, MN—DAY

Molly's dad, Lou, unpacks fishing gear from the back of his
Suburban. Molly, in civilian clothes, sits on the tailgate,
looking out at the snow. Her prowler is parked nearby.

                         LOU SOLVERSON
          I got two kinds of sandwiches. Tuna and turkey.
                         (beat, off her)
          Tuna's for the fish. Unless ya think they'd think that's
          cannibalism.

Molly doesn't answer. Lou offloads a cooler.

                    LOU SOLVERSON (CONT'D)
          Ya know, I been looking for some more help at the
          restaurant. Someone to seat customers. Answer the phones.

                    MOLLY
                    (absently)
          A hostess.

                    LOU SOLVERSON
          That what they call it? Anyway, not sure if that was
          somethin you might be interested in.

                    MOLLY
                    (this gets a look)
          I'm a police officer, Dad.

                    LOU SOLVERSON
          Well, sure. I know that. I also know that people in this
          world are less inclined to shoot a hostess, than, say, an
          officer of the law.

                    MOLLY
                    (beat)
          That's true.

He kicks snow off his boots.

                    LOU SOLVERSON
          So, does that mean you're gonna help yer old man out?

                    MOLLY
          No. But maybe you could put that in the ad.

Molly jumps down from the tailgate.

                    MOLLY (CONT'D)
          On second thought, I'm gonna head in ta work. Rain check on
          the fishin?

He nods. She kisses his cheek.

                    MOLLY (CONT'D)
          Love ya, Dad.

                    LOU SOLVERSON
          Love ya too, hon.

Molly walks to her cruiser. Her father watches as we . . .

          FADE TO WHITE:

          END OF PILOT

Far · go (fär go)

1. A city of eastern North Dakota on the Red River east of Bismarck. Founded with the coming of the railroad in 1871, it is the largest city in the state. Population: 105,549.

2. A unique brand of true crime story, part tragedy, part farce, in which simple, good-hearted people come face-to-face with something monstrous.

THIS IS THE STORY of a **CRIMINAL** who meets a spineless insurance salesman and agrees to kill his bully, mostly because he wants to see how far he can push the insurance salesman before he snaps.

IT'S THE STORY of an **INSURANCE SALESMAN** who asks the criminal to kill his bully, then beats his own wife to death, and lies and cheats and steals to get away with it.

IT'S THE STORY of a young, **FEMALE POLICE DEPUTY** trying to figure out who killed the insurance salesman's wife, Who shot the police chief, Who stabbed a local trucking boss in a whorehouse, and who exactly is the dead naked guy in the woods.

IT'S THE STORY of a widowed STATE PATROLMAN who lets the criminal escape, and then feels compelled to track him down.

IT'S THE STORY of the SUPERMARKET KING of Minnesota, a man with a secret, who hires the criminal to figure out who's blackmailing him. Only to realize that may have been a mistake.

IT'S THE STORY OF A CRIME SYNDICATE in Fargo, North Dakota, that sends **TWO MEN**—a stone-deaf killer and his sign language interpreter—to Minnesota to figure out who killed the trucking boss. The two men find their way first to the insurance salesman, and then to the criminal, with grisly results.

IT'S A STORY about **CONSEQUENCES**, about what happens when a civilized man puts on his mukluks and tromps out into the wilderness. And how the wilderness he brings back infects him and the world around him.

IT'S THE STORY of a **PLACE**, where the sedate innocence of unremarkable American life collides with the lawless frontier. Mall food and frozen tundra. Pee Wee hockey games on thin ice.

IT'S THE STORY of the **PEOPLE** we long to be (simple, kind, neighborly) versus the people we fear the most (hardened, vicious, unfeeling).

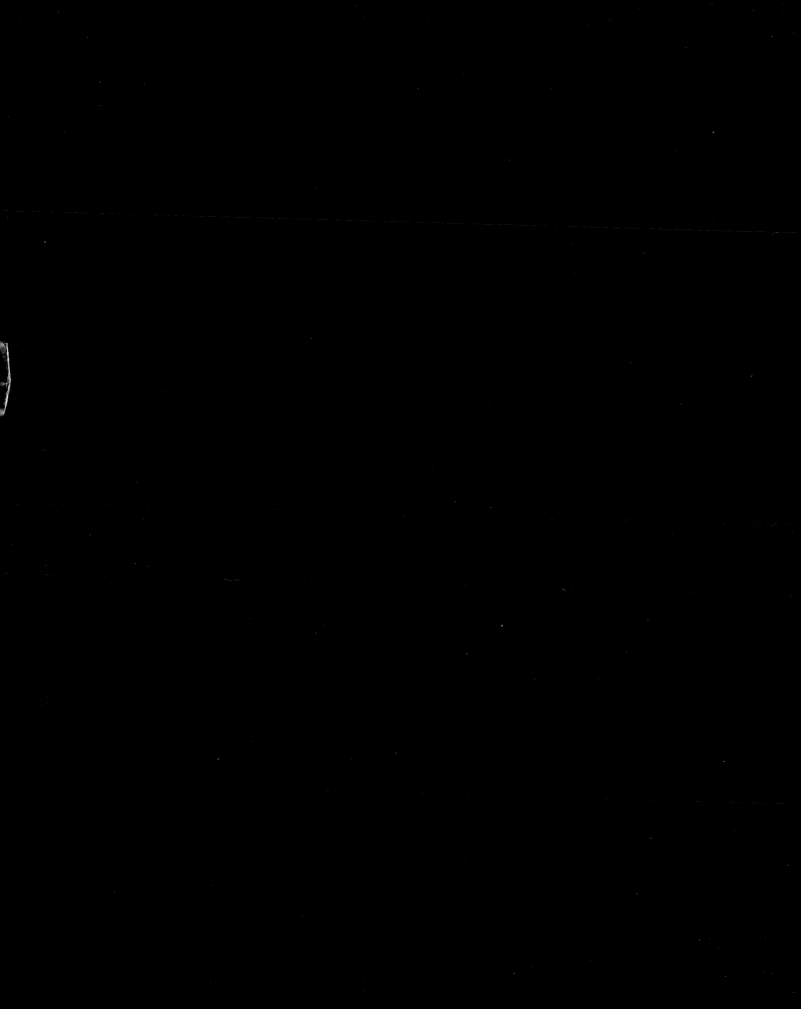

Yes, we have problems,
in other words. But look
who's solving them.

in CONVERSATION with CAROL CASE
(Series Costume Design Seasons 1–3)

NOAH: Early on, when asked what he thought he might wear, Billy basically said black. Then you and I talked about trying to avoid having any black clothes in the show. That iconic coat he wore, you made it, and it was a combination of an overcoat and then the fur was added in later.

CAROL: I think that coat is one of the things we remember the most from the show. Just because of how it evolved. The good thing with Billy and you, you both let me try other things moving out of the realm of classic bad guy looks. And Billy was great, once he saw where we were going; he just seemed to let it happen. He was quite lovely to work with that way. Collaborative but not demanding.

LORNE MALVO

PICTURE THIS: YOU AND YOUR WIFE GO to a party. There's a man there you've never seen before. He's charming. He tells great stories. When you talk to him you find yourself telling him things you wouldn't tell your closest friend. As does your wife. But on the way home you and your wife have a huge fight. In fact, after the party there are three divorces, one rape, and a suicide.

Here's a word. Instigator. Here's another. Anarchist. If Malvo were a religious man, he would worship Loki, the Norse god of mischief. He is the opposite of a brooding sociopath, a man capable of great charm. Malvo is what you might call a freelance criminal, a man you hire when you want something done that is not exactly legal. He has a broker, Mr. Rundle (whom we met in the pilot), a broker who fields requests—figure out who robbed me, murder my business partner, et cetera—and sends Malvo around the country.

Malvo is a collector, not of things, but of moments—moments where otherwise moral people are pushed to do immoral things. Malvo chases these moments. He manufactures them. They are more important to him than sex or love or money.

Which, as we saw in the pilot, means that, basically, he really likes fucking with people.

INT. INTERVIEW ROOM. POLICE PRECINCT.
DULUTH, MN—DAY

Malvo sits at the table. He has transformed himself into a mild-mannered local. Schmidt and Oswalt enter.

> LIEUTENANT SCHMIDT
> Ya. I'm Lieutenant Schmidt. This is Bill Oswalt, chief over Bemidji.

> MALVO
> Ya, Frank Peterson. I'm the minister up in Baudette. Go Bears.

Schmidt and Oswalt look at each other.

> LIEUTENANT SCHMIDT
> A minister.

> MALVO
> Ya. Baudette Lutheran. Six years now. Frank Peterson. Aberdeen fore that. So, ya know, not used ta havin a firearm stuck in my face, which — I know the Lord tests us in all kinda ways — but hoo partner, that's a heart stopper.

Oswalt has a CASE FILE in front of him. He looks down at the PHOTO from the parking garage.

ANGLE ON THE PHOTO

Grainy, black and white. Oswalt looks at it, then looks at

> MALVO
> with his top button done, squinty eyes, and his side part. If Malvo notices the photo (he does) or recognizes where it was taken (he does), he gives nothing away.

> BILL OSWALT
> frowns. The man in front of him doesn't look much like the man in the picture.

> LIEUTENANT SCHMIDT
> Cut the shit. You were pulled over Tuesday night driving a stolen car.

> MALVO
> Nossir. Think I'd remember that. Plus, Tuesday is bingo night at the church. Had

a full house. Florence Nightgarden won the whole pot, if I'm not mistaken.

> BILL OSWALT
> And we can check that?

> MALVO
> Yessir. Call Florence herself. Or Jim Avery. He's our alderman.

> LIEUTENANT SCHMIDT
> Deputy Grimly —

> MALVO
> Ya, that's the fella. Pulled his pistol, pointed it right at me. Thought I was gonna have a heart attack. But, ya know, after he mentioned those homicides over Bemidji, I thought — Frank, ya can't blame the guy fer bein a little jumpy. A horror show like that.

CUT TO:

> GUS GRIMLY
> watching the interview through the glass. He can't believe the performance he's watching.

> GUS
> That son of a bitch.

CUT TO:
INT. INTERVIEW ROOM. POLICE PRECINCT.
DULUTH, MN—CONTINUOUS

Bill Oswalt tries to press Malvo.

> BILL OSWALT
> So you weren't in Bemidji last week? If I show yer picture around, yer sayin no one'd recognize ya?

> MALVO
> Me? Nossir. Got a cousin lived in Bemidji back in the nineties. Out near Leech Lake. Moved ta Anchorage in oh three. I said: what, not cold enough fer ya in Minnesota? We had a good laugh bout that.

> BILL OSWALT
> And also yer sayin you didn't get pulled over fer speedin.

MALVO
Nossir. I'm a cautious driver by nature, on
accounta my eyesight's poor. Glaucoma
they say. Just in the one eye, but ya can't
be too careful. I tell my parishioners that.

LIEUTENANT SCHMIDT
Deputy Grimly . . .

MALVO
Forgiveness. That's at the heart a the
good book. Turn the other cheek. Second
chances. Amen. So I don't hold a grudge
against the deputy, though at the same
time — lucky I had my nitroglycerine pills,
I'll tell ya. Uffda.

Beat. Malvo is very convincing. Schmidt looks
at Oswalt. What do they really have on the guy?

LIEUTENANT SCHMIDT
Okay. Well, sit tight. We're gonna make
some calls, check yer story.

MALVO
Pick a name outta the phone book.
Everybody knows me up there.

CUT TO:
INT. POLICE PRECINCT. DULUTH, MN—DAY

Malvo heads for the exit. Gus Grimly
approaches him.

GUS
How could you do that?

MALVO
(still in character)
What's that, son?

GUS
Just — lie like that.

Malvo doesn't break character.

MALVO
I sure do hope you find the fella killed all
those people. I'll be prayin on it.

Malvo walks away. Beat. Gus calls after him.

GUS
Lorne Malvo.

Malvo stops, turns, reassessing Gus.

MALVO
(beat)
Did you know the human eye can see
more shades of green than any other
color?

GUS
What?

MALVO
I said did you know the human eye can
see more shades of green than any other
color? And my question to you is why?

Gus is stunned.

GUS
Now just — hold on.

MALVO
When you figure out the answer to my
question, you'll have the answer to yours.

He walks out the door. Gus watches him go.

If you're a man who likes to push others to the breaking point, then Minnesota is a darn good place to be. Because polite societies like this one—societies where people repress bad feelings, where they bury them under a sweet red gelatin of Minnesota nice—are also the most violent. Put enough pressure on a man like Lester, as we saw, and he's going to snap.

After the events of the pilot and his run-in with Patrolman **GUS GRIMLY**, Malvo arrives in beautiful downtown Duluth. He ditches Lester's car and reports for work. Work, in this case, being a freelance assignment: figure out who is blackmailing Stavros Milos, the Supermarket King of Minnesota. The blackmail note reads *I know about the money*.

But knows what? And who knows it? There's clearly a big secret there, but Stavros isn't talking.

INT. CAR (TRAVELING). DULUTH, MN—NIGHT

Malvo drives Stavros home. He looks at him in the rearview mirror.

> MALVO
> It was the Romans, wasn't it?

Beat. Stavros is lost in thought.

> STAVROS
> (confused)
> What are you saying?

> MALVO
> Saint Lawrence. Your window. The Romans burned him alive.

> STAVROS
> They did.

> MALVO
> (beat)
> You know why?

> STAVROS
> Because he was Christian.

> MALVO
> Maybe.
> (beat)
> But I think it's cause the Romans were raised by wolves. Greatest empire in human history, founded by wolves. And what do wolves do? They hunt. They kill. That's why I never bought into *The Jungle Book*. A boy raised by wolves and he makes friends with a bear and a panther? I don't think so.

Stavros thinks about this.

> MALVO (CONT'D)
> I knew a guy once, had a hundred-and-ten-pound Rottweiler. One night this girl thought it'd be funny to get down on all fours and let the dog hump her. Dog still had its balls. Well the dog gets up there, but he's not in on the joke. This is a bitch in heat as far as he's concerned and he's not leaving till he gets what he came for. Now the girl — too late — realizes the kind of mistake she's made, wants to get up. But the dog had other ideas.
> (beat)
> Had to shoot it behind the ear to get it off.

> STAVROS
> I don't —

> MALVO
> I'm saying the Romans, raised by wolves, they see a man turning water into wine, what do they do? They eat him. Cause there are no saints in the animal kingdom. There's only breakfast and dinner.

Stavros looks out the window, thinking.

STAVROS
(beat)
Every year I think, Are people gettin stupider? My own son, all he thinks about is fruit.
(beat)
I used to think about fruit. And vegetables. And where the paper products should go. Which aisle. And I used to stand by the front door and say good morning to people. By name.
(beat)
That's after I went to church to give thanks for what the Lord had given me. Before I was a big man.
(*what a joke*)
Big man.
(beat)
We're all the same size in the ground.

MALVO
sees something in the road ahead.

ANGLE ON A MAN
in the street. It's GUS GRIMLY. He's looking around, trying to figure out why Malvo was on this street earlier today. He turns towards the approaching car.

MALVO
thinks about what to do. He's so close to getting Stavros's money, he can't afford to see Gus now. For a second we think Malvo might hit the accelerator, run Gus over. Instead . . .

ANGLE ON THE DASHBOARD

Malvo turns on the BRIGHTS.

GUS
THROWS up his hands, BLINDED, as . . .

THE CAR
passes him.

MALVO
drives a few hundred feet. He checks the . . .

REARVIEW MIRROR
Gus is shaking his head, still blinded.

MALVO
turns into Stavros's driveway.

So Malvo starts to dig.[1] Is the blackmailer Stavros's head of security, former farm league hockey goon WALLY SEMENCHKO? Is it Stavros's simple son, DMITRI, or his bitter ex-wife, HELENA?

It's not until after Malvo finds Stavros's blackmailer (spoiler alert: Helena's Curves trainer, **DON CHUMPH**—an orange spray-tanned buffoon) that we realize his real agenda. Because rather than put a stop to the plan, Malvo takes over the blackmail scheme. Why take a small fee, when you can have the whole pot? Besides, Stavros is rich, and rich men have secrets, and men with secrets are vulnerable. And Malvo, as we know, thrives on the vulnerability of others. How far can Malvo push him? How far can he push Chumph?

1   Not realizing that as he digs, St. Cloud Police Deputy Molly Solverson is on his trail, putting together the pieces of Lester's and Malvo's crimes, first getting a photo of Malvo, then a name.

INT. DON CHUMPH'S HOUSE. DULUTH, MN—DAY

Don Chumph works desperately to peel the tape off of his mouth, rubbing his face against his shoulder. Over and over he does it, working the tape loose with his tongue. Then he sees . . .

SHADOWS
passing in front of the windows as the SWAT team gets in position.

CLOSE ON DON CHUMPH

Oh fuck. He redoubles his efforts, manages to loosen the tape.

DON CHUMPH
(muffled)
Wait!

TWO FLASH BANGS
crash through the window and roll to a stop.

CLOSE ON DON CHUMPH

He has time to widen his eyes. Then THE GRENADES GO OFF, stunning him, blinding him, and bursting his eardrums (along with all the windows in the house).

The KITCHEN DOOR CRASHES OPEN, and the Tactical Team enters.

ANGLE ON DON CHUMPH

From their POV HE IS BACKLIT. All they can see is a MAN standing in front of them with a shotgun.

COP
Gun!

The cops RIDDLE Don Chumph with bullets. He "dances" for a full minute, held up by the tape.

Finally the cops run out of bullets. The room is full of smoke. Slowly . . .

A COP
creeps forward, and for the first time sees

the strange sight of a MAN TAPED TO AN EXERCISE MACHINE, full of bullet holes.

There will be no Turkish Delight for Don Chumph.

But Malvo has a problem (two problems, actually, but we'll get to the second in a minute). And his problem is Gus Grimly, the Duluth patrolman who pulled him over. Because Gus realizes he made a mistake when he let Malvo go. He becomes a fly, a mosquito, buzzing around, threatening to ruin everything Malvo is trying to accomplish.

EXT. STREET. DULUTH, MN—CONTINUOUS

The prowler STOPS abruptly at an odd angle. Watching it, Malvo calmly buttons the top button of his shirt. Gus tumbles out of the car, fumbling for his sidearm. Malvo dials his cell phone.

GUS
Freeze! Don't —

Gus gets his gun out, AIMS it at Malvo, who has the phone to his ear. With his other hand, Malvo smooths his HAIR into a SIDE PART. (He is subtly changing his appearance.)

GUS (CONT'D)
Hands where I can — where I can see 'em.

MALVO
Just making a call.

GUS
I'm tellin ya, drop the phone.

MALVO
Absolutely. Soon as I —
          (into the phone)
This is Duluth. Package requested. Frank Peterson.

Malvo hangs up, shows Gus his hands.

MALVO (CONT'D)
See? All good.

GUS
Drop it!

MALVO
It's a new phone.

GUS
Now!

MALVO
Okay.

Malvo drops the phone, which shatters on the cement.

MALVO (CONT'D)
What's this about, Officer?

GUS
It's — you know what it's about. Now, uh, face the car. Hands on the car.

Malvo turns, puts his hands on the hood. Gus edges over, trying to figure out how to keep his gun on Malvo and cuff him at the same time.

GUS (CONT'D)
Gimme yer, put yer left hand behind yer —

Malvo does. Gus manages to get the handcuff on it.

GUS (CONT'D)
Now the other — slowly.

Gus clicks the cuff on Malvo's wrist, holsters his weapon. The relief on his face is palpable. He turns Malvo around.

> MALVO
> Am I under arrest?

> GUS
> Yer handcuffed. Course yer under —

> MALVO
> On what charge?

Gus realizes he has acted impulsively, and doesn't have a strategy here.

> GUS
> It's — we'll figure that out at the station.

Gus grabs Malvo's arm, leads him over to the prowler. He tries to pull the BACK DOOR open, but it's LOCKED. Gus has to get the CLICKER out of his pocket, unlock the doors, to get Malvo inside.

And then there's Malvo's second problem. The actions he took with Lester are about to catch up with him. Because Lester has told the hired killers that it was Malvo, not him, who killed Hess. And just as Malvo is about to collect the blackmail money, he is ambushed by Mr. Wrench and Mr. Numbers.

It is the first time we've seen Malvo at a disadvantage, and he barely escapes with his life. Malvo abandons his blackmail scheme—because money has never been his primary goal—and goes after the men who sent Wrench and Numbers.

EXT. CHINESE RESTAURANT. FARGO, ND—DAY

<u>The following is one long tracking shot.</u> We are across the street from the restaurant. We see EIGHT MEN exit. They include MR. TRIPOLI, MR. CARLYLE, AND MR. JERGEN (aka the Fargo Crime Syndicate).

Mr. Jergen is picking his teeth with a toothpick.

MR. JERGEN
— so he's got the stick in his mouth, right? Bitin down — and I grab the arrow —

The men turn left down the sidewalk. The CAMERA TRACKS RIGHT WITH THEM—parked cars and street traffic between us.

MR. JERGEN (CONT'D)
And Craig's in the car, laughin his ass off. Thinks the whole thing's hi-larious, which — that's my cousin out there, right? So I slip the knife outta my boot.

The men reach the ENTRANCE of a three-story office building (windows opaque or mirrored). The camera stops. The men enter the building, and the CAMERA DROPS STRAIGHT DOWN to find TWO MEN sitting in a parked car directly across the street. These are FBI AGENTS WEBB PEPPER and BILL BUDGE.

PEPPER
And lunch is over.

Budge makes a note of this in his log book.

BUDGE
I don't know how they eat that crap every day.

Pepper takes out a hoagie.

BUDGE (CONT'D)
Speaking of.

Pepper unwraps the sandwich.

PEPPER
What? It's fresh.

BUDGE
Do you know the conditions of a modern fast-food restaurant? I'm not just talking hygiene.

PEPPER
Get bent.

As they talk, the CAMERA MOVES around to the front of the car, facing the windshield, and as it does, we see LORNE MALVO approaching from the rear along the passenger side of the car. He

wears a long coat. Underneath it is a KEVLAR VEST. We may also see evidence of some of the MANY WEAPONS Malvo's got on him.

BUDGE (O.S.)
They did an experiment once. Scientist took two glasses of water.

As Malvo reaches the curb in front of the FBI car, the camera continues to turn and RISE, until we LAND IN a CLOSE UP.

Malvo looks up at the office building the eight men entered. If he's scared by what he's about to do, he doesn't show it.

BUDGE (O.S.) (CONT'D)
He cursed at one of them, just called it all kinds of names.

Malvo steps into the street. We LET HIM GO, ROTATING to catch him from behind as he approaches the front door of the building.

PEPPER (O.S.)
You're making this up.

Malvo enters the front door. Instead of following we stay on the front door.

We HEAR THE FOLLOWING:

RECEPTIONIST (O.S.)
Good afternoon, sir, how can I help you?

We HEAR A SCREAM. A GUNSHOT. The sound of running feet. Then a series of GUNSHOTS. It's clear the occupants of the building are fighting back.

The camera TRACKS RIGHT—and though we can't see Malvo inside, we realize we are following his spree through the building.

Meanwhile, we ALSO HEAR Pepper and Budge continue their conversation, oblivious to the fire fight going on inside.

BUDGE (O.S.)
Swear to God. He yells at one of the water glasses and whispers sweet nothings to the other.

They're oblivious to the YELLS and

GUNSHOTS we're hearing. We TRACK ALONG the first floor of the building. MEN YELLING. GUNSHOTS.

> BUDGE (O.S.) (CONT'D)
> A week later —

> PEPPER (O.S.)
> Just stop it.

Then we HEAR the sound of a STAIRWELL DOOR OPENING. The sound quality changes, becoming echoey. As Malvo CLIMBS, the camera rises with him to the SECOND FLOOR.

> THUG (O.S.)
> Stop!

A GUNSHOT. The sound of THE DEAD THUG FALLING down the stairs.

> BUDGE (O.S.)
> A week later the glass he yelled at — it's tinted green. The other glass — still crystal clear.

Then we HEAR the second-floor STAIRWELL DOOR OPEN.

> THUG #2
> He's here!

More GUNSHOTS.

Now the CAMERA TRACKS LEFT, as Malvo kills his way across the second floor. GUNSHOTS, RUNNING, YELLING.

> PEPPER (O.S.)
> (spills something)
> Shit. That's gonna stain.

> BUDGE (O.S.)
> My point is, it's not just what's in the food. It's how it's made. The conditions.

The CAMERA STOPS. We hear a DING and the sound of elevator doors opening. We RISE STRAIGHT UP with Malvo, hearing the soothing sounds of ELEVATOR MUSIC.

DING, we arrive on the TOP FLOOR.

> THUG #3 (O.S.)
> Hold him!

GUNSHOTS.

> THUG #4 (O.S.)
> No, please.

GUNSHOTS. A MAN CRASHES through a window, FALLS out of our sight-line. Through the window we see our only glimpse of what's going on inside the room. Malvo has entered through a door camera left. He will exit through a door camera right, but right now he lowers the smoking shotgun (the one he used to blow Jergen through the window) and lifts a semi-automatic weapon in time to SHOOT a thug who is leaping at him.

The door ahead of him opens and a THUG with a gun steps in, FIRES a shot at Malvo. It goes wide. Malvo BLOWS the GUY AWAY, then steps over his body and exits the room.

And we PAN PAST THE ROOM and are back on dark glass.

Over this we hear:

> PEPPER (O.S.)
> Jesus!

> BUDGE (O.S.)
> Was that —

The SOUND of a CAR DOOR opening.

> PEPPER (O.S.)
> Call it in!

We continue to TRACK RIGHT past the broken window, as Malvo reaches the far end of the building.

> MR. TRIPOLI (O.S.)
> You want a piece of me? Come on then!

A FINAL FLURRY OF GUNSHOTS. Beat. Then we HEAR ANOTHER STAIRWELL DOOR open.

We HEAR Malvo climb a short flight of stairs to the ROOF. We RISE with him and ARRIVE ON THE ROOF as he emerges from the DOOR.

He is BLEEDING from a few cuts on his face.

Malvo winces, takes off his bulletproof vest. He drops it down an airshaft. He checks his abdomen. There is a bullet hole in his side, blood coming out.

We HEAR SIRENS in the distance.

Malvo breaks down his pistols, drops them down the airshaft. He goes to the edge of the roof and JUMPS onto the adjoining roof of the next building.

As we watch, Malvo OPENS the ROOF DOOR and disappears.

      CUT TO:
EXT. STREET. FARGO, ND—DAY

Pepper and Budge stand over Mr. Jergen's twisted body. The SIRENS are close now.

            PEPPER
Shit.

            BUDGE
Mother of —

POLICE CARS SCREAM TO A HALT. COPS jump out, drawing their weapons. Pepper and Budge hold up their badges.

            PEPPER
FBI! We're FBI!

We FIND MALVO as he exits the neighboring building. A CROWD is gathering outside. THE COPS PUSH THEM BACK.

            COP
Back! Get back!

Malvo buttons his coat, turns, and walks off down the street. We watch him go.

Then, when he learns that it was Lester who gave the men his name, Malvo goes back to St. Cloud to get revenge.

What he doesn't realize though, is that the Lester he met is gone. In his place is a very different man, a man capable of anything.

in CONVERSATION with CAROL CASE
(Series Costume Design Seasons 1–3)

NOAH: Martin Freeman, in his own life, is such a clotheshorse and such a natty dresser that I have to believe that his sartorial instincts really rebelled against that flat Midwestern style.

CAROL: He never gave us any trouble. But I think the orange parka was the thing he had to get over in the beginning.

NOAH: It was very important to me that there was a Charlie Brown factor to him and the orange coat was that for me.

LESTER NYGAARD

THINK OF LESTER AS PATIENT ZERO and Lorne Malvo as the Plague. The two men meet by chance in a hospital waiting room. One is weak-willed, a harborer of petty resentments and jealousies, tired of being pushed around by life. The other is a biblical snake, cold-blooded, manipulative, a being of pure id. In their accidental contact an infection is passed from snake to worm. As a result, all of Lester's *why me* resentments, his punching bag repressions, are switched from passive to active.

Then, when Malvo kills Hess—Lester's iconic childhood bully—a fuse is lit within Lester. He has spent his entire life believing his problems to be unsolvable. Now a single act of brutal violence shows him the truth. Any problem can be solved as long as you are willing to do what it takes. No one in this world is going to give you respect. You have to take it.

So Lester beats his wife to death and tries to frame Malvo for it, but everything goes to hell. So now here's Lester, new to sociopathy, trying to cover his ass and stay out of jail. In the days after his wife's death he is just getting the hang of it—the lying, the manipulation, the willingness to do whatever it takes to get your way.

The truth is, he feels bad about what happened to his wife. Still harbors some regrets over Hess. Don't worry. This will pass.

INT. BEDROOM. LESTER'S HOUSE—DAY

Everything is as it was when Pearl was alive, half-empty water glass, slippers by the bed. And yet everything has changed.

Lester doesn't know what to do with himself. He opens his wife's CLOSET and tries to summon up grief. It doesn't come. He touches her clothes, then STEPS INSIDE, burying himself in her shirts and dresses. An animal noise comes out of him. It is a primal sound, but maybe also a little forced. A performance.

The DOORBELL rings. Lester immediately snaps back to normal and heads downstairs.

                    CUT TO:
INT. LESTER'S HOUSE—DAY

Lester answers the door to see Molly and Bill.

                    BILL OSWALT
          Heya, Lester.

                    LESTER
                    (unnerved)
          Bill.

                    MOLLY
                    (jumping right in)
          Mr. Nygaard, we have some questions
          we'd like ta —

                    BILL OSWALT
          This is Molly.

                    MOLLY
          Deputy Solverson.

                    LESTER
          Sure. Nice ta meetcha.

                    MOLLY
          Like I was sayin — we got some questions.

                    BILL OSWALT
                    (interrupting)
          How ya holding up, Lester? How's the head?

                    LESTER
          Yeah, it hurts. Got a little double vision
          still.

                    BILL OSWALT
          Jeez. Well, ya know, if now's not a good
          time . . .

                    LESTER
          No. I mean, I was just — I wanna help, ya
          know — but there's just so much work ta
          do.

                    MOLLY

          It'll only take a second.

                    CUT TO:
INT. KITCHEN. LESTER'S HOUSE—DAY

Lester sits across from Bill and Molly. She has her CASE FILE out. There is a glass of grape juice in front of each of them. Lester's skin feels electric. He knows that at any moment he could say or do the wrong thing, and then they would know the truth. That he killed his wife. That he knows who killed Vern and Hess. That he is responsible.

                    LESTER
          All I got's grape juice. Hope that's okay.
          Pearl says it reminds her of bein a kid.
                    (beat)
          Said.

                    BILL OSWALT
          Remember that gum? That grape gum.
          They had it when we were kids. Heck.
          What was that called?

                    MOLLY
                    (ignoring him)
          So, we got yer statement from the
          hospital.

                    LESTER
          Yeah, I was real thorough with those
          fellas. I mean, what I could remember.
          Doctor says I got a concussion. Says if I
          was hit any harder my brain coulda swole
          up, leaked right out my ears.

                    BILL OSWALT
          Thank gosh that didn't happen.

MOLLY
In yer statement you said ya came home
and found yer wife — that she was
already dead.

LESTER
Downstairs. Yeah. I heard the washer
going. The spin cycle. And I — well, she
was on the floor, ya know, and there was
a lot of — and — I never even heard the
guy. Just — one minute I'm looking at her
and the next —

MOLLY
So you don't remember Chief Thurman
comin to the house.

LESTER
No. I feel sick about that really. I guess he
saw the guy breaking in.

MOLLY
No, Mr. Nygaard. Chief Thurman came
to talk to you. About a man you may
have met in the emergency room the day
previous.

LESTER
(freaked, covering)
Ya don't say.

BILL OSWALT
Lester, if it's too hard for you, just give
the —

MOLLY
(pressing)
We got a witness says she saw you and
this other fella arguing — about Sam
Hess.

LESTER
Who?

MOLLY
Sam. Hess.

BILL OSWALT
You remember Sam. Used to beat you up
in high school.

Molly turns to Bill. This is news to her, and
definitely a clue.

MOLLY
What?

BILL OSWALT
Oh yeah. That Sam — he had a thing fer
old Lester. Used to chase him around
the schoolyard until one or the other ran
outta gas.
(to Lester)
You remember. Big kid. What was that he
called you? *Lester Nigg . . .*

LESTER
Oh, yeah. Sam. Heh heh. That was a long
time ago.

MOLLY
But you were talking about him in the
emergency room. What's the story there?

Under the table Lester fidgets with the wound
on his hand.

LESTER
I — you know — it's real fuzzy. I may have
said *my face is a mess*. Mess. That sounds
like Hess. Probably the — yer witness —
just misheard.

BILL OSWALT
That's possible.

MOLLY
Can you describe the fella? Height, eye
color, that kinda thing.

LESTER
(sweating)
It's, uh — the last few days — they're real
fuzzy.

BILL OSWALT
Reason we asks is we got an operating
theory — this being the work of a drifter
or drifters. Possibly drug related. So I'm
thinking this fella you met at the hospital,
maybe he followed you home.

MOLLY
That's not — we don't both share that
theory.

LESTER
Well, uh, I'm a little — scrambled right now? Doctor says I got a concussion. Not sure if I said that. So things are kinda fuzzy.

Beat. Lester is really sweating now. Molly watches him. Lester looks like he may crack. Suddenly, Bill stands.

BILL OSWALT
Ya know what? I'm satisfied.

MOLLY
Well, I've got a few more . . .

Bill lifts her out of the chair by the elbow.

BILL OSWALT
Thanks for the grape juice, Lester. Takes me back, I'll tell ya. And I'm gonna look up the name of that gum when I get home.

LESTER
Hubba Bubba.

BILL OSWALT
(smiles)
That's it. Hubba Bubba. We used to crack up about that. Hubba Bubba.
(to Molly)
You remember Hubba Bubba?

MOLLY
(not amused)
No.

Lester sees them to the front door.

BILL OSWALT
You need anything, Lester, you just let us know. This is a tragedy. A straight dyed-in-the-wool tragedy.

Lester nods. The outline of Vern's body looms behind him.

LESTER
She was a good woman, ya know. A good wife. I just keep asking myself — who coulda done a thing like this?

If Lester had any doubts, the positive reinforcement he gets from his brother—showing up at the hospital, expressing concern, inviting Lester to stay with them—shows Lester that he has made the right choice. In his own twisted way he takes two separate things—his wife's murder and his brother's love—and conflates them. Killing his wife, in other words, rewarded Lester with brotherly love.

And that klieg light of unconditional love—a love he has never known before—is a light that, once felt, becomes addictive to Lester. He has killed his wife and aided in the death of two others, and as a result has secured a family. What wouldn't he do to keep that?

But living a lie isn't easy. And the deeper Lester gets, the more lies he finds himself telling. At first just to the police. But then two men show up in town, hired killers looking for Hess's murderer. And suddenly Lester finds himself being squeezed tighter and tighter.

INT. BO MUNK INSURANCE SHOP. BEMIDJI, MN—DAY

Mr. Wrench and Mr. Numbers are standing in the empty shop looking at him. Lester jumps a little, seeing them there.

LESTER
Ho. Ya scared me there. Thought the place was —

Wrench and Numbers stare at him.

LESTER (CONT'D)
I was in the —

Wrench and Numbers just stare at him. Beat.
Lester's desk PHONE RINGS. He flinches.

LESTER (CONT'D)
Uh, just —

He goes to his desk, answers.

LESTER (CONT'D)
(answering)
Yello.

VOICE (O.S.)
Lester Nygaard, please.

LESTER
This is Lester.

VOICE (O.S.)
Ya, Mr. Nygaard, this is Duluth impound.
Just wanna let ya know we got yer car.

Lester is surprised, but also aware that he is
being watched.

LESTER
Pardon?

VOICE (O.S.)
Yer car.
(looking it up)
License 62863QI. Got towed yesterday
from Phoenix Farms on Elm.

LESTER
In Duluth?

VOICE (O.S.)
Yessir.

Numbers doesn't like being ignored. He
reaches out and SPINS the pamphlet RACK
without looking at it. It needs oil and makes a
grating sound as it spins. *Eek, eek, eek.* But he
doesn't stop.

LESTER
(to Numbers)
Take anything ya like.
(into phone)
Well, so what do I gotta —

VOICE (O.S.)
Just need proof a current registration and
a hundred fifty dollars and we'll release
the car to ya. Cash only, course.

Eek, eek, eek. Numbers spins the rack,
watches Lester. Lester thinks about asking
more, but can't figure out how without giving
things away. *Eek, eek, eek.* Mr. Numbers spins
the rack of insurance pamphlets. Mr. Wrench
leans against the wall and looks at Lester.

LESTER
(distracted)
Okay. Thanks fer callin.

VOICE (O.S.)
Remember. Cash only.

Lester hangs up, looks at Wrench and
Numbers.

LESTER
So. What can I do fer you fellas then?

Beat. Numbers spins the pamphlet rack. *Eek,
eek, eek.* Wrench stares at Lester.

LESTER (CONT'D)
Cause, uh, we're pretty busy right now.

Beat. It's obvious business is dead. *Eek, eek,
eek.*

Mr. Wrench SIGNS something to Lester.

MR. WRENCH
(signs)
Little man.

LESTER
What's that?

MR. WRENCH
(signs)
Small time, small town. Nobody.

Eek, eek, eek. It's obvious he's saying something important, but Lester doesn't understand.

LESTER
I'm sorry, I —

Mr. Numbers is watching them, spinning the rack. *Eek, eek, eek.*

MR. NUMBERS
Sam Hess.

LESTER
(testicles retracting)
Are you — uh, fellas, family of his?

Wrench SIGNS angrily.

MR. WRENCH
(signs)

I've killed lions. Kings. But you? You're a joke. A bug.

Lester looks at Numbers, who finally STOPS spinning the rack. The silence is both a relief and a sign of escalation.

MR. NUMBERS
We saw you with the widow. Looked like you were having a party. Celebrating, maybe?

The two men advance on Lester from either side, cornering him. Violence is in the air.

LESTER
(appealing to them)
I got a deaf cousin.

They've got him against the wall now. Violence is imminent. There is A KNOCK on the door. The three turn. Molly Solverson is standing at the glass. She waves. Lester, looking relieved, waves back.

He SQUEEZES between Wrench and Numbers and unlocks the door.

Lester's desperation increases, the scale of lies he'll tell. Darker thoughts arise.
    What will it take to make his problems disappear? A mob war? A dead cop? Maybe the answer is to stop defending and start attacking. To become less like Lester and more like Malvo.

INT. INTERVIEW ROOM. POLICE PRECINCT. BEMIDJI, MN—DAY

LESTER NYGAARD sits alone. He looks nervous. But at the same time, he looks better than we've seen him since episode one. His nose and face are healing. His hand is better.

We sit with him for a moment. Maybe he gets up, walks around the room, trying to keep his fears in check. Is he under arrest? Did his gambit at Chazz's fail?

Finally, the door opens and Chief Bill Oswalt

comes in with a FILE FOLDER. The last two weeks have taken a toll on Bill, his positive nature, his faith in humanity. He sits, looks through the file. Lester sits across from him, nervous, waiting.

LESTER
Busy morning?

Bill goes through the folder.

LESTER (CONT'D)
Is there a — some kinda development in the case? Is that why I'm —

in CONVERSATION with JEFF RUSSO
(Series Composer, Seasons 1–3)

NOAH: In the first season we started the idea of themes for characters that continued throughout, and you would write themes for characters that sometimes would be used for different characters. I liked the idea of percussion—straight percussion—for Wrench and Numbers.

JEFF: Which was one of the best musical ideas for the show that there was, I think. And even bringing it back in season 3, because the only character that appears in all three seasons is Mr. Wrench.

Beat. Lester looks around.

> LESTER (CONT'D)
> Where's the — female deputy? Is she —

> BILL OSWALT
> She got shot, Lester.

> LESTER
> She got —

> BILL OSWALT
> In Duluth.

Lester reacts to *Duluth*—where Malvo is, where he sent Wrench and Numbers—but tries to cover. Luckily, Bill's not looking at Lester. He's lost in thought.

> BILL OSWALT (CONT'D)
> I should be up there right now, but then there's this mess —

He stares at his paperwork. Lester tries to get a look at the file, but Bill holds the folder so he can't see.

BILL OSWALT (CONT'D)
I don't even know where ta start. It's like
ya see on the news where a boat sinks in
India and three hundred people drown.
And you think, Do I know three hundred
people? Or some African massacre.
Twelve-year-olds with machetes. And they
kill — heck, ya can't even count that high.
(beat)
We lost sixteen people in nineteen twenty
to the flu. I looked it up. In seventy-eight,
pharmacy fire took six. But nothin like
this. Ever. Three people murdered in two
days, includin the chief a police. Lenny
Potts missing. A cop shot. And now a kid
brings a gun ta school.

This hits Lester. Elation. Did his plan work? He
covers.

LESTER
A kid —

BILL OSWALT
It was Gordo, Lester.

LESTER
Gordo? My Gordo?

BILL OSWALT
Had a handgun in his backpack. Unloaded,
thank gosh, but still. Ya can't — not with
the current climate.

LESTER
Is he in trouble?

BILL OSWALT
He's — he brought a gun ta school. At the
same time, Gordo's the leasta this. We
searched the house —
(beat, hard for him)
And I gotta be honest with ya, Lester, I
don't know whether ta — I'd like ta think
after all those years — that you coulda —
come to me. As a friend. Coulda trusted
me with —

Lester doesn't know Bill's angle, so he waits.
Bill collects himself.

BILL OSWALT (CONT'D)
We know you were in the room when Vern
was shot. You had a shotgun pellet in yer
hand. Same as killed Vern.

Lester nods, waiting to see what Bill says next.
Beat. Bill looks Lester in the eye for the first
time.

BILL OSWALT (CONT'D)
Lester, was yer wife havin an affair?
(beat)
With Chazz?

Beat. Lester nods. Bill shakes his head.

BILL OSWALT (CONT'D)
He had a photo of her. Photos. At his
place. Suggestive.

LESTER
I don't wanna —

BILL OSWALT
Boudoir pictures. Plus a pair a —

LESTER
Bill.

BILL OSWALT
And look. I know ya loved her. I remember.
Ninth grade science class. Mrs. Nagutuck.
And Pearl comes in, first day a class, sits
down. And you look at me. *I'm gonna
marry that girl one day.*

Beat. Lester is surprised that this memory hits
him as powerfully as it does.

BILL OSWALT (CONT'D)
But she was always — and I know it's
outta line — but I mean, we all knew, ya
know, the stories — but ta sleep with yer
own brother.

LESTER
I know.

BILL OSWALT
Yer own — and then she what? Tells him
it's over and he — I mean, yer brother
always did have a temper.

LESTER
Broke a guy's nose once, just fer crackin
wise at the state fair.

BILL OSWALT
Ya. I remember that. Had ta do community
service. And so Pearl, what, she cuts it
off, the affair, and he —

Beat. This is it. The moment of truth. If Lester
can sell the lie, he will walk free.

LESTER
(beat)
All I know is, I came home from work and
they were arguin. In the basement. I heard
the voices and I thought — *Is that Chazz?*
And so I go to the top a the stairs — ta
hear, ya know. And she says *is that what
you think this is? Love?* — or somethin like
that — and then she laughs. And says,
ya know, *yer not half the man yer brother
is.* And then I hear this sound. This — I'll
never forget it. And I run downstairs, and
there's Chazz — and he's got a hammer in
his — and he looks up at me and says, *aw
jeez, Lester. What did I —*

Lester lets this hang in the air. *Aw jeez, Lester.
What did I—*

LESTER (CONT'D)
And we're — I'm upset, and tryin ta go ta
Pearl, ya know. See if she's — and Chazz
says, *it was an accident, huh?* And I'm —
an accident? Ya hit her with a hammer.
And Chazz, he lifts the hammer again
— lookin at me. And I don't know if he's
gonna — so I say, something like, *Chazz,
what the heck are ya —*
(beat)
And then the doorbell rings.

BILL OSWALT
Vern.

Lester nods.

LESTER
I wanted to say somethin, Bill. Swear. But
Chazz, ya know, he —

BILL OSWALT
You were afraid.

LESTER
I was afraid. And Chazz, ya know, he's my
brother. My —

BILL OSWALT
(beat, gets it)
So what happens then?

LESTER
It's — we go upstairs, and Chazz says,
take care of it. And he goes inta the livin
room.

BILL OSWALT
Where you kept the shotgun.

Beat. Lester nods.

LESTER
I shoulda thouta that — the shotgun —
but I was in shock, ya know. And so I
let Vern in, and right away I think ta tell
him, say what happened — cause maybe
Pearl's still alive downstairs. Maybe
there's time ta — but then Chazz comes
outta the living room with the shotgun.
(beat)
I shoulda stopped him. I shoulda said
right away, ya know, Chazz's in the house
and he — but I was afraid, like you said.
And now —

Beat. Lester decides to make a big play.

LESTER (CONT'D)
— Bill, if you think that makes me guilty a
somethin — well, then I want ya ta throw
the book at me. Send me ta prison. Cause
I loved her, ya know. Pearl. Despite all —
she was my wife. And not a minute goes
by I don't —

He shakes his head, grief-struck.

BILL
thinks about this, about his relationship with
Lester and how he just doesn't want to live
in a world where the man he's known for
decades is a criminal.

It is from this notion that Lester will grow into true villainy. It is a path that will put him on a collision course with the original source of his infection. Our true villain, Lorne Malvo. And in this way we will see if the student can surpass the master.

INT. LOBBY/ELEVATOR. HOTEL—NIGHT

The elevator doors open and Malvo and his party get on. Malvo glances out into the lobby to make sure Lester isn't following.

BURT
He was a piece of work, huh?

MALVO
Who's that?

BURT
The guy from the bar. You sure you don't —

Malvo pushes the door close button.

MALVO
Oh, people nab me all the time. Just one of those faces, I guess.

The doors start to close. Then . . .

A HAND
shoots out and stops the doors. They open. Lester climbs aboard, winded.

LESTER
(worked up)
No. Ya hear me? No. You don't get to —
(to everyone else)
— and I'm sorry for interrupting — but it's not right, and when something's not right — well, the old Lester, he woulda let things slide, but not this guy.

He waves his award at them.

LESTER (CONT'D)
I've worked too hard, ya know? Come too —

MALVO
Lester. Stop.

LESTER
Oh, so now you <u>do</u> know me.

Beat. Malvo laughs. *You got me.* Lester laughs too.

JEMMA
Honey?

MALVO
(to Lester)
Is this what you want?

LESTER
(thrown)
I —

BURT
Hey, Mick Mike, lighten up, huh?

But Malvo is focused on Lester.

MALVO
Is. This. What. You. Want?

BURT
Mick Mike —

MALVO
(focused on Lester)
Yes or no.

Beat. Lester nods. He is the new Lester, a maker of choices.

LESTER
Yes.

Without looking away, Malvo pulls out a PISTOL with a SILENCER and SHOOTS BURT in the head. WEEZY SCREAMS. Malvo turns and SHOOTS HER too.

JEMMA
(in shock)
Oh my God. Oh my God.

Without a second thought, Malvo SHOOTS JEMMA. She drops. Three people dead in under five seconds. The elevator looks like an abattoir.

LESTER
stands frozen in shock and horror.

LESTER
Oh my —

Malvo holsters his gun, coolly fixes his hair.

MALVO
That's on you.

LESTER
(in shock)
I —

The elevator arrives at the third floor and dings. Malvo pulls his gun, ready to shoot anyone in the hall. Beat. The doors open. Luckily no one is waiting. Malvo pockets the gun, presses B. The doors close.

MALVO
Six months I worked that guy, Lester. Six months. Can you imagine the number of sewer mouths I put my hands in? The gallons of human spit. Not to mention a hundred-thousand-dollar bounty down the toilet.
(beat)
Still, the look on his face when I pulled the gun. Classic.

The elevator doors open on the basement level. We see a long, empty concrete hallway.

MALVO (CONT'D)
Grab the fat guy's feet. We'll throw him in a dumpster.

He bends down, gets Burt under the arms.

LESTER
looks at the back of Malvo's head, then at the Salesman of the Year Award in his hand. He SWINGS, connects. Malvo grunts, falls, not unconscious, but dazed. He struggles to get up.

MALVO (CONT'D)
Shit, Lester.

Lester jumps over him, hurries off down the . . .

INT. BASEMENT HALLWAY. FLAMINGO HOTEL. LAS VEGAS—CONTINUOUS

It's a narrow space and darkly lit. Lester runs, panicked, expecting to be shot, chased, caught, killed. Beat. Then Malvo's voice echoes after him.

MALVO (O.S.)
I'll see you soon, Lester.

MOLLY SOLVERSON

THERE IS A SIMPLICITY TO life when you grow up in a small town. Simplicity to a place where the graduating high school class has less than a hundred people in it. A place where time is measured in generations. America is a big country, and Minnesota is a big state, especially in winter. But when you live in a small town like St. Cloud it can feel as if you live on an island surrounded by endless snow. Like you live in a place the rest of the world can't touch.

Which is what Molly Solverson likes about St. Cloud. She was never the girl who dreamed of moving to the big city. Molly is Scandinavian after all, and an Episcopalian to boot. Humble to a fault. Smart, but not a showoff. She likes her victories quiet, her progress slow.

Molly has no desire to make the Big Case that gets her into the FBI. Instead, she just wants everything in its right place. Which is why she became a law enforcement officer. Because crime is the antithesis of order. It's a B & E that leaves behind a broken home, except the home in this case is society. And so criminals have to be put in their right place, which is prison.

But then Lorne Malvo comes to town. And the rules of order and society go out the fucking window.

INT. INTERVIEW ROOM. POLICE PRECINCT. BEMIDJI, MN—DAY

Molly has a whiteboard of the case up. Nothin fancy. Names, pictures, places. A more organized version of what she drew on the window at the hospital in Duluth.

Bill comes in with Deputy Knutson, sees it. His heart sinks a little, but he covers.

                    BILL OSWALT
          There she is. The gunfighter.

                    MOLLY
          Hey, Chief.

He looks up at the wall.

                    BILL OSWALT
          Nice collage. You take up basket weavin
          too in yer downtime?

                    MOLLY
          Just some loose ends. Wanted ta —

                    BILL OSWALT
          Look, before ya — I just want you ta know
          — I'm not too proud ta say I was wrong.
          On the Lester case. I had the wrong idea.
          Thought it was a drifter thing. Which —
          was the wrong way ta go, clearly. But look
          — some good police work and we caught
          the guy. So —

                    MOLLY
          Well, see, that's the problem. Yer still —

She stops.

                    BILL OSWALT
          Still what?

                    MOLLY
                 (reluctantly)
          Wrong. I mean, no disrespect. But it
          doesn't make sense. The brother? I mean,
          with all the things we know are true. And I
          been lyin in bed just thinkin, ya know? So,
          fer example, I mean, if it was the brother,
          how do you explain the phone call from
          Lester's to the motel the night a the
          murders?

Bill doesn't want to get into this all again.

                    BILL OSWALT
          Molly, now — darnit. Just — stop. Can't
          keep havin the same — it's time. Gotta
          let it go. We did our jobs. The brother
          Nygaard is locked up. He killed the wife
          and cornered and shot the chief. Lester
          was coverin for him on accounta the
          brother thing, which explains the —
          and we had drinks to celebrate. I had a
          greyhound and Knutson had, what was
          that — had a cherry in it?

                    DEPUTY KNUTSON
          Rob Roy.

                    BILL OSWALT
          Right. A Rob Roy. Had a few of 'em if I'm
          not —

                    MOLLY
          What about the Hess case?

                    BILL OSWALT
                 (suspicious)
          What about it?

                    MOLLY
          Still open, yeah?

                    BILL OSWALT
          Yeah. No. Look, we're checkin ta see
          maybe the hooker had a boyfriend.
          Jealous type. Didn't like her gettin
          tooled by every Tom, Dick, and Jane. But
          otherwise —

                    MOLLY
          Who's workin that now?

                    BILL OSWALT
          Terry.

                    MOLLY
                 (nods, carefully)
          Well, that's good.
                 (beat)
          Cept Terry don't know what end of a mop
          ta wash the floor with.

BILL OSWALT
(thinks about that)
He's not the brightest bulb. I'll give ya that. But he's soldierin through.

MOLLY
Good fer him.
(beat)
Cept I'm back now —

BILL OSWALT
No.

MOLLY
Chief.

BILL OSWALT
Molly, Deputy — I'd give it to ya. I would. Except we both know I'd be back in this room in two days with you pointin at names on a whiteboard, stirrin things up, and me chewin on my tie.

It's too much. Frustration gets the better of her.

MOLLY
Just — fer Pete sake, I got evidence that puts Lester Nygaard in a room with a known killer the day of the Sam Hess murder, and the next night Lester calls the guy. He calls him at the —

BILL OSWALT
(interrupting)
Look. Look. That's how it is sometimes. Life. Ya go to bed unsatisfied. They call the lottery numbers on TV and you get the first few and in your head yer already buying a jet or a fjord or whatever, but it's not meant ta be. It's just not meant ta be.
(moving on)
Look, we're all glad yer back. Yer a heck of a police officer. Guys are gonna have a cake fer ya later. Try to look surprised. It's really somethin else. Got an assault rifle on top, made a frosting. Not sure how they do that.

Off Molly: unsatisfied, but trying not to show it. We PUSH PAST HER to the CASE DIAGRAM laid out on the wall.

It's all there, the true crime. Why is she the only one who can see it?

For Molly, emotionally, the first season will be about coming to terms with the fact that the frontier she polices is a feral and lawless place. And that when you get right down to it, some things—like Lorne Malvo—don't have a right place. The things Molly sees—violence, cruelty, senselessness—will make her question her role as a law officer, a job that exposes her to the worst of human nature.

INT. LOU'S COFFEE SHOP. BEMIDJI, MN—DAY

Molly Solverson has lunch with her dad.

LOU SOLVERSON
So, how's it goin?

MOLLY
Well — turns out Lester and Hess went ta high school together. And Hess used ta beat him up.

LOU SOLVERSON
A learn-ed detective might call that a clue.

MOLLY
That's what I said. But Bill's a big believer in coincidence, apparently.

LOU SOLVERSON
What he lacks in common sense he makes up in self-esteem. Bill have a theory?

MOLLY
Says it was a spree. A drifter or, quote,
"gang of drifters." Like it's 1942. Like
drifters are a national threat. Hoboes.

LOU SOLVERSON
Well, he's chief now. So he sets the
agenda. Same as it's always been.

MOLLY
Ya. I know. But here we got a car crash with
a dead man in frozen panties nearby. And
the driver gets a head injury and maybe
ends up in the emergency room talking
to Lester about Sam Hess. Then within
twenty-four hours there's Sam Hess dead
and the fracas with Lester's wife and Vern.

Beat. Lou watches her push food around on
her plate.

MOLLY (CONT'D)
Course Bill wants me to focus on random
strangers instead.

Beat. Lou watches her push food around on
her plate.

LOU SOLVERSON
Not sure if ya remember, but when you were
five they had ta put you under anesthesia to
fix yer teeth. They gave ya that mask, and
gas that smelled like tutti frutti.

MOLLY
I sorta remember that.

LOU SOLVERSON
And you were so brave, didn't cry or
nothing. My soft little girl in a hard world
of drills and needles.

MOLLY
I'm thirty-one, Dad. I carry a gun.

LOU SOLVERSON
I know, but it's relative, ya know? There's
the things a schoolteacher gets exposed
to — truancy and the like. And there's the
stuff a cop sees — murder and violence
and general skofflawery. And then there's
the kind of deal you're looking at now.

MOLLY
Which is.

LOU SOLVERSON
Which is — if I'm right — savagery, pure and simple. Slaughter and hatred and devils with dead eyes and shark smiles. And one day yer gonna get married and have kids and when you look at them, their faces, you need to see what's good in the world. Cause if you don't, how are you gonna live?

Beat.

MOLLY
You talk a lot, you know that?

LOU SOLVERSON
It's always been a problem.

Chief Bill Oswalt comes in, sees them, approaches.

BILL OSWALT
Lou.

LOU SOLVERSON
Chief.

BILL OSWALT
Molly, could I have a word?

MOLLY
Sure. Pull up a chair. Ya want a cup a coffee or —

BILL OSWALT
Ya. No. I'm — Look, Lester Nygaard called me. Ya. He's super upset.

MOLLY
Well, now I thought he might do that.

BILL OSWALT
And, ya know, we talked about this. And I thought we were — I thought I was clear that we were gonna focus on the drifter angle, and not, ya know, harass the victim.

MOLLY
I'm not — I didn't harass him. I just — I've got questions.

BILL OSWALT
Well, ya know, I'm the chief now. And I gotta — everyone's gotta line up behind me. Tow the line, ya know?

MOLLY
Ya, of course, but —

BILL OSWALT
And we talked about this and all. And now
I gotta take ya off the case.
          (off Molly)
I just — we all know how ya felt about
Vern. Heck, who didn't? But maybe it's
best if ya just — and this'll be good for ya
career-wise — I'm makin ya head of the
inquiry on the frozen fella. The naked one.
That's — I'll make ya lead on that one.

Lou watches his daughter absorb this.

MOLLY
Bill. Listen —

Bill stands.

BILL OSWALT
Ya, so that's my decision. Have a good
night.

He exits. Lou and Molly sit for a bit in silence.

MOLLY
Okay then.

She stands. Lou hates to see her go through
this, but he knows that anything he says will
only embarrass her further.

LOU SOLVERSON
See ya fer dinner?

She nods, heads for the door. Then stops,
turns.

MOLLY
Drills and needles.

He nods. She exits and we DRIFT OFF into the
snow.

But luckily Molly won't be alone in her journey. Her father, Lou, is by her side,
a quiet, comforting presence.
          And along the way Molly will meet the man she's going to marry, Gus
Grimly. The Norm to her Marge. And with these two at her side, Molly can face
anything.

INT. LOU'S COFFEE SHOP. BEMIDJI, MN—DAY

LOU SOLVERSON is at the counter. MOLLY
SOLVERSON comes in, in uniform. Lou pours
her a cup of coffee.

LOU
Back to it then?

MOLLY
Looks like. Doc cleared me fer duty.

He shows her a glass bowl holding a flower
arrangement, wrapped in colored cellophane.
There's a card on a plastic trident inside.

LOU
More flowers came for ya at the station.
From Duluth.

She smiles, looks at the card.

LOU (CONT'D)
A smarter man'd think you were being
wooed.

MOLLY
I don't know what you're talkin about.

He puts the flowers on the counter.

MOLLY (CONT'D)
Take the paper off at least so they can
breathe.

He does. She drinks her coffee.

LOU
Got a strategy? On this Lester thing?

MOLLY
Just gonna walk in and say *Bill, we
gotta* —

LOU
If you think that's best. The direct
approach.

MOLLY
I mean, you tell me my options here.

Lou refills the sugars.

LOU
Seem ta remember you going out to Uncle
Packy's once. Maybe eight years old. You
remember?

MOLLY
Remember Aunt Septema smelled like
cigarettes.

LOU
Third day you were gone, Packy called,
said he took you ice fishin. Said the two a
you went all day, caught not a thing. So he
starts packin up, but you said *not leavin
till we catch a fish*. Said you had this look
on yer face, same as yer mother used ta

get. No point in arguin, he figured, so he
put down his stuff, built a fire. Sun went
down. Somewhere around one a.m. you
finally got a nibble. Packy was nappin.
Said you woke him up, fish in hand, said
now we can go.

MOLLY
Yer point bein?

LOU
Got no point. Just tellin a story.

She takes her coffee, stands. She goes to the
door.

LOU (CONT'D)
(calls after her)
You keep fishin, okay?

Molly stops, looks at him, nods. Somehow he
always makes her feel better.

MOLLY
Will do. Thanks, Dad.

GUS GRIMLY

A MAN-BOY'S WIFE DIES AND LEAVES HIM with a little girl to raise. The man-boy isn't a slacker so much as a half-grown man who hasn't yet decided if he has a purpose. But now, a single parent, he must focus. So the man-boy gets his hair cut and learns how to change a diaper. He looks around for a job that pays well and offers good benefits, but one with flexible shifts, so that he can spend time with his daughter. In this way he becomes a state cop. In this way he becomes a man. He realizes he likes the structure of it, the hierarchy of the force and the rules it offers. Gus has always benefited from structure. Something that keeps him from drifting.

Over time, Gus's daughter grows out of diapers and learns to read. She watches *Star Wars* for the first time and wears a plastic fireman's hat for 363 days straight. She goes to elementary school and then middle school. Her dad is her best friend.

The two live next door to an orthodox Jewish family. Because their houses are side by side, Gus and his daughter can see into their neighbor's home. On Friday nights and High Holidays they watch the family—father, mother, and two daughters—observe the seder. It is a fascinating peek into another world.

INT. KITCHEN. GUS GRIMLY APARTMENT—
LATER

Gus and Ari sit across from each other,
drinking milk.

                    ARI
          The winter is cold, but I can't complain.
          My socks have holes, but again, do I
          complain? I do not. The oldest needs
          braces and the youngest once sneezed
          for three days straight, but who could
          complain? They're gifts.

                    GUS
          Children?

                    ARI
          All of it. The cold, the holes.

Gus thinks about that.

                    GUS
          Hey, so I got a question. Spiritually, I
          mean. Or not spiritually, but — I don't
          know, of like an ethical nature?

                    ARI
          Please.

                    GUS
          Well, let's say I know a person is guilty
          — committed a crime — but can't, ya
          know, prove it. Like he has everybody
          else fooled, but I know. What am I s'posed
          ta —

                    ARI
          Find the proof.

                    GUS
          Ya, okay. But here's the thing. I'm no
          detective. I mean, Molly, she's — amazing.
          But I just — and then there's Greta, ya
          know? And should I put myself in danger?
          Or do I just — I don't know — let it go?

Beat. Ari looks at him.

                    ARI
          A rich man opens the paper one day. He
          sees the world is full of misery.

                    GUS
          Is this a —

                    ARI
          It's a parable. A rich man opens the paper
          one day.

                    CUT TO:
INT. DINING ROOM. PENTHOUSE—DAY
(PARABLE)

A handsome MAN, in a suit, sits at his
breakfast table, reading the newspaper.
Around him is evidence of wealth.

                    ARI (O.S.)
          He sees the world is full of misery. He
          says, *I have money. I can help.*

The man <u>mouths the words</u> along with Ari.

                    CUT TO:
INT. AUDITORIUM—DAY (PARABLE)

Onstage are UNDERPRIVILEGED CHILDREN in
folding chairs. The man hands an OVERSIZED
NOVELTY CHECK to a WOMAN in a SKIRT
SUIT.

                    ARI (O.S.)
          So the man gives away all his money. But
          it's not enough.

          CLOSE ON THE MAN
looking out at the clapping audience. We can
tell from his face he doesn't feel the happiness
he thought he would.

                    ARI (O.S.) (CONT'D)
          For people are still suffering.

                    CUT TO:
INT. KITCHEN. SHABBY APARTMENT—DAY
(PARABLE)

The man, now poor, sits at a ramshackle
kitchen table, reading the newspaper.

                    ARI (O.S.)
          Then one day the man sees another
          article.

CLOSE ON NEWSPAPER

The headline reads: *Organ Donors in Short Supply.*

CUT TO:
INT. DOCTOR'S OFFICE—DAY (PARABLE)

The man sits across from a SURGEON.

ARI (O.S.)
The man decides he was foolish to think just giving money was enough. He goes to the doctor, and says, *Doctor, I want to donate a kidney.*

Again, the man mouths the words as Ari says them.

CUT TO:
INT. SURGERY—DAY (PARABLE)

The man lies on the table. Doctors perform surgery.

ARI (O.S.)
So the doctors do the surgery.

CUT TO:
INT. HOSPITAL ROOM—DAY (PARABLE)

The man lies in bed, recovering, a bandage on his abdomen. He stares out the window forlornly.

ARI (O.S.)
After, he knows he should feel good, but he doesn't. For people are still suffering.

CLOSE ON THE MAN'S FACE

Even as the woman thanks him, we can see he feels he hasn't done enough.

CUT TO:
INT. DOCTOR'S OFFICE—DAY (PARABLE)

Again the man sits across from the surgeon.

ARI (O.S.)
So the man goes back to the doctor. He says, *This time I want to give it all.* The doctor says, *What does that mean, give it all?*

(The man and doctor mouth the words.)

ARI (O.S.) (CONT'D)
The man says, *Now I want to donate my liver, but not just my liver. I want to donate my heart, but not just my heart. I want to donate my corneas, but not just my corneas. I want to give it all away, everything I have. All that I am. It's the only way. The only way to stop the suffering.*

CLOSE ON THE DOCTOR
who becomes irate.

ARI (O.S.) (CONT'D)
The doctor tells the man he's crazy. He says a kidney is one thing, but you can't give away your whole body, piece by piece. It's suicide. So he sends the man home.

CUT TO:
INT. BATHROOM—DAY (PARABLE)

The man lies in a BATHTUB filled with ICE WATER.

ARI (O.S.)
But the man cannot live knowing that others are suffering when he could help.

The man lifts a STRAIGHT RAZOR from the edge of the tub. As he does, we RISE UP along the WHITE TILES.

The words "ORGAN DONOR" have been written on the tile.

ARI (O.S.) (CONT'D)
So he gives the only thing he has left, his life.

A SPRAY OF RED arcs up the white tile.

CUT TO:

A HEADSTONE
in a CEMETERY. The headstone reads *Here lies Jeremy Hoffstead, who gave everything.* We PUSH IN on the headstone and into the gray stone . . .

                    GUS (O.S.)
And does it work? Does the suffering stop?

. . . and we find ourselves back in . . .

INT. KITCHEN. GUS GRIMLY APARTMENT. DULUTH, MN—NIGHT

Ari sits across from Gus.

                    ARI
You live in the world. What do you think?

Beat. Gus thinks about this.

                    GUS
So he killed himself for nothing?

                    ARI
Did he?

                    GUS
                    (beat)
Well, I mean — are ya sayin — what are ya sayin?

                    ARI
Only a fool thinks he can solve the world's problems.

                    GUS
But you hafta try, don't you?
                    (beat)
Don't you?

But listen, Gus Grimly didn't get into law enforcement because he was a law and order guy. He doesn't suffer from a need to seem tough, doesn't get off on power. He's scared a lot of the time at work, because fighting crime is scary. And because the stakes for survival are too high. The daughter has no one but him. So Gus can't afford to get himself killed.

Which is why one snowy night he lets a psychopath drive away from a routine traffic stop. And yet, Gus has been a police officer by this point for ten years. He has developed a strong sense of right and wrong, a strong sense of responsibility. Which is why that night he wakes knowing he made a mistake.

And so Gus sets off to find the man he let go, Lorne Malvo. But by pursuing Malvo, Gus puts himself (and his daughter) at risk. Was he right to walk away from death the first time? Or right now in pursuing it? Was saving his own life for the sake of his daughter a coward's act, or a hero's? And will he survive the pursuit?

INT. RECEPTION AREA. POLICE PRECINCT. BEMIDJI, MN—NIGHT

Gus comes in with Greta.

                    GUS
Sit there, and, uh, I'll be back in a —

                    GRETA
Just tell the truth and say yer sorry.

That's what you always tell me.

                    GUS
                    (nods)
Yer a good girl.

                    GRETA
As far as you know.

She sits, opens her book. Gus goes to the

FRONT DESK.

> GUS
> Ya, hi. I'm, uh, I drove over from Duluth
> PD. Need ta talk ta someone about Lester
> Nygaard.

Molly has just come out of Bill's office and
is walking by, carrying her case file. She
overhears.

> MOLLY
> Ya, hey there. I'm Deputy Solverson. What
> can I do fer ya?

Gus gears up his courage.

> GUS
> Well —

Molly glances over at Bill's office.

> MOLLY
> Why don't we talk at my desk?

He nods. Molly leads Gus to her desk. She sits.

> MOLLY (CONT'D)
> Have a seat. Ya want some coffee? The
> guys just brewed a pot.

> GUS
> No. I gotta —
> (gestures)
> I'm good.

He sits.

> GUS (CONT'D)
> So, uh, three nights back I was on patrol,
> ya know. And I pull this guy over — silver
> Taurus. Ran a stop sign. And I, uh, let him
> go with a warnin, see. But then — I don't
> know — I had a feelin.

> MOLLY
> What kinda feelin?

GUS
Bad feelin. Real suspicious-like. So I run his plates. And — turns out the car's registered to one a yer victims.

Molly sits forward.

MOLLY
What?

GUS
Ya. Uh, Lester Nygaard.

MOLLY
Son of a — he said his car was in the shop.

GUS
Oh ya? Well, here's the thing. It wasn't Lester drivin. I know that now cause I ran the plate. But at the time —

Molly pulls out the photo of Malvo.

MOLLY
Is this the fella?

GUS
Holy cow. Ya. That's — I think that's him — how did you — ?

MOLLY
Security camera caught him over St. Paul kidnappin an accountant.

GUS
No kiddin.

MOLLY
Ya, but so, uh, one thing I'm not clear on — ya say you only found out later it wasn't Lester driving. But, I mean, ya looked at the fella's license and registration, didn't ya?

GUS
Well.
(long beat)
See uh. I asked, but he uh — threatened me? And uh — I mean, there's no excuse — but I just — he seemed like a real dangerous fella. Had these real scary uh eyes, and I uh —

Greta comes over.

GRETA
Dad. Could I get a dollar fer the vending machine?

Beat. Molly looks at Greta, and in that moment she understands why Gus let Malvo go.

MOLLY
Here. They give us these tokens.

She opens her drawer, hands a coin to Greta.

MOLLY (CONT'D)
Just put it in the coin slot.

GRETA
Great. Thanks.

Greta goes over the vending machine.

MOLLY
How old?

GUS

Greta? Ya, twelve. She's a real good girl.

MOLLY

Her mom at home?

GUS

No, uh — it's, uh, just us. Ten years now.

Greta comes back with a candy bar.

GRETA

They're outta M&M's.

Molly looks at Gus and his daughter. It's clear he's a good guy who feels terrible for what he did.

MOLLY

So you guys drove all the way from Duluth, huh?

GUS

Ya.

MOLLY
(beat)
Well, I was just gonna grab some dinner. There's a good burger place close. Think maybe you wanna join me fore you head back?

Gus looks at Molly. He's so grateful for her niceness he might cry.

GUS

Well, I mean, we don't wanna be a bother.

MOLLY

No bother. We can talk about the guy, what ya remember. Maybe a clue drops out.

She stands, and they do as well.

MOLLY (CONT'D)
— it's Lou's, couple blocks up the street. Just let me get this APB out and I'll be over.

WHO AND/OR WHAT IS OUR MIKE YANAGITA?

FARGO, THE FILM, IS A TRUE CRIME STORY THAT ISN'T TRUE. Or—that is to say—somewhere, sometime, a man may have paid other men to kidnap his wife, but *Fargo* is not a fact-by-fact reenactment of that crime. And yet the events and characters of the film—though mostly invented—are portrayed as real, in a truth-is-stranger-than-fiction manner.

Because, as we know, real life doesn't unfold along conveniently linear plot lines. It is filled with dead ends and random non sequiturs. To make the events of the film feel truer, the Coens have added narrative elements that detour from the central story. The biggest of these is Mike Yanagita.

In the film, Marge is asleep when the phone rings. The caller is Mike Yanagita, an old high school acquaintance. It takes her a while to figure this out. Later, she agrees to meet him for lunch in the Twin Cities. There, he tells her he married another classmate of theirs, but that she died. Mike Yanagita breaks down and tries to sit next to her. *I'm just so lonely*, he says.

Later, Marge is talking to an old friend on the phone. When she mentions Mike and the tragedy he's suffered, the friend tells Marge it isn't true. The woman in question is very much alive, and not only didn't she marry Mike, she took out a restraining order against him. The whole story has a *you can't make this stuff up* quality to it.

Which is why, when it's added to a true crime story, it makes the crime elements seem truer.

So the question for us in translating the film to series is *Who or what is our Mike Yanagita?* And because the season evolves over thirteen episodes and follows multiple characters, my instinct is that, rather than create a single narrative detour, we must spread "real-life" characters and moments throughout the story in unexpected ways. Like the naked man in the trunk or Gus Grimly's Jewish neighbors, or the *Be the One* poster, or the group of Sudanese Lost Boys who moved to St. Cloud five years earlier and pop up in our story from time to time, et cetera.

Accidents happen in the Fargo universe. Randomness is ever present. The point is not to create meaninglessness. It's to show that meaning in the universe is open to interpretation. As Larry Gopnik is told in *A Serious Man* when he tries to make sense of the strange twist of events that has become his life:

ACCEPT THE MYSTERY.

INT. FILE ROOM. FBI BUILDING—FARGO,
ND—DAY

One year later, the place is now wall-
to-wall files. The taped-up picture
of Malvo that was once the only
thing on the wall is now obscured by
requisition forms, a calendar, etc.,
like a memory suppressed. Webb Pepper
stands at a cabinet trying to file a
stack of folders. Bill Budge bounces
his (now ancient) tennis ball against
the wall.

          BILL BUDGE
The file room.
       (beat)
A room full of files.
       (beat)
Say you took one of the files out.

          WEBB PEPPER
Took it where?

          BILL BUDGE
Doesn't matter. Say you take one
file. Is it still the file room?

          WEBB PEPPER
      (ignoring him)
Pizza day, right? In the
cafeteria. Or meatloaf.

          BILL BUDGE
I'm saying we both agree that the
file room minus one file is still
the file room.
       (beat)
Now say you took another file.
Then another. If the file room

minus one file is still the file
room, and you keep subtracting one
at a time, you could end up with
zero files. Logically, I'm saying.
Or even negative files, and it
would still be the —

          WEBB PEPPER
How do you have negative files?

          BILL BUDGE
I'm just saying — logically.

          WEBB PEPPER
Except no one's taking files. They
just bring more.

          BILL BUDGE
       (beat)
Or take a cemetery. Remove one
body, it's still a cemetery. But
a cemetery with no bodies, what's
that?

          WEBB PEPPER
Condos.

Budge throws the ball against the
wall one last time, and all at once
<u>everything falls off</u> EXCEPT the
picture of Malvo.

The two men look at it. Both agents
step forward. Seeing it is like
waking from a spell.

          ANGLE ON THE PHOTO

Where is Malvo?

IN CONVERSATION WITH
BILLY BOB THORNTON
Lorne Malvo

NOAH: As you said, we sent you that first script and I came in to pitch you what the show was. And my memory is I started it and you were like, "I don't want to know too much. If you wrote this we're good."

BILLY: Exactly. The fact of the matter is you can tell. When I read the script it's like, yeah, who in their right mind wouldn't want to do this? I loved the character. So the thing about it was that I really loved what you'd written, and when I met you and Warren [Littlefield] it was like, wow. The energy is right and the script is amazing.

The thing I always tell people when they ask what attracted me to it is that Noah managed to make a new thing out of something that was revered. And yet, keep what the thing was that was revered. I said you're not tackling *Saved by the Bell*, you're tackling fucking *Fargo*. Anybody can write a script and I read it like I'm reading a brand-new thing. And yet I felt like I had just read *Fargo*. That's a fucking magic trick.

And so I knew I was dealing with people who were, creatively, people I could be on the same page with. The funny thing is that, all you do is look up Charles de Gaulle's birthday and the next fucking thing you know you're in a chatroom and you see yourself on it and you're like, how the fuck did I find this? I got on something one day and it was a *Fargo* deal and a bunch of these creeps are rating *Fargo*. It's like the movie, season 1, season 2, and season 3. Pretty much across the board the number one was season 1 or the movie. That was usually the order and then a couple people liked season 2 better than season 1. But the fact that it became a thing that they would even consider rating as opposed to saying fuck you guys we love the movie. That's not what they did.

So it really became a phenomenal piece of art, this thing. Everywhere I go now, it's always been *Sling Blade*, *Bad Santa*, and *Monster's Ball*, and now *Fargo* is a thing that people come up to me about and go, "My God that character in *Fargo* is literally the best character I've ever seen on TV." I mean, I get it all the time.

NOAH: You can't ask Joel and Ethan how to make a Coen brothers movie. They don't want to talk about their work. Also, they write a lot of scripts that other people direct that aren't Coen brothers movies. So there's clearly something in the transformation that I had to figure out in the process. For me a big part of it was realizing they write a lot of things they think are really funny but aren't meant to be comedy on-screen.

BILLY: I talk to Jim Jarmusch sometimes about why I left Arkansas and why he left Ohio. And I said to tell you the truth, when I was eleven years old and I heard my first Mothers of Invention album I was like, there's something else out there. In other words, I already knew the Mothers of Invention—never heard of them. But when I saw it and I heard it I was like, that's what I do! So, somebody does do this. So, Steve Martin comes along and nobody had done that. And you go, oh okay. Nobody had done *All in the Family*, whatever it is. All the things that sort of haven't been done before, people are out there who are already that and they understand it. It's their sensibility and their sense of humor and when it comes along they come out of the woodwork. And that's what people did with the Coen brothers. It's like, oh here's that thing that I can't explain to anyone, but these guys do it and I plug into that.

NOAH: And a lot of people try to do it and they do it terribly. Because they always make it too comedic and think that's what it is.

BILLY: They were the executive producers and I think wrote the final draft of the first *Bad Santa* and they wanted nothing to do with it. I think a lot of time, when people aren't in charge of something, you have a feeling you want to distance yourself from it. Maybe out of self-protection and also a little bit of envy. What if it works and we didn't do it. They wanted to do a stage Broadway show of *Sling Blade*. Not with me, with some other guy, and I was like, I don't know about that. You know what I mean, even though it may be brilliant. Who knows.

But yeah, they [the Coen brothers] are different kind of guys. But it's like when people ask you, you mentioned earlier, when people ask me as an actor "What is your process?" I don't fucking know. How am I supposed to tell you what my process is? And by the way, if I did know what it was, if it was a formula or a trick, I wouldn't tell you. But they want to hear it, they want to hear how I can be like you. What is this thing that you do? You tell me the secret. Like in acting class, it's like when they are interviewing an actor for some overearnest talk show, they want to hear the actor talk about that shit. "Well, what I did is I took my grandfather and I would go at night to this diner I would go to . . ." It's like they want to hear that shit because they want to believe that there aren't people who are born with it. They don't want to know that.

NOAH: Yeah, where it's actually just a thing that happens when you go in.

BILLY: With Lorne Malvo, I had critics call him the protagonist and they would ask me how I did that. What am I going to say to that? "How can we feel that way when he is so evil?" I didn't particularly see him as evil. It's like, do you think Lorne Malvo is evil? You didn't get all the references to the animal kingdom? Lorne Malvo was eating.

NOAH: And playing with his food first, fascinated by "How far can I push this guy?" And with Lester, it was the first time he was ever surprised. Where he was like, "Oh this is interesting, I'm willing to shoot these three people I've been working with for six months, because this guy is interesting."

BILLY: Yeah exactly. He was like, "How does a guy like this make his life interesting?" And he did. I even looked at Malvo as almost like Santa Claus or a ghost or something. Where it's like, is Lorne Malvo even real? Or is he just this force that came into all these people's lives that fucked them up.

NOAH: There was this Richard Matheson short story, "The Distributor," that I read right around the time that I was writing this. It's about a guy who moves into a suburban neighborhood who just starts screwing with everybody. He takes a guy's lawnmower and puts it in the other neighbor's garage. And it just seemed like a great subversive element for a character because the world is full of antagonists. I never wanted him to be one of those Tarantino, mustache twirly, articulate guys. I think it was something about the guy that goes in and they go, "Do you have a pet?" And he's like, "A fish? How about a cockroach? How about a bacteria. You've got this dumb rule. Let's talk about it."

BILLY: Well, Ed Crane, in *The Man Who Wasn't There*, could have easily been Lorne Malvo. It's almost the same guy, but one guy did it and the other one wanted to. I mean, their morals were pretty much the same. I think Ed actually was probably darker in a lot of ways because he was pretty humorless. But people say, and I guess it's a thing to be flattered by, it's like asking John Lennon if "Lucy in the Sky with Diamonds" is LSD because that's the initials? And it's like no, my kid drew a picture in school. And so they would say to me, well, why is his name Lorne Malvo? I said, well, I don't know for sure, but I can tell you this, when I look at that guy, his name is Lorne Malvo. That's all I can tell you. I would not be affected by this guy as much if his name were Peter Johnson. He's Lorne Malvo. And they say well, we think Noah called him Lorne Malvo because of Malvo the sniper in D.C.

NOAH: No, not at all. That's news to me.

BILLY: I said, "I don't know for a fact because I didn't ask him. But I can tell you for a fact that I'm 99.99 percent sure that that's not true because it's too easy. I think his name is Lorne Malvo because when you are writing the characters, they tell you what their name is."

NOAH: Yeah, and there is something about the mouth feel of it. The long O and the guy from *Bonanza*. There is something funny about the guy and he needed to have a throwback name. You can't really analyze it. I didn't really. You never know. If you're lucky they speak to you and if you're not, you have to name them and then those names never feel right.

BILLY: Well, Karl Childers in *Sling Blade*. You look at the fuck and you go, his name is Karl Childers.

NOAH: Yeah, and I mean it was. That first year [of *Fargo*] was really a great experiment. And it's sort of an odd thing structurally now that I have some distance from it. When Malvo comes to town we have this huge episode with you and Martin Freeman. And then you drive off into this whole other movie with Oliver Platt for four hours. And then finally the original movie crashes into you when Wrench and Numbers show up shooting. But yeah, it's interesting looking back. I like that idea that it feels more realistic—this was a stop on the way somewhere. And then what is nice is that Joel and Ethan have that theme you see a lot in their work, which is consequences and the past is going to catch up with you.

I remember seeing Glenn Howerton, who played Don Chumph. It was after the episode aired where he met his end and you taped him onto that thing with the gun and called the SWAT team, et cetera. He told me that he watched that episode with his wife and during that scene she started crying because it was so awful what was happening to him. And he said, "You know I was such a minor character and you gave me this oper-

atic death that was so disproportionate to my importance to the show." I never wanted the violence in the show to be entertaining. What I liked about that moment is that it seems fun, "Oh, it's Malvo, he's fucking with these guys and the cops, he shoots out the window and tapes him up and he backlights him." And it starts to play out and there's part of you where you're like, "This is great" and then, at a certain point, things slow down and the Gregorian chant comes in and the glass is flying. This guy is scared out of his mind, he finally gets the tape off and the cops kick open the door and then they just drill him. And then it's just a tragedy. What's comedic becomes tragic in a way that makes you really uncomfortable.

BILLY: Oh yeah, it was like a whole opera. It was fucking amazing. I loved that. And the thing about Malvo, he never indicated anything that he was going to do. So, there was never a moment looking around like, "Oh, I know what I'll do." Every time I was in a scene, you never wrote it. That's the thing that drives you crazy, if you write the descriptive stuff and directions in the script it's like, who's going to do that. And then you get back actors and they'll do it and then you're fucked. But Malvo just did his stuff. So it was a very methodical thing. The thinking had already been done and then he walks away.

NOAH: You talk about indicating and it's the one conversation we had about that last hour. Where you said, "I haven't

said anything all year, I just think there are easier ways to get close to these guys." Because in the original version of the script, he went to all this trouble to pretend to be an FBI agent to get close to these FBI agents. You saw what the plan was, you saw what was going to happen, and then it happened. Yeah, so it changed and it became the kidnapping of the car lot guy and the car pulling in while these guys walk out of the woods while these guys were distracted. It was much better.

BILLY: That brings all those scenes back to me. I have to say, it was such a good experience on all levels. Somehow, if you are shooting in the cold and you are doing something shitty, it's colder. If you're doing something great, it somehow becomes your pal.

NOAH: It's never been that cold again. The second year was balmy and the third year was kind of cold, but it's never been that cold again. And that was crazy. The guy who was supposed to climb out of the trunk in his underwear and run through the snow. The first day we were supposed to shoot that it was forty below.

BILLY: I asked that fucking guy, he was Canadian, and he just said "Oh it's okay." Just like the guy on the show.

NOAH: You've got to protect him from himself. For something that was that high degree difficulty of a dive it just felt right. It didn't feel stressful. It felt like we were all doing what we were supposed to do. We had the blueprint and it was relatively easy honestly. The hard part was in the conception. Once I had you and Martin and Allison Tolman and Carradine. You had that scene with Carradine. "I haven't had a piece of pie like that since the garden of Eden."

BILLY: I loved that scene with Keith. Every second of the scene you feel the crackle. A lot of that has to do too with the fact that it was me and Carradine who instantly have a natural thing together. Also, two guys who have been around a long time are suspicious of people anyway. I loved working with him.

NOAH: You and Allison didn't have a single scene together through the whole [season].

BILLY: I saw her through the snow once. Absolutely, it worked perfectly.

NOAH: It was a process to get her too. Through MGM and FX because I think they worried that she was too comedic and they had certain ideas in their heads. So, I had to kind of game the system to get her to New York for callbacks. And then when they saw it, they saw it. I agree I think she and Colin, that combo was . . .

BILLY: Oh, I think it was great. Speaking of Colin, do you know the most talked about scene in season 1? Me in the car with Colin pulling me over. That scene struck a chord with people in such a way. And what I say to him is something they point out. That dialogue and that story, it's chilling.

NOAH: There will be dragons . . .

BILLY: Once again, that is so finely tuned because you put that dialogue in another character's mouth, it's not right. That's the great thing about good writers, they know tone. It's like you get a fucking amplifier and put two AC30s next to each other and play through both of them. But it's like, "You know what, this one's got something. I know it's the

same year and the same fucking amp but something about this one . . . "

NOAH: It's also the fact that it's very unorthodox the way that hour is structured. You have this whole movie with Martin Freeman and then you drive out of town, and it's only then that you see Colin Hanks in one scene. And he's just some cop in a car, we shouldn't care about him at all but because we've seen what you've done to this town, we know he's in real danger." We shot that scene onstage and then his side of it outside.

BILLY: I think it was colder onstage than it was outside. That was one of the coldest scenes I did. I swear to God, I had to put the heater on in between takes because it was fucking freezing.

NOAH: Well you weren't there when Oliver Platt took a blood shower on that stage. You're like, close the goddamn door. The water can be warm, but it's twenty-five degrees in this stage.

BILLY: I loved Oliver, I loved what he did with it.

NOAH: Well, he was funny, because the first conversation that I had with him when he came on board was like, "I just want to apologize now because I'm not going to say a single line that you wrote." But he said every line that I wrote but there was a process. There were the crickets, and the store, and this moment at the beginning. This flashback where he said "God is real," and he was like, "I don't want to say that I don't want to say it, I think it's a different line." Take after take it was this or that and then he'd land back on the line that was scripted. And it's like just say the line in the first place.

BILLY: Sometimes guys have to come in and kind of piss on the rug.

NOAH: It's fine but it is a funny process.

BILLY: I have to say it's the least I have ever done in terms of saying, "Hey maybe this scene should be this or that." I said a couple of things the whole time and if I didn't think it was a good idea I would shut up then. But people ask me a lot because I have a reputation of doing different dialogue and I tell them, "Ask Noah Hawley, I didn't change his shit."

NOAH: I say, "What do you mean you're having a problem with Billy? Billy is easy."

IN CONVERSATION WITH
ALLISON TOLMAN

Molly Solverson

NOAH: So, I was thinking, I don't think you and Billy had a scene together the whole season, did you?

ALLISON: No, we didn't. We had one day on set together. We had a scene where I was coming in the front door and he was leaving out the back door of the diner. That was the only day we were ever on set at the same time. That's when we took our one selfie together was that day. Because we were never together again.

NOAH: Seems crazy in retrospect that I did that. But I think it was right. And that scene with Keith, that pie scene turned out to be pretty iconic.

ALLISON: Yeah it did! Sinister, it was good.

NOAH: I can't be offended, but did you watch the other *Fargos*?

ALLISON: I do, well I watched the second season. But I haven't watched the third season yet. I watched the first episode but I was waiting for my show, for *Downward Dog* to start, and I was so stressed out. I was like, "This is not safe for me. I can't watch the new season of *Fargo* while I'm this stressed out about waiting for my show to start." So, I set it aside and I haven't come back to it yet. I think it's still sitting on our DVR.

NOAH: I just wondered if it was weird for you to suddenly have it be called the same thing you did but suddenly have other people in it. Did you recognize it watching the second one? Had you watched the first one?

ALLISON: I did, I watched the first one in real time with everyone else when it was on TV. Which was fun. And then I did watch the second season. I liked the second season a lot. I think there was some distance there because of the time period shift. And I couldn't come to the premiere at the ArcLight because I was working. But I still kind of felt like part of this family. But then by the end of the second season and then sort of rolling into the third season, it started to just sort of feel like, I think at one point in time I said, "It's like watching a train leave the station." And you're like, "But that was my train. I drove that train for a while." So, it is strange. Especially for me. That was where I started from. It was such an auspicious beginning but also such a blessing and a curse because it was one job. One season's worth of work and then sort of thrown into Hollywood.

NOAH: Right, it must have been quite a beginning. Then you move onto other things and go, "Oh no this is how it actually works." Obviously, that second season was sort of like the Allison Tolman origin story in a way—The Solversons. That was kind of fun. The third season my goal was to have no real connections to either season until, of course—well, I won't spoil it.

ALLISON: Yeah, exactly. I know about the spoilers! I saw pictures!

NOAH: Oh, okay, good! Yeah, we brought Russell [Harvard] back. He was great.

ALLISON: If I could name a person who I would most want you to bring back and give more work to, it's Russell. He's such a nice guy and is so talented. So that's really cool.

NOAH: Yeah, he was great. Obviously, this was your first sort of screen credit, I believe. But you never would have known when you showed up that you didn't necessarily know what a mark is.

ALLISON: Yeah, I didn't know anything.

NOAH: You faked it real good. And you certainly didn't show any intimidation if you felt any from, say, spending your first day acting on-screen with Keith Carradine. But yeah, it was a good school to go to I would think.

ALLISON: It was and I think I have to give a lot of that credit to those guys and that cast that you assembled. People ask me all the time, "How was that experience and how was that cast?" I think people are kind of digging for some drama. But I don't know how I got so lucky. I feel like I was in the safest, best group of men who were so endlessly patient with me. And literally taught me everything that I needed to know within the first two weeks of shooting. It was a crash course and they were also so kind and treated me like a peer. I think that helped me be able to fake that as well as I was able to for that whole first season.

NOAH: You would never know. Well, it's got to be the hardest thing because whatever your training, you have a sort of natural timing and rhythm. To bring that into that high-pressure situation and just still be yourself on some level is a testament to just how much you don't give a shit, I think.

ALLISON: Thank you.

NOAH: Yeah, and then Colin; obviously, working with him and finding him so that by the end it was that great family unit. It was really lovely.

ALLISON: Yeah, I remember that when I realized this was a connection that was going to happen. I think it was shooting that scene in the lobby of his building. I come over to say like, "Something happened" and he was like, "I'll go get changed and we'll go do police work." And I can remember like nervously patting down my hair thinking, "Do I look okay for this man, for Gus?" And then thinking, "This is like a little love story—this is so sweet." I love that scene for that reason.

NOAH: Yeah and you know—trying to just understate all of it and you guys just knew instinctually to let it be simple. The most romantic it ever got was the phone call where he asked you out, which immediately transitioned into a year later.

ALLISON: You pulled a good trick on me with that year later thing!

NOAH: Yeah, it was a good trick. You guys were in bed watching something. I can't remember . . .

ALLISON: Something about a female detective!

NOAH: Oh, right—yeah, something we found . . .

ALLISON: *Kitty* something . . . yeah, you found something about a female detective.

NOAH: Old Hollywood where they never cut so they just had nine people in like a nine-shot.

ALLISON: Yeah. Standing around behind a couch.

NOAH: Funny. And obviously, you worked a lot with Odenkirk as well. That sort of obstructionist, he didn't want to believe that the world was with bad people. And you're like, "But we're cops." Yeah, what was that experience like?

ALLISON: I feel like Bob and I meeting was so auspicious and so lucky. His wife is now my manager and is just invaluable to me as I'm trying to navigate this weirdo world. As with Bob, we actually have kept in touch and see each other for dinner and try to keep up with each other, et cetera. I instantly felt so at home with him, which I think is helpful when you're going to be butting heads for that many episodes. He's just so perfect for that character and that he manages to still be likable while being such a buffoon is a testament to both the casting and his work as an actor. And that character is a perfect foil for Molly as well.

NOAH: I think he was just surprised. He thought he was just the comic relief and then realized that he was basically the moral center of the show. I remember he had a day that was I think eight to ten pages of dialogue. He had a huge scene with Martin walking him through the frame of Chazz. And then he had a big scene with you at the whiteboards about, "you gotta let it go." I remember he was sweating because he was so focused to get it right.

So you had some very dramatic moments with him but also obviously with Martin Freeman. You had that last scene with him telling him about that story about the gloves. In the original script, you explained what the story meant, but then when we were on set filming it I cut that part out because my thinking was—if he can't figure out what the right thing to do is, then you're not going to help him.

ALLISON: Right, I remember that day because I think we were doing second units at that time and I think you were actually directing that day. I remember feeling a lot of pressure to get that story right. I mean, good pressure, not like I was like, "how to do it" but like, "This is not the same thing as delivering lines." And I knew how to be Molly at that point in time but I didn't really know how to be Molly telling a parable. I remember really feeling like, how do I dial in and how do I find this character in this circumstance. And I realized she was just trying her dad's approach—like she was going to try to do what her dad would do in that situation. He would tell a story that seemingly had nothing to do with anything. And once I kind of decided that was the route to go, I was like, "Oh, now this is just so much fun." Now that I know that I'm just channeling Keith, then it kind of all dialed in for me. I think that it ended up being such a great scene and I really enjoy watching it. But when I remember doing it I was like, "How do I do this, I'm not sure that I know how to do this."

NOAH: There were so many parables that year, with their heightened reality—the most obvious example being fish falling from the sky. But also Colin was given a parable in episode four about the man who wanted to give away everything. It was more grounded in some ways than some

of the things we ended up doing. But still there were those moments where in that first hour where Malvo kills Verne and went into the basement and Martin ran down to warn him and Malvo was gone.

ALLISON: Yeah, there was a little bit of magic.

NOAH: We had an executive from MGM who said, "Well, should we show an open window or something? How did he get out of the basement?" And I was like, *Exactly, how did*

he get out of the basement!? That's the whole thing. Because remember in *No Country for Old Men* when Tommy Lee Jones goes back to that motel room after Brolin is killed, and you can see Anton Chigurh on the other side of that door. And then when he opened it the room was empty. And you think, "I know he was there, the camera told us he was there, so did he disappear or was that just TLJ's fear?" So, I always felt like we have license to play with that stuff.

Are there moments that really stick out for you in your memory in terms of the production or specific themes or moments?

ALLISON: Yeah, shooting the scene in the bed with the lady detective show on with Colin was really special. We were in that old, old house with the creaky floorboards and we had a really smaller crew just in that bedroom. Had the blue light from the TV and it was cold outside that night. Who directed that episode?

NOAH: That was eight, so Scott Winant I believe.

ALLISON: Yeah, and he just urged us to take our time and that it so rare I think. It's so rare for me. I tend to really chew on things and make discoveries and decisions while I'm on camera. And I'm constantly being told to speed up and take the air out of things. And having Scott give us permission to really sit in that silence and really live in that moment was really special I think for me as a performer. It felt really like a gift. That day was really special. That day out on the frozen lake was really cold. It was so cold. I stepped out of the warming van and my hair froze from the tips up. I just froze like icicles.

NOAH: I remember Keith Carradine saying, "Am I talking, because I can't feel my face." And then of course the next day was the day it was forty below and we couldn't shoot.

ALLISON: Yeah, and it was the day before Christmas break, so we all just went home early.

NOAH: You were on a frozen lake and it was twenty-five below, but that wasn't too cold. The next day *was* too cold.

ALLISON: Yeah, the next day was too cold. But we actually all came to work. Remember we came to base camp, but we had to call it because it was so cold that electrical cords kept snapping. So, we didn't have power at base camp because things kept shattering.

NOAH: My joke is you learn a lot of science at forty below. Propane turns to a liquid, the porta-potties freeze. It's never been that cold again. The second year was balmy and the third year it was cold, but nothing like that. That was a crazy polar vortex year. But you could see it on-screen, it worked, it looked great.

ALLISON: And I still lived in Chicago at that point in time, so I was like, yeah, it is cold but not terrible. And all the guys in from California were like, this is the worst thing in the world.

NOAH: And then we shot that blizzard episode in the sun. Where we just had to fake that it was a blizzard. And you running off and him shooting you. And I remember Adam Goldberg, we just grabbed like nine or ten pieces in the same courtyard, and he was like, "You're going to see I'm in the same place." We said, "No, don't worry about it. It's all going to be snow."

ALLISON: And they did. That blizzard looks amazing. That's John [Ross], right? It came together. I do remember shooting it and being like, "Well, I can see him." Honestly,

I feel this way about all filmmaking. I have no ability to see how things fit together. I'm such a theater actress that I'm like, I don't understand what side of the line to look at. I truly have no sense of it whatsoever. I was just like I guess it will look like a blizzard and boy did it look like a blizzard when you guys were all done with it!

NOAH: That was Colin Bucksey, the director. He got an Emmy for that one.

ALLISON: Yeah, he did and deserved it.

NOAH: You spent a lot of time that year trying to convince people of what the truth was and no one would believe you. Obviously, Keegan [Michael Key] and Jordan [Peele] showed up and they believed you and that was a huge moment of validation. Do you remember that big scene?

ALLISON: I do remember that scene in the diner. When I sit down with them and I'm just like, "Blah blah blah, I've sent someone out." She's been calling and leaving messages and now they are doing their due diligence and they've sent some people out. I remember doing that scene and being told what a huge moment that is and to allow that to be a huge moment when she realizes that these two men are here because they've heard what she's been saying for over a year now. And what a relief to get to play that and then to get to go do that wonderful scene in front of the board with poor Bob showing them all of this evidence. It was just such a gift.

I remember I had a joke in there. I don't remember what it was, but I said something to Bob at the end of that scene. And you cut that line. And I was like, "It's literally Molly's only joke, she never tells jokes ever ever." And you were like, "It's got to go, I'm sorry." And I was like, "Aw man, she never gets to be funny on purpose." I don't even remember what the line was now. But I remember when I read it I was like, "Oh, it's a joke, and it was cut!"

NOAH: Well, I know it. It was consistency.

ALLISON: You were right though. It came out right!

NOAH: That said, you were funny the whole time, you just weren't jokey funny. I remember the final scene of the season. I had had a conversation with John Landgraf at the network on the day we were shooting the final scene. He said, "Look I think the last scene that you've written is good. All I know is that the last scene of the movie is sublime. And I don't know." Because all it was, was that you got a phone call that he was dead and you went in and sat on the sofa and you guys watched TV.

I said, "Look, let me cut it together and I'll show it to you because it wasn't the last day of production, and if you think we need to do more then we'll do more." Then I drove over to set and basically took over the set from Matt Shakman, who was directing. And I said let's do it as a one-er, the whole thing. Because I guess I had this instinct that what made that last scene so sublime was how simple it was. And that I'd written this last scene that you would go in and he would be dead and you would sit on the sofa and Colin was getting a citation and it was *Deal or No Deal*. I remember that was essential to me that you were watching *Deal or No Deal*, I don't know why.

The one thing that I knew that I didn't tell the network was that it was the only place in the whole season that I was going to use the original Carter Burwell theme music. I didn't tell FX because why would you ruin that impact to know it's coming. Anyways, the story goes they had no notes and they loved it. I remember that evening as everything we were racing at the end. And so it was one of those moments where you are racing the clock and so you say okay, well, take your time and let's pretend we are not racing the clock.

ALLISON: Yeah, I remember that night and remember the decision to shoot it in one and I remember you making the decision on the call. And coming in that night and being like, "Okay, Noah's on set and we have to wrap this up with a bow and all hands on deck." And the movie ends in the same way. I think it's hard to find an ending that's satisfying, and also leaving you wanting more. I think it's hard to strike that note and also be really satisfying. I can't imagine anybody watching that and feeling like, "Oh, but I wanted more and needed more to feel like the story has come to a conclusion." It's just a satisfying end.

NOAH: It feels like it wraps up for you guys as well. And what made the movie so great was that she had this crazy case and tomorrow was going to be a normal day. And that feeling with Molly and Gus and that was it! You saw the worst that their lives ever got and they are okay now.

ALLISON: I remember you telling me that that was the plan. That we weren't going to come back for a second season because if we were going into the pretense that this is a true story, then how many crazy Mad Cow cases can one person have in their life. Then I remember I was like, "Okay,

so here's what you should do. You should use the same cast but write us all new roles and then I can be like a prostitute villain." And you were like, "No."

NOAH: Ryan Murphy has been using the same cast in different roles. It's hard to have something that works so perfectly and then walking away from it. My joke is you never see a major corporation do a mic drop after a success. I was really proud of FX and MGM that despite the fact that we won every award ever invented and we had this major impact, they never said out loud that maybe two seasons with Molly and Gus and then we can switch. You just have to be true to what you are doing and yes the money is nice and the accolades are nice, but we were rewarded because we took risks and we have to keep taking them.

But yeah, it's always very odd, because obviously that first season I lived up there and was immersed in it every day. But there came a moment halfway through season 2 where I was like, "Wait, we made another *Fargo*? With this cast and this group?" And then season 3 was the same and you know you reach the middle point, and it's you and Ewan McGregor, David Thewlis, and Carrie Coon and are like, well *this* is *Fargo*. Isn't this what it's always been? It's very odd but hugely rewarding. I've never gone back and watched a single hour after we've wrapped. That first season lives in a bubble in my mind. It would be interesting to go back and see it after having made twenty more hours. To be like, oh, right, I was just figuring something out here. I feel like it worked pretty well.

Fargo

SEASON 2

THIS IS A TRUE STORY

POLICE LINE - DO NOT CROSS

2016 EMMY® NOMINATION HIGHLIGHTS

Outstanding Miniseries

Kirsten Dunst—Outstanding Lead Actress in a Miniseries or Movie

Jesse Plemons—Outstanding Supporting Actor in a Miniseries or Movie

Bokeem Woodbine—Outstanding Supporting Actor in a Miniseries or Movie

Jean Smart—Outstanding Supporting Actress in a Miniseries or Movie

Bob DeLaurentis—Outstanding Writing for a Miniseries, Movie, or Dramatic Special ("Loplop")

Noah Hawley—Outstanding Writing for a Miniseries, Movie, or Dramatic Special ("Palindrome")

Noah Hawley—Outstanding Directing for a Miniseries, Movie, or Dramatic Special ("Before the Law")

2016 GOLDEN GLOBE NOMINATIONS

Best Limited Series or Motion Picture Made for Television

Patrick Wilson—Best Performance by an Actor in a Limited Series or Motion Picture Made for Television

Kirsten Dunst—Best Performance by an Actress in a Limited Series or Motion Picture Made for Television

in CONVERSATION with DANA GONZALES (Director of Photography, S 1–3)

NOAH: My guiding principal was that Joel and Ethan Coen have never made the same movie twice—so why should we? In the second year we went back to the seventies so a lot of the lens choices and the old glass informed the look. But also, we just happened to luck out, I think, that the first year was really white and wintery and the second year was just really brown. It gave that second story a completely different look. You would never look at a still image from any season and confuse it with the other seasons.

DANA: When people tell me they love *Fargo*, one of the things they love is the feeling of every aspect of it coming together. It's pretty hard on a normal show to coordinate. For a TV show to do that as successfully as we did it on *Fargo*, the audience feels it. And I think now with where TV is going, soon it's going to be better than cinema, in some respects. It has to have that level.

Episode 1

WAITING FOR DUTCH

```
          FADE IN:

EXT. BATTLEFIELD. SIOUX FALLS, SOUTH DAKOTA—DAY (1862)

A snowy field, surrounded by pine trees. A GREAT BATTLE has
been fought here. Smoke rises. The bodies of the SIOUX DEAD
lay scattered amid Union TROOPS, splayed and bloody, near the
occasional horse corpse.

A crow lands and begins to scavenge. STRINGS SWELL as we PAN
ACROSS the snow.

We are in BLACK AND WHITE.

Over this image an old-fashioned chyron—

MASSACRE AT SIOUX FALLS . . .

—fades on- and off screen.

The CAMERA finds a Sioux Warrior, RUNNING BEAR (30s), dressed in
skins and wearing full war paint. He stands alone, rubbing his
hands together and stamping his feet to stay warm.

Beat. He looks out past the camera.

                    RUNNING BEAR
     Am I — what are we waiting for?

Someone yells something from off screen.

                    RUNNING BEAR (CONT'D)
     What?

A white man, SYD SCHWARTZ (30s), enters frame. He is dressed,
incongruously, in slacks, a cardigan and scarf. SYD is the
FIRST A.D. of the movie Massacre at Sioux Falls. The year is
actually 1952.

                    SYD SCHWARTZ
     The arrows. Gayle's putting in the arrows. On Reagan.

He indicates a body riddled with arrows.

                    RUNNING BEAR
     I know, but they said — Jenny came by the trailer and said
     five minutes, so —

                    SYD SCHWARTZ
     Well, there's a lot of arrows.
```

                    RUNNING BEAR
                         (beat)
     So should I go back to my —

                    SYD SCHWARTZ
     No. It's — Jenny said —
                         (calls off screen)
     What did Jenny say?

A young woman, BRENDA, enters frame.

                    BRENDA
     They're putting in the arrows.

                    SYD SCHWARTZ
     Yeah, I know, but how long?

Beat. Brenda doesn't know.

                    SYD SCHWARTZ (CONT'D)
                         (frustrated)
     Doll, just — go find out, will ya? The chief's wearin
     moccasins and it's goddamn February.

Brenda hurries off. Syd and Running Bear both stamp their feet,
trying to stay warm.

                    RUNNING BEAR
                         (beat)
     That's offensive, you know.
                         (off him)
     "The chief." I've got a name.

                    SYD SCHWARTZ
     I meant your character.

                    RUNNING BEAR
     Oh.
                         (beat)
     What's he like anyway?

                    SYD SCHWARTZ
     Who?

                    RUNNING BEAR
     Dutch. Reagan.

                    SYD SCHWARTZ
     Ronnie? He's a prince. A real class act.

A CORPSE, lying nearby, suddenly sits up.

                              CORPSE
     Can I get a blanket?

Syd gestures to A MAN off screen, who enters frame and lays a
blanket over the "corpse," then exits.

                         SYD SCHWARTZ
                            (beat)
     This is the actual field they tell me.

                         RUNNING BEAR
     What?

                         SYD SCHWARTZ
     The actual battlefield. *Massacre at Sioux Falls.* I think
     three hundred of your people — braves — died here, what? A
     hundred years ago.

                         RUNNING BEAR
     I'm from New Jersey.

                         SYD SCHWARTZ
     Sure, but you're — an Indian, right? So that's gotta be —

                         RUNNING BEAR
                            (beat)
     — gotta be what?

                         SYD SCHWARTZ
     No, I'm just saying. This battle — the last big battle of
     the — and then what came after. And, look, I'm a Jew, so
     believe me, I know tribulation.

Syd takes out a pack of cigarettes.

                         SYD SCHWARTZ (CONT'D)
     Smoke?

Running Bear takes one. Syd lights them up.

                         SYD SCHWARTZ (CONT'D)
     We got a lot in common is all I'm sayin. Our *tribes*.

They stand there, smoking. Beat.

                         SYD SCHWARTZ (CONT'D)
                            (smoking)
     Any minute. He'll be out.

We FADE TO BLACK as they wait.

CUT TO:

EXT. ALLEY. FARGO, ND—DAY (1979)

Two men stand in an empty alley, DODD GERHARDT and OHANZEE DENT.
It's cold and they've been there awhile. As they wait, we see
the following text:

*This is a true story. The events depicted took place in
Minnesota in 1979. At the request of the survivors, the names
have been changed. Out of respect for the dead, the rest has
been told exactly as it occurred.*

Dodd checks his watch.

                                     DODD
    Is he kiddin me?

Hanzee sees something behind Dodd, nods—*there he is.* Dodd turns.

       ANGLE ON RYE GERHARDT

approaching. He looks worried.

                                       RYE
    Hey there. Sorry.

Dodd moves towards Rye.

                              DODD
          Are you kiddin me?

                              RYE
          Said noon, yeah?

Dodd closes on Rye, blind with anger.

                              DODD
          Are you kiddin me?

                              RYE
                         (oh shit)
          Hold on now.

But Dodd's not waiting. He grabs Rye in a headlock, chokes him
for a bit.

                              DODD
          Said eleven. Not noon.

                              RYE
          What?

Dodd squeezes.

                              DODD
          Say that again.

                              RYE
                         (ow, fuck)
          Okay. Okay.

Dodd lets him go with a shove. Rye stumbles, tries to regain his
dignity.

                              DODD
          Where's the goddamn money?

                              RYE
                         (lying)
          Gave it to Ollie, like, yesterday.

                              DODD
          Don't lie.

                              RYE
                         (flinches)
          I mean, I'm gettin it. Just a little late.

                              DODD
          The hell you say. I did the rounds. Everybody paid.

                              RYE
          Course they're gonna *say* that.

                              DODD
          So you got the money.

                              RYE
          Well — ya know — maybe I need it for me, fer something I
          got —

Dodd points at him. *Watch it.*

                              DODD
          No. You earn for family. Not for yerself.

                              RYE
          Yeah, but yer oldest and then Bear. And that's the throne.
          What am I ever gonna be except the kid brother ya send out
          fer milk?

                              DODD
          Yer a Gerhardt.

                              RYE
          That's like Jupiter telling Pluto — *hey, yer a planet also.*
          If I'm this — royalty, how come ya got me doin bullshit
          collections like some nobody chump?

                              DODD
          Everybody earns. That's the law.

                              RYE
          Yeah, but what if I got dreams, ya know? Ambitions.

                              DODD
          Ya wear short pants till you prove yer a man.

                              RYE
          I'm a man.

                              DODD
          Yer the comic in a piece a bubblegum.

This stings.

                              RYE
          Well — I mean, says you — but maybe I got a plan, ya know?
          Somethin in the works. Maybe I start an empire a my own. Be
          a king too.

Dodd looks at him. *What are you talking about?*

                              DODD
          Ya got till tomorrow ta bring in the collection money ya owe.

                          RYE
         Or what?

Dodd nods to Hanzee. The two walk to Dodd's car. Dodd stops at
the door.

                          DODD
         You make me wait for ya again, I'll cleave yer skull.

He and Hanzee get in, drive away. Rye stands there, shaken, but
also pissed.

         CUT TO:

EXT. GERHARDT HOME. FARGO, ND—DAY

A ranch house in rural North Dakota.

         CUT TO:

INT. KITCHEN. GERHARDT HOME. FARGO, ND—DAY

The camera moves along a long kitchen table towards OTTO
GERHARDT, 60s, who sits at the head. He is the gangster warlord
of the plains states—the Winter Lion—and has ruled this land for
thirty years, crushing all who oppose him.

His son, BEAR, sits to his right. To Otto's left is his wife,
FLOYD. There is a Native American HOUSEKEEPER cooking in the
background.

Floyd has the business ledger out. She slides it over and shows
Otto the figures for the month.

                              FLOYD
          This is the month's cash — all in. You'll see the problem
          right away.

He looks at the books.

                              OTTO
          Light.

Dodd enters with Hanzee.

                              OTTO (CONT'D)
          About time.

                              DODD GERHARDT
          Gimme a break.

Dodd comes over—gives Bear a look—*you're in my chair*. Bear
stands, leans against the wall over Otto's shoulder.

                              OTTO
          Soon as you ladies are done dancin —

Dodd makes a gesture—*go ahead*.

                              FLOYD
          You're right. We're light. Even though transport dollars
          went up. It's the local business — drugs, gambling, whores.

Otto glares at Dodd and Bear.

                              OTTO
          Meine keine gute Söhne?

                              DODD GERHARDT
          Don't pin this on me.

                              BEAR
          Or me. We earned.

                              OTTO
                          (lasering in)
          But not Rye.

                              FLOYD
                          (reluctant)
          No. But even without his nut we shouldn't be this short.
          It's like we're a balloon leakin air all over.

Otto turns to Bear, glaring.

                              OTTO
          Well, spit it out. What are we talkin about here?

Bear doesn't want to say. Looks at Dodd.

                              OTTO (CONT'D)
          Tell me, Goddamn it.

                              BEAR
          There's another outfit.

                              DODD GERHARDT
          I'm takin care of it.

                              BEAR
          From the south. Not sure where.

                              DODD GERHARDT
          I said I'll handle it.

                              BEAR
          They're comin hard.

Otto can't believe it.

                              OTTO
          Son, I am the iron fist of God. There's not a sane man in
          three states who would dare ta —
                         (getting worked up)
          — some pissant crew from south-no-place? — you bring me
          these hirnlose mutter fotzen and I'll grind their bones ta
          make my —

          CLOSE ON OTTO

As a blood clot breaks free from somewhere deep in his arteries
and shoots like a bullet into his brain. One of his EYES
DILATES, the pupil drifting left.

          ANGLE ON HIS HAND(S)

As they reach out and GRIP the ends of the table.

                              OTTO
forces himself up through sheer willpower into a stand, as if
even his own body can't kill him. Then he sputters, chokes, and
<u>falls to the floor</u> into a full-blown seizure.

Floyd drops beside him, getting her knee under his head.

                              FLOYD
          Hold him!

Dodd grabs his ankles. They try to contain him, but he's thrashing. Floyd looks at Bear.

                    FLOYD (CONT'D)
        Call a doctor. Go now!

Bear hurries out. We leave Floyd there holding her fallen husband.

            CUT TO:

EXT. RURAL ROAD (TRAVELING). FARGO, ND—DAY (1979)

We are looking over the hood of a red 1973 Mustang, driving down a rural snowy road, the yellow lane lines sharking towards us.

We CUT TO a DIFFERENT ROAD, closer to town, but the camera mount and the car's hood remain unchanged.

A THIRD ROAD, more residential, the camera mount and the car's hood unchanging.

Now we are on A COMMERCIAL STREET. The car turns right into a parking space, the camera framing CARRIAGE TYPEWRITERS in front of us.

We see a SIGN on the plate glass.

GRAND RE-OPENING . . . SOON.

The car comes to a stop.

      REVERSE ON THE CAR

As RYE GERHARDT (28) climbs out. Rye sees himself as a big
swinging dick (being the youngest son of the Gerhardt crime
family), but in reality he has zero class or gravitas. A small
dog, in other words, who barks big.

Rye looks up at the shop, wipes some WHITE POWDER remnants from
his mustache.

      CUT TO:

INT. CARRIAGE TYPEWRITERS. FARGO, ND—CONTINUOUS

An old-world, small-town store in the middle of a "modern"
remodel. New shelves stand half-finished.

SKIP SPRANG (40s), the owner, talking to CLYDE BUTTERWORTH
(50s), a carpenter, dressed in dusty overalls.

And here's what you should know about Skip. He's a man
chronically on the verge of Hitting It Big. The problem is, his
instinct for what the Next Big Thing is is always wrong.

And yet—God bless him—his fervor remains undaunted, his absolute
certainty that success, validation, and riches are right around
the corner.

He speaks to Clyde as Albert Einstein might address a cow.

                    SKIP
          I'm saying tomorrow has never been closer than it is right
          now.

                    CLYDE
                (*don't bullshit me*)
          It's eleven o'clock in the morning.

                    SKIP
          Metaphorically, I mean.

The door opens. Rye comes in. Skip sees him, isn't happy about
it, but covers.

                    SKIP (CONT'D)
                (to Rye)
          Hi, friend. Be with you in a —

Clyde won't be put off.

                    CLYDE
          The check never came is my point. I'm owed for work I did.
          Me and the boys. We're owed —

Rye whistles softly to get Clyde's attention. Clyde stops, looks
over.

                    RYE GERHARDT
          Giddy-up there, cowboy.

Clyde looks at him.

                    CLYDE
          Wait yer turn, short round.

                    RYE GERHARDT
          What did you say?

                    CLYDE
          You heard me.

But Rye has been disrespected enough today. He PULLS A REVOLVER,
points it at Clyde, cocks it. Clyde glares at him, but there's
fear now. Skip intervenes.

                              SKIP
         Jesus — just — it's in the mail okay? The check. Just —

He moves Clyde to the front door. Rye keeps the gun on him.

                          SKIP (CONT'D)
         — if it hasn't come by Tuesday, I'll write ya another.

At the door, Clyde gives the two of them a look of disdain,
walks out.

                          RYE GERHARDT
         Yeah, that's right. You better run.

Skip closes the door, locks it, turns back to Rye, who is
putting the gun back in his belt. And the look on Skip's face
says he's questioning his choice in new partners.

                              SKIP
         Come on now. He could call a cop.

                          RYE GERHARDT
         He's not callin anybody. Guys like that — they're just big
         on the outside. So where's this miracle contraption that's
         gonna make us both rich?

Skip shakes off the mood, shows Rye an electric typewriter.

                              SKIP
         Behold. The future on a pedestal. I'm talkin money, hand
         over fist.

                          RYE GERHARDT
                          (unimpressed)
         A typewriter.

                              SKIP
         The self-correcting IBM Selectrics Two _electric_ typewriter
         with patented high-speed typeball. They're not just for
         women anymore.

                          RYE GERHARDT
         And you're sure we're the only —

                              SKIP
         Sole distributor, Midwest region. Assuming — you're willing
         to — _forget_ certain debts owed to yer family — from the,
         uh —

                          RYE GERHARDT
         Gambling.

                              SKIP
         Yeah, which — ya know — I'm not proud.

                    RYE GERHARDT
You said fast money off this, right? Like overnight?

                    SKIP
Well — soon as you talk to the judge and she unfreezes the
accounts — well, then we can turn on the money spigot.

                    RYE GERHARDT
The what?

                    SKIP
The spigot. It's like — where you hook up a hose.

                    RYE GERHARDT
Like a fire hose?

                    SKIP
Any hose. I'm sayin once we get those typewriters — the
money — there'll be no stopping it.

                    RYE GERHARDT
You better not be lyin ta me.
                    (off Skip)
But assumin yer right — fast money first and then somethin
steady, well — a man could get used ta bein called Boss.
                    (beat)
Which judge again?

                    SKIP
Mundt. She's driving to South Dakota tonight. Clerk told
me she has a nephew in the Crippled Children's Hospital. A
cripple, I guess.

                    RYE GERHARDT
You got a picture?

Skip hands him a photo of the judge. Rye studies her.

                    RYE GERHARDT (CONT'D)
May have to get a little rough with her. Uptown broad like
this.

He pulls his gun, lays it on the counter.

                    RYE GERHARDT (CONT'D)
Probably have ta show her who's boss.

Skip looks worried.

                    SKIP
Yeah. But don't —

                    RYE GERHARDT
I won't.

<pre>
                          (beat)
         Unless I have to.

              CUT TO:

EXT. COURTHOUSE. FARGO, ND—DAY

Judge Mundt exits the courthouse—walks from out of focus into a
close up. We PULL BACK as she starts down the steps. We FIND Rye
Gerhardt watching her. He gives her a few steps, then follows.

              CUT TO:

EXT. RURAL ROAD. MINNESOTA—NIGHT

Snowy, barren. We see a sign LUVERNE, MN 10 miles. The judge's
CAR passes. Beat. A SECOND CAR follows.

              CUT TO:

INT. RYE'S CAR (TRAVELING). RURAL, MINNESOTA—NIGHT

Rye follows the judge. His radio is on, playing "Children of the
Sun," by Billy Thorpe. He takes out a cigarette, lights it off
the dashboard.

              ANGLE ON THE JUDGE'S CAR

As it signals right and pulls off the road into the parking lot
for the WAFFLE HUT.

              CUT TO:

EXT. WAFFLE HUT—CONTINUOUS

The judge's car pulls in, parks. Judge Mundt gets out, goes
inside. Beat. Rye's car pulls in.

              CUT TO:

INT. RYE'S CAR—CONTINUOUS

Rye Gerhardt sits in the driver's seat. He watches as . . .

              ANGLE ON THE JUDGE
the judge enters the diner. She is met and seated by a WAITRESS.

              RYE GERHARDT
takes a glassine envelope out of his shirt pocket, pours some
white powder on the meat of his left thumb, snorts it.

As he does we RUSH INTO A CLOSE UP.

Ding!
</pre>

```
                HARD CUT TO:

INT. WAFFLE HUT—MOMENTS LATER

. . . as the front door opens and Rye enters. The same song is
playing on the jukebox. Rye looks around.

        ANGLE ON THE DINER

The CAMERA PANS left to right with his eyes. There is a FAMILY
OF FOUR at a back booth. The judge sits two booths forward,
reading her menu.

A FRY COOK works behind the counter. As the camera turns, it
finds THE WAITRESS standing in front of Rye (us), waiting.

                    WAITRESS
        Welcome to Waffle Hut! Table or booth?

Rye, cranked, jumps a little.

                    RYE GERHARDT
        Shit, lady. Just, uh, the counter.

        RYE

nods his head to the counter, goes and sits. The waitress comes
around behind the counter, lays a menu in front of him.

                    WAITRESS
        Special's tuna melt and fries. Pie's humbleberry.

                    RYE GERHARDT
        Just coffee.

The waitress heads off. Rye watches the . . .

        ANGLE ON THE FRY COOK

A BLACK MAN in a hair net, working the grill. He reads an order
slip, puts a burger patty on the grill.

Laughter makes . . .

        RYE
turn

        ANGLE ON THE FAMILY

Meal finished. The KIDS are up, horsing around. MOM scolds them,
as DAD puts on his coat. The Camera DRIFTS to Judge Mundt as the
waitress brings her a milkshake.
```

ANGLE ON RYE'S RIGHT FOOT

tapping nervously on the floor.

          RYE

smooths his mustache. Behind him <u>The Family</u> walks to the
register. The waitress meets them.

                    WAITRESS
     How was everything?

                         DAD
     Oh yeah. Real good.

Dad pays. The waitress opens the register, gives Dad his change.
They exit. Rye watches as they . . .

          ANGLE ON THE FAMILY

. . . climb into their station wagon.

                    WAITRESS (O.S.)
     Sugar?

          RYE TURNS

The waitress is there, smiling, holding a sugar container.

                    RYE GERHARDT
     You're freakin me out a little.

She leaves. Rye wipes his nose nervously, glances at the judge,
who is examining her burger suspiciously. It's now or never. Rye
stands and crosses over and SLIDES INTO the booth across from
the judge.

                    RYE GERHARDT (CONT'D)
     Hi.

The judge doesn't look up.

                    JUDGE MUNDT
     No.

                    RYE GERHARDT
     Whatdya mean no?

                    JUDGE MUNDT
     Whatever yer sellin, I ain't buyin.

                    RYE GERHARDT
     First of all, I'm not sellin anything. Second —

The judge turns and signals for the waitress, who comes over.
The judge offers up her plate.

                    JUDGE MUNDT
        He needs to make me another burger. This one's a coaster.

                    WAITRESS
        Yes, ma'am.

The waitress leaves.

                    RYE GERHARDT
                    (undermined)
        Look, yer majesty —

Rye sits across from her, trying to change the momentum in his
favor.

                    RYE GERHARDT (CONT'D)
        Yer gonna change yer mind about somethin. A case.

                    JUDGE MUNDT
        Or what?

                    RYE GERHARDT
Or you'll find out is what. I'm not someone ya *triffle* with.

                    JUDGE MUNDT
Trifle.

                    RYE GERHARDT
What?
                    (off her)
Look, yer queenship, yer gonna change yer mind here. This
isn't one of those optional "check A or B" scenarios.

The judge sighs. It's one of those. She balls up her napkin,
puts it on the table.

                    JUDGE MUNDT
One day the devil came to God and said, *Let's make a bet, you
and me, for the soul of a man.* And from on high they looked
down on Job — a devout man, religious — and the devil said,
I can change his mind, make him curse your name. And God
said, *Try and you will only fail.* So the devil begins. He
kills Job's herds and takes his fields. He plagues him with
boils and throws him on the ash heap. But Job's mind remains
unchanged. And so I ask you, son, if the devil couldn't
change Job's mind, how the hell are you gonna change mine?

Beat. Rye doesn't know what to make of any of that.

                    RYE GERHARDT
Huh?

                    JUDGE MUNDT
You're a little dim, aren't ya?

                    RYE GERHARDT
Listen, this is — there's two ways this can go —

                    JUDGE MUNDT
Is one of them the hard way?

                    RYE GERHARDT
— easy and, uh — Ya know what? There's a fella needs ta get
his hands on some typewriters — and yer gonna —

                    JUDGE MUNDT
Christ, you're with that fool.

                    RYE GERHARDT
Yer gonna —

        ANGLE ON THE JUDGE'S PURSE

next to her on the booth's bench. The judge turns calmly and
opens her purse. We see the CAN OF RAID inside.

She takes it out, puts it on the table.

      ANGLE ON RYE

He looks at it questioningly.

          RYE GERHARDT (CONT'D)
  What —

          JUDGE MUNDT
  Son, I'm givin you three seconds to pick your ass up and get
  outta here, or I'm gonna squash you like a bug.

          RYE GERHARDT
  Look, bitch — I'm the one doin the —

The judge calmly picks up the can of Raid and SPRAYS Rye in the
face. He screams, scrambles to his feet, pawing at his eyes.

          RYE GERHARDT (CONT'D)
  Aghh! You — goddamn — my eyes!

The judge puts the can back in her purse.

          JUDGE MUNDT
  Now scram before I call the cops.

                    RYE

fumbles A GUN from his pocket. He aim-squints through the bug
spray, half blind.

          ANGLE ON THE JUDGE

Blurry. She sees the pistol, realizes she brought bug spray to a
gun fight.

                    JUDGE MUNDT (CONT'D)
          Crap.

Rye SHOOTS HER dead center. The judge rocks backward and slumps
over.

                    RYE

rubs his burned eyes, weeping, in pain. Then . . .

                    FRY COOK (O.S.)
          Ahhhhh!

Rye turns, just in time to see the Fry Cook charging him with an
IRON SKILLET.

Rye SHOOTS HIM. The Fry Cook goes down hard. Rye hears <u>glass</u>
<u>shatter</u>. He turns.

          THE WAITRESS

is standing there, screaming. She has dropped her coffee pot on
the floor, shattering it.

THE CAMERA RACES TOWARDS HER, as RYE FIRES. A bloom of blood
appears above her right breast. The waitress drops.

          REVERSE ON RYE

who suddenly SCREAMS himself, and turns, a STEAK KNIFE in his
back.

          THE JUDGE IS STANDING THERE

not dead after all, just wounded. She has stabbed him, and looks
ready to do it again.

                    JUDGE MUNDT
          I'm gonna skin your prick and eat it, you hairy piece of —

          RYE SHOOTS HER

. . . *one, two, three* more times, knocking her off her feet and
into the next booth.

ANGLE ON THE JUDGE

lying prone on the table, wisps of smoke coming off her, now
completely and totally dead.

RYE TURNS

trying to reach the steak knife, like a dog chasing its tail.
Beat. He screams in frustration, finally grabs it, and drops it
on the floor, stands panting, half blind.

> RYE GERHARDT
> Son of a bitch.
> (beat)
> Son of a bitch.

He wipes his face, eyes red and swollen, then takes in the
damage.

ANGLE ON THE DINER

Blood everywhere, bodies. It's a goddamn massacre.

RYE

tries to think. This could <u>not</u> have gone worse. He holsters his
gun, walks to the register, opens it.

ANGLE ON HIS HAND

scooping out the cash. Behind him he hears:

Ding!

RYE TURNS

The FLOOR where the waitress lay is now empty.

ANGLE ON THE FRONT DOOR

as we find the waitress, outside, hobbling bloody through the
snow towards the road.

> RYE GERHARDT (CONT'D)
> Shit.

RYE

hurries to the door.

CUT TO:

EXT. WAFFLE HUT—CONTINUOUS

Rye stumbles out into the snow. He raises his gun.

        ANGLE ON THE WAITRESS

over his gun barrel, only seconds to live.

Click.

        ANGLE ON RYE

flustered. The gun is empty.

                RYE GERHARDT
    Shit. Shit.

He fumbles to reload.

        ANGLE ON THE WAITRESS

almost to the road, dragging her right leg a little. Five more
steps, four, three.

BLAM!

Blood sprays into the snow. The waitress falls.

        RYE

walks over to her, gun up, leaving a blood trail of his own from
the knife wound. He looks down on her, prepared to fire again,
but she's dead. That's when . . .

        A STRANGE LIGHT

envelops Rye, a kind of **BLUE GLOW**. With it, all sounds of life
(frogs, crickets) stop.

Slowly, Rye looks up.

        ANGLE ON THE LIGHT

in the sky, hovering.

        RYE SQUINTS

What is that? It's not a helicopter.

        ANGLE ON THE LIGHT

as it begins to descend, as if in a dream. It's bright, flaring
the lens, but around it maybe we see a telltale **SAUCER SHAPE**.

Suddenly, the light begins to strobe, flashing blue, then
yellow, then red.

                    RYE

hypnotized, steps towards it, into the road. He is having a
transformational moment—*Is this God? Proof of something bigger
than me in the universe?* He is filled with awe and wonder.

                    THE LIGHT

drifts slowly backwards, and disappears behind the trees.

                    RYE

now back in the dark, stands for a moment, blinking. The sounds
of nature return. Suddenly, a HARD WHITE LIGHT hits Rye from
behind. Is the UFO back?

Rye TURNS. At the last second we . . .

          CUT TO:

INT. MOLLY'S BEDROOM. SOLVERSON HOUSE. LUVERNE, MN—NIGHT

LOU SOLVERSON (33) is in bed, reading to YOUNG MOLLY SOLVERSON
(4). It's the nightly bedtime ritual. Lou is a clean-cut
man, four years back from the navy. He was a lieutenant on
a swift boat in Vietnam. A humble man, competent, used to
responsibility.

He reads from a book.

                    LOU SOLVERSON
          "*Oh Whocky!*" cried Joel. "See what you've done Polly
          Pepper?" But Polly didn't hear. Over the big flat door-
          stone she sped and met Ben with little David coming in
          the gate. His face was just like Phronsie's! And with a
          cold, heavy feeling at her heart, Polly realized this was
          no play. "Oh Ben!" she cried, flinging her arms around
          his neck and bursting into tears. "Don't! Please. I wish
          you wouldn't. Phronsie's got em' and that's enough."
          "Got what?" asked Ben, while Davie's eyes grew to their
          widest proportions. "Oh, Measles!" cried Polly, bursting
          out afresh. "Hatefulest, horridest measles and now you're
          taken!" "Oh, no, I ain't," responded Ben cheerfully, who
          knew what measles were. "Wipe up Polly. I'm all right. Only
          my head aches, and my eyes feel funny." Polly, only half
          reassured, gulped down her sobs and the sorrowful trio
          repaired to mother. "Oh, dear me," *ejaculated* Mrs. Pepper,
          sinking in a chair at the dismay at the sight of Ben's red
          face, "Whatever will we do now?"

He turns the page.

                    LOU SOLVERSON (CONT'D)
          This is a funny book, huh?

BETSY SOLVERSON comes in.

> BETSY SOLVERSON
> Phone call, hon. It's the shop.

Lou kisses Molly.

> LOU SOLVERSON
> Okay, you. Sleep, huh?

He stands. Betsy turns to Molly.

> BETSY SOLVERSON
> Be back in a minute ta tuck ya in.

> CUT TO:

INT. KITCHEN. SOLVERSON HOUSE—CONTINUOUS

Lou walks to the phone (the handset resting on top of the hooks). Betsy follows.

> BETSY SOLVERSON
> Murder, Eunice says. Three of 'em. Over at the Waffle Hut.

Lou picks up the phone, pauses.

> LOU SOLVERSON
> Hey, you had your thing today?

> BETSY SOLVERSON
> Yeah. This mornin.

> LOU SOLVERSON
> You feel okay?

> BETSY SOLVERSON
> Compared to what? Love Canal?

He nods—what else is there to say—picks up the handset.

> LOU SOLVERSON
> Solverson.
> (beat, listening)
> Yeah, okay. Tell him don't go inside. Hank on his way?
> (beat, listening)
> Okay. Me too.

He hangs up.

> LOU SOLVERSON (CONT'D)
> Gotta go, hon. You okay getting her to bed?

                    BETSY SOLVERSON
          She's four. Not, ya know, Pol Pot.

He kisses her.

                    LOU SOLVERSON
          Okay. Call if you need — whatever.

          CUT TO:

EXT. WAFFLE HUT. LUVERNE, MN—NIGHT

As it was, except for a big rig cab is parked out front, a
TRUCKER standing next to it. A STATE POLICE CAR pulls up. Lou
gets out.

The trucker approaches him.

                    TRUCKER
          I left my rig there. Hope that's okay.

Lou sees the dead waitress, approaches her body, flashlight up
and on.

                    TRUCKER (CONT'D)
    I'm the one called it in, see? Stopped fer waffles, ya know.
    With the blueberries. Come frozen this time a year, I know,
    but —

Lou ignores him, crouches next to the waitress's body. She's
been covered up.

                    TRUCKER (CONT'D)
    I put my coat on her. Seemed only right.

Lou lifts the collar of the coat, looks under it.

                    LOU SOLVERSON
                    (to himself)
    Yeah.

                    TRUCKER
    "Yeah" it's okay about the coat, or —

Lou shines his light on the snow.

            ANGLE ON A BLOOD TRAIL

Two actually (Rye's and the waitress's), leading from the
waitress's body back to the front door of the restaurant.

            LOU

. . . straightens, walks to the entrance, the trucker following.

                    TRUCKER (CONT'D)
    Hell of a thing. Just really wanted some waffles, ya know?
    Been driving since Brunswick — Maine — and —

Lou stops, gives him a look. The trucker stops. Lou climbs the
steps, goes inside.

            CUT TO:

INT. WAFFLE HUT. LUVERNE, MN—CONTINUOUS

Lou enters. He looks around.

            ANGLE ON THE CRIME SCENE

The bodies have drained, the blood has started to congeal. The
camera FINDS a POOL OF BLOOD (where the waitress first fell).
There are BLOOD SMEARS (from where she got up) and BLOODY
FOOTPRINTS back past Lou to the front door.

            LOU

notes this.

                              LOU SOLVERSON
                              (to himself)
     Yeah.

He approaches the fry cook, lying prone on the linoleum.

          ANGLE ON THE FRY COOK

One leg bent under his body, arms thrown up, as if in surprise.

          LOU

nods.

                         LOU SOLVERSON (CONT'D)
     Yeah.

He steps over the body carefully, goes to the judge.

          ANGLE ON THE JUDGE

She lies on her back, half on a table, shot multiple times.

          LOU

studies her, the blood spray around her. His eyes go to . . .

          ANGLE ON THE WINDOW

behind her. There is a BULLET HOLE surrounded by spider cracks.

          LOU

nods, looks down.

          ANGLE ON SHELL CASINGS

on the floor. A BLOODY STEAK KNIFE lies beside them. There is
a small pool of blood, with blood dots leading back to the
counter.

          LOU

follows them with his eyes.

                         LOU SOLVERSON (CONT'D)
                              (assessing)
     Yeah.

He walks over to the checkout counter.

          ANGLE ON THE CASH REGISTER

drawer open. Blood on the plastic, a bloody DOLLAR BILL still
under the metal flap. Below this we see . . .

        ANGLE ON THE FLOOR

A small pool of blood has formed—where Rye stood for a moment
and took the cash—it leads to the front door.

The CAMERA FOLLOWS (as Lou's POV) the blood trail to the front
door. As we land, the DOOR OPENS. SHERIFF HANK LARSSON (60)
comes in. Hank is the sheriff of Rock County. He is a big man,
experienced, who makes Lou look like a chatterbug.

Hank looks around, pushes up his hat.

                HANK LARSSON
        Well, this is a deal.

Lou nods.

                LOU SOLVERSON
        I count three dead.

                HANK LARSSON
        You saw the waitress in the parking lot?

Lou nods.

                LOU SOLVERSON
        Think she caught one over there, then staggered out. Gunman
        followed, made things permanent.

Hank steps over the blood and goes to the fry cook.

                HANK LARSSON
        That's Henry Blanton. Got the single season touchdown record
        in tenth grade. Thirty-one. Still stands.

Beat. Hank steps over the body, goes and examines the judge.

                HANK LARSSON (CONT'D)
        Yeah. Don't know her.

                LOU SOLVERSON
        North Dakota plates on the Ford outside.

                HANK LARSSON
        A tourist, you're thinking.

Lou shrugs.

                HANK LARSSON (CONT'D)
        How's Betsy?

                    LOU SOLVERSON
You didn't call her on the way over?

                    HANK LARSSON
Well, yeah. Just bein polite. Give ya a chance ta talk about
yer feelings, should you be so disposed.

                    LOU SOLVERSON
She's good. Ordered this kit of recipe cards. Saw it on TV.
So now every night we eat delicacies of the world.

                    HANK LARSSON
Some men like that. Variety.

Lou nods. He's not one of those guys.

                    LOU SOLVERSON
She put a soufflé on the table last night. Perfectly good
casserole. Then lit it on fire with a kitchen match.

                    HANK LARSSON
                  (takes all kinds)
Huh.

Lou nods.

                    LOU SOLVERSON
Which reminds me. You're invited for dinner tomorrow.

                    HANK LARSSON
Six?

Lou nods.

                HANK LARSSON (CONT'D)
I'll bring a suit of armor.

        CUT TO:

EXT. WAFFLE HUT. LUVERNE, MN—NIGHT

Other police cars have arrived, deputies setting up yellow crime
scene tape. Lou and Hank stand over the dead waitress.

                    HANK LARSSON
Based on the number of bodies, I'm thinkin we got one car too
many in the parking lot.

                    LOU SOLVERSON
Saw that.

                    HANK LARSSON
Victim missing maybe.

                    LOU SOLVERSON
Or the shooter had an accomplice in a second car. Left his
behind.

                    HANK LARSSON
See. That's big-time state police thinkin.

Lou sees BLOOD DROPS in the snow, leading to the ROAD. He walks
to the blacktop, looks left, then right, sees something on the
asphalt.

                    LOU SOLVERSON
Skid marks.

Hank comes over.

                    HANK LARSSON
I see 'em. Course, connecting those to this deal here would
be what we call "jumping to a conclusion."

Lou sees something.

          ANGLE ON A BLOODY $20 BILL

in the slush on the side of the road.

        LOU

crouches next to it.

                   LOU SOLVERSON
                   (to himself)
Yeah.
                   (beat, to Hank)
So the shooter's got a wound or two in him from the steak
knife. Two blood trails lead out, one to the waitress, now
deceased, the other to the road here — where he absconds,
leaving a few dollars behind.

                   HANK LARSSON
And why not take his own car?

                   LOU SOLVERSON
                   (beat, thinks)
Unclear at this time.

Beat. They think about that. Hank looks up. Something's up in a
tree. He shines his flashlight on it.

        ANGLE ON A WHITE PENNY LOAFER

In a high tree branch.

                   HANK LARSSON
There's a shoe in that tree.

Lou looks up at it.

                   LOU SOLVERSON
There sure is.

Beat. They think about that.

                   HANK LARSSON
S'pose we oughta get that down.

                   LOU SOLVERSON
Could be unrelated.

                   HANK LARSSON
Like the skid marks.
                   (beat)
Well — are we calling this a local matter or do the state
police want it?

                   LOU SOLVERSON
We do not.

                    HANK LARSSON
                      (nods)
Local matter it is.

                    LOU SOLVERSON
Course, any support the state can provide.

                    HANK LARSSON
Course.
                      (*well . . .*)
See you tomorrow then.

                    LOU SOLVERSON
Six o'clock.

He walks back to his car, turns.

                    LOU SOLVERSON (CONT'D)
Be ready for anything.

Hank nods, stands there, thinking about the case. He looks up at
the shoe again.

                    HANK LARSSON
That's a shoe all right.

        CUT TO:

EXT. BUD'S MEATS. LUVERNE, MN—NIGHT

A small-town butcher shop, near closing time.

        CUT TO:

INT. BUD'S MEATS. LUVERNE, MN—CONTINUOUS

BUD JORGENLEN is behind the meat counter, covering the meat with
butcher paper. NOREEN VANDERSLICE is behind the cash register,
reading *The Myth of Sisyphus*. ED BLUMQUIST (30s) comes out of
the back room, hangs up his apron, gets his coat.

                    ED BLUMQUIST
Okay then.

                       BUD
Okay then.
              (beat, Ed puts on his coat)
Noreen?

                     NOREEN
               (doesn't look up)
Mmmm?

                              BUD
          Ed's leavin.

                            NOREEN
                       (doesn't look up)
          Okay then.

Ed reaches the door. Bud finds something in the case.

                              BUD
          Oh, hey. You may as well take these.
                       (holds up a package)
          Boolie Hendricks paid, but never picked em up.

Ed reaches across the counter, takes them from Bud.

                          ED BLUMQUIST
                       (guessing by weight)
          Chops?

                              BUD
                            (nods)
          Wasted meat's a crime. Or should be.

                          ED BLUMQUIST
                        (a polite beat)
          Okay then.

                              BUD
Okay then.

                            NOREEN
                        (doesn't look up)
Okay then.

Ed exits.

          CUT TO:

INT. VETERANS OF FOREIGN WARS HALL. LUVERNE, MN—NIGHT

A small-town gathering place for veterans. It's been here since
the twenties. There's a bar, a small stage. Card tables are set
up around the room. Drinkers tend to gather by war. You've got
the older WWII vets, middle-aged Korean War vets, and a few
scraggly Vietnam vets. In back we even see a ninety-one-year-old
veteran of the Spanish American War.

It's BINGO night. There is a MAN, BJORN GRUFFENSON (50s), up
front calling numbers. Everyone has a board in front of them.

                       BJORN GRUFFENSON
     B-8. B-8.

Sitting alone at a table we find KARL WEATHERS (40s) and SONNY
GREER (30). Karl is the town lawyer, a heavyset big talker,
who spends most of his days lightly soused. Korea was his war.
The last real war, he calls it. None of this "Police Action"
bullshit of Vietnam.

He cracks peanuts and eats them from a bowl as he talks.

Sonny is an auto mechanic, deaf in one ear from a Vietnamese
landmine. He's never been the smartest fella. A round hole,
square peg kind of guy. Never felt bad about that though. He's
as smart as God made him, he figures.

The conversation we come in on has no beginning or end.

Sonny and Karl absently check their boards.

                             SONNY
     So Ho Chi Minh —

                             KARL
     Jesus, kid. Keep up. Ho Chi Minh was just a front man. Enemy
     number 1, straight outta central casting. Aka a stuffed
     shirt for the military industrial complex.

                             SONNY
     The what's that now?

                    KARL
Jesus, Mary, and Joseph. Ike's farewell address? The military
industrial complex. Wheels inside wheels. Special interests.

He gets some peanut shell on his tongue. Works to get it off.

                BJORN GRUFFENSON
N-33. N-33.

Sonny looks around.

                    SONNY
I thought there was a band tonight.

Lou Solverson comes over with a beer, sits.

                LOU SOLVERSON
Boys.

                BJORN GRUFFENSON
I-17. I-17.

Karl thinks he has that. Doesn't.

                    KARL
Balls.
                (to Lou)
Tell this dipshit pissant about Ike's farewell address.

                LOU SOLVERSON
You mean the military industrial complex?

                    KARL
                (to Sonny)
See? He knows.

                LOU SOLVERSON
Course we've been to war. Nothing complex about it.

                    SONNY
How come you're in uniform then, Lou? Didn't you work this
morning?

                LOU SOLVERSON
Three dead at the Waffle Hut.

                    KARL
No shit.

                LOU SOLVERSON
A real mess. Women too. Hank's thinking botched robbery.

                    KARL
Oh sure. That's what they want you to think.

                    SONNY
Who?

                    KARL
They. Ya know, the powers that be. It's a classic story.
Oswald acted alone. The girl in the polka-dot dress.

                    SONNY
The what now?

                    KARL
The girl in the — after Kennedy the other was shot — Robert,
in L.A. — people saw a woman in a polka-dot dress run out of
the hotel yelling "We got him." But who do they arrest? An
A-rab. Racist pricks.

                    LOU SOLVERSON
It's a diner robbery in Minnesota, Karl. Not a presidential
assassination.

                    KARL
Oh sure. That's how it starts. With somethin small, like
a break-in at the Watergate Hotel. But just watch. This
thing's only gettin bigger.

                    BJORN GRUFFENSON
G-53. G-53.

Sonny looks around.

                    SONNY
The flyer said there'd be a band. Paul Garvey and the
Woodchippers. Sunday night at eight.

                    LOU SOLVERSON
There's yer problem. It's Saturday.

                    SONNY
Well, that explains it.

Lou finishes his beer, stands.

                    LOU SOLVERSON
Well, better get home. Betsy had her chemo today.

                    KARL
               (suddenly angry)
Goddamn it.

                              SONNY
           What is it, Karl?

                              KARL
           It's just — goddamn — unacceptable is what it is. A woman
           like that — in the prime of her — with a young daughter —

           He drinks, overcome by sadness, then rallies.

                          KARL (CONT'D)
           Tell her if John McCain could hold out five and a half years
           against Vietcong thumbscrews, she can beat this cancer
           bullshit in her sleep.

                        LOU SOLVERSON
           I'll make sure ta mention that.

                   CUT TO:

           INT. KITCHEN. PEGGY AND ED'S HOUSE—LATER

           The first thing you notice about the house is that it has
           style. Not taste, per se, but style. As in, Peggy cares about
           her things and the way they look. It's part of her identity,
           the life she wants to live. The home she wants to have. As if
           her house is a slice of the bigger world here in small-town
           Minnesota. An oasis.

The second thing you notice about the house is that it's cluttered. There are STACKS OF MAGAZINES visible in every room. As styles change and decorating tastes progress, Peggy has tried to keep up. But without necessarily getting rid of the old things.

Peggy, we will come to realize, is a hoarder. Nascent, maybe, not bad yet, but on her way.

Peggy is at the stove cooking. The table is set behind her. The front door opens.

                    ED BLUMQUIST (O.S.)
     Hey, hon.

                    PEGGY BLUMQUIST
                       (calling)
     In the kitchen.

Peggy is upbeat now, filled with energy. Her husband, ED BLUMQUIST, enters the kitchen. He is a big man, but gentle, and affable. A cow, basically. Which sounds like a judgment, but is simply his classification in the animal kingdom.

Where Peggy is a Dreamer with Big Plans, Ed is already Living his Dream. He got Peggy, didn't he? The small-town knockout? And he's got his job at the Butcher Shop, and Bud's gonna retire, and then Ed will take over. And soon they'll start having kids. And Ed wants a lot of kids. Six even. Boys and girls.

Sure, maybe Peggy's not ready yet. But she'll come around. Ed has no doubt, because deep down he's a Blue Sky Guy.

So here's Ed, coming home from work, home to his Happily Ever After. He's carrying meat wrapped in white butcher paper, puts it on the counter.

                    ED BLUMQUIST
     Boolie Hendricks paid for chops, never picked em up. So I
     figured —

He kisses her cheek.

                    PEGGY BLUMQUIST
                       (exasperated)
     Hon. Yer gettin blood on the tile.

          ANGLE ON THE MEAT

Blood is, in fact, leaking through the paper. Ed picks it up.

                    ED BLUMQUIST
     Sorry. I'll put 'em in the fridge.
                       (looks in the pan)

Hamburger helper?

                    PEGGY BLUMQUIST
          And tater tots.

                    ED BLUMQUIST
          Yum.

He goes to the fridge, puts the chops inside. She starts plating
their food.

Ed approaches his chair. There's a <u>large stack of magazines and
papers</u> on it. Ed goes to move them.

                    PEGGY BLUMQUIST
                      (noticing)
          Hon. Don't — I just got that stuff organized.

                    ED BLUMQUIST
          Yeah, but it's my chair. Where am I s'posed ta —

She pulls over an old kitchen stepladder.

                    PEGGY BLUMQUIST
          Sit there, huh? I'll move that stuff tomorrow. Promise.

They sit and start to eat for a comfortable moment.

          CUT TO:

EXT. SOLVERSON HOUSE. LUVERNE, MN—NIGHT

Lou pulls up out front in his prowler. He gets out, goes inside.

          CUT TO:

INT. SOLVERSON HOUSE. LUVERNE, MN—NIGHT

Lou takes off his coat and boots. Betsy approaches.

                    BETSY SOLVERSON
          So you think there was an accomplice in a getaway car?

Lou kisses her.

                    LOU SOLVERSON
          Your dad called?

                    BETSY SOLVERSON
          You know him. He likes to talk things through before he goes
          to bed.

They go into the . . .

in CONVERSATION with Warren Alan Young
(Production Design, Seasons 1–2)

NOAH: For season 2, the 1979-ness of it was a huge part of the identity of the story. What is your way in when you start to think about that time period?

WARREN: There's a lot out there about what we think the seventies were. But how did others really experience it? How did I experience it and my parents and others? What did they really see? At one point, I remember Dana Gonzales saying to me, "Hey, I hope you're not afraid to go with those colors of the seventies because some people might think it's kitsch." And I said, "No, this is what it was." Especially with Peggy's house. We were re-creating what was true.

```
          CUT TO:

INT. KITCHEN. SOLVERSON HOUSE—CONTINUOUS

Lou gets a carton of milk out of the fridge, drinks straight
from it.

                    BETSY SOLVERSON
     We got glasses.

                    LOU SOLVERSON
     Tastes different in a glass.

He puts the milk back.
```

>   LOU SOLVERSON (CONT'D)
> Molly go down okay?

>   BETSY SOLVERSON
>   (nods)
> Ya know, forgot earlier. She made you something at school
> today.

She hands him a clay ashtray. It looks like a four-year-old made
it.

>   LOU SOLVERSON
> She knows I don't smoke, right?

>   BETSY SOLVERSON
> You could start.

He rubs his face, tired. He's seen things tonight he doesn't
much care for.

>   LOU SOLVERSON
> Your dad said he'd be over on Sunday in a suit of armor.

>   BETSY SOLVERSON
> Jeez. Ya light one soufflé on fire . . .

He smiles. She smiles back. Love.

>   CUT TO:

INT. KITCHEN. PEGGY AND ED'S HOUSE—NIGHT

They sit and eat.

>   PEGGY BLUMQUIST
> So I'm gettin excited about this seminar.

>   ED BLUMQUIST
> The which?

>   PEGGY BLUMQUIST
> Ya remember, hon. It's next weekend. Constance is takin me.
> Lifespring. Everybody's doin it.

>   ED BLUMQUIST
> Oh ya.

>   PEGGY BLUMQUIST
> Ya. I really think this course is gonna help me actualize,
> ya know, fully. Re-examine reflex patterns. The ones that
> keep my life from workin.

>   ED BLUMQUIST
> From (working?) — cause we're doin great, yeah?

                    PEGGY BLUMQUIST
     Oh yeah. Course. I just mean me. Ya know. As a person.

Beat. He eats.

                    ED BLUMQUIST
     Well, Bud asked again if I was interested in maybe takin
     over the butcher shop. Said he's thinkin of retirin the end
     of the year.

                    PEGGY BLUMQUIST
     Just had the end of the year, huh?

                    ED BLUMQUIST
     Yeah, I guess he means this year. Wouldn't that be great? Me
     ownin the shop. And maybe you take over the salon one day,
     unless — ya know — we've got a whole litter a kids by then.

Beat. The idea of children clearly makes her uncomfortable.

                    PEGGY BLUMQUIST
     Yeah, that's — we talked about that. We're trying, but it
     takes time, ya know?

                    ED BLUMQUIST
     Yeah, course.
                         (beat)
     Though, uh — hon — "tryin" —
                         (delicately)
     I mean, last time I checked, there's just the one way ta
     make a baby, ya know —

Beat. She forces a smile, keeps eating.

                    PEGGY BLUMQUIST
     Did that last weekend, didn't we?

                    ED BLUMQUIST
                         (thinking)
     Bear Lake last weekend. You said ya didn't want ta — not
     with Kevin and Sally in the next —

                    PEGGY BLUMQUIST
                         (*please stop*)
     Hon —

                    ED BLUMQUIST
     Point is, I'm twenty-nine. My dad was nineteen when I was
     (born) — and I just — love ya, is all. So much. And our
     kids'd be (amazing) —

A THUD from the other side of the garage door. Not loud, but
audible. Ed turns.

Peggy, panicked suddenly (realizing what that must be), knocks
her glass off the table to get Ed's attention. It breaks/spills.

                    PEGGY BLUMQUIST
        Oh, shoot.

Ed jumps up.

                    ED BLUMQUIST
        Here, hon. Lemme —

He grabs a rag.

                    PEGGY BLUMQUIST
        No, it's — I'm just such a bumble sometimes.

Another SOUND from the garage, louder.

                    ED BLUMQUIST
        What the heck?

Peggy grabs his arm.

                    PEGGY BLUMQUIST
        I love you too, hon. So, so much. Maybe we should — maybe do
        it right now.

This gets his attention.

                    ED BLUMQUIST
        Here?

                    PEGGY BLUMQUIST
        No, silly. In the bedroom. Come on.

She starts to drag him that way. We HEAR A CRASH from the
garage. Ed stops.

                    ED BLUMQUIST
        Jeez. I better see what —

                    PEGGY BLUMQUIST
                        (wait)
        No.

Ed pulls away, walks to the kitchen door. Peggy is after him,
trying to block his path.

                    PEGGY BLUMQUIST (CONT'D)
        Prolly just a raccoon or —

Ed reaches the door to the garage.

PEGGY BLUMQUIST (CONT'D)

— we can —

      CUT TO:

INT. GARAGE. PEGGY AND ED'S HOUSE. LUVERNE, MN—CONTINUOUS

A two-car garage half filled with junk, stacks of boxes turning
it into a one-car garage. Ed turns on the light. Peggy is behind
him, afraid to look.

PEGGY BLUMQUIST

— I'll wear that nightie you —

Then Ed sees Peggy's car.

      ANGLE ON THE CAR

driver's door open, windshield smashed. Blood on the exterior
and the dash.

      RYE IS GONE.

      ANGLE ON ED

stunned on seeing the bloody, bashed car.

ED BLUMQUIST

What the —

Behind him, Peggy is both relieved not to see Rye and <u>very worried</u>. Where did he go?

                    PEGGY BLUMQUIST
     It's — uh, I hit a — didn't I tell you? I kind of hit a —
     deer.

                    ED BLUMQUIST
     You hit a —

Ed turns to her, concerned.

                    ED BLUMQUIST (CONT'D)
     Hon. Are you —

                    PEGGY BLUMQUIST
     No. I'm fine. Just — ya know, shook up mostly.

Ed turns, approaches the car. And the whole time we're thinking—
Where's Rye?

                    ED BLUMQUIST
     Well, insurance should cover —

A MOAN from behind a TOWER OF BOXES near the front-left bumper.
The clutter has created a well in the back corner of the garage
that is <u>not visible</u> from here.

Peggy hears the sound, panics.

                    PEGGY BLUMQUIST
     Actually, I, uh, think I need to — sit down. Can we go in
     the —

The MOAN repeats. Ed takes a step towards it.

                    PEGGY BLUMQUIST (CONT'D)
                         (warning)
     Hon.

          ANGLE ON A TRAIL OF BLOOD

On the floor, leading around the front bumper.

          ED

glances back at Peggy.

                    ED BLUMQUIST
     Heck, did you — bring the deer home?

The MOAN comes again, longer this time.

                PEGGY

stands frozen.

        ED

turns and walks around the front of the car.

        ANGLE ON THE DARK WELL

behind the boxes, from Ed's POV. We move towards it slowly. As
we close, we hear another moan, but also now a <u>shuffling sound</u>
and a faint *thump, thump, thump.*

                    PEGGY BLUMQUIST
        Hon. Don't. Come back.

But . . .

        ED

grabs a FLASHLIGHT off a shelf. He tries to turn it on, but the
batteries are low. He hits the flashlight once, twice. The light
COMES ON BRIGHT.

        ANGLE ON THE WALL

as a beam pierces it, revealing Rye Gerhardt. He is facing the
far wall, arms down by his sides. The shuffling and thumping
we heard was <u>Rye trying to walk through the wall</u>. He shuffles
forward, hits the wall and bounces back.

        ED

is stunned.

                    ED BLUMQUIST
        Aw jeez.
                (calling)
        It's a — there's a — man in the —

At the sound of his voice, <u>Rye turns</u>. His face is bloody and
broken.

                    RYE GERHARDT
                (rage)
        You —

We realize he is HOLDING A KNIFE.

        ED

stumbles back into a stack of boxes.

                      ED BLUMQUIST
      Holy Christ. Call the —

           RYE

moves towards Ed, knife coming up. Ed tries to run, but gets
hung up on the clutter. Rye LUNGES, STABBING. Ed barely manages
to grab Rye's wrist, but it's slippery with blood.

Peggy screams.

                      ED BLUMQUIST (CONT'D)
      Call the police!

But . . .

           PEGGY

doesn't move, as . . .

           ED

struggles with Rye. Ed reaches out desperately, looking for a
weapon of his own.

          ANGLE ON A GARDEN TROWEL

dirt still on it. Ed grabs it, STABS RYE with the garden trowel.

          ANGLE ON THE TROWEL

too dull to penetrate deeply. Meanwhile . . .

          ED

has his left arm up high, Rye dances with him, a kind of zombie
strength surging through his bones. We can see from Ed's face
that he knows he is seconds from being killed.

Ed puts all his weight into . . .

          THE TROWEL

It <u>breaks through Rye's ribs and into his heart</u>.

Beat. Then . . .

          RYE

dead, falls against Ed, his head resting on Ed's shoulder,
like they're sweethearts at a dance. Ed stands there, swaying,
adrenaline coursing through him.

Beat. He realizes there's a corpse on him, shoves Rye away. Rye
falls to the floor.

                    ED BLUMQUIST (CONT'D)
                      (under his breath)
          Oh my God. Oh my God. Oh my God.

          PEGGY

creeps cautiously across the garage towards Ed.

                    PEGGY BLUMQUIST
          Hon?

Ed stands unhearing. He has been ambushed by a crazed zombie in
the middle of dinner. No words can describe the level of freaked
out he is right now.

Peggy touches his arm. He WHIRLS around, his ELBOW HITTING HER
in the EYE. She recoils in pain.

                    ED BLUMQUIST
          Aw jeez! Sorry.

It hurts but she pushes through it.

> PEGGY BLUMQUIST
> No. It's — I'm fine.

Ed is trying to catch up with what's happened.

> ED BLUMQUIST
> Who — who —

> PEGGY BLUMQUIST
> You gotta believe me — I thought he was dead.

> ED BLUMQUIST
> (blinking)
> What?

> PEGGY BLUMQUIST
> When I hit him. I thought he was —

> ED BLUMQUIST
> (putting it together)
> You hit him? With the car?

> PEGGY BLUMQUIST
> He just ran out inta the road.

                              ED BLUMQUIST
        You said a deer —

              CUT TO:

INT. CAR (TRAVELING)—EARLIER

We are looking over a car's dashboard, through the windshield at
Rye Gerhardt in the road ahead of us. There is only a second or
two before THE CAR HITS HIM, going 35 MPH.

Rye rolls up the hood and CRASHES through the windshield.

EXT. ROAD. LUVERNE, MN—CONTINUOUS

The driver's door CREAKS OPEN. Peggy climbs out. She looks
around.

              ANGLE ON THE ROAD

Trees line the two-lane blacktop. No cars or people are visible.
The GLOW from the Waffle Hut is distant, but visible.

              ANGLE ON PEGGY

Beat. What should she do? Go to the hospital? The police? She
climbs back into the car.

INT. CAR—CONTINUOUS

              PEGGY

sits in stunned silence. She is a small-town beautician who
Knows Things. Hollywood Things and Style Things and Gossip
Things. Not in a shallow way. But as a means of escape. Peggy
Blumquist—a small-town beautician, married to a small-town
butcher, fending off the gravitational pull of Settling Down, of
Having Children—is committed to the Real Now (what's current in
the big cities, not the small-town fall behind).

She reads the magazines. She watches the shows. In her mind she
is living a bigger life than just Luverne, Minnesota. She is
Going Places. Maybe not today. But one day.

Unless, of course, she kills someone and goes to jail.

              ANGLE ON RYE

stuck half-in, half-out of the windshield. There is blood
everywhere. No one could have survived that.

She unbuckles her lap belt, leans over.

```
        ANGLE ON RYE

His head is a bloody mess, one arm flopped down into the
interior dripping blood onto a spread of TRAVEL MAGAZINES,
marring the azure blue waters.

Rye's other arm is caught under him, his stomach impaled on the
jagged broken glass of the windshield.

        PEGGY

reaches out to touch him, then doesn't. Instead, she PICKS UP
whatever magazines haven't been stained by blood and puts them
on the seat out of harm's way.

        CUT BACK TO:

INT. GARAGE. PEGGY AND ED'S HOUSE. LUVERNE, MN—NIGHT

Ed's having a hard time figuring this thing out.

                ED BLUMQUIST
        You hit him. Why — why didn't you go to the police? Or the
        hospital?

                PEGGY BLUMQUIST
        He ran out into the road, hon. What was I supposed ta do?

                ED BLUMQUIST
        Yeah, but you brought him home. You made dinner. Hamburger
        Helper.

        CUT TO:

INT. GARAGE. PEGGY AND ED'S HOUSE. LUVERNE, MN—EARLIER

ANGLE ON THE GARAGE DOOR

as it opens. Peggy's car pulls in towards us, Rye's body still
half-in, half-out.

        ANGLE ON RYE'S BACK

as it touches a TENNIS BALL hanging from the ceiling (there to
help her park). The car stops. Inside . . .

        PEGGY

turns off the car. We hear the ticking of the engine. Being
careful not to look at the body, she picks up her magazines
and climbs out of the car. Leaving her door open, she walks
around behind the car to a short flight of stairs leading to
an INTERIOR DOOR.
```

Peggy climbs to the door and opens it.

        ANGLE ON THE LIGHT SWITCH

as she turns off the garage light and goes inside, without
looking back.

        CUT TO:

INT. PEGGY AND ED'S HOUSE. LUVERNE, MN—NIGHT

She lays her magazines on a pile, makes her way over the shag
carpeting to the stairs, goes up.

        CUT TO:

INT. BEDROOM. PEGGY AND ED'S HOUSE—NIGHT

Peggy comes in and sits at her vanity. She's got a lot of
nervous energy. As a woman of the region, who's been raised
to stay chipper and positive no matter what, Peggy is working
overtime to keep that attitude up.

She picks up a hairbrush and starts to brush her hair,
determined to keep up appearances. *Fake it till you make it.* She
sees something in the mirror.

        ANGLE ON HER SHIRT

There is a bloodstain on her collar.

        PEGGY

rubs at it, but the blood is still wet. It smears. Peggy
unbuttons the shirt, takes it off. She sits there in her bra,
brushing. We PUSH IN on her reflection. In one corner of the
vanity we see a POSTCARD. A white sand beach, sunbathers, green
palm trees lined up before a boardwalk. Over the blue sky it
reads *Hollywood Beach* in a red cursive.

We PUSH IN on it.

        CUT BACK TO:

INT. GARAGE. PEGGY AND ED'S HOUSE. LUVERNE, MN—NIGHT

        PEGGY BLUMQUIST
  — That's — I panicked, okay? But look. Look. Nobody saw.
Nobody. I was careful. I drove the back way all the way
home.

        ED BLUMQUIST
You drove the — a man is dead and people are gonna — We
gotta call the police. An ambulance. Maybe he's not —

                              PEGGY BLUMQUIST
No.

                               ED BLUMQUIST
No? Whatdya — ?

                              PEGGY BLUMQUIST
I ran over the guy. A hit-and-run. And then you stabbed
him with a gardening tool — the cops — do you really think
they're gonna believe us?

                               ED BLUMQUIST
I don't know. People are gonna look fer him.

                              PEGGY BLUMQUIST
That's why we hafta clean it up. Tell people I hit a deer
or —

          ANGLE ON PEGGY

as it hits her. An idea. The idea.

                         PEGGY BLUMQUIST (CONT'D)
We could run.

                               ED BLUMQUIST
What?

                              PEGGY BLUMQUIST
Go to California.

                               ED BLUMQUIST
Cali — no. We're — we have a life here. Family. I'm gonna
take over the shop and —

                              PEGGY BLUMQUIST
Start again, I'm sayin.

                               ED BLUMQUIST
I don't wanna —

                              PEGGY BLUMQUIST
Then hon, look at me. The only way we're gonna get clear of
this is to clean it up. Pretend it never happened. Cause if
this comes out — then all that — the things you want — that
we want — that's — over — I go to jail. And you maybe also.
And then there's no shop and no family. No kids.

Ed hears her. Beat.

                               ED BLUMQUIST
                                (quietly)
Okay.

                         (he turns to her)

Okay. We clean it up.

Beat. She nods.

                    PEGGY BLUMQUIST
     We clean it up.

They sit there for a moment, considering the magnitude of what
that means.

          CUT TO:

INT. BEDROOM. SOLVERSON HOUSE—NIGHT

Betsy is in bed, reading. Lou stands by the window, in white
boxers and a white t-shirt, looking out. He has a LENGTH OF ROPE
in hand and he's tying and untying a knot—thinking.

Beat. Betsy puts the book down.

                    BETSY SOLVERSON
     Well — should we call that Saturday?

Lou nods, puts the rope on the dresser, comes over and climbs
into bed.

                    LOU SOLVERSON
     S'pose we better. She'll be up at five anyway, wantin to
     play dolls.

Betsy smiles, kisses him.

                    BETSY SOLVERSON
     And I know how fond you are of your doll playin time.

He nods, turns off the light. Beat. Then, from the dark . . .

                    BETSY SOLVERSON (CONT'D)
     Goodnight, Mr. Solverson.

                    LOU SOLVERSON
     Goodnight, Mrs. Solverson and all the ships at sea.

          CUT TO:

INT. OTTO'S ROOM. GERHARDT HOME. FARGO, ND—NIGHT

Otto is in bed. Floyd sits in a chair beside her husband,
holding his hand. Dodd and Bear stand on either side of the bed.
We are far back in the room, PUSHING IN on them. We move slowly,
steadily into a CLOSE UP of FLOYD.

          CUT TO:

INT. GARAGE. PEGGY AND ED'S HOUSE. LUVERNE, MN—NIGHT

Half lit. We are floor level, drifting inside. We CATCH UP to the BLUE TARP being dragged across the floor. We follow it, catching only Peggy and Ed's legs as they drag it. Then the body is LIFTED up out of frame.

The CAMERA RISES, revealing a long white MEAT FREEZER. As Peggy and Ed turn away and leave frame, we arrive at the freezer's open mouth in time to see RYE's partially covered face.

The freezer door slams shut.

      CUT TO:

INT. BOARD ROOM. OFFICE BUILDING. KANSAS CITY, MO—DAY

We are looking at a SLIDE PROJECTED ON A WALL. The sound we heard is of the slide carriage changing slides.

The slide reads:

The Kansas City Group TM

Northern Expansion Strategy

1979-1980

We are in a nondescript boardroom. The overhead fluorescent lights are off. The venetian blinds are drawn. The SLIDE PROJECTOR rests on top of a large CONFERENCE TABLE.

In the room, we see the shapes of MEN in suits, smoking.

JOE BULO (40s) steps in front of the slide—meaning part of the image is now on him.

Sitting in the shadows on his flanks are his men, MIKE MILLIGAN (30s) and THE KITCHEN BROTHERS (20s). Just shapes in the dark now.

We don't see the BIG BOSS (HAMISH BROKER), whom Bulo is addressing.

>   JOE BULO
>   So, as you see on page sixteen of the prospectus, the main
>   component of our Northern Expansion Strategy involves the
>   absorption of the Gerhardt Family Syndicate, headquartered
>   in Fargo, N.D.

Ka-chunk-chunk.

The SLIDE CHANGES to a COLLAGE OF PHOTOS arranged in a family tree. At the top is OTTO GERHARDT (63) and his wife, FLOYD (60).

Below them are their THREE SONS, DODD (40), BEAR (35), and Rye.

Below Dodd we see FOUR GIRLS, including SIMONE (20). And under Bear we see CHARLIE (19).

>   JOE BULO (CONT'D)
>   The Gerhardts control trucking and distribution for the
>   entire northern Midwest.

Ka-chunk-chunk.

The SLIDE CHANGES to a MAP of GERHARDT distribution routes, with lines running from Winnipeg in the north, east to Ohio, and west to Wyoming. The southern edge of their operation is South Dakota.

>   JOE BULO (CONT'D)
>   It's a family business started in 1931 by —

Ka-chunk-chunk.

The SLIDE CHANGES to an old black-and-white PHOTO of a very angry, GERMAN-looking MAN.

>   JOE BULO (CONT'D)
>   — Dieter Gerhardt — now deceased — and taken over in 1940 by
>   his son —

Fargo, season 2 . . . in which a typewriter salesman, a butcher, and a beautician get caught in a war between two crime syndicates.

Ka-chunk-chunk.

The SLIDE CHANGES to a PHOTO of Otto. No friendlier.

>   JOE BULO (CONT'D)
>   Otto. Not in the report, but of relevance to this meeting
>   — old Otto had a stroke yesterday on the family compound in
>   North Dakota. A bad one.

A voice from off screen.

>   HAMISH (O.S.)
>   Leaving who in charge?

Ka-chunk-chunk.

The SLIDE CHANGES to a PHOTO of FLOYD. A stern, Midwestern-
looking woman in her sixties.

>   JOE BULO
>   Unclear. His wife, Floyd, is a possibility. She's tough, but
>   — you know — a girl. Then there are three sons, who all want
>   a shot at the throne.

Ka-chunk-chunk.

The SLIDE CHANGES to THREE PHOTOS. The Gerhardt boys: Dodd,
Bear, and Rye.

>   JOE BULO (CONT'D)
>   Which, the boys in research think provides a tactical
>   opportunity for us to move aggressively to acquire or absorb
>   their operation.

>   HAMISH (O.S.)
>   And if you can't and the current business owners resist?

>   JOE BULO
>   We liquidate.

A long beat.

>   HAMISH (O.S.)
>   Good.

Bulo smiles, snaps his fingers. The slide projector is turned
off, plunging us to BLACK.

All hell is about to break loose.

                    End of Episode 201

LOU SOLVERSON

A STATE POLICE OFFICER, married to Betsy, father of Molly. Well, what can you say about Lou really? He doesn't like to talk about himself or his feelings. People talk too much, is his opinion, and especially these days with the "Me Generation," always going on about self-help and self-improvement.

Lou is a veteran who served as a lieutenant on a swift boat in the navy, patrolling the Mekong Delta. He's seen things, sure, done things—things that men do in wartime—and he can live with those, he supposes, as his father did in World War II and his father before him. That's what men do. They go to war and come home. And then they try to define themselves by who they are in peace.

INT. LIVING ROOM. PEGGY AND ED'S HOUSE. LUVERNE, MN—CONTINUOUS

Ed leads Lou into the living room, Peggy following. Ed takes off his coat. Peggy removes her hat. Ed and Peggy share a look.

     ANGLE ON PEGGY

What's he want?

     ANGLE ON ED

I don't know.

     PEGGY
I could make some coffee.

     LOU
None fer me. Thanks.
        (gets right to it)
Saw yer car. At the shop.

     ED
Yeah. Slipped on some ice on the way ta work.

     PEGGY
My fault really. I was goin on about somethin.

ED
Went into the ravine, hit a tree. Lucky Peggy wasn't killed.

Ed smiles, then looking past Lou his eyes focus.

ANGLE ON THE FIREPLACE

    THE SCREEN HAS BEEN MOVED.

    ANGLE ON ED
curious. *Was it like that this morning?* Then Ed sees something else.

    ANGLE ON A FOOTPRINT
on the shag carpet. A big footprint made with ash from the fireplace.

    ED
looks around, suddenly afraid. Somebody's been in the house. Beat. Lou notices.

LOU
Somethin wrong?

ED
No, just — no, sir. I'm sorry. What were you —

LOU
I wanna be clear about somethin — I can help you. But ya gotta be straight with me.

Ed looks at Peggy.

ED
What?

Lou sizes him up.

LOU
If I check the car — the interior — I'm not gonna find blood?

PEGGY
I mean, Ed hurt his neck.

ED
(re: neck brace)
That's why I'm wearin the —

PEGGY
But no blood.

They look at him "openly." Lou studies their faces.

LOU
You didn't fight, did you, Ed? In the war.

ED
No, sir. 4F on accounta I got the one kidney.

LOU
There's a look a boy gets when he's been shot. Or a landmine takes off his legs. And he's layin there in the mud, tryin ta get up. Cause he doesn't feel it yet.

ED
Sir, I don't —

LOU
His brain hasn't caught up with the reality — which is he's already dead.

PEGGY
Ed. He's scarin me.

LOU
But we see it. The rest of us. And we lie. We say, *Be still. Yer gonna be fine.* And if you'd been ta war you'd know the look. See you and Peggy — you've got the look. You still think it's Wednesday. You have no idea what's comin.

ED
Lou, Officer, I'm trying ta be straight with ya here —

PEGGY
We hit some ice. That's all. Coulda happened to anyone. Ed wasn't even speedin.

LOU
That man you hit. His name was Rye Gerhardt.

ED
Hit a tree. We told ya.

But his voice has weakened, his conviction.

PEGGY
We were arguin and Ed turned his head.

Happened in a flash.

LOU
Rye Gerhardt. And his family hurts people fer money. And they're comin. May be here already. And I checked the log — cars stopped outside the crime scene — we know you were outside the Waffle Hut the night a the murders. Yer truck. And now Peggy's car turns up with damage matchin our theory. And my point is — cause I'm tired a talkin — if you did somethin — made a mistake, panicked and maybe covered it up — now's the time ta say. Cause we can still fix this. But if I'm right — that window is closin. And you may already be dead.

Ed looks at Peggy. She shakes her head.

ED
Look —

PEGGY
This is — yer outta line and we — we want ya ta leave. No offense. But we're askin you ta leave.

Lou looks at Ed.

LOU
Is that true, Ed? Are you askin me ta leave?

Beat. Ed is tied up in knots.

ED
Prolly fer the best. It was an accident is all. That's all it was.

Lou puts on his hat, goes to the front door.

LOU
Okay. Do yerself a favor, lock the door.

He exits. Peggy closes the door behind him. They look at each other.

Lou is a traditional man with a traditional marriage. He is unimpressed and unaffected by the radical reinvention of the sixties. That great social upheaval of a generation preoccupied with making the world over in their own image. As far as Lou's concerned, the old world was just fine—with its emphasis on hard work and responsibility. Its focus on family.

Lou is the silent majority that Ronald Reagan will unleash. His values are family values—not religious wackery or evangelical bluster—but simple, honest, American do-it-yourself-ism. There isn't a thing on hell or earth he wouldn't do for the people he loves.

INT. MIKE MILLIGAN'S SUITE. PEARL HOTEL. FARGO, ND—DAY

Lou sits across from Milligan. Gale Kitchen stands behind Milligan, ready for anything.

MIKE MILLIGAN
So is this a conversation about how it's time for me to pack up and go home?

LOU
No. Don't hafta go home. It's a big country. Just maybe don't be here.

MIKE MILLIGAN
(beat, thinks)
Are you familiar with the phrase "manifest destiny"?

LOU
Yeah, see here's the thing — I own two pairs a shoes. A summer pair and one fer winter.

Mike likes that.

LOU (CONT'D)
We're not meant to have more than we
can handle, is my point. So this need for
conquest, ya know — to own things that
aren't meant ta be owned —

MIKE MILLIGAN
Like people?

LOU
That's an example. But also places.
Believin we can tame things. That's a
problem, right? Not a solution.

MIKE MILLIGAN
You're sayin capitalism is a problem.

LOU
No. Greed. Makin this thing all or nothin.

Milligan thinks about that. Schmidt comes in,
walking funny.

LOU (CONT'D)
What happened to you?

SCHMIDT
Let's just get this over with.

Lou turns back to Milligan.

LOU
So, you got a response? To my all-or-
nothing line?

MIKE MILLIGAN
(beat, thinks)
Sometimes there's a man —

SCHMIDT
What man?

MIKE MILLIGAN
Just a man, works in a factory. And
the boss — one day he gets the idea
that this man is stealing from him, so
every night at the gate they search the
guy's wheelbarrow. But they never find
anything.

SCHMIDT
Pat him down.

MIKE MILLIGAN
Oh they do, even strip him naked —
nothing.

SCHMIDT
So he's not stealin.

MIKE MILLIGAN
(come on, this is easy)
Sure he is.

Beat. He waits. Schmidt doesn't know what
they're talking about. Suddenly Lou "gets it."

LOU
Wheelbarrows.

MIKE MILLIGAN
Thank you. That's right. He's stealing
wheelbarrows.

SCHMIDT
(doesn't get it)
What?

MIKE MILLIGAN
My point is, sometimes the answer is
so obvious you miss it because you're
looking too hard.
(beat)
See — we can't leave, because we're the
future and they're the past. And the past
can't become the future any more than
the future can become the past.

Lou stands. This is pointless.

LOU
Okay. We said our peace.

He goes to the door, then stops, turns.

LOU (CONT'D)
Just don't be offended next time if I don't
say hello before I shoot.

He and Schmidt walk out. Milligan sits back,
feeling squeezed.

BETSY SOLVERSON

Lou's wife, daughter of Rock County sheriff Hank Larsson. Betsy grew up as the daughter of a cop. She has sat in the car at crime scenes coloring and doing her homework while her dad walked the clues. She has spent hours talking his cases through with him, first as a girl, and now as a grown woman and mother of one.

So it was only natural she married a cop, except Lou doesn't like to bring his work home with him. He likes to keep a healthy distance between worlds. He has also never really discussed the war with her; the occasional story here or there, but none of the dark stuff, the things he's done or seen.

Betsy is a sturdy plainswoman, pretty but firm. She knows how to jump-start a car and make a casserole. She can clean a gun and the gutters of her home. She is a feminist of common sense, apolitical, while at the same time knowing the limitations of men, their often dim and violent natures, their inability to see things long term, their pettiness and fear. It is women who bear the next generation, who nurture and educate, who love and reward.

Betsy doesn't believe her stay-at-home mothering makes her a second-class citizen. After all, what job is more important than hers?

PEGGY
BLUMQUIST

A BEAUTICIAN, WIFE OF ED.
Peggy is a hoarder, a girl who started collecting travel magazines when she was sixteen.

Peggy allowed herself to be wooed by and ultimately married a local butcher's assistant, Ed Blumquist, who has worshipped her since high school. But her hoarding behavior only grew, travel magazines becoming beauty magazines, becoming anything and everything that could stem—at least for a moment—the trapped anxiety she felt every day.

INT. KITCHEN. PEGGY AND ED'S HOUSE.
LUVERNE, MN—NIGHT

Peggy and Hank stand in the kitchen. The place is its normal mess. The chairs still have magazines stacked on them.

> PEGGY
> I got coffee from this mornin. Could heat it up.

> HANK
> Please.

Peggy crosses to the stove. Hank looks around for someplace to sit. There isn't one. He picks a chair covered in magazines.

> HANK (CONT'D)
> I'm gonna move these, okay?

> PEGGY
> Actually, can you —

She drags over the stepladder.

> PEGGY (CONT'D)
> I just got it all organized.

Beat. Hank considers this.

> HANK
> No problem.

He sits. Peggy leans against the counter.

> HANK (CONT'D)
> You collect these then?
> (looks)
> Beauty and travel magazines.

> PEGGY
> No. Not collect. I just — gotta stay up on the latest trends, yeah? In my line a work.

> HANK
> That explains the beauty mags.

> PEGGY
> Oh, well — there's more ta life than just Minnesota, ya know.

She pours coffee for both of them, hands him his.

PEGGY (CONT'D)
Do you think — I mean, I know there's lots a questions, but I got this seminar Saturday. Lifespring? I'm s'posed ta drive over ta Sioux Falls first thing.

Hank finds it interesting she doesn't seem more alarmed about what happened.

HANK
Well now, I got five dead since Saturday, includin one tonight in the burned-down butcher shop. And yer husband's currently in jail. So, I wouldn't count on gettin there early.

PEGGY
No, I mean it's terrible, all the things that've — but what can Ed — I mean, a robbery attempt, those two men at the shop — and you said you arrested one of 'em, so —

HANK
Wasn't a robbery, Peggy. Those men came fer yer husband. Came ta kill him.

PEGGY
That's — ya don't know that fer a fact, Sheriff. Yer just bein dramatic. Tryin ta scare me.

HANK
I assure ya, I am not. When I say five dead I'm only talkin about inside the city limits. Reports are fifteen more bodies up in Fargo. A turf war between the Kansas City mob and this Gerhardt family you've gotten yerself mixed up with.

PEGGY
Stop sayin that. Ed and me, we're just bystanders. Not even. Dis-connected. Him with the shop and me — just tryin ta actualize fully, ya know? Be the best me I can — because these are modern times, yeah? And a woman, well, she doesn't have ta be just a wife and mother no more. She can be — there's nothin she can't be.

Hank sips his coffee, studies Peggy.

HANK
Yer a little touched, aren't ya?

PEGGY
(flustered)
What?

HANK
Different, I'm sayin. It's not there's anything wrong with that. Don't get me wrong. It's just the time and place in which yer —

PEGGY
No, I mean — I got dreams if that's what ya — and yeah, maybe I don't see it all like everybody else — but I got plans. We, I mean. And ya can't just come in here and derail —

HANK
Peggy. They tried ta kill yer husband. They burned down his shop. Ya think that's the end of it?

PEGGY
Well, I mean, look, right? Ed really — he loved that place, yeah — but life's a journey, ya know. That's what John Hanley Senior says. He's the founder a Lifespring. Life's a journey, and the one thing ya don't do on a journey is stay in one place, right? So — I mean, maybe we'll — I don't know — go ta California, or —

HANK
California.

PEGGY
Or someplace — I mean, now the shop's gone —

HANK
Well, Peggy, before ya go makin plans — you should know — I got a forensic team comin down from the Twin Cities in the morning. And I know it's been repaired, but we're gonna check yer car for blood. Microscopically, I mean. Which — you'd be amazed at what they can find on the atomic level these days.

This stops her short.

PEGGY
No — I mean, course ya can't do that without permission, ya know, from the owner. So —

HANK
Oh, we got permission — bout an hour ago.
(off her confusion)
Ya sold the car ta Sonny Greer, didn't ya? Earlier? At the body shop? So he's the owner a record now. And Sonny was more than happy ta —

PEGGY
No. No. Ya can't just — now hold on — that's not —

HANK
So — Peggy — I'm serious now — better ya tell me — before I get a fistful a evidence — what happened that night — when you hit Rye Gerhardt with yer car?

Peggy dreams of going to Hollywood and being a hairdresser to the stars. Every year on her wedding anniversary she goes to the bus station and buys a ticket. And every year she sits and watches as the passengers board and the bus pulls away. Then she goes home and puts the bus ticket in a box among her many things.

The truth is, she is too afraid to escape on her own, so she pads her cage with travel magazines, like a hamster.

INT. BASEMENT. PEGGY AND ED'S HOUSE. LUVERNE, MN—NIGHT

We are in a GOAT PATH of stacked magazines, PUSHING FORWARD, as if moving through the folds of Peggy's mind.

We see the following text:

This is a true story. The events depicted took place in Minnesota in 1979.

At the request of the survivors, the names have been changed.

Out of respect for the dead, the rest has been told exactly as it occurred.

As the last line fades we EMERGE FROM THE PATH to FIND—

PEGGY BLUMQUIST
sitting at the bottom of the stairs. DODD GERHARDT is sitting on the floor, back to a post, bound, unconscious.

The dead goon (gut shot) Is lying on the stairs above her, frozen in death. Peggy sits on the steps below, holding the cattle prod. She is lost in thought, in shock possibly, or something more profound.

ALBERT (O.S.)
Peggy?

She turns. Nobody's there. Beat.

ALBERT (O.S.) (CONT'D)
Peggy?

Peggy turns again. Nothing. But when she turns back, instead of Dodd, we see a man in a suit and tie, sitting in a sixties analyst chair, lit from above. Let's call him Albert.

ALBERT (CONT'D)
Have you actualized? Fully?

If Peggy thinks this is strange, she's too polite to say anything.

PEGGY

What?

ALBERT

Have you actualized? Fully?

PEGGY

I don't know. I mean — I'm trying.

ALBERT

Do you feel cold sometimes, even when
it's hot?

PEGGY

Sometimes.

ALBERT

Do you understand the difference
between thinking and being?

PEGGY

What do you mean?

ALBERT

Do you understand the difference
between thinking and being?

PEGGY

I, um —

ALBERT

To be is simply to exist. Try it. Try simply
being.

A long beat. She doesn't know what to do.

PEGGY

I'm sorry — what's the — I mean — how
is just — sitting here going to help me be
the best me I can be?

ALBERT

Ah. You want an explanation.

PEGGY

Well — kinda.

ALBERT

The human mind, aroused by an
insistence for meaning, seeks and finds
nothing but contradictions and nonsense.

PEGGY

Okay.

(beat)

It's just — practically, I'm sayin. As a
married person — a woman — who's
worried she's not living up to her full
potential.

ALBERT

Think or be. You can't do both.

PEGGY

(beat)

You're sayin don't think about the person
I want to be — just be that person?

ALBERT

Peggy?

PEGGY

Yes?

ALBERT (O.S.)

Peggy?

A HAND touches her shoulder. Peggy turns.
Ed is standing on the steps above her, out of
breath.

ED

Are you okay? Come on. We gotta —
they'll be here any —

Peggy looks back at Albert, but he's gone.
Instead, Dodd sits there, eyes open, watching
them.

PEGGY

We just — we were talkin, and finally it all
makes sense.

Ed looks at Dodd.

ED

You were talkin to —

DODD

This lady's lost her mind, brother.

ED

Shut up.

DODD

She's seein people who aren't there.

ED

I said shut up.

Dodd struggles against his ropes.

> DODD
> And here I am — tied up for no reason. Just a concerned citizen walkin past — heard a cry fer help.

Ed studies him.

> ED
> No. Yer a Gerhardt.

> DODD
> And yer some shit on my shoe. Come here. Lemme wipe you off.

Ed comes over and KNOCKS DODD OUT.

> ED
> We gotta go, hon.

> PEGGY
> (docile, still in shock)
> Okay.

He takes her arm, helps her up.

> ED
> The cops are comin and who knows who else. There's no time ta pack. Just the clothes on our back.

Ed looks at the goon on the steps.

> ED (CONT'D)
> Did you —

> PEGGY
> No. It was him. He's the leader, I think.

Ed looks back at Dodd.

> ANGLE ON DODD
> unconscious.

> ANGLE ON ED

He makes a choice.

> ED
> Then we take him with us.

in CONVERSATION with Jeff Russo *(Series Music, Seasons 1–3)*

NOAH: There was a lot of comedy to season 2. But I feel like we had sort of shied away from scoring it as much in season[s] 2 and 3 as we did in the first year.

JEFF: I think that we utilized songs more for some of the funnier moments. But even so, I grew more and more to believe that the comedy for this particular show was always best served by not trying to play comedy.

Carol Case *(Series Costume Design, Seasons 1–3):* [on Ed Blumquist] We did make some adjustments for the seventies, but it really was the kind of clothing that you imagine that your dad wore. Or that uncle that you really love to see at Christmas. That was my approach with him. It's the guy that you really think you want your daughter to marry. That sort of steadiness.

ED BLUMQUIST

A BUTCHER'S ASSISTANT, husband of Peggy. Ed is "a good guy," friendly, reliable. He is guilty of only one sin and that is loving Peggy Blumquist too much, and also maybe deluding himself into believing that she loves him just as much. The truth is Ed is *Old Yeller*, which is to say a loyal dog, who just wants to grow old and die lying at Peggy's feet.

But Ed is a big man, who never went to war because of his lone kidney. And he hasn't been tested, the way that those men have been tested, but if he had gone to war, had learned to fire an M1 and carry a bayonet, if he had had to hump a pack through the muck and brush, to shoot and stab and kill and die, to face the specter of his own death every day, I think most of the people who knew him would be surprised at the pluck he showed, the fortitude and grit. Because deep down, Ed is willing to fight for the things he loves. And what he loves most of all is Peggy Blumquist.

INT. HUNTING CABIN. RURAL SOUTH DAKOTA—DAY

Dodd watches Peggy putter in the kitchen. He tests his bonds, but they're too tight. For a moment the frustration gets him and he struggles, but there's no getting out of these ropes.

ANGLE ON PEGGY

She looks over.

PEGGY
Foot's on the other shoe now.

DODD
Shut up.

PEGGY
Oh now. That's just rude.

He struggles against the ropes, a trapped animal.

DODD
Come on, fer shit sake.

PEGGY
Ed'll be back any minute, so don't get any ideas.

DODD
I got four daughters, ya know. I'm not a bad guy.

PEGGY
You called me a whore. I heard.

Dodd has had enough.

DODD
I swear ta Christ, the minute I get free you'll be talkin to the back a my hand.

Peggy frowns. She goes into the kitchen, opens a drawer.

ANGLE ON THE DRAWER FULL OF KITCHEN TOOLS.

We see a boning knife.

Peggy grabs it, walks back over to Dodd.

PEGGY
We're gonna be together for some time, possibly. So you should be civil.

DODD
Go ta hell.

Peggy STICKS THE KNIFE in Dodd's left shoulder.

DODD (CONT'D)
Ah. Bitch, you bitch.

PEGGY
(frowns)
What did I just say?

She STICKS HIM in the other shoulder, deep. He clamps down against the pain.

PEGGY (CONT'D)
Are you gonna be nice?

DODD
Yeah, okay. Okay.

She pulls out the knife. He's bleeding from both wounds.

PEGGY
Good. Now, I'm makin beans. You want beans?

Dodd is beginning to worry he's trapped with a lunatic.

DODD
No.

PEGGY
No, what?

DODD
(beat)
No, thank you.

PEGGY
That's better.

Peggy goes over to the stove, stirs the pot.

PEGGY (CONT'D)
I gotta say, this whole thing — and I'm sorry about yer brother. I am. But it was an accident — and this whole thing has just been so — well, ya know, I try ta be positive. That's somethin you'll — if we spend any time together — you'll see about me. "Positive Peggy" they call me. But this whole thing has been super hard on Ed.

She spoons beans into two bowls.

PEGGY (CONT'D)
He's more delicate, ya know. And I mean, sure he's a big guy, but — deep down, ya know — well, this whole thing's just been really hard on him.

She brings the bowls over, puts them on the table, then pulls a chair over. She sits in front of him, prepared to feed him.

PEGGY (CONT'D)
And it's my fault. I know that.

She gets some beans on the spoon, lifts them to his mouth.

DODD
No —

But she's not really listening. She pushes the beans against his lips, smearing them. He has no choice but to open up.

PEGGY
I mean, I hit the guy — yer brother — and again, I'm sorry about that, but he just — he stepped right out inta the road. Didn't even look where he was —

Another spoon full of beans. He has to open up.

PEGGY (CONT'D)
— goin, so — all Ed did was clean it up, ya know? And then ya sent those other fellas, and — I mean —

Another spoon full.

PEGGY (CONT'D)
— what were we s'posed ta do? So I'm hoping — we're both hopin — that, ya know, now we can just — smooth things out, and everyone goes back ta normal.

Another spoon full. He's got beans all over his mouth at this point. Then she remembers.

PEGGY (CONT'D)
Wait, now you said ya didn't want beans, didn't you?

DODD
Don't worry about it. They're — thanks. They're good.

PEGGY
No. You said, and I shoulda —

She sits back, starts eating his beans herself.

PEGGY (CONT'D)
— but with everythin that's goin on — and here I am tryin ta actualize fully — which — that's no small thing. Ta review and reflect, contextualize — not just stick ta old patterns.
(beat, realizes)
Will ya listen ta me — natterin on.

The door opens. Ed comes in.

PEGGY (CONT'D)
Hey, hon. We're — ya want some beans? I just made 'em.

Ed comes over.

ED
No, just —
(sees the wounds)
Jeez. What happened ta him?

PEGGY
(looks at Dodd)
Well now, we don't need ta talk about that, do we? Water under the bridge.

Ed looks at Dodd more closely. He's bleeding from the stab wounds.

ED
I mean, those look like — hon, did you stab the hostage?

DODD
Yes.

PEGGY
No.
(off Ed)
I mean, I — had ta teach him some manners, is all. If we're gonna spend time together. And him so angry.

She takes her bowl to the sink.

PEGGY (CONT'D)
I mean, we're the ones who should be —

DODD
(to Ed, quietly)
Keep her away from me. She's crazy.

PEGGY
(still going)
— when ya get right down to it. It's our shop they burned, our house we had ta leave behind.

Ed stares at Dodd, then turns to Peggy. Dodd's eyes say—Dude, she's crazy.

ED
Hon — they're not gonna want him back if we cut him up too much.

PEGGY
Oh, I hardly stuck him at all.

DODD
I'm hurt pretty bad.

ED
Shut up.

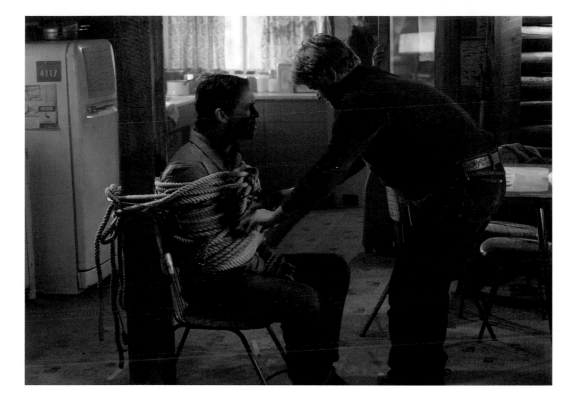

DODD
I think she got my lung.

PEGGY
(calls)
How'd it go with the family? They gonna
negotiate?

Ed glances at Dodd, comes over.

ED
(quietly)
Had ta leave a message.

PEGGY
You said we had him?

ED
Yeah, but it was like a flunky or somethin.
I said I'd call back.

PEGGY
Okay, well — maybe there's — sounds like
there's some kinda war goin on up there
— so maybe they're busy.

ED
Yeah, but, I mean — if he's such an
important guy —

PEGGY
Don't go doubtin yerself, Ed. That was
my undoin. It's a good plan. Sound. See
it, then be it, right? So just — have some
beans and call back. They'll be home next
time fer sure.

He nods, sits. She puts a plate of beans in
front of him. He eats. She stands beside him,
looking at him lovingly.

PEGGY (CONT'D)
Good?

ED
(nods)
Gotta stop stabbin him, hon.

PEGGY
Well, he needs ta be nice.

FLOYD
GERHARDT

THE MATERFAMILIAS, THE matriarch. She has run the family after Otto's stroke. Floyd came to the U.S. after World War I, when she was a girl. There is still a trace of the German in her. She has the strong back and sturdy work ethic of an immigrant and she and Otto built a small trucking business into a criminal empire that spans the upper Midwest.

Floyd is happy with the size and scope of the operation. She sees their job as to maintain the syndicate and not take risks. But the next generation is waiting in the wings, especially Dodd, and year after year she finds herself fighting harder and harder to keep the peace.

INT. CONFERENCE ROOM. PEARL HOTEL. FARGO, ND—SAME TIME

Floyd is seated across from Joe Bulo.

FLOYD
Thank you for sittin with me today. And for givin us time ta consider yer offer. I've asked the bank to arbitrate, as neutral party.

JOE BULO
Whatever makes you comfortable. This is your town.

FLOYD
(looks around)
And where's Mr. Milligan?

JOE BULO
Another matter. Back in Kansas City.

He sits forward, small talk over.

JOE BULO (CONT'D)
So — we've given you forty-eight hours to consider. Do we have a deal?

Beat. Floyd is cool.

FLOYD
No. But I have a counteroffer. A respectful
one. Instead of a straight sale, us to
you —

CUT TO:
EXT. PARKING LOT. DOCTOR'S OFFICE.
FARGO, ND—SAME TIME

The nurse pushes Otto's wheelchair to the
front door, the two guards on the lookout for
trouble.

FLOYD (O.S.)
— we pay you one million. Cash money.
Plus twenty percent of our territory in
Minnesota, including smuggling on the
Indian reservations.

CUT TO:
INT. CONFERENCE ROOM. PEARL HOTEL.
FARGO, ND—SAME TIME

Floyd is laying out her terms.

FLOYD
We'll also discount transportation fees
on Kansas City merchandise — twenty-
five percent for the first five years. In
exchange, we retain full control of our
remaining operations. The Gerhardt
family still runs North Dakota, but with
Kansas City. A partnership, not a sale.
That's our offer to you. And we believe it's
more than fair.

JOE BULO
I see.

FLOYD
Now — I don't know — maybe when you
look at me you see an old woman. And I'm
sixty-one.

She holds up her hands, coarse and strong.

FLOYD (CONT'D)
But I been workin since four years old.
Hands in the earth. I've born six children.
Had three miscarriages. Two of my sons
are here today. Two were stillborn. My
firstborn, Elron, was killed in Korea —

gook sniper took off half his head. The
point is — don't assume just because I'm
an old woman that my back is weak and
my stomach's not strong. I'm makin this
counter, because a deal is always better
than war. But no mistake, we'll fight to
keep what's ours to the last man.

Beat. Joe thinks about this.

JOE BULO
You're a good woman. I wish I'd known
your husband.

FLOYD
No. My husband would have killed you
where you stood the first time you met.
So be glad you're talking to his wife.

Bulo laughs.

JOE BULO
Then that's what I'm glad for.

He stands.

JOE BULO (CONT'D)
And if it were up to me, I'd take your
counter — partner up — except — I gotta
admit — I just wonder — if we make this
deal. Split the territory. And we move in?
Can you guarantee your boys will abide?

FLOYD
My sons listen to their mother.

JOE BULO
Good. Okay. Except — here are two of my
men, assaulted just this morning in the
appropriation of doughnuts by your oldest.

ANGLE ON BUNTZ AND TAYLOR
looking worse for wear.

JOE BULO (CONT'D)
Attacked in peacetime, during a period of
deliberation — without provocation.

FLOYD
looks at Dodd, who stares at Bulo with the icy
cool of a madman.

DODD
Oh, I was provoked.

Warren Alan Young *(Series Production Design, Seasons 1–2)*: Part of my goal with this location was to reflect that energy that you felt when you walked into this abandoned, forgotten hotel. We wanted that room to feel somewhere around six to ten years older than the present time. The series reflects a big change in American society at that point. We had gone through Nixon and the aftermath and we're into Carter. There was a tremendous amount of change happening. At my age back then, the threat of nuclear war was on my mind—we tried to reflect some of that mentality in the show.

FLOYD

Hush.

(to Bulo)

My sons will abide.

But Bulo is looking at Dodd, who stares back defiantly.

JOE BULO

See — that's the problem with a family business. One of my men defies me — puts a deal in Jeopardy — I take his arm. If he talks out of turn — I take his tongue. But you — your children, your grandchildren — what are you willing to do to show us you're committed?

Floyd's jaw is tight.

> FLOYD
> I'll deal with my son. This partnership will hold.

But Dodd can't hold his tongue any longer.

> DODD
> Come on. You're gonna let this guy come in here and disrespect us. Disrespect Pop.

> FLOYD
> Quiet!

> DODD
> A bunch a fruits in ties with pocket protectors? I'll pick my teeth with 'em.

Floyd turns to Bear.

> FLOYD
> Take him out. Now.

Bear grabs Dodd, pulls him struggling out of the room.

Beat. Floyd turns, trying to retain her authority.

> FLOYD (CONT'D)
> I apologize.

> BULO
> (reasonably)
> He's a proud man. His father built an empire, and he wants what's his.

> FLOYD
> He'll fall into line.

Bulo thinks about this.

> JOE BULO
> No. I don't think he will.

CUT TO:
INT. DOCTOR'S OFFICE—FARGO, ND—DAY

OTTO GERHARDT sits on the doctor's table in a blue smock, his ass hanging out the back, as DOCTOR MAYNARD TIKKANEN (50s) hands Otto's NATIVE HELPER a stack of pills.

Ollie and Duke stand guard just outside the door.

EXT. PARKING LOT. DOCTOR'S OFFICE. FARGO, ND—SAME TIME

Doctor's visit over, Otto's nurse wheels him back across the snowy parking lot. In the lead, Ollie suddenly holds up his hand to indicate they should stop—

> OLLIE
> Hold up.

They all stop, stare at something.

> OLLIE (CONT'D)
> Who's the dumb-ass?

> REVERSE POV—

A BRONCO has parked too close to their car on the driver's side, blocking the door. Ollie calls to Duke.

> OLLIE (CONT'D)
> Go around to the passenger seat. Slide across.

Duke ambles over to the passenger door, opens it. The car on the other side is too close as well—the passenger door SLAMS against it—but there's room to get in.

Duke wedges himself inside the car, his belly fat pushing tightly against the door jam until he POPS through.

> ANGLE ON OLLIE
> outside the car. He looks around nervously, doesn't like being out in the open, exposed.

> OLLIE (CONT'D)
> (to Duke)
> Hurry up.

> DUKE
> Yeah, yeah . . .

Duke slides over into the driver's seat. He puts the key in the ignition.

> CLOSE ON THE KEY

He turns it. The car just farts a few times but doesn't turn over.

Ollie looks up.

> ANGLE ON A BLACK CAR DRIVING PAST

It slows.

> OLLIE
> slides his hand over his gun, readies himself.

The car CREEPS past, stops.

Ollie's hand tightens on the grip of the gun.

> THE BLACK CAR'S DOOR OPENS—

A WOMAN steps out, kisses her husband goodbye, before heading into the building.

> OLLIE
> lets out a deep sigh, loosens his grip on the gun. He turns his attention back to Duke inside the car.

> OLLIE
> What's the holdup?

> DUKE
> Think maybe I flooded it.

Duke turns the keys again. This time it starts. He puts the car in reverse, slowly backs out. He only gets a few feet before—

> REVERSE THROUGH THE WINDSHIELD

as GALE KITCHEN steps out from behind a parked car and SHOOTS Duke through the windshield.

> DUKE
> jerks back, slumps, his—

> FOOT
> SLAMS DOWN on the gas pedal.

> THE CAR
> ROARS backwards, almost hitting Otto and his helper before SLAMMING into a parked car.

> OLLIE
> (to the nurse)
> Take him inside! GO!

But the nurse panics, runs off alone, leaving Otto behind.

Ollie draws his gun just as—

> WAYNE KITCHEN
> moves in behind him, puts a gun to his head, pulls the trigger. BAM!

Ollie goes down.

THE NURSE
runs frantically across the parking lot. She
gets to the front door of the building.

ANGLE ON THE FRONT DOOR
as it opens in slow motion. A MAN is there. It's
Mike Milligan. He smiles, reaches out a hand
as if to help her—then a DERRINGER springs
out of his sleeve into his hand.

BAM!

THE NURSE
falls backwards, dead. Milligan walks across
the snowy parking lot to where Otto sits,
parked in his wheelchair, helpless.

Mike leans in only inches from Otto's face.

MILLIGAN
Joe Bulo says hi.

He slaps Otto gently on the cheeks. Otto can
only GRUNT in anger.

Beat. We think Milligan is going to kill Otto.
Instead, he turns and he and the Kitchen
Brothers walk off as we—

RISE UP TO AN OVERHEAD SHOT
OF—

OTTO

Sitting in his wheelchair, an old man in the
freezing cold, surrounded by three dead
bodies lying on the ground, the snow around
them turning blood red.

CUT TO:
INT. CONFERENCE ROOM. PEARL HOTEL.
FARGO, ND—SAME TIME

Joe Bulo sits at the table across from Floyd.
A GOON comes over, whispers in his ear,
withdraws. Bulo turns to Floyd.

JOE BULO
Your counter is rejected. And now
we're lowering our price by two million.
Because I respect you and your family,
I'm gonna give you the night to think it
over. Anything other than unconditional
surrender and we'll wipe every last
Gerhardt off the face of the earth.

He stands with his men and exits.

ANGLE ON FLOYD
She made her play and lost.

DODD GERHARDT

Dodd is the oldest surviving son, the kid who taped fireworks to frogs. He is an impatient man with a temper. He hates waiting, which is what he's doing, waiting for his parents to die. Dodd has ambitions. He wants to expand, to build an empire out of a kingdom. He is opportunistic and believes his whims are at the center of the universe.

INT. HUNTING CABIN. RURAL SOUTH DAKOTA—CONTINUOUS

Ed enters, stops short.

REVERSE ON THE CABIN

Dodd's chair is empty, surrounded by rope. Behind the sofa we see PEGGY'S legs— Unconscious? Dead?

ANGLE ON ED
as he starts to react, a NOOSE DROPS OVER HIS HEAD, and he is HAULED UP OFF HIS FEET.

ANGLE ON DODD
behind him. He has thrown a rope over a ceiling beam and is pulling Ed up into the air.

ED'S FEET
kick wildly, free of the ground.

DODD
hauls him up, ties the rope off, leaving Ed to hang. Dodd comes around to the front of him.

DODD
Son, ya got yerself a woman problem.

Ed kicks wildly.

DODD (CONT'D)
How I know is — they been plaguin me
my whole life. What's the joke? Can't live
with 'em, can't turn 'em inta cat food?
Personally, I don't see the value — all
that talkin, the mood swings. It's the lack
a rational thinkin — which, brother, your
bitch's got that in spades.

ANGLE ON PEGGY

as she wakes up. She's out of it, groggy. She
rises up behind the sofa. From her POV we
see—

ED

As we clear the back of the sofa—out of focus,
swinging, legs kicking—he's pawing at the
noose. Only minutes left to live.

DODD (CONT'D)
See the male a the species, he's got the
potential fer greatness. Look at yer kings
of old. Napoleon, Kublai Khan, Sampson.
Giants hewn from muscle and steel. But
the women? Even in the Bible ya see it —
Delilah, Scheherazade —
		(looks Ed in the eye)
I'm gonna tell ya my own private belief
here.
		(beat, for effect)
I think Satan is a woman.
		(huh? Am I right?)
Think about it. With her snake tongue,
always underminin.

ANGLE ON THE BONING KNIFE

It's lying on the floor—knocked there during
the struggle we didn't see.

PEGGY
grabs it. The movement catches

DODD'S EYE

He looks over, sees she's awake.

DODD (CONT'D)
See? No matter what ya do to 'em — these
goddamn twats just won't die.

He comes for her, and when he gets close,
Peggy STABS the KNIFE through his LEFT
SHOE—the blade sinking into the floor. The
HANDLE SNAPS OFF.

DODD
howls, drops to pull out the blade—his hands
going to the blade.

PEGGY
sits up, looks around wildly for something else
to help him with.

ED
swings, the life choking out of him.

DODD
searches for some part of the blade he can
pull out, but all he does is bloody his hands
on the broken blade. He tries to pull his foot
up, but the blade gets fatter at the top, and a
fresh wave of PAIN goes through him.

ANGLE ON ED
losing his battle for life. His leg kicks become
weaker, his hands flailing without accuracy.

PEGGY
sees the fireplace pokers. She goes to them,
picks one up.

DODD
slowly pulls his foot off—the blade fatter at
the top. He yells at the effort.

PEGGY
runs over as—

DODD
rips his foot clear and starts to rise—

PEGGY
brains him in the BACK OF THE HEAD with
the fireplace poker. Dodd falls. Peggy drops
the poker, breathing hard. A moment of relief.
Then she becomes aware of the CREAKING
SOUNDS of the ROPE. She looks over.

in **CONVERSATION** with Elisabeth Williams *(Series Production Design, Seasons 2–3)*

NOAH: One of the bigger challenges of the show is the nondescript or unremarkable quality. You are trying to capture Midwestern blandness and yet it can't appear to be bland because then it's boring to look at.

ELISABETH: Well, we assume and we've seen from our research that realism is bland in the Midwest and actually in most parts of the world, but we want to make it aesthetic and pleasing to the eye. And we also wanted to follow a thread of aesthetic throughout the entire show and therefore through every single set. That's the challenge and at the same time that's where the art comes in.

ED
is hanging, almost dead.

PEGGY
runs to the kitchen, grabs another knife, runs over and CUTS HIM DOWN.

ED COLLAPSES IN A HEAP
sucking AIR. Peggy goes to him, helps him get the rope off.

PEGGY
It's okay. Yer okay.

He coughs. She helps him sit up.

ED
Is he dead?

PEGGY
I don't know.

SIMONE GERHARDT

Dodd's daughter. Simone is that crazy girl otherwise sane men destroy their lives for. The only girl in a pack of boys, Simone is spoiled and easily bored. She lives hard, does drugs, beds men, but only men she can control. Though her grandmother, Floyd, has taken over, Simone resists all overtures to learn the family business. She just doesn't have the attention span.

INT. BEAR'S TRUCK (TRAVELING). RURAL, ND—DAY

Bear drives. Simone sits uncomfortably in the passenger seat. The silence is killing her.

> SIMONE
> Any word from Grandma?
> (beat)
> I saw they took her. The police.
> (beat)
> She's tough though. It's not like they'd —
> (beat)
> And, like I said, I was just — ya know,
> Dodd told everybody on our side not ta

sell ta me — weed, ya know — and so —
> (beat)
> I mean sometimes a girl just wants ta bust a nut, ya know?

She tries a laugh. It comes out forced.

> BEAR
> (beat)
> How come ya don't ask about Charlie?

> SIMONE
> What?

BEAR
Ask about Floyd and yer dad, but not about Charlie.

SIMONE
Well, I mean — sure, how's he —

BEAR
In the state pen, waitin fer trial.

SIMONE
We should, I mean, visit. Except, maybe Dodd —

BEAR
Dad.

SIMONE
What?

BEAR
His name's not Dodd ta you. It's Dad.

SIMONE
Bullshit. After everythin he did — that you seen him do to me, which — you don't even wanna think about what he does when yer not —

BEAR
Not defendin him, just tellin you what he is ta you.

SIMONE
And what's he ta you?

Bear doesn't answer, except to slow the car and turn off the main road onto an unmarked access road, heading into the woods. Simone doesn't like this.

SIMONE (CONT'D)
Where are we —

Bear ignores her, drives.

BEAR GERHARDT

Dodd's younger brother, the middle child of three after Otto and Floyd's oldest son, Elron, was killed in action during the Korean War.

Bear is a calming presence at the center of the Gerhardt clan. An articulate man, a sensible man, Bear is not quick to anger. Nevertheless, like his namesake, he can be dangerous when provoked. Alongside his mother, Bear is the glue that holds the Gerhardts together. But even the most reasonable man has his limits.

EXT. WOODS. RURAL NORTH DAKOTA—DAY

The truck pulls in. Bear climbs out.

> BEAR
> Come.

> SIMONE
> No.

> (scared)
> That's not —

Bear comes around, opens her door.

> BEAR
> Come.

SIMONE
Yer scarin me.

Bear grabs her, pulls her out of the truck. He pushes her towards the trees.

SIMONE (CONT'D)
Stop.

But he doesn't, looming over her, cold, and she surrenders, walking into the trees. He walks behind her.

BEAR
He took my boy. Used his snake tongue and took him. Walked him right out the door. That's what yer dad is ta me.

They walk.

SIMONE
Look — I didn't — it wasn't against you. What I did. I didn't — mean fer —

BEAR
Doesn't matter what ya mean. It's what ya do. Sleepin with the enemy. In France after the second war they shaved a lady's head if she bedded the Germans, then ran her outta town. Or worse.

He walks Simone deeper into the trees. And the farther they go, the more Simone knows what's going to happen.

SIMONE
I can help. They trust me. I could — I don't know — I could give them information — fake — information and you could —

BEAR
Not our way.

SIMONE
Yeah, but, I mean, they're — how many dead now? They're kicking our ass.

BEAR
That's on you. Yer uncle, yer own grandfather. That's you.

She stops, turns.

SIMONE
No. You don't do that. Put this on me. Grandma wanted ta negotiate, but Dodd —
(off Bear)
Dad — wouldn't let her. He made it war. He did this. He's a snake, like you said. A rat. He took Charlie, not me. I was just — I'm the victim here — what was I s'posed ta —

Bear pulls a pistol from his waistband.

BEAR
Kneel down now.

Simone stares at the gun. It is the death of hope.

SIMONE
Please. Please.
(beat)
It's not — we're family.

He spits.

BEAR
None of us are family anymore.

He raises the pistol. She kneels, cowering away from the gun.

SIMONE
Please, please, please. Just — banish me. Like you said. Shave my head, run me outta — and I'll go — I'll go away and never — you don't hafta —

BEAR
Hush now.

SIMONE
Please.

BEAR
It's already done.

She looks at him, crying. He points the gun at her, and maybe now he's crying too—not hard, not out loud, but a simple leaking humanity.

CUT TO:
EXT. CLEARING. RURAL NORTH DAKOTA—
DAY

We are back at the truck staring at the trees they first walked into. We hear the cold snap of a gunshot. The CAMERA PUSHES slowly towards the trees. After a while, Bear emerges from the woods alone. He walks to his truck.

He reaches for his door with his cast arm, but can't get it. Then all his frustration pours out and he smashes his cast against the bed wall of his truck over and over until the cast is off.

Beat. Bear pulls himself together, climbs into his truck.

We close on him, sitting there behind the wheel. This is how it is now. All his life he did things for a reason and today he realized that his reasons were a lie, that he was tricked, the sucker in a long con called "family."

Beat. He starts the car, drives away.

OHANZEE "HANZEE" DENT

Ohanzee is half Dakota, half white. He was "adopted" off the street by Otto Gerhardt in his youth and so grew up with the Gerhardts—alongside the family, but never part of it. Given his sway in politics, Otto kept his sons out of Vietnam, but Ohanzee volunteered and went to fight. He was a combat tracker who went deep in country. *Ohanzee* means "shadow," and that's what he became, a vengeful spirit stalking the jungle taking Vietcong ears and wearing them around his neck.

He came back a changed man, intense, quiet, and returned to his position with the family, but everyone could tell there was a darkness in him now that troubled even these bad-hearted people. Everyone except Dodd, who believes the best way to keep Ohanzee in his place is to grind him down under his boot.

INT. HANZEE'S TRUCK (TRAVELING). RURAL
SOUTH DAKOTA—DAY

A moving POV through a windshield.
Driveways line the road.

 REVERSE ON HANZEE
looking for Dodd's car. He drives for a while,
then sees something through the woods.

 ANGLE ON DODD'S CAR
seen through a stand of trees.

 CUT TO:
INT. HUNTING CABIN. RURAL SOUTH
DAKOTA—DAY

Ed kneels beside Dodd, who is starting to
come around.

  PEGGY
 Watch him, Ed.

  ED
 Yeah. My eyes are open now.

Dodd groans.

  ED (CONT'D)
 Yer scheme failed, mister. Probably
 thought we were a pair a patsies. And
 now I'm gonna sell ya ta Kansas City.
 Could almost hear this Mike Milligan fella
 droolin through the phone.

He rolls Dodd over to hog-tie him.

  DODD
 Ah. Stop. My neck.

  ED
 Yeah, think how mine feels.

  DODD
 No, I'm serious. Somethin's wrong.

Just then the door behind them SWINGS
OPEN.

Peggy and Ed turn.

  ANGLE ON HANZEE

standing in the doorway.

PEGGY
Ed!

Ed starts to rise. Hanzee shows him a GUN.

HANZEE
Step away from him now.

Dodd sees Hanzee.

DODD
Thank Christ. Get me outta here.

Ed and Peggy exchange a look.

HANZEE
On the sofa, both a ya.

ED
What if we say no?

DODD
Just shoot 'em, ya half-breed. I'm really
hurt here. I can't — I don't think I can feel
my legs.

But Hanzee is focused on Peggy. He steps
towards her. She shrinks back.

HANZEE
Thinkin a gettin a haircut.

PEGGY
What?

HANZEE
Somethin professional. Shorter, like on
the sides and back.

PEGGY
(glances at Ed)
Oh, well, that'd be — I mean, ya got the
bone structure.

DODD
Jesus, ya mongrol. Just shoot these
fucking two and get me to a goddamn
hospital.

Hanzee turns and CASUALLY SHOOTS DODD
in the HEAD. Dodd slumps over, dead.

PEGGY
Oh my God. Oh my God.

Hanzee turns back to Peggy.

HANZEE
Can ya do it?

PEGGY
Huh.

HANZEE
The haircut. Can ya do it?

ED
Look, we — thank you — that's —

HANZEE
Shut up.
(to Peggy)
Can ya do it?

Peggy pulls herself together.

PEGGY
Yeah. Yes. I can — lemme just —

She pulls a dining chair into the open space.

PEGGY (CONT'D)
You sit and — lemme get some scissors.
Ed, will ya — our guest may be thirsty.

ED
What? Oh. Sure. Ya want a pop or —

Hanzee turns the chair so he's facing them—
his back to the front window—then sits,
resting the gun in his lap.

HANZEE
No pop.

He nods to the sofa behind Dodd.

HANZEE (CONT'D)
You take a knee.

Ed doesn't want to be close to the body, but
he sits.

Peggy searches through the kitchen drawers,
finds a pair of scissors.

PEGGY
Not sure how sharp they are.

She comes over.

HANZEE
No funny tricks.

PEGGY
No, I mean — ya saved us — we're —
grateful. Aren't we, Ed.

ED
Sure are. Could we — anything we can do
ta repay ya.

Peggy steps up, moves his hair around.

PEGGY
Professional, ya said?

HANZEE
Yeah. Tired a this life.

Peggy and Ed exchange a look. Should she try
to stab him? Ed shakes his head. Just cut his
hair. So Peggy finds a length of hair and raises
the scissors to it.

ANGLE ON ED

His eyes go to the window behind Hanzee.

ANGLE ON THE WINDOW

We see Lou Solverson's prowler pull into the
driveway.

ANGLE ON THE SCISSORS

closing on the hair.

ANGLE ON HANZEE

as he sees Ed's eyes. He stands, turning.

ANGLE ON THE SCISSORS

as, in slow motion, the hair rises up past the
blades and the scissors close on air.

ANGLE ON HANZEE
raising his gun.

ANGLE ON LOU AND HANK
approaching the house.

Hanzee fires through the front window.

LOU AND HANK

duck, as the bullets whizz past them. Lou
crouches, fires back.

PEGGY
sees an opportunity, STABS the scissors into
Hanzee's back. He turns, shoves her.

Ed charges him, but Hanzee ducks him and
runs for the back door, bursting through it and
from inside the cabin we see him run off into
the trees. Then . . .

REVERSE

to see Lou BURST through the door, gun up.
And then he sees . . .

PEGGY AND ED

who slowly put their hands up, caught.

FUTURE DREAD
OR "THE COMING STORM"

THE YEAR 1979 WAS THE VERGE OF THE MODERN. FIVE YEARS AFTER THE END OF THE VIETNAM WAR. Ten years after Charles Manson killed the sixties. It was Jimmy Carter's last gasp, the peanut farmer president focused on creating a "just plain decent" America, while Ronald Reagan, the first modern president—telegenic, conservative, evangelical, a literal product of Hollywood—waited in the wings.

There is a running dread to season 2, a sense that things are changing and not for the better. *No Country for Old Men* had some of this. Set in 1980, it featured a lot of talk about how with "the nature of crime today, it's hard to take its measure." Anton Chigurh and the Mexican cartel represented something new, a level of violence unmoored from reason or reciprocity.

There will be a similar dynamic here, the Massacre at Sioux Falls representing a previously unconsidered savagery, rejecting all the formerly agreed upon rules of combat. It is the Vietnam War coming home, a guerrilla battle devoid of all the protections of the Geneva Convention. In 1979, the American criminal has become the black-pajama-clad, tunnel-rat sneak attack. He is the massacre at My Lai, the secret bombing of Cambodia. He is napalm and Agent Orange. Sioux Falls is his scorched earth.

POLICE LINE - DO NOT CROSS

INT. SHERIFF'S STATION. LUVERNE, MN—
CONTINUOUS

Karl enters. (Through the running
monologue that follows he makes his
way through the main room, down a
hall and to the interview room, never
pausing.) There's a RECEPTIONIST
behind the front desk. TWO OTHER
DEPUTIES, Bluth and GARFIELD, are on
duty (in addition to Lou, who isn't
visible).

                    KARL
        Greetings and salutations. I have
        made the pilgrimage this night
        from the Hall of Veterans, as
        George Washington once forded the
        Delaware, steely in my resolve,
        prepared to battle unto my dying
        breath for —

                    DENISE
                    (calling)
        Lawyer's here.

                    KARL
        — hey Denise — for the rights of
        free men. Rights that were —

DEPUTY GARFIELD comes out from the
back.

                    DEPUTY GARFIELD
        Hey, Karl. Ed's in back.

Karl doesn't pause or stop talking. He
heads for the back hall.

                    KARL
        — squeezed from British oppression
        like water from a stone. That all
        men are created equal, free from
        the jackboot tyranny —

Karl enters the—

                    HALLWAY

heading for the Interview Room.

                    KARL (CONT'D)
        — and gulag magic tricks of
        nameless, faceless committees.

Lou approaches.

                    LOU
        Hope they didn't wake ya.

                    KARL
        Out of my way, tool of the state.
        For I have come to comfort and
        counsel my client, even as you
        seek to terrorize and imprison
        him.

                    LOU
        Well, whatever yer gonna do, ya
        got thirty minutes.

                    KARL
        Don't dictate terms to me,
        you rogue. I and only I shall
        determine the extent of my
        client's need to —

                    LOU
        Careful there, Karl.

Karl takes it down a notch. He opens
the door to the interview room.

                    KARL
        — for the law is a light on a
        hill —

        CUT TO:

INT. INTERVIEW ROOM. SHERIFF'S
STATION. LUVERNE, MN—NIGHT

Karl enters mid-sentence. Ed looks up.

                    KARL
        — calling to its breast all those
        in search of justice.

Karl closes the door behind him.

                    KARL (CONT'D)
        To whit, this poor, mottled wretch
        in front of me.

                    ED
        Hey, Karl.

                    KARL
        Edward, what a sad but fortuitous
        day — you chained ta that table
        and me —

Ed raises his hands, shows him.

ED
No. I'm not cuffed.

KARL
Chained in thought, if not action
— at the mercy of a cold and
venal —

ED
I didn't do this thing they're
sayin. Ya hafta —

KARL
No, don't tell me. The
establishment has ears everywhere,
even here.

ED
Ears?

KARL
Instead I shall simply ask, G or
NG, and you — my client — will
shake your head in the affirmative
for the letter or letters that
best describes your status.

ED
Shake my head yes?

KARL
Let's say, for the purposes of
the cameras that are no doubt
watching, that a negative shake,
side to side, shall in this case
be a positive affirmation.

ANGLE ON ED

confused.

ED
So —

KARL
Remember — only shake once — G —
or — NG?

Through this Ed kind of half shakes
his head for both, not knowing exactly
what he is agreeing to.

ANGLE ON KARL

Similarly unclear what has been
established here, but too far down
through his roll to stop now.

                    KARL (CONT'D)
          Well, son, rest assured — no
          matter your status — I shall
          defend you till your last breath.
          I mean my last breath — excuse
          the obvious death penalty snafu.
          I am slightly inebriated. And now
          I must bid you adieu so that I may
          polish my armor and sharpen my
          sword.

Karl opens the door, turns.

                    KARL (CONT'D)
          Give up neither confidence nor
          hope. And for God sake, keep yer
          trap shut.

                    CUT TO:

INT. HALLWAY. SHERIFF'S STATION—
CONTINUOUS

Karl comes out, closes the door. Lou
is waiting.

                    LOU
          Still got twenty-six minutes.

They walk and talk, Karl in a hurry to
get back to his hooch.

                    KARL
          And that, by no strange
          coincidence, is the amount of time
          it will take me to rouse Judge
          Peabody from his bed and have him
          dismiss these unfounded charges —

                    LOU
          No charges as of yet.

                    KARL
          Held without charges. Even better.
          Then I shall have to tell His
          Honor ta boost my client from the
          baseless restrains you've —

He stumbles a little going out the
doorway into the—

INT. MAIN ROOM. SHERIFF'S STATION.
LUVERNE, MN—CONTINUOUS

Lou steadies him.

                    KARL
          — shackled him under.

                    LOU
          Not drivin, are you?

                    KARL
          My choices outside this building
          are none of yer — but no, Sonny
          valeted me here tonight — and now,
          now —

Karl reaches the front door.

                    KARL (CONT'D)
          I bid you all adieu and admonish
          you to watch your proverbial
          butts, for I shall be back with
          the sledgehammer of justice,
          prepared to lay Joseph waste to
          these four walls —

                    CUT TO:

EXT. SHERIFF'S STATION. LUVERNE, MN—
CONTINUOUS

Karl steps out onto the landing,
closing the door behind him.

> KARL
> — if you so much as touch a hair
> on my client's —

Karl turns outward. As he does
HEADLIGHTS HIT HIM in the face. The
CAMERA CHARGES HIM, as his eyes widen.

ANGLE ON THREE CARS PARKED
OUTSIDE,

and standing beside those cars are TEN
GERHARDTS with guns, Bear Gerhardt at
the front. As the CAMERA FINDS HIM he
RATCHETS his shotgun. Click-clack!

ANGLE ON KARL

Without pausing, he turns on his heels
and goes back inside.

CUT TO:

INT. SHERIFF'S STATION. LUVERNE, MN—
CONTINUOUS

Karl closes the door behind him. As
Lou and the others watch, puzzled, he
goes over and grabs the VISITOR BENCH
and SLOWLY DRAGS IT (scraping sounds)
ACROSS THE FLOOR. Placing it in front
of the door. Then, winded, he sits on
it.

> LOU
> Karl?

> KARL
> The Jackboots are upon us.

Lou goes to the window, looks out.

ANGLE ON THE GERHARDTS
OUTSIDE

Bear points to the corners of the
building. TWO MEN break off in each
direction, flanking the building.

> LOU

lowers the shade.

> LOU
> Deputy Bluth, I need you ta
> lock the back door. Do it now.
> Garfield, kill the lights in back.

The deputies hurry off. Lou doesn't
pause.

> LOU (CONT'D)
> Denise — get on the horn to
> HQ. Tell 'em we need every man
> available yesterday. There's a
> lynchin party outside.

> DENISE
> Shouldn't call the sheriff first?

> LOU
> You can try. Somehow I don't think
> he's gonna answer. But if he does,
> tell him not to try anythin heroic
> until reinforcements arrive.
>
> (looks at Karl)
> You okay there, Counselor?

> KARL
> It's possible I soiled myself.

> LOU
> Well, I need ya ta stand up now,
> so I can get out.

> KARL
> There are large men with larger
> guns out there.

> LOU
> It's neither the size of the man
> nor the gun, but what is in his
> heart that counts.
> (beat)
> I hope. Now get up.

Karl stands. Lou pushes the bench out
of the way.

And facing the new brutality, are our heroes, Lou Solverson, Hank Larsson, and Ben Schmidt. Decent men, some (like Lou and Hank) tested in battle. Men who've been to war and seen the horrors and came home, believing that those horrors were specific to war. But now realize that the war has followed them home. The savagery has been domesticated.

EXT. RURAL ROAD. LUVERNE, MN—
CONTINUOUS

Hank Larsson hitches up his pants, approaches the silver Skylark.

Gale Kitchen sits in the driver's seat. His brother Wayne is in the passenger seat. Mike Milligan sits in back, behind Gale.

Hank raps on the driver's window. Gale ignores him, keeps his eyes straight ahead. Behind him, Milligan rolls down the back window.

                    MIKE MILLIGAN
          Help you, Officer?

                    HANK
          Sir, please roll up your window.

He raps on the driver's glass again. Beat. Nothing. Gale Kitchen keeps his eyes forward.

                    MIKE MILLIGAN
          My friend in front doesn't like to
          talk to strangers.

                    HANK
          Well, he's gonna talk to me.

Milligan glances at Hank's prowler.

                    MIKE MILLIGAN
                    (reading)
          Rock County. It's like — what's
          the town on The Flintstones.
                    (beat, likes that idea)
          Is that where we are? On The
          Flintstones?

Beat. Hank doesn't like this.

                    HANK   HANK
     That's it. Outta the car. All a   From Kansas City.
     you.
                                                       MIKE MILLIGAN
Beat. Milligan leans deeper into the   What's this about, Sheriff? If I'm
car, says something to the Kitchen   okay to ask.
Brothers we can't hear. Is he telling
them to come out shooting? Then he   HANK
turns back, smiles at Hank, opens   (all business)
his door and climbs out. But Hank's   If I search you three, am I gonna
focus is on the Kitchen Brothers, who   find weapons?
haven't moved.
                                                   MIKE MILLIGAN
               HANK (CONT'D)   Well, that depends. What's the law
     Your friends too.   in Minnesota concerning knives?

Beat. Mike raps once on the roof of   HANK
the car. The Kitchen Brothers open   It's fairly liberal. Unless yer
their doors, climb out. Both put their   a police officer affecting a
hands up without being asked.   traffic stop who finds himself
                                           outnumbered.
               HANK (CONT'D)
                 (to Wayne)   Milligan likes that.
     Come around the driver's side.
                                                   MIKE MILLIGAN
Wayne comes around, hands raised.   Well, sir, you've got nothin ta
                                           fear from us. We're just passin
               HANK (CONT'D)   through town on our way to points
     Lemme see some IDs.   south. Thought we might stop fer
                                           some waffles. Gale's idea. Heard
               MIKE MILLIGAN   there was a good place round here.
                 (take it easy)   So imagine our surprise to see it
     I'm gonna put my hand in my   closed and apparently the scene of
     pocket.   a crime.

Milligan reaches carefully into his   Hank glances at the men's feet.
coat, pulls out his wallet. Hank
stands ready to act if Milligan pulls   HANK
out something else. Beat. Milligan   What size shoes do you boys wear?
hands over his wallet.
                                                   MIKE MILLIGAN
               HANK   Now that is a truly odd question.
     Now them.   (thinks)
                                           I was a ten, last time I checked.
The Kitchen Brothers hand over their   (to the Kitchen Brothers)
wallets. Hank takes them, trying to   Boys?
keep out of their reach, should they
decide to make a move. He glances at   Both brothers hold up two fingers.
one license after another, trying not
to look away from the three men for   MIKE MILLIGAN (CONT'D)
too long.   I'm gonna go ahead and guess my
                                           friends wear a size eleven — and
               HANK (CONT'D)   not a two, which would make them
     Mike Milligan and, uh, two named   toddlers.
     Kitchen. Brothers?   (off Hank)
                                           Now, unless we've broken some
               MIKE MILLIGAN   kind of law, I believe my friends
     Yessir. That's us.   and I should get going. I told

in CONVERSATION with Warren Alan Young
(Series Production Design, Seasons 1–2)

NOAH: Minnesota in 1979 is also kind of Minnesota 1964 or Minnesota in 1948. It catches up a lot slower and it holds on to things a lot longer.

WARREN: Correct. And I was keen on showing the pace of time or the lack of pace through the vehicles. We didn't want any cars that were too new, too hip, or too forward. We had the odd VW Beetle. But to reflect that time, again, how did people, particularly in this part of the world, see themselves? And what did they see when they looked out of their window or down the street?

their wives I'd have 'em home fer
supper. And I am, if nothin else,
a man of my word.

Beat. Hank has nothing to hold them
on. He hands them back their licenses.

         .HANK
Okay. I got yer names and yer
plate number. I'm gonna radio
ahead to make sure you make it
outta state. If not, I'm gonna put

out an APB, and have you rounded
up. And then we're gonna talk
again. You understand?

        MIKE MILLIGAN
I do. And isn't that a minor
miracle? The state of the world
today, the level of conflict and
misunderstanding. That two men
could stand on a lonely road in
winter and speak to each other
calmly and rationally, while all

around them people are losing
their minds.

Hank has nothing to say to that. He
watches as the three get back in their
car.

> MIKE MILLIGAN (CONT'D)
> You have a nice day now.

He rolls up his window.

> ANGLE ON HANK

He knows these guys are fishy. He
looks at Gale, driving.

> ANGLE ON GALE

He turns and gives Hank a chilling
smile, then pulls away.

> ANGLE ON HANK

watching them go. After they're gone,
we see he's trembling.

INT. CARRIAGE TYPEWRITERS. FARGO, ND—
DAY

Still in some disrepair, stopped mid-
remodel. SKIP SPRANG is behind the
counter, on the phone. There is a fat
old manual typewriter in front of him.

> SKIP SPRANG
> (heated, into phone)
> Ya, I know, we — you said all
> that, but my point — what I'm
> tryin ta — I've got the money, see
> — I've got —

The front door chimes. Mike Milligan
enters with the Kitchen Brothers. Skip
sees them and is unsettled.

This theme is best represented by the battle between the **two crime syndicates** around which the season is structured.

The first is a traditional family (the Gerhardts) who run trucking and prostitution in the upper Midwest (out of Fargo).

The second isn't a family at all. It's the Kansas City Group, run by Joe Bulo out of a chain of funeral parlors. Bulo is a drug kingpin and the face of the new criminal corporation—where money is the only priority and there is no faith or love or loyalty.

The Gerhardts still obey the traditional rules and morays of crime (an eye for an eye, no wives and children). The KC Group, on the other hand, represents "savagery pure and simple," where the ends always justify the means.

SKIP SPRANG (CONT'D)
I mean, I will have — and so ya just need ta — hold the Selectrics for me, until — uh — So just — hold 'em, okay? Don't — and I'll call ya back.

He hangs up, turns to Milligan, forcing a smile.

SKIP SPRANG (CONT'D)
Hi, there.

MIKE MILLIGAN
Money troubles?

SKIP SPRANG
What? Oh — no, that's — he double billed me fer somethin is all. Just — straightenin things out.

MIKE MILLIGAN
I see.

The Kitchen Brothers wander the store, looking around. Skip watches them nervously.

SKIP SPRANG
Yeah. We're not really — open, is the thing. Waitin for the — for new models to come in. So closed — temporarily.

MIKE MILLIGAN
That's okay. We're not really customers.

An awkward beat.

SKIP SPRANG
Okay, well —

MIKE MILLIGAN
(interrupting)
Rye Gerhardt.

Skip reacts to the name, tries to
cover it.

SKIP SPRANG
Is that — yer name, or —

Milligan stares at him.

SKIP SPRANG (CONT'D)
— are you fellas maybe friends a
his?
(off Milligan)
Or —
(off Milligan)
I mean, jeez — I met the guy, a
course. Once or, uh, twice. Were
you — did you — need a character
reference or —

Milligan laughs. He likes this funny
little guy.

MIKE MILLIGAN
That's good. I like that. A
character reference.
(leans in)
How bout you just tell me where he
is. Seeing how he's working for
you. Isn't that what you told Big
Jim Suggs?
(off Skip)
At the Pig 'n Poke yesterday? Had
a few drinks. Told him you had a
Gerhardt in yer pocket.

SKIP SPRANG
(looks at all three)
I never —

Milligan GRABS SKIP by his tie, pulls
him forward and ROLLS the end of his
TIE under the platen (roller) of the
big old manual typewriter, which rests
on the counter between them.

SKIP SPRANG (CONT'D)
Ow. Hey.

Milligan hits the carriage return
again and again, until Skip is bent
forward uncomfortably, his tie half
swallowed by the typewriter.

MIKE MILLIGAN
Kids today like to talk on the
phone, but I'm a big believer
in correspondence. Friendly
or otherwise. If you've got a
complaint, is my motto, put it in
writing. Like last week I bought
an automatic coffee machine at
Sears? Ya know, one of those new
ones, got a clock inside? And it
was — pardon my French — a real
piece of shit. So what do I do?

He starts typing.

MIKE MILLIGAN (CONT'D)
Dear General Electric. The coffee
maker I bought at Sears on eleven
March makes a noise when it brews
that sounds like a fat man havin a
heart attack.

He hits the carriage return lever, and
Skip is pulled farther down.

SKIP SPRANG
Stop.

MIKE MILLIGAN
You can imagine my dismay, dear
Executive — both as a consumer and
a shareholder in your fine company
— that a product listed on the box
as "whisper quiet" sounded instead
like a box of rocks fallin down a
flight a stairs.
(carriage return)
And it forces me to ask — is this
the reason our once proud country
is in the crapper?

He ratchets the carriage return—once,
twice, three times—and now SKIP's tie
is in the guts of the typewriter up to
the knot.

Skip starts to choke.

SKIP SPRANG
Guhh, guhh.

MIKE MILLIGAN
Yours in peace and harmony, Mike
Milligan.

SKIP SPRANG
(gasping)
The judge.

MIKE MILLIGAN
(stops typing)
Go on.

SKIP SPRANG
All I said was talk to her.

MIKE MILLIGAN
What judge?

Beat. Skip doesn't want to say.
Milligan reaches for the carriage
return.

SKIP SPRANG
Mundt. Judge Mundt.

From behind him, Wayne Kitchen makes
a sound to get Milligan's attention.
Milligan crosses to him. Wayne leans
over, whispers something in his ear.
Milligan glances at him, surprised.
Really? Wayne nods.

Milligan comes back over.

MIKE MILLIGAN
Talk to her. That's what you said?

SKIP SPRANG
Yeah.

Milligan shakes his head, then turns.
The three men head for the exit,
leaving Skip stuck in the typewriter.

SKIP SPRANG (CONT'D)
(calling)
Why? What happened?

KNOTS

LOU SOLVERSON, A NAVY MAN WHO SERVED ON A SWIFT BOAT IN VIETNAM, KNOWS THE VALUE OF A STRONG KNOT. He spent so much time practicing his knots in war that now it is the only way he can relax, and so he carries an old length of rope with him and when he has time or needs to think something through he takes out the rope and starts tying.

The knot is a tool invented by man to conquer and control his environment. But it's also a symbol of problems both physical and spiritual, problems that are complex, messy, and sometimes impossible to solve.

Men tie knots to bind the world together. They use them to try to hold on to things that want to drift away. And yet knots can be a prison, both physical and emotional—to be tied up in knots is to be trapped in a problem that can't be solved.

The hangman ties a knot.

But a good knot, the right knot, firmly tied, in the face of forces that want to tear things apart, can save your life. So when Peggy and Ed Blumquist got married, they "tied the knot," creating a bond that was meant to be unbreakable.

As did Lou Solverson and his wife, Betsy. But how unbreakable is it?

```
INT. BATHROOM. DINER. RURAL, MN—LATER

Lou is peeing at a urinal when someone
enters and steps up to the urinal
right next to him. Lou glances over—

          RONALD REAGAN

is at the next urinal, relieving
himself next to Lou.
```

```
          RONALD REAGAN
     Ohhh, that's good. Been holding
     it since Ortonville. My wife puts
     this potpourri in the bus toilet,
     can barely breathe in there.

          LOU
     They do like their scents.

Reagan notices a POW/MIA pin on Lou's
jacket lapel.
```

RONALD REAGAN
Where did you serve, son?

LOU
Mekong Delta, swift boat patrol.
Three tours.

Beat. Reagan nods knowingly.

REAGAN
Well, I sure appreciate your
service. Every generation has
their time.
        (then)
I remember back in '42. America'd
just joined the war. I was in the
middle of — think it was called
Operation Eagle's Nest . . . for
Paramount.

Reagan gets a far-off look in his
eyes, like he's remembering an actual
battle.

RONALD REAGAN
I got dropped behind enemy lines
— trying to rescue Jimmy Whitmore
and Laraine Day from this SS
commando — Bob Stack was on loan
from Selznick. That Nazi bastard
had us cornered, we were done for.
But in the end, with a little
American ingenuity we managed to —
        (beat, thinking)
No, now wait a minute . . .
        (beat)
Come to think of it, I don't think
we made it out of that one.
        (another beat)
Or did we? Shit, I can't remember.

Either way, it was a fine picture.

Reagan zips up, flushes, and goes to
wash his hands. Lou does the same.

LOU
Governor — I don't mean ta — but
what we did over there — the war —
and now — my wife's got lymphoma.
Stage three. And lately — the
state a things — well, sometimes —
late at night — I wonder if maybe
the sickness of this world — if it
isn't inside my wife somehow. The
cancer.

(beat)
I don't know what I'm sayin except
— do you really think we can get
outta this mess we're in?

Reagan looks at Lou, directly, as a
person.

RONALD REAGAN
Son, there's not a challenge on
God's earth that can't be overcome
by an American. I truly believe
that.

ANGLE ON LOU

He nods. This supports his basic human
belief in the power to overcome.

LOU
Yeah. But how?

Reagan smiles, walks out.

WHO OWNS PEGGY BLUMQUIST?

THERE ARE FOUR WOMEN AT THE HEART OF THIS SEASON:
PEGGY BLUMQUIST (a hairdresser in Luverne, Minnesota); **BETSY SOLVERSON** (Lou's wife, mother of Molly); **FLOYD GERHARDT** (matriarch of the Gerhardt crime family); and **SIMONE GERHARDT** (Floyd's promiscuous, femme fatale granddaughter). Each represents a different side of 1970s feminism.

Betsy is the traditional woman, wife, and mother, smart and capable, but rooted in the past.

Floyd is the new "have it all" woman, the CEO of a criminal empire, mother to strong boys, clearly in charge.

Simone is the dark side of the sexual revolution—the femme fatale of the Midwest, devoid of any maternal instincts. To her, *Deep Throat* was an empowering movie.

Peggy is the limbo in between all these paradigms. She is married and has a job but feels in control of neither. Marrying Ed was Ed's choice. He wants to stay in small-town Luverne and raise a family. Peggy has a dream of going to California and being a hairdresser to the stars, but she is too afraid to act. Meanwhile, her boss, Constance, wants Peggy to leave Ed and move in with her. Everywhere Peggy turns someone thinks they know what's best for her.

This season of *Fargo* will be Peggy's declaration of independence, beginning with the accidental murder of Rye Gerhardt and snowballing, as Peggy sees the point of no return and races towards it.

INT. LOU'S PROWLER (TRAVELING). RURAL MINNESOTA—NIGHT

Lou drives. Peggy sits in the middle of the backseat. A long beat.

          PEGGY
  Do ya think — is there any chance
  I could be tried federal?

Lou looks at her in the rearview mirror.

          LOU
  Why?

          PEGGY
  I thought — maybe they'd let me
  serve my time in California. There
  was this report on the TV, how
  there's a penitentiary just north
  of San Francisco that looks out
  onto the bay. Doesn't that sound
  nice? Maybe see a pelican?

Beat. Lou drives.

          LOU
  We'll see what we can do.

Beat. He drives.

          LOU (CONT'D)
  I was there at the end, ya know.
  After the war, when Saigon fell.
  On the USS *Kirk*, patrolling the
  coast. And when the country went,
  it went fast. So we had to get
  everybody out in like twenty-four
  hours. Not just Americans, but our
  allies — the South Vietnamese —
  packed onto boats and helicopters.
  And we stood on the deck and waved
  'em in. So they'd land, unload,
  and then we'd push the whirlybirds
  into the sea. Damnedest thing. But
  then this Chinook comes, and those
  things — well, ya just can't land
  one on a ship this size. So we
  wave him off. But this pilot's got
  his whole family inside, and he's
  runnin outta fuel, so it's now or
  never. So he — hovers over the

deck and people start — jumpin —
scared or not — onto the ship. And
there's a baby. Literally, a tiny
baby. And the mother just — well,
she drops him. And one of my boys
— like catching a ball — he just
sticks out his hands and —
(beat, *the things we do to survive*)
And so now everybody's out and I'm
thinking, How the heck is this
pilot — how's he gonna get out?
But he maneuvers off the port bow
and hovers there for the longest
time — doin — we learn later,
takin off his flight suit — then —
somehow — he lays the bird on its
side and — just before it hits the
water — jumps. Six thousand pounds
of angry helicopter flyin apart
around him. But somehow he made
it.
      (still haunts him)
How did he do that?

Beat. Peggy doesn't understand.

          PEGGY BLUMQUIST
What are you sayin?

          LOU
Yer husband. He said he was gonna
protect his family, no matter
what, and I — acted like I didn't
understand, but I do. It's the
rock we all push. Men. And we call
it our burden. But it's really our
privilege.

Beat. She thinks about that—his
clarity and conviction.

          PEGGY
I never meant fer any of this
ta happen, ya know. Not to Ed.
Not anybody. I just wanted ta be
someone.

LOU
Well, yer somebody now.

PEGGY
No. See. I wanted ta choose. Be
my own me. Not defined by anyone
else's (expectations) — But then
that guy — that stupid guy —
walked out inta the road. Why'd he
hafta do that?

LOU
You mean the victim?

PEGGY
No. That's not fair. Cause I'm a
victim too. Was a victim first.
Before him.

LOU
Victim a what?

PEGGY
(beat)
It's — yer a man. You wouldn't —
(beat)
It's a lie, okay? That you can
have it all. Be a wife and a
mother, but also this — self-
made career woman — like there's
thirty-seven hours in the day.
And then when ya can't, they say
— it's you. Yer faulty. Like yer
inferior somehow. Like if you
could just get yer act together —
until yer half mad with —

LOU
People are dead, Peggy.

Beat. She thinks about that. Beat. She
nods. What else is there to say?

Absurdism

Similar to nihilism, absurdism is a strain of philosophy that focuses on the absurdity of existence in the face of death. As Camus writes in *The Myth of Sisyphus*, everyone lives as if no one knew they were going to die. But death is inevitable and final for all living things. Human beings spend all their time in a pointless search for "meaning" in the universe, but the universe is indifferent to us. That is the absurdity of life.

Job wants his suffering to *mean something*. But in the end his life is just a joke. His suffering arbitrary. That makes his life absurd, and him an absurd figure.

NOREEN VANDERSLICE, the seventeen-year-old girl who works with Ed at the butcher shop, reads Camus and Kafka, and has decided that life is ridiculous and nothing means anything. One day she finds a severed finger in the butcher shop. She keeps it in an empty tin of mints and looks at it from time to time.

We are left to wonder, Are the values of small-town American decency also absurd and outdated? Or are they ideas worth fighting for?

INT. CARRIAGE TYPEWRITERS—FARGO, ND—CONTINUOUS

Lou comes in slowly. His gun's not drawn, but he can get to it quickly.

ANGLE ON THE MAIN ROOM

Empty. But there's a light on in the back office (and are those VOICES?). Lou heads for it slowly. Then, just as he's about to look in, the SOUND of a TOILET FLUSHING. And a DOOR to his LEFT OPENS.

Gale Kitchen comes out, holding a magazine. There's a SHOTGUN leaning against the wall next to the door—left there when Gale went in to take a dump.

ANGLE ON LOU

in a bad spot. He's turned towards Gale now, putting the office to his right. And from the sound of it, there are at least two guys in there as well.

Gale Kitchen sneaks a hand towards his shotgun.

Lou shakes his head, his hand unclicking the button on his holster. *I will shoot you.* Then . . .

MIKE MILLIGAN (O.S.)
    Jesus. What are ya —

Mike Milligan steps out of the office.

        MIKE MILLIGAN (CONT'D)
    — havin a baby in there?

He sees Lou and Gale. The moment Mike appears, LOU PULLS HIS REVOLVER, takes a step back, trying to cover both of them.

                MIKE MILLIGAN (CONT'D)
                     (unfazed)
          Hello.
                     (to Gale)
          You didn't tell me the family was
          in from outta town.

Wayne Kitchen appears behind Milligan, SHOTGUN UP, pointed at Lou.

                MIKE MILLIGAN (CONT'D)
          Whoops.

                LOU
          Gotta ask you yer business here.

                MIKE MILLIGAN
          Maybe I'm the owner.

                LOU
          No. Met the owner this mornin.

                MIKE MILLIGAN
          That so? Maybe tell us where he
          is. Make a few bucks.

                LOU
          I was gonna ask you the same.
                     (beat)
          Say, you wouldn't by any chance
          be Mike Milligan and the Kitchen
          Brothers, would you?

                MIKE MILLIGAN
                     (tickled)
          Makes us sound like a prog rock
          band. Ladies and Gentlemen, Mike
          Milligan and the Kitchen Brothers.

He mimics the roar of the crowd.

Gale Kitchen, taking advantage of the distraction, GRABS his SHOTGUN off the floor, levels it at Lou, who turns to cover him.

                MIKE MILLIGAN (CONT'D)
          Double whoops.

                LOU
          Easy.

Milligan studies Lou.

                MIKE MILLIGAN
          Minnesota cop. You know we're in
          North Dakota, right?

                LOU
          Musta got lost on the way to the
          lake.

                MIKE MILLIGAN
          Where'd you say you saw old Skip?

                LOU
          At yer mother's house, I think,
          goin in the back door.

Milligan looks at the Kitchen Brothers.

                MIKE MILLIGAN
          I like him.
                     (to Lou)
          I like you. Met this other
          Minnesota fella yesterday. Big
          guy. Sheriff, I think. Liked him
          too.

                LOU
          We're a very friendly people.

                MIKE MILLIGAN
          No. That wasn't it. Pretty
          unfriendly, actually. But it's the
          way yer unfriendly. How polite you
          are about it, like yer doin me a
          favor. In my parta the world we
          don't like you, we just bust your
          head and leave you bleedin on the
          curb.

Lou eyes the Kitchen Brothers, guns high.

                    LOU
          Well, this has been enjoyable, but
          I better get goin.

                    MIKE MILLIGAN
          What did Nixon call it? Peace with
          honor.

                    LOU
          Somethin like that.

He takes a step back. The Kitchen Brothers put their shotguns to their shoulders. *Don't move.* Beat. Milligan looks at Lou.

                    MIKE MILLIGAN
          Naw. You stay. We've seen what
          there is to see.

He nods to the Kitchen Brothers. Guns still raised, they move with Milligan past Lou, who keeps his gun up. Then Milligan turns and does a Nixon impression with both hands making the V for victory.

                    MIKE MILLIGAN (CONT'D)
          I am not a crook.

They back out, guns raised. When they're gone Lou lowers his revolver, feeling shaky in the knees.

The Vietnam War

It is a war that started with a lie (the Gulf of Tonkin incident) and ended with a Declaration of the Absurd, that we had achieved—in our retreat—*Peace with Honor*.

It was the first war televised day by day to the people back home. The brutality of it, the senselessness, took Americans by surprise—having always been shielded from the true nature of war in the past. These were monstrous acts, and the men who committed them, by definition, had to be monsters. And yet weren't they also our sons, our brothers?

Two men went off to fight that war: **LOU SOLVERSON** and **OHANZEE DENT**. They fought hand to hand in the jungles, seeing the worst men are capable of, the brutality and the indifference.

The first man, Lou Solverson, returned believing war was an abomination, and that man's natural state is peace. Ohanzee, the second man, returned believing that war *is* man's natural state. He believes that every social interaction is a battle, that the world is kill or be killed. There is no such thing as peacetime, only a time where the peaceful man sleeps and the warrior haunts his dreams.

A man of peace and a man of war, on a collision course. The first believing they are in a time of peace. The second knowing they are at war. Can the peaceful man survive?

THE UNIDENTIFIED FLYING OBJECT

THERE WILL BE TWO CRITICAL JUNCTURES IN THIS SEASON WHERE A UFO PLAYS AN IMPORTANT ROLE. The first is in the opening episode, after Rye Gerhardt has killed the judge and then sees a strange light in the sky. The light draws him out into the road, where he is hit by Peggy's car.

The second will be revealed later.

The UFO represents not just a "Mike Yanagita" element (consistent with the UFO runner in *The Man Who Wasn't There*), but also plays into a larger dread of the moment. This sense, in 1979, that there were forces greater than us at work. That there were secrets our government knew and was keeping from us. And that God had been replaced by something alien, something sinister.

The year 1979 is the morning after, when the drugs wore off and we realized that we weren't in Nirvana after all. We were in a loony bin. Post-Nixon, post-Vietnam, post-hippy.

Star Wars came out in 1977, as did *Close Encounters of the Third Kind*. Aliens and space travel were very much part of the American psyche.

EXT. ALLEY ACROSS FROM THE MOTEL.
SIOUX FALLS, SD—NIGHT

The Gerhardt convoy pulls in—
headlights off. The cars stop. The
men get out. Floyd too. The motel is
across the street.

          HANZEE
  Two rooms upstairs. Three down.

He points them out.

          HANZEE (CONT'D)
  They got Dodd on the bottom next
  to the office. That's their man
  on guard. Milligan's on the second
  floor.

Bear nods to Hanzee.

          BEAR
  Stay with Ma.

Beat. Hanzee shrugs. Floyd hugs BEAR.

          FLOYD
  You fly like an arrow — straight
  and true — let nothing turn you
  from yer path. Or the next grave
  they dig'll be for me.

Bear releases her, gestures to his
men. They move out.

          ANGLE ON THE STREET

As the Gerhardts cross, guns high.

          CLOSE ON THE MEN

coming towards us in slow motion.

          CUT TO:

INT. HANK'S ROOM. MOTEL. SIOUX FALLS,
SD—SAME TIME

Hank sits up.

          HANK
  Screw this.

He stands and starts to put on his
uniform.

          CUT TO:

EXT. MOTOR MOTEL. SIOUX FALLS, SD—
CONTINUOUS

Carol Case (Series Costume Design, Seasons 1–3): Personally, I think Jean Smart gave an incredibly strong performance and it felt like the performance really matched the look. She really did embrace it. Even the red coat that she wore at the end, that's an old Hudson Bay coat probably from the forties or fifties. It was something that just happened at the last minute. It was like, "Oh, you need a coat." And that coat happened to be sitting around and we just happened to have doubles.

We are CLOSE ON the GUARD, asleep in his chair. A SHADOW falls on him. He stirs. But then a hand covers his mouth and Ricky stabs him, holds him while he dies.

ANGLE ON BEAR

He points to the stairs. FOUR MEN break off and move quietly (in pairs) to the two staircases.

TWO MEN move to a room on the first floor.

BEAR and Ricky move to the room beside the office.

ANGLE ON FLOYD

and Hanzee watching from beside Bear's truck.

CUT TO:

INT. LOU'S PROWLER (TRAVELING). RURAL SOUTH DAKOTA—SAME TIME

Lou has lost the Gerhardt convoy and he doesn't know where the motel is. He prowls the streets looking.

CUT TO:

INT. PEGGY AND ED'S ROOM. MOTEL. SIOUX FALLS, SD—NIGHT

Lying in bed, Peggy sees MOVEMENT.

ANGLE ON THE WINDOW

as two shadowy figures walk past towards their door. She sits up.

CUT TO:

EXT. MOTOR MOTEL. SIOUX FALLS, SD—SAME TIME

All the men are in position.

ANGLE ON BEAR

He sees this, lifts his arm to give the signal.

CUT TO:

EXT. MOTOR MOTEL. SIOUX FALLS, SD—SAME TIME

Bear drops his arm and RICKY KICKS OPEN the door.

ANGLE ON CAPTAIN CHENEY

and the other trooper. The trooper sits up. RICKY shotguns him out of bed.

Cheney sits up, terrified.

>   CAPTAIN CHENEY
>   No.

Bear BLASTS HIM.

CUT TO:

INT. MILCH'S ROOM. MOTEL. SIOUX FALLS, SD—SAME TIME

Playing cards.

>   TROOPER MILCH
>   Yeah, but okay — why is pissin in
>   the pool so much worse than pissin
>   in a kitchen sink?

>   CHIEF GIBSON
>   Well, first of all, son, were
>   there other people in the pool at
>   the time?

Suddenly, they HEAR the SHOT, rise, as the DOOR FLIES OPEN.

ANGLE ON THE GERHARDT MEN

who shoot.

ANGLE ON THE COPS

Milch falls, but the others dive for their guns. Gibson returns fire.

CUT TO:

INT. LOU'S PROWLER (TRAVELING). RURAL SOUTH DAKOTA—SAME TIME

He passes the cross street of the motel, HEARS GUNFIRE, turns.

CUT TO:

INT. HANK'S ROOM. MOTEL. SIOUX FALLS, SD—SAME TIME

We are looking at the door as it's KICKED IN.

REVERSE ON HANK

Gun up. He fires.

ANGLE ON THE GERHARDT MEN

The first falls, shot. The second returns fire.

CUT TO:

INT. CAPTAIN CHENEY'S ROOM. MOTEL. SIOUX FALLS, SD—SAME TIME

Bear steps inside, gun up—looking for Dodd. Ricky stays at the door.

>   BEAR
>   Brother?

He approaches the bathroom (door half open, light on inside)—and we realize he means to SHOOT DODD when he finds him.

Bear toes open the door, goes in fast, gun up.

          ANGLE ON THE BATHROOM

empty.

          ANGLE ON BEAR

What the fuck? Where's Dodd?

          CUT TO:

EXT. PEGGY AND ED'S ROOM. MOTEL. SIOUX FALLS, SD—SAME TIME

The TWO MEN kick open the door.

          REVERSE ON THE EMPTY ROOM

Where did Peggy, Ed, and Schmidt go?

          ANGLE ON THE BATHROOM DOOR

Closed.

          THE TWO MEN

approach it, guns up.

          ANGLE ON THE FRONT DOOR

As it swings slowly closed, revealing SCHMIDT. He BACKSHOOTS the men. They fall. Schmidt slams the door.

                SCHMIDT
      All clear.

ANGLE ON PEGGY AND ED

as they come out of the bathroom.

SCHMIDT

goes to the blinds, peers out.

SCHMIDT (CONT'D)
Oh Christ.

ANGLE ON PEGGY

She looks at Ed. *Now's our chance.*

ED

shakes his head.

ANGLE ON SCHMIDT

He lowers the blinds, then turns. And is HIT with a SHOTGUN BUTT. He falls. Peggy lowers the gun.

ED
He was protectin us.

Peggy hands Ed the shotgun.

PEGGY
Don't need protection. We're fully realized.

CUT TO:

EXT. MOTOR MOTEL. SIOUX FALLS, SD—NIGHT

Bear emerges from Cheney's room. From his POV we see—

ANGLE ON THE HENCHMAN UPSTAIRS

who's in a shootout with Hank.

HENCHMAN
They're cops!

ANGLE ON FLOYD

watching. She hears this. Her worst fears are realized. We see Hanzee standing behind her. She turns.

FLOYD
My son is dead, isn't he?

Hanzee moves as if to hug her—

ANGLE ON THE KNIFE

going into Floyd under the ribs.

Floyd feels it—her end. She inhales—the last great leader of a dying empire.

HANZEE

holds her while she dies. Then he lets her fall, grabs a RIFLE out of the truck, crosses the street.

ANGLE ON BEAR

He SEES HIS MOTHER FALL.

BEAR
No!

Then a BULLET TAKES OFF HIS LEFT EAR.

ANGLE ON LOU

charging across the parking lot, gun up.

BEAR

touches his missing ear. If he feels it, he doesn't show a thing. He CHARGES LOU.

ANGLE ON RICKY

who sees the tables turning. *Fuck this.* He DROPS HIS GUN, runs off, as—

ANGLE ON LOU

Bear charges him. He GETS OFF TWO MORE ROUNDS.

ANGLE ON BEAR

as the bullets hit him, but don't stop him. And then BEAR IS ON LOU and they go down.

ANGLE ON HANZEE

as he reaches the parking lot and joins the fray. He SHOOTS GIBSON, who falls, then SHOOTS the GERHARDT GOON Gibson was fighting, making his way for the stairs. He is heading for Peggy and Ed's room.

ANGLE ON LOU AND BEAR

grappling on the ground. Lou is a strong guy, but Bear is—well, Bear.

Behind them we see the COPS from the card game shooting it out with some Gerhardt men.

Bear has the upper hand on Lou—who has lost his gun. Bear HITS HIM—once, twice—stunning Lou.

Then Bear begins to STRANGLE LOU. This is it. The end.

CUT TO:

EXT. STREET. SIOUX FALLS, SD—SAME TIME

as MILLIGAN'S CAR pulls in. Gale and Milligan climb out, stare at the melee.

ANGLE ON THE BATTLE

from their POV.

MILLIGAN

watches, then something catches his eye. He turns.

ANGLE ON FLOYD

dead in the alley.

ANGLE ON MILLIGAN

What a strange turn of events.

GALE KITCHEN

pulls his shotgun, ready to get into the mix. Milligan puts a hand on his arm. *Wait.*

CUT TO:

EXT. SECOND FLOOR. MOTEL. SIOUX FALLS, SD—SAME TIME

Hanzee, gun up, heads for Peggy and Ed's room. Ahead he sees—

TWO DEAD GERHARDTS

killed by Hank. Hank's door is open. Then HANK POPS OUT and gets off a shot.

ANGLE ON HANZEE

It misses. He BLASTS HANK.

ANGLE ON HANK

as he falls.

Hanzee reaches Peggy and Ed's room.

He raises his gun. Then an instinct has him MOVE FAST TO THE SIDE as

A SHOTGUN BLAST

blows a hole in the door.

CUT TO:

EXT. PARKING LOT. MOTEL. SIOUX FALLS, SD—SAME TIME

Down below, Bear strangles the life out of Lou.

CLOSE ON LOU

struggling, weakening.

Then—

A LIGHT HITS THEM FROM ABOVE

flooding the entire parking lot with
light.

All around the motel, EVERYBODY STOPS
fighting, looks up.

ANGLE ON HANZEE

upstairs, getting to his feet. The
LIGHT turns his head just as Peggy and
Ed's DOOR OPENS and—

PEGGY

is there. She THROWS the boiling
contents of the MR. COFFEE into
HANZEE'S FACE.

He drops the gun, grabs his face. Then
ED comes out and SLUGS HIM. Hanzee
drops.

ANGLE ON BEAR

down below. DROPS OF FALLING WATER
HIT HIS FACE, bringing him out of his
blood rage. He looks up and sees the
light. He loosens his grip, looks up.

ANGLE ON A UFO

circular, hovering above the motel. It
is warmer than the air and has mist
around it. THREE LIGHTS on the bottom
create pools of light in the parking
lot. LIGHTS on the SIDES revolve.
Condensation DRIPS OFF OF IT.

ANGLE ON THE PARKING LOT

All the fighting has stopped—cop and
Gerhardt alike staring into the sky.

ANGLE ON LOU

as his hand finds his pistol. He raises it and—as Bear stares in awe at what he's seeing—LOU SHOOTS HIM UNDER THE CHIN, the bullet passing through the top of Bear's head.

BEAR FALLS and with him the Gerhardt legacy.

CUT TO:

EXT. STREET. SIOUX FALLS, SD—SAME TIME

Milligan and Gale are looking agape at the UFO. Milligan hears the shot, looks over, sees Bear fall.

GALE KITCHEN

raises his shotgun to, what, shoot the UFO?

MILLIGAN

puts a hand on his arm, lowers the gun. Gale looks at him. Milligan shrugs—what can you do? He gets back in the car. Gale gets in too and they drive away.

CUT TO:

EXT. SECOND FLOOR. MOTEL. SIOUX FALLS, SD—SAME TIME

Ed stares at the UFO. Hanzee is on his knees, stunned. Peggy grabs Ed's arm.

> PEGGY
> Gotta make a break for it.

> ED
> Are you seein this?

> PEGGY
> It's just a flyin saucer, Ed. We gotta go.

He lets her drag him away and they run, as—

Hanzee regains his senses, rises. The lower half of his face is badly burned.

ANGLE ON LOU

—down below—as Bear falls off of him. Slowly, he rises to his feet, shielding his eyes against the bright light.

Then the LIGHT GOES OUT.

ANGLE ON THE SKY

as the ship moves away.

UPSTAIRS

Peggy and Ed jump over the balcony onto the roof of the office. A SHOT hits the wood behind them.

ANGLE ON HANZEE

in pursuit. He runs to the end of the balcony.

ANGLE ON PEGGY AND ED

in the alley now, running.

HANZEE

raises the rifle to shoot them. Then BULLETS hit the wall around him; he ducks and turns.

ANGLE ON LOU

firing at him from the parking lot.

HANZEE FIRES BACK

pinning Lou—who dives behind a car.

HANZEE

jumps over the railing onto the roof, drops into the alley and runs off after Peggy and Ed.

ANGLE ON LOU

prepared to follow—but then he hears a
voice.

                    HANK (O.S.)
          Officer down!

Lou runs to the stairs, ascends.

ANGLE ON HANK

lying in the doorway. He's shot bad.
SIRENS are audible, getting closer.

                    HANK (CONT'D)
          Shoulda gone home with you.

                    LOU
          Turns out I didn't go.

                    HANK
          Grateful fer that. Ed and Peggy?

                    LOU
          On the run, with the Indian in
          pursuit.

The sirens are almost on them.

                    HANK
          Go. I can make it.

Lou doesn't want to, but he can't
leave Peggy and Ed to their fate.

                    LOU
          Dinner Sunday?

                    HANK
          I'll be there — in a suit of
          armor.

Lou nods, stands. Reluctantly, he runs
off. We stay with Hank, trying to keep
the blood in his body with his hand.

ANGLE ON THE PARKING LOT

as TWO POLICE CARS (reinforcements)
arrive.

                    LOU

reaches the bottom of the stairs and
doesn't slow. He runs to the alley—on
Hanzee's trail.

IN CONVERSATION WITH
PATRICK WILSON
Lou Solverson

PATRICK: I guess this is the million-dollar question: Is this the end of it or are you doing more? Or is that not a topic to discuss yet?

NOAH: No, we can. I guess I have the beginnings of another idea. I mentioned it to FX and of course they ran out and announced it. But it's not something I'd film until probably the end of 2019 because I'm still planning to make a movie this summer and then I have to write the damn thing. There's sort of something about this type of story that you can really do something with that you can't do with anything else, in terms of the movie pieces and the characters thematically, etc. So I sort of thought it might be more of a period piece. We'll see. It's fun to start to think about, but I can really only see it out of the corner of my eye. I'm not trying to look at it directly.

I talked to Allison [Tolman] yesterday and I've chatted with some other folks. It's funny because whenever you're in that first year, I felt like well this is all *Fargo* has ever been. And then we got halfway through it the second year, and it's like, "Wait, we made another one of these?" And then I got into the third year and it's like, "It's always been David Thewlis and Ewan McGregor." But it's fun that way and it's always different. For all that people liked that first year, that second year felt really special to a lot of people. I remember the first time you and I spoke, you were at your dad's and you were trapped in a car by a Pomeranian or something.

PATRICK: I was! That dog has since died. Parker aka what the hell is his other name. In typical backwoods fashion, that dog had attacked my father a couple of years before. This is a neighbor's dog, and of course no one has a leash or a fence down there. And so that dog attacked my dad, then apparently attacked other people and the police came to look for the dog. And then they showed up and the dog was there and being very obedient because his master was there. And the police asked if that was the dog and they said, "Oh no," and they renamed him on the spot. This is a true story and so the dog had an alias so we always got very paranoid about it.

I remember that conversation so vividly because I was sitting in that car and there was literally a dog and so much weight behind this conversation. I'm talking to you about this potential huge job and I'm in the mountains. I never really think about any type of work there, and there are these tiny teeth staring at me. As soon as I have to hang up the phone, I have to get out and deal with this dog. And it became this metaphor, like Address the Fucking Dog.

NOAH: Obviously, I said the right things and you came to do it. There's a huge alchemy to casting, there is no scientific formula, but certainly the combination of you and Cristin Milioti was really special. Had you ever met her before or worked with her before?

PATRICK: No, and I had seen her in *Once*. And if you told me the girl from *Once* was going to play my cancer-stricken wife, I would have thought, "Oh, no, that girl was some immigrant singer." That sounds stupid to say, but in a testament to her, after working with her and meeting her, I couldn't even see the person that I saw in *Once*. And I loved her in *Once* and remember thinking, "God this girl is amazing." And then it was probably the second month in working together, I was like, wait, "You were in *Once*?" I felt so stupid I hadn't googled her or IMDB[ed] her or something. I said to her then and was sitting with her feeling like, "You've got like Meryl Streep quality." First of all, she can do any accent, but she just floats so effortlessly in and out of roles and is so convincing and relaxing. Other people can swing a big stick and make bold choices as an actress, but it was just all sort of feathered in there. I just think she is just amazing, I really do.

NOAH: I do as well. She came in and auditioned for Peggy, and I told her she had to play Betsy, Molly's mom, and she passed. And I said, "No, I don't accept your pass," and I had a much longer conversation with her and she ended up doing it. Sometimes you have to say, "Look, you don't know what you're talking about. I know that you think that you're doing the right thing, but you're doing the wrong thing. Let me save you from yourself." I remember that first hour, that scene that you guys had in the house in the kitchen, and the ashtray that your daughter made you. Just in that moment, the ease and the feeling like, "Oh yeah, these guys have been married forever." I learned so much from watching that scene as a director and a writer, in terms of leaving room for the actor. It's a simple scene but it tells you everything.

PATRICK: In those first few episodes there was so much of that. Not that I ever have, but anytime you get an offer when you're away from your family, all I can think of is, "Fuck, I've got to go away again." And so you don't look at it from your head. I remember this coming to me when I was working on something in the winter in Cincinnati or something, and feeling like, "I don't know." While I loved the first few episodes, that was before I had talked to you and it was both my wife and my agent who were like, "Dude, you have to do this, you have been wanting to do things of this caliber, etc." Then it was like, okay, let me take this a step further, and you sealed the deal. Sometimes you're sort of reading words on a page and you're not seeing the big picture. If you had told me, "Hey by the way, this is going to be one of the best roles you have ever done and may ever do," I would have said you're crazy. But it was, and it is.

NOAH: What's deceptively simple is that it's a role in which it takes nine hours for you to get to a place where you're going to speak your peace in that scene with Peggy in the car. There is that sort of Lutheran humility and understatement. I can imagine reading the role and thinking, "Well, I'm not sure there's enough there." Because he takes it as it comes and you can't really shake him. He's more Gary Cooper and a lot of that depends on the filmmaker and that relationship where you're able to fill that space and no one is forcing you to be *Die Hard*. But it is a lot harder because some of the more character-y roles are much flashier on the page. But you get to that scene with Mike Milligan and the Kitchen Brothers in the typewriter shop—I mean, why would you want any more lines than that?

PATRICK: That's why with Lou, you had to be in a moment of crisis to understand. Like going to the Gerhardts, it's like, "Okay, now I got it." And I'm sure you saw this, which is why we reshot it—those first scenes in the first episode, we didn't really know how to play it. And you were in and out; I guess I should say, we were sort of like, "How funny do we do this?" We didn't quite know tone. It was so reactionary it kind of just felt silly looking at us.

NOAH: There was that layer that you guys had to get through with someone who was sort of telling you wrong. But we stuck the landing at the end. My feeling with the Lou Solverson role, which was sort of much like I had told Colin Hanks when he played the good guy in the first year, is that those are always so much harder than the flashy award-winning roles because you have to do all that stuff and still be grounded. Your performance I hold up against anyone in any medium. That's what a leading man is, and you carried the weight that was given to you. There was such a nobility and honor in it, and you never complained. It was the sort of American hero that you don't see that much anymore.

PATRICK: Yeah, no it's true. You don't. It's funny, I thought I had played a lot of people that were understated and a lot of roles that weren't flashy. Then you get actors and directors who go, "Hey I know those roles are hard and you don't get all the accolades." And obviously you don't do roles for awards, but I didn't know the whole role in its entirety, but in a strange way I didn't know that that role was missing. I thought I had played good strong guys, and then I was like, "I have never played anyone like him. Sometimes you play guys and you're like, "Oh, this will be fun to play this guy again, I like this guy." But there was something with Lou where I was like, "God, I love this guy." A lot of it sounds so simple, but I love the fact of just going in to work and knowing I was going to put on my maroon uniform and I wasn't going to take shit from anybody.

You're a Texas guy, and I was born in Virginia—it's very Americana and sort of just grounded, open, and earnest but steadfast. I play good guys and at some point, they turn or they've got this deep secret but that wasn't Lou, and that was really exciting. You could put him in any moment of crisis and I was like, "Oh, I can't wait to see what he does here, and I can't wait to see what y'all come up with."

NOAH: There's this axiom that conflict equals drama and everyone tries to put conflict everywhere. And I just don't agree, especially with *Fargo*. When this guy goes home the audience needs a place where we can feel safe with the people we like. So Cristin's character had cancer obviously, but you guys never fought and there was no conflict there. You were just doing the best you could.

PATRICK: Yeah, that is so true.

NOAH: It makes the story more dramatic in my opinion.

PATRICK: Yeah and is that because you've got so much darkness outside of that home with each of these characters and problems? And it's like okay, this has to be the rock here and they've got to be solid.

NOAH: I think so. And I ended up in a sort of similar thing with Allison and Keith Carradine and Ewan McGregor and Mary Winstead. I don't know if you saw that third year, but they had this dynamic. He's a parole officer and she's his parolee and you can certainly play it a number of different ways. Most of which involve her conning him or turning on him or policing him and I just wanted them to be in love. Like, why would this beautiful woman fall for this crazy loser? And you do it, because then the audience falls in love with them, and I felt there was that with you and Cristin. It just felt like "Oh, I can't wait to go home where everything is safe." Because yeah, when you put the boots on in the morning and go out with Angus, Jeffrey Donovan, and Bokeem and there is a UFO. You fought everything. We had no shortage of villains for you to face down.

PATRICK: No, that was fun.

NOAH: There are so many moments that stick out in my mind, but the one that really goes to what you are talking about is in that ninth hour. The new police chief comes in and kicks you out and you are just like, "This is wrong," and you could go home, but you took an oath to protect these people and you're going to do it no matter what. That's what I love. That moment where the state trooper escorts you to the state line and you go, "Fuck it," and you go back.

PATRICK: Yep. I loved that. I did.

NOAH: And of course, we the audience had seen Cristin fall and we don't know is she dead or alive; she's not answering but you go back and that's what the hero does.

PATRICK: Well, also I remember—I don't know if this was conversations with you—but I always felt like, he can't win the cancer fight. He is helpless, but he can win this one because he can do something. It fields it. So I'm sure it's not something that Lou could consciously say. He'd say it was just a feeling that he had to go back. But if somebody could sit back and analyze it they'd go, "Yeah, it's probably because of that." He's not the type of person to talk about it, at least I don't think so. But I always felt that as the hours went on, that was burning in him. He's got to say something, goddamn it; he's got to say something.

NOAH: Yeah, and then obviously we know the future because you are playing the younger version of a character that we've met and we know that Mom's not around anymore. We don't know how or when, but yeah, I think that was what is really interesting too. That Keith Carradine echo. And I don't know if you did, but it wasn't my intention for you to try to play Keith Carradine; I just wanted you to play the character.

PATRICK: That freed me up because I love the first season and I love Keith, but you said that very early on. I remember that you said I don't want you to play Keith Carradine playing Lou Solverson. I almost left that up to you. Meaning, I'm going to leave my words to be the similar thread. I also didn't want to do his dialect. He's just different and it freed me up to be a little more focused on letting me find how my Lou sounds and then we can pick those moments. Sitting on the porch with a shotgun. Those moments where we knew: "I bet that's something that he does the same way. I bet he's always that guy who crosses his legs like that." That stuff I remember very specifically and having all those episodes on my iPad from season 1. But as far as acting and dialogue stuff, I was very glad. You were probably right in directing me that way too, because then you are getting my instincts with Lou instead of my instincts through Keith through Lou. And then again, for what? It's not really worth it.

NOAH: Yeah, it was interesting to me. How did this guy turn into that guy?

PATRICK: Absolutely.

NOAH: Because that's what happens to people, they change over time. And how uninteresting would it be if he was always the same.

PATRICK: These events shaped him. He got much calmer, and talk about stoic and solid and steadfast in season 1. I mean, those scenes with him and Billy Bob are just locked in. But there is an ease that he has that Lou doesn't have at this point in his life.

NOAH: Yeah, and the idea of being a veteran and of Ted's character being a veteran and having come back from war just recently. We talked about this idea of moral injury. This idea that you've done things in wartime that if it was peacetime it would be considered immoral and how do you rationalize that. Especially with a war where you think, I don't know what I did that for. And that idea that you had seen the madness of war enough to recognize it when it started to appear at home. Which all of that, thematically, whatever intellectual I had certainly a very playable undercurrent I would hope.

PATRICK: Absolutely, that was in there.

NOAH: All building obviously to that last scene with you and Kirsten in the car, which feels like it must have been a hundred-page dialogue scene or something. It was a crazy monologue you had and she had. I will say, and I told this to Kirsten, I think the best acting I have ever seen happened in that car between the two of you on that day. The place that you went after nine hours in the show finally being able to say, "You know what, this is what bothers me and this is where I come from." And then for her to tell her story and the difference is people are dead and she is responsible. And there is a moment that happens on her face after you say that that is truly priceless.

PATRICK: God, she is so good in that scene.

NOAH: It's that idea for me that *Fargo* for me is tragedy with a happy ending. And the tragedy is that you are there in this car and you tried to warn them and now Ed is dead. And for what? It's that classic *Fargo* scene, for a little bit of money or, you know, whatever it is. But then you go home to your wife and your kid and it's going to be okay at least for a while for you. I think that's better than a sort of simplistic "Good wins the day" or "Evil wins the day." It's like, no, it sucks. Some people really got fucked and Milligan's got to spend the rest of his life in an office with that typewriter.

PATRICK: Speaking of that scene in the car, how conscious were you with echoing the last scene of the movie?

When Frances is driving and storming away but they are so far apart. He shot through the rearview mirror and the cage in the back. Then you look at our scene and she and I have become so close that she is just sitting there. Yes, she's in the backseat but there's no cage and I don't think she was cuffed or anything. I love the movie and I thought that it was a nice nod but these characters were so close. When you were shooting that, was it like a conscious decision of like, "Hey listen, there shouldn't be a cage here. We shouldn't feel like she's a trapped animal." Or was that even mentioned?

NOAH: Yeah, we talked about all of that. There are these echoes that are deliberate on a lot of levels, those echoing *Fargo* and other Coen brothers' moments where they are both familiar and unfamiliar at the same time. It creates this interesting dynamic in the audience. They are watching something that they feel like they've seen but it's not like they've seen. They are both remembering a different scene but also watching this one. And obviously, here, the genders are reversed and she's in the back and you're in the front. And Kirsten is not a monster that Peter Stormare was and there is empathy. It's a testament to Kirsten, that there is no point in the ten hours where the audience turns on Peggy. And it's because she's so aspirational and she's like, "Maybe they will put me some place where I can see a pelican." You can't hate her.

PATRICK: No, you can't. It's so true!

NOAH: She becomes a kind of amoral character and yet you're there to say, "I know, but people are dead." And there is that moment where it finally registers on her and there's nothing to say after that. But then you get to go home and have the other big scene with Ted. That hour, we had about twenty minutes of action and then it was all denouement afterwards. It was one of those things I felt like the audience needs to process what's happening and they need to be back in that safe space with that family and have Ted talking about angels having the faces of his children. And feel like, "Okay, well, maybe we'll turn this America experiment around and get it righted again."

PATRICK: Right.

NOAH: You guys got a relatively mild year. That first year was crazy cold and last year was cold as well.

PATRICK: Was it? I wondered that.

NOAH: Plus, you rocked the maroon like no one could rock the maroon.

PATRICK: I remember being super cold episode one, but then it was shipping snow back in using the white carpet or whatever they brought out there. I remember being out at the Gerhardts' and when we were shooting there, in the morning, it was covered in snow and it looked very beautiful. But I remember them sort of being very self-conscious, like, "Yeah, we are not going to shoot that yet because it's going to melt." And then I think it took a whole different turn when you saw the just plains of the sort of like golden field. It became a much different feel, which obviously production design had to sort of adapt to. I remember the typewriter scene and all that stuff where people would run in with shovels of snow to put by the signs to give it some sense of winter. We got lucky.

NOAH: One thing I decided early on is that you just can't stress about the weather because you can't control it at all. I realized, very quickly, that it was actually a blessing that there wasn't much snow the second year. I love the idea that just looking at a still photo, you knew what season it was. And it's why in our third year it was very important to figure out what's the look of this year. If the first year is sort of frigid white, and the second year was winter brown. We ended up doing a process in the third year where we pulled all the blue-channel out of the film and created a very specific look. And again, if you look at a still photo from that you'll never think, Oh that's season 2 or season 1. I think it allows you to have owned a *Fargo* experience that was unique. Even though Ewan and Carrie Coon were up in Calgary also, it was a very different experience for them.

PATRICK: I'm such a fan, but I haven't even ever met anyone from the other seasons. We've never talked. I know I stayed in Martin Freeman's old place, that much I know, but I didn't know anything else. So my wife is shooting a TV show with Kieran, and it's been so long since we had done the show, and in my mind I thought, "Oh, I didn't get to meet him because his stuff was done by the time I showed up." Forgetting when they came back and reshot his scene.

So I said, "Oh, tell him sorry I didn't meet him."

And of course, he says to my wife, "Not only did we meet, we had a very long conversation. I was hungover and I felt really bad because he embarrassed me. Here he was in his cop uniform being all stoic and I thought he was really judging me for being a little hungover." I had just forgot because we were in our own little world. Everybody got along swimmingly, but you tend to hang out with who your scenes are with because you're sort of going, "Hey, let's get something after work." So the good guys hung out with the good guys. Every now and again, because I knew Angus from *Insidious*, so we'd go out. But you're really stuck with good guys go out with good guys and bad guys go out with bad guys. I swear to you, Noah, we didn't start hanging out until in the script I had caught them and was trying to save them. Then we started to go out and get drinks and play poker and stuff. It wasn't anything conscious, but I didn't really spend any time outside of school until we were all in these scenes together.

NOAH: It's unconscious, but I think it's good for the work to keep that tension for the screen in some ways to work out that relationship.

PATRICK: It's true.

NOAH: Are we going to get along? Are we going to be friends?

PATRICK: And it's certainly not conscious, but it helps.

NOAH: Well you should know, for months after we wrapped, Warren Littlefield was pushing me to do the Lou Solverson spin-off. He made a really good argument, but at the end of the day it says it's a true story. And the Lou Solverson show is a great show but it's a TV show at the end of the day. But I'm very proud of that role in the midst of all that chaos. If there was no Lou Solverson, we would have had to build him in a lab. And Ted also; between you and Ted and Cristin there was just this ironclad sense of right and wrong. I can't imagine having created that season without it. Otherwise, it would have just been chaos.

PATRICK: Well, I know from the acting perspective, every character that stepped foot on that show got their moment—their character-defining moment. At least one, some of us more than one, but everybody who spoke on that show got a payoff. And I always loved that. It was such great words for actors to come in and chew on. And those of us who were there the whole time just knew that. I think sure, you were glad for our confidence, but me and Ted and Cristin were so glad to be able to say the words. It was certainly a blessing.

IN CONVERSATION WITH
KIRSTEN DUNST and JESSE PLEMONS

Peggy and Ed Blumquist

NOAH: I remember you saying that when you work you kind of like to stay away from your life.

KIRSTEN: Very much so. I don't like people visiting me. I only let them visit when I know, if I am working, that it's going to be an easy week for me or an easy day that leads into the weekend so they can come hang out and we can still have fun. But yeah, I don't like people on set. I don't like visitors unless I know it's a good time.

NOAH: I remember we did a panel where everyone was like, "No, I didn't watch the first season." Had you guys seen any of it?

JESSE: I did after it came up. And I had a similar reaction before I saw it to *Friday Night Lights*, and I was like, this is a terrible idea. Then I watched it and was like, "Oh, wow." I really think, weirdly enough, Bob Odenkirk's performance is what made me want to do season 2. And the way it was shot obviously really captured the Coen brothers' essence. But I loved his performance in that first season.

NOAH: Bob was great. He came in and auditioned, which I thought was kind of crazy given *Breaking Bad,* and then I think he signed on thinking he was just going to be her obstructionist boss—kind of a joke role or whatever. But then he ended up being kind of the heart and moral center of the show.

KIRSTEN: Wasn't he her father?

JESSE: No, he was a deputy.

NOAH: Keith Carradine played her dad.

KIRSTEN: Oh, okay, I just got confused for a second because I watched all the first season. I think I watched a couple, read the episodes you sent me, I think two, and then met you. I remember getting phone calls in the car on the way home like, "Noah wants you to do this," and it was like happening as I was driving home. But I had that good feeling too when I left, like, "Oh, we are doing this together."

NOAH: For me, I always feel like casting is really just an instinct for people who feel right for the role. It doesn't mean you can't transform yourself into someone you're not, but there's just something that just feels like, "Well, if this person feels right, then you're not going to go wrong." But that said, I feel like the roles were challenging in different ways. I mean, we had this conversation going into maybe episodes three and four about that sort of energy of acceptance versus denial.

JESSE: Yeah!

NOAH: Because you said, "I killed someone, shouldn't I see his face every day?" And I was saying, "No, that's the energy of acceptance—I did this. *Fargo* is the energy of denial. Everything's fine." Nothing to see here. You're trying so hard to deny it ever happened that you become manic.

JESSE: Yeah, compartmentalizing it. I think Peggy rubbed off on me in a big way!

NOAH: She's very good at that.

KIRSTEN: That's so funny!

JESSE: There was also a turning point. I don't know what episode, but there were these checkpoints it seems like. Where it was like, "All right, how is he still rationalizing this?" Even though I know people like that where once you're in they love you—that's it, no questions asked. There is also something before the cabin where Peg started getting a little nutsier. Then I watched *Melancholia* for the first time and something snapped in my head where I was like, "Oh no, he's genuinely worried about her too and would rather stay as close as possible to make sure she doesn't go off the deep end." But it really did feel like this crazy journey he went on.

KIRSTEN: Yeah, things are coming back to me. In the car, when we were going to the cabin, that was such a good bridge of energy. I remember Jesse was just playing that same song in the car over and over again. It was exciting!

NOAH: Yeah, talking over each other and you're running through the plan. You're fully actualized, fully realized.

JESSE: Yeah, well, it felt real.

KIRSTEN: Real!

JESSE: I think that's part of being up there too. In Calgary. There are very few distractions. Which is a good thing.

NOAH: You talk about the landmarks and that moment after the fire at the butcher's shop. Where you come home and you've got the check and you're having that conversation.

KIRSTEN: You know what I was just thinking of too? Side note, nothing to do with the *Fargo* book. We were Christmas shopping, and remember that guy came up to us and he was so nice. Remember that guy who was like, "Your season of *Fargo* was the best TV show I've seen in my life. I don't even know what to watch these days because it was so good." We get good compliments.

JESSE: People love it.

KIRSTEN: They are going to be happy about this book. Side note.

NOAH: Part of what's fun for me is giving you guys this range. Sometimes you play a dramatic role and sometimes you play a comedic role. I like to take someone like Bob Odenkirk and say let's give him the dramatic role, and you get to play the whole range of it over the course of the ten hours.

JESSE: That's also just people. You're not going to make it if you don't find some way to see the irony in something or see the humor in it.

KIRSTEN: Especially female characters too; you really wrote a full female role. When I read things now, I would actually be put in Jesse's position more so in a way. We probably would have flipped roles if it was a normal movie.

JESSE: Yeah, you are absolutely right.

NOAH: You were the doer.

KIRSTEN: Yeah, Jesse was like, "Oh shit," which is usually the women's role.

JESSE: Yeah and that middle part.

KIRSTEN: Wait, which middle part? Oh, that middle part!

NOAH: Right, I remember that. We did that hair and makeup test and I was like, "Ah, Jesse, I think it's gotta be a middle part." It was hard to accept, I know.

KIRSTEN: Oh gosh. I mean, you just giggle when you see those two. I think like a year later or something my girlfriend was like, "Let's put on a scene from *Fargo* to see you guys together, now that you are together." She was getting a kick out of it so we did it. It just put such a smile on my face because I have such good working memories and they also are such a funny two to watch together. It really gives you so much pleasure.

NOAH: "It's just a flying saucer, Ed, we gotta go."

JESSE: Side note too: I don't think there's a moment that I've experienced on set that rivals watching Kirsten run out of that butcher freezer. That moment with Patrick. I was dead so I could only hear it, but I watched it on playback.

NOAH: Yeah, it was intense. I remember that.

JESSE: You were also pissed about having to go there I think.

KIRSTEN: I know. I was pissed about how I was asked.

JESSE: Adam went like this: "I think it's more . . . "

NOAH: Oh, he gave you a line reading. That's funny

because I was there that night and I didn't see that. No, it's hard. Cycling those directors in and . . .

KIRSTEN: It does bond you though. I remember all of us having breakfast. Whatever it is, you'd had your close-knit group. I don't know; we always had dinners with everyone new that would come on. It [was] kind of like the new kid . . .

NOAH: Yeah, I thought they all did really good. What was hard about you guys is that the first hour was so poorly done. Then we had to reshoot a lot of it. So you guys actually didn't see anything until we wrapped. Literally, it was like the day of or the day after.

KIRSTEN: Oh yes, you showed us the day of the wrap party.

NOAH: Which is crazy because Ewan and Mary and that lot, I showed while we were shooting episode three. They saw that first hour. So you had to do the whole thing on faith.

KIRSTEN: Oh, really. I wouldn't want to actually. Would you? I'd feel weird to already see something. I'd want to do my own journey with it. We only redid the garage scene I thought in ours.

NOAH: There were a lot of pieces. Then there was so much in finding the editorial style and the split screens and all that. And then I ended up changing, because originally in the script you hit Kieran and then you got out of the car and then we went home with you. Then I changed it so that the car hit him and no one got out. Then I added that scene in the butcher shop. The "Okay, then" scene. Which then the network when they read it were like, we feel like we are missing an opportunity to really get to know these characters. And I was like, "No, no, this is all you need." Then when we went home with Ed and met you, just like making dinner, it changed the whole thing.

KIRSTEN: Normal. It really did. It makes me want to imagine it. I don't mean it in a narcissistic way, but when I think about it it's almost like a home movie now.

JESSE: It's really good memories.

NOAH: It's amazing because people have seen him get hit by a car, but when people hear that noise from the garage they think, "Oh, she's having an affair." There's this weird thing where they sort of forget until they see the car. But yeah, it was a really magical year. Everyone. Jean [Smart], I still work with Jean.

KIRSTEN: I love Jean. We were supposed to go to her Christmas party, then she got sick, then we were in Austin.

NOAH: And Jeffrey Donovan was great. I know that cabin was a tough shoot on some levels.

KIRSTEN: We still see Angus sometimes.

JESSE: I don't think Jeffrey likes me anymore.

NOAH: Yeah well, he went with it in the moment.

KIRSTEN: I just remember lying dead on the floor hearing it all. I was worried about it. It looked very real and I remember Jeffrey being upset. I think Jesse spit in his face on one take.

NOAH: For the record, Jesse nodded.

JESSE: I mean, it felt like I had to.

KIRSTEN: Yeah, he knocked me out!

NOAH: Well, that's true. That's obviously part of the process. Working stuff out in advance. Or sets are different or actors are different. I don't know.

JESSE: At that point, it just meant so much to me. It was four months in and it was not difficult to release myself there at that point.

NOAH: And you must internalize to some degree that journey you'd taken. These fucking guys who want to kill you and those feelings. It was literally five days that were nights mostly. We were on a stage shooting a set, and it sucked that the days started at two o'clock in the afternoon and then went until the morning.

KIRSTEN: But it worked. It was so good that it did. That was perfect that it was nights. It just makes everyone delirious and their guards are down. I always feel like night is such a good creative space. There's no phones and no one's trying to make something else happen. I've always liked night shooting if you are on schedule and you aren't totally out of it.

JESSE: It's like free time.

KIRSTEN: Yeah, it's like the world's sleeping.

JESSE: And not waking up at five in the morning.

NOAH: Well, right, that's what is great about being in Austin is that L.A. doesn't really wake up until noon my time, so I can get so much done.

KIRSTEN: Oh, I love that too when we're in Austin. I'm so much more on it, it seems, when I'm in Austin. Maybe we shouldn't be putting all this money into the house.

JESSE: Well, we're going to need it.

NOAH: We had a meal on that wrap party night and we got talking about who you wanted to work with again and that you were surprised it was Ted Danson.

KIRSTEN: I loved working with Ted. I've grown up watching Ted in movies and on *Cheers* and stuff. But I also hadn't seen Ted in this kind of role and Ted is such a good actor. I loved working with him. He's such a generous actor and so with you in the scene.

JESSE: Ridiculously present.

KIRSTEN: Yeah, he is! It's almost like, I don't know if he does or not, but one would think he would meditate every day or something. I loved working with Ted.

NOAH: He just brings goodwill to the set.

KIRSTEN: He's very presidential.

NOAH: He's the mayor of television.

KIRSTEN: Yeah, he has a very mayor quality.

JESSE: He really does!

NOAH: I love that scene where he says, "You're a bit touched." I also have to say that last scene with you and Patrick in the car is one of the great acting moments I've ever been a part of.

KIRSTEN: Thanks, Noah.

NOAH: "Maybe they'll put me somewhere where I can see a pelican." You know what I mean. Both of her feet aren't on the ground. It was sad in the freezer that night. The night of the Nazi movie and . . .

KIRSTEN: Oh yeah, I forgot about all that. That was hard.

NOAH: Yeah, it was hard with the fake smoke.

KIRSTEN: And real pigs were in that freezer too.

NOAH and Jesse: Oh yeah, they were!

NOAH: It was like real animals hanging.

KIRSTEN: They were, but what were they so they weren't smelling?

JESSE: They were smelling.

KIRSTEN: But they cured them in a certain way or something. There was a lot of cured meats in there and huge pigs hanging.

JESSE: It was some fake but a lot of it was real.

NOAH: I guess it's cheaper in the end to go to the supermarket or the butcher. I mean, we didn't slaughter them for the movie or anything, but yeah.

KIRSTEN: I think with Peggy, she believed it. I also think she's coming from a good place. Whatever that place was in her own deranged mind.

NOAH: I always thought she knows there's more out there, she just doesn't know what it is. She was just about to find out when she hit that guy. And then her choices were taken away and she refused to accept that. Literally, the whole rest of the time is her going, "No, I'm going to actualize myself."

JESSE: And the idea that everything was coming to a head, had she never hit that guy, something was bound to happen.

NOAH: It's interesting because I think about Peggy a lot with this *Lucy in the Sky* movie because it's about this woman who goes to pieces in a certain way. And yet, I didn't want to make a film about a professional woman who falls apart because she's too emotional about a man. So I had to change it in the end to something different from the real story.

KIRSTEN: But even if it is that, it's not that anyway. I didn't read it, but I think she's probably messed up because she's been to space.

NOAH: Yeah, you don't send poets to space, right? You send engineers and they go up and have these celestial experiences and then they come back and it's like, how can I just go back to eating at Applebee's? I've seen the whole universe.

KIRSTEN: Big picture.

NOAH: No matter how complicated the universe is, it's still simpler than life on earth. So all those things go into it. I think about Peggy a lot because we managed to thread that needle where you never turned on her. She got justice and eventually she ran into the consequences of her decisions, but we never disliked her. I don't think.

KIRSTEN: No, I don't think so either. But I think that's a lot of how you cast because the essence of a person you can't get rid of in general. So when you cast someone like Rachel McAdams playing a bitch in a movie. You will always love her because you can tell her essence is good. So even though she's playing a bitch it's exciting and fun to watch her play that because you are with her still. And with Peggy, I feel like you were right because you would be on the ride with her and understand her. And you wouldn't dislike her because my motives came from a genuine place.

NOAH: I agree. Positive Peggy.

KIRSTEN: I feel like audiences and we are all treated like we are not as smart as we are most of the time. Oh my God, there's so much bad talk I want to say about that. Even when Jesse got *Black Mirror* I kind of felt bad for his character still.

NOAH: Because in the narrative they created empathy for him early on.

KIRSTEN: But also because it's him playing it. If it was someone who you could tell was demanding on set or just has an air about them. You hate the character just by the pure essence he is as a person.

NOAH: And my experience working with both of you is that there is no drama.

KIRSTEN: It's unnecessary.

NOAH: And I also feel like because it's more of an ensemble, people can't have too big of an ego because it's not a show named after their character or anything like that. And I know Jeffrey Donovan; I worked with him his first day on set. He was great so I didn't give him much, and he went home that night thinking he was going to be fired. Which is weird for an actor who starred in a show for that many years to feel insecure on that level. But I think I just am not a dramatic guy, and my feeling is that if I cast it right, I shouldn't have to say too much.

KIRSTEN: And I also don't like to over-talk about things either as a person. Let's just do it and then if it's that wrong, then we can talk about it. It's my job to come with my artillery stacked and ready too. I don't want to have to have those conversations about what's wrong.

The thing is that the more invested you are and the farther along the process is, if anyone even comes near you with something when you know you've been working so hard, and you're so passionate about it and you're so involved. It's like your baby if someone says something, and you can get very ticked off very easily depending on the way things are said.

JESSE: I felt that about the last day. Everyone was like, "Fuck, it's the last day of school."

NOAH: Yeah, we ended on some big stuff.

KIRSTEN: Yeah, running and the car.

NOAH: And the other thing is that it's basic cable. We don't have as much time as we need. We are asked to do eight pages of dialogue in a day. It's crazy.

JESSE: And the crew too. The show would not work.

NOAH: Daryl [Hartwell, first camera operator] is down here this week. I think he's going to come by. He was great.

KIRSTEN: He was a good constant to check in.

NOAH: That was the thing. We went up to Calgary, and it turned out there were a lot of artists up there. And Justin [Onofriechuk], who did our props, and you see that guy on the street and you wouldn't think he has this sweet artistic soul. But that guy would work tirelessly and have great ideas. And Daryl a lot of the crew. And they don't get to do much up there. A lot of westerns.

KIRSTEN: I haven't shot in L.A. in ten years or eleven years. Don't you wish you could shoot your movie in Austin?

NOAH: Yes.

KIRSTEN: Is there no tax incentive anymore?

NOAH: No, there's very little.

KIRSTEN: Why does that happen to a city? Why wouldn't you want people to make their films there?

NOAH: Because let's say you are a very conservative state, you go, "Why are we giving these Hollywood liberals money?" But I'll get back there.

KIRSTEN: By the way, I kept my script next to the Bible in the Marriot in the drawer.

NOAH: Oh yeah?

KIRSTEN: I kept it on top of my Bible in the drawer in the Marriot before I switched to the apartment buildings because I figured it was a good Lutheran mojo to keep together. The script and the Bible. I forgot that I did that.

NOAH: It's a spiritual show.

Fargo

SEASON 3

THIS IS A TRUE STORY

2017 EMMY® NOMINATION HIGHLIGHTS

Outstanding Miniseries

Carrie Coon—Outstanding Lead Actress in a Miniseries or Movie

Ewan McGregor—Outstanding Lead Actor in a Miniseries or Movie

David Thewlis—Outstanding Supporting Actor in a Miniseries or Movie

Noah Hawley—Outstanding Directing for a Miniseries, Movie, or Dramatic Special ("The Law of Vacant Places")

Noah Hawley—Outstanding Writing for a Miniseries, Movie, or Dramatic Special ("The Law of Vacant Places")

2018 GOLDEN GLOBE AWARD

Ewan McGregor—Best Performance by an Actor in a Limited Series or Motion Picture Made for Television

2018 GOLDEN GLOBE NOMINATIONS

Best Limited Series or Motion Picture Made for Television

David Thewlis—Best Performance by an Actor in a Supporting Role in a Series, Limited Series, or Motion Picture Made for Television

in CONVERSATION with Dana Gonzales *(Director of Photography, Seasons 1–3)*

NOAH: We made a deliberate choice in Season 3, to say, "Well, how is this one visually going to distinguish itself?" and *Inside Llewyn Davis* was a big inspiration.

DANA: Bruno Delbonnel, who shot *Llewyn Davis*, came up to me and said, "I need to talk to you. What you're doing on *Fargo* is fucking amazing. I really love this year." So, there is the guy who did that, and he loved it. Stripping out the blue spectrum and then picking the colors in the production design to work with, that instantly gave it that tone and atmosphere so you know where you are. You are in a different story.

EPISODE 1

THE LAW OF VACANT PLACES

INT. STASI INTERVIEW ROOM. EAST BERLIN—DAY (1988)

The room is sparse, with a single HARDBACK CHAIR positioned across from a DESK, under a hanging MICROPHONE. A tabletop reel-to-reel tape recorder is on the desk. There is a drain in the center of the concrete floor.

A MAN (50), meticulous, wearing glasses, sits behind a desk, wearing a Stasi police uniform. This is Colonel HORST LAGERFELD. He is eating a sandwich that has been wrapped in waxed paper.

A knock at the door.

                         HORST
          Kommen.

The door opens. A young STASI OFFICER stands there holding the arm of a fat, balding man, JAKOB UNGERLEIDER, in his mid-forties. (The following exchange takes place in German.)

                     HORST (CONT'D)
                  (barely looking up)
          In the chair.

Horst returns to his lunch as the officer sits the man in the chair, then withdraws. A long, tense silence. Horst eats. The man, JAKOB, looks around.

          ANGLE ON A REEL-TO-REEL RECORDER

Light off, reels still.

          ANGLE ON JAKOB

in the chair, nervous, sweating. He looks up.

          ANGLE ON THE MICROPHONE

hanging down from the ceiling.

          ANGLE ON JAKOB

in the chair. He looks at—

          ANGLE ON HORST

He finishes his sandwich, licks his fingers, then carefully refolds the waxed paper for future use. He opens his desk drawer, puts the waxed paper inside, pulls out a FILE FOLDER, slides the drawer closed. He opens the folder, looks inside, then reaches over and turns on the recorder. The light comes on, reels begin to spin. Finally, Horst looks up at the man.

                    HORST (CONT'D)
You are Yuri Boiko.

                    JAKOB
No, sir. My name — thank goodness — my name is Jakob
Ungerleider. There is some misunderstanding.

Horst studies the file, tsking to himself, unconcerned.

                    HORST
You live at 349 Hufelandstraße.

                    JAKOB
Yes, sir.

                    HORST
Well then — Yuri Boiko is the registered occupant of 349
Hufelandstraße. So if that is your address, then your name
is Yuri Boiko, and you are a twenty-year-old émigré from the
Ukraine.

Jakob blinks. He is a forty-six-year-old father of two.

                    JAKOB
Sir, I am from Stuttgart. A German citizen. As you can
plainly see, I have not been twenty years old for a very
long time.

Horst studies the file, tsking to himself.

                    JAKOB (CONT'D)
                    (cautiously)
Perhaps — if I may — I have only lived at this address —
349 — for six months. So, perhaps Yuri was the previous —

Horst holds up his hand. Jakob stops talking.

                    HORST
                    (beat, tsking)
This is a problem, you understand? Because for you to be
right, the state would have to be wrong. Is that what you're
saying? That the state is wrong?

                    JAKOB
                    (trapped)
No, sir.

                    HORST
Good. Then you admit that you are Yuri Boiko. And your
girlfriend's name is Helga Albracht.

                    JAKOB
                 (taken aback)
My — no, sir. I don't have —
                 (reluctantly)
I mean, *my wife*, she is in fact named Helga, yes, but not —

                    HORST
Excellent.

                    JAKOB
— Albracht —

                    HORST
                 (not listening)
Now we are getting somewhere. And was it this morning or
last night that you strangled her?

                    JAKOB
What?

                    HORST
Your girlfriend. *Helga Albracht.* You killed her last night
or this morning?

                              JAKOB
          Sir — please. This must be — I do not — as I said before —
          I do not have a girlfriend. I have a <u>wife</u>, and though she
          <u>is</u> named — coincidentally — she is named Helga, yes, but
          Helga *Ungerleider*, not — and also, believe me — Helga, my
          wife, is very much alive. In fact, when your men came to
          pick me up only an hour ago, she was home. My wife was home,
          and offered them tea. Ask them. Your men. My Helga. She is
          alive.

Horst tsks some more, absently. Jakob sweats. Horst finds a
photograph in the file, holds it up. In it, a YOUNG WOMAN lies
dead on a riverbank.

                              HORST
          And yet here is a body, found earlier today. *Helga Albracht*.
          Strangled manually — and left on the banks of the Spree.

                              JAKOB
                           (horrified)
          Sir, I don't know what to tell you. My wife — as I said —

Horst holds up his hand. Jakob stops talking.

          CLOSE ON HORST

He leans forward.

                              HORST
          Herr Boiko, be reasonable. I have shown you a body, purple
          in the face and cold to the touch. I have seen this body
          with my own eyes. Her death is a fact. What you are giving
          me are words. This "wife," who is "alive," with a "different
          last name." That is called "a story." And we are not here to
          tell stories. We are here to tell the truth. Understand?

Horst offers a small smile, as if to say—*see how simple things
can be?* The camera PANS slowly past him, finding a framed
photograph, hanging on a wall. It shows a snowy field, a lone
tree in the distance.

          CUT TO:

EXT. FIELD. EDEN PRAIRIE, MINNESOTA—DAY (2010)

We are outside, suddenly, in the same snowy field, looking at
the lone tree, rolling hills. We TRACK RIGHT across the snowy
ground.

We see the following text:

This is a true story.

We PAN RIGHT and FIND some kids playing, building a snowman and realize we are in our contemporary world.

The events depicted took place in Minnesota in 2010.

PANNING FARTHER we see the back deck of a MANSION.

At the request of the survivors, the names have been changed.

It has been set up for a party with heat lamps and a bar. A BANNER reads HAPPY ANNIVERSARY STELLA AND EMMIT.

We find a WAITER heading for the back doors. We follow him.

Out of respect for the dead, the rest has been told exactly as it occurred.

                    EMMIT (O.S.)
     Honestly, Buck. It's a little embarrassing.

          CUT TO:

INT. STUDY. EMMIT STUSSY'S HOUSE. PRAIRIE, MN—CONTINUOUS

An important man's lair. Emmit sits in a puffy chair. Sy Feltz leans against the credenza. Emmit and Buck are smoking cigars. Sy has a pipe.

                    EMMIT
     We called the number. They said if there was ever a problem
     we should call the number. And, well, we called it.

          ANGLE ON BUCK OLANDER

sitting on the sofa, facing them. He's a heavyset man, former head of the Chamber of Commerce.

                    BUCK
     And?

                    EMMIT
     A series of clicks and buzzers.

                    BUCK
     A series of —

                    EMMIT
     Clicks and buzzers. That's what we got — which —

                    SY
     Couldn't even leave a message.

                    EMMIT
     No message possible. So we thought —

                              SY
          We thought get Buck back in here. After all, he vouched for
          'em.

                              BUCK
          Well now — let's be — call a spade a spade — don't know 'em.
          Don't vouch for 'em. I was just a conduit for information.
          Like you said, *Buck, we tried all the normal channels — need
          a bridge loan ta — last year, fer Pete sake* — and I'd met
          this fella at the Shriners —

                              EMMIT
          Sure, okay. And everything worked out great when we met the
          broker, a Mr. Ermentraub, if I'm not —

                              SY
          Right. Rick Ermentraub. I got his card in my — (rolodex)

                              EMMIT
          — and now, we're in the black again, so we call the number
          ta arrange payback and — clicks and buzzers.

                              SY
          Maybe there's another number, we're thinkin.

                              EMMIT
          Another number where we could at least leave a darn message.
          It's a lotta money.

                              SY
          A heck of a lot.

                              EMMIT
          And it's just sitting there on the books — which —

                              SY
          Can't have that.

          Beat. Buck thinks about it.

                              BUCK
          Wish I could help. But this Ermentraub fella, like you said,
          I met him at Mussbaum's last year — shared a pilsner out on
          the veranda. That's about the extent of our —

                              EMMIT
          It's real peculiar. That's all we're sayin. Ta lend out
          money and then —

                              SY
          So if you had another number, or —

          A long beat. Buck doesn't.

                              EMMIT
          Okay then. Well, thanks for coming in.

Buck stands.

                              BUCK
          Course. And did you think about what I asked? The Widow
          Goldfarb. She wants to meet.

                              EMMIT
          The who?

                              SY
          I was gonna tell ya. She's the so-called storage queen,
          sniffin around fer a possible silent partner type
          arrangement.

                              BUCK
          She seems like the real deal. Money ta burn.

                              EMMIT
          Where was she two years ago?

From offscreen we hear a MAN'S VOICE, giving a speech to a crowd
of people.

                              EMMIT (O.S.)
          Friends — and Dave —
                    (a big laugh from the room)
          — I'm not lying when I tell ya — I still remember that first
          date — twenty-five years ago.

INT. GRAND ROOM. EMMIT STUSSY HOUSE. EDEN PRAIRIE, MN—DAY

FIFTY GUESTS are gathered to celebrate the twenty-fifth wedding
anniversary of EMMIT and STELLA STUSSY. All are dressed up,
holding cocktails. Various big-game heads hang on the wall.

They are all facing the grand staircase, where EMMIT STUSSY
stands on the steps beside his wife, STELLA.

                              EMMIT
          Took her to *Fiords* in St. Paul, my Stella. Bought her a
          lobster the size of a car. Cost me two weeks' salary from the
          Red Robin. But it was worth it.

Laughter from the crowd.

                              EMMIT (CONT'D)
          And so over shellfish she says: *So — where do ya live?* Ya
          know, just makin conversation. And I tell her the address.
          Two-thirteen Monroe. And she gets this funny look on her
          face and says, *What apartment?* And I say *sixteen.* And now
          the look gets even funnier, and she says —

                              STELLA
          I say, *what are the odds? I lived in that same apartment for
          three and a half years.*
                                   (to the crowd)
          I still had the key.

The coincidence gets a reaction from the crowd, as if a magician
has pulled a rabbit from a hat.

                              EMMIT
          Course she didn't tell me that part. So I come home a week
          later and *what the heck?* She's moved in.

People laugh.

          ANGLE ON A COUPLE

Standing in the back of the crowd. The MAN looks remarkably like
Emmit, except he's pudgier and balding, wearing a mismatched
jacket and slacks. This is RAY STUSSY (47), Emmit's younger
brother. (Note: Emmit and Ray should be played by the same
actor.) Ray is a parole officer, blue collar in body and mind.

To use a sports analogy, if Ray is a journeyman catcher with bad
knees, Emmit is the owner of the team. In other words, one has
power, the other bad luck and excuses.

The WOMAN next to Ray seems similarly out of place in this crowd, being young and beautiful, dressed in a short skirt and low cut top, with a punk rock attitude. This is NIKKI SWANGO (28). If she were a plant she'd be the sarracenia, which lures insects inside with its sweet smell, then drugs them and digests them slowly.

A WAITER passes by with a tray of canapés. Nikki stops him, takes one, then another, then a third. Each time the waiter tries to move on she stops him.

            ANGLE ON EMMIT STUSSY

Mid-speech.

                    EMMIT (CONT'D)
        And now, somehow, it's twenty-five years later, and here we
        are. And we got Grace and her husband, Dennis.

            ANGLE ON GRACE AND DENNIS

GRACE (23), like her mother, is short and heavyset. Her husband, DENNIS (27), is skinny and nervous. Not a great catch, but loyal, like a golden retriever.

                         EMMIT (CONT'D)
     And life has been good to us. More than good. So raise a
     glass — to my Stella, still lovely as the day we met.

He drinks, as does everyone.

          ANGLE ON RAY

He dumps his drink into a ficus tree. A MAN approaches. This
is SY FELTZ, Emmit's consigliere. If Sy were a plant—well, *who
are we kidding?*—Sy Feltz would never be a plant. He'd be the
bulldozer that plows the land so condos can be built. He looks
like what would happen if a hockey goalie was thrown out of the
league for beating out a guy's eyeball and started preparing tax
returns.

                         SY
     I got you five minutes.

He nods towards the hallway, moves off. Ray looks at Nikki.

                         NIKKI
     Go get 'em, tiger.

          CUT TO:

INT. ANTECHAMBER. EMMIT STUSSY'S HOUSE—DAY

Ray sits on a bench, losing his cool.

          ANGLE ON THE WALL

across from him. We see framed magazine covers and plaques
commemorating all of Emmit's good works.

The study door opens. Sy steps in.

                         SY (CONT'D)
     Ray?

          CUT TO:

          ANGLE ON A POSTAGE STAMP

vintage, behind glass, inside a frame. We pull out to find we
are in—

INT. STUDY. EMMIT STUSSY'S HOUSE—CONTINUOUS

The stamp is hanging on the wall behind an expensive desk. Emmit
Stussy sits behind the desk. Sy Feltz stands nearby.

                    ANGLE ON RAY

in the chair on the other side of the desk.

                              RAY
          Ya know, congratulations and all that.

                              EMMIT
          Thank you.

                              RAY
          Place looks good.

                              EMMIT
          We had the floors redone.

                              RAY
          Yeah? That's — uh —

He shrugs—*what's he gonna say? They're fucking floors*. Beat.

                          RAY (CONT'D)
          I saw the — Stella's mom. Guess you got her on the oxygen
          now.

Emmit exchanges a glance with Sy.

                              EMMIT
          So — what can we do for ya here, Ray?

                              RAY
          No. Nothing, just — wanted to pay my respects. Twenty-five
          years and all that.
                             (beat)
          You said Grace got — that's her husband now? Dennis?

The implication being, *Why wasn't I invited to the nuptial?*

                              SY
          It was nothin, barely even a wedding.

                              EMMIT
          We did it in Cabo. On the beach. They said — invitation said
          no shoes — can you imagine — wearin a suit with no shoes?
          Still — real nice.

                              SY
          But small. Only, like, ten people.

                              RAY
          But <u>you</u> went.

                              EMMIT
          We had some meetings.

                              SY
          The next day. Potential investors.

                              RAY
          In Cabo.

                              SY
          It's like a resort. Super high-end.

                              EMMIT
          International businessmen and the like.

                              SY
          Exclusive.

                              RAY
          Not for parole officers, ya mean.

                              EMMIT
          Don't take offense.

                              SY
          Yeah, Ray. Jeez. Don't take offense. We're just explainin
          what happened.

          Beat. Ray stares at the stamp over Emmit's shoulder. Emmit
          glances back.

                              EMMIT
          How's the Corvette?

                              RAY
          It's a car.
                         (looks at Emmit)
          Look, I'm gettin engaged.

                              EMMIT
          Again?

                              RAY
          Don't say that.

                              EMMIT
          I'm sorry — I just —

                              RAY
          She's real sweet. Nikki. We're in (love) — ya know.

                              SY
          You meet her at work?

                              RAY
          At work, yeah.

                              SY
          So — embezzler? Drug mule?

     Beat. Ray turns to Emmit.

                              RAY
          Why's <u>he</u> here? He doesn't need to be here.

                              EMMIT
          Sy's always here when the conversation's about money. That's
          what this is, right? A conversation about money?

     Ray stares at the stamp, fumes.

                              RAY
          I wanna buy her a ring.

                              EMMIT
          So — serious.

                              RAY
          And the way I figure it is — you still owe me from —

                              EMMIT
          I owe you?

                              RAY
          — from what happened when we were kids, so —

                              SY
          Well now, Ray, that's — I gotta say yer math seems shaky
          there. I mean, after the — what was it? Last quarter we
          fronted ya eight-fifty fer car repairs and —

                              EMMIT
          — on top a co-signin the mortgage so you could get yer
          apartment — not that I mind. Glad to help. Really, but —
          where does it (end) —

                              RAY
          No. See. That's not — the way I see it, that's you payin me
          back fer —

                              EMMIT
                         (not again)
          Ray.

     Ray fumes.

                              SY
          The thing is, Ray — even if we wanted ta — we're —

                              EMMIT
          What Sy's sayin is — it's not the best time.

Ray fumes. There is a defining injustice between them that Ray
is trying to let slide, but can't.

                        RAY
     How bout you just gimme my stamp and we call it square?

                        SY
     Ray.

                        RAY
     I'm talkin ta my brother.
                    (beat, to Emmit)
     Ya know, yer lucky I don't sue. I mean, a legal document
     which delineates things, bequeaths them to specific parties.
     A father, dead in the driveway. An older boy takin advantage
     of a younger, playin on his —

                        EMMIT
     Nobody took advantage — it was a trade. If I had a time
     machine, you'd see. I'd play back the tape. *Emmit, come on.*
     I'm beggin ya. Take the stupid stamps already. Gimme the
     car.

                        RAY
     No. *You* said — that was you — *trickin me* —

                        EMMIT
     Ray.

                        RAY
     What did you get for them anyway? The whole collection. I
     never asked. Two, three dozen stamps? Vintage.

Now Emmit is pissed. Sy sees it, intervenes.

                        SY
     Ray —

Ray sits back, wanting to show he has the power now.

                        RAY
     No. She's a nice girl, a catch, and she deserves a sweet
     ring. Pricey. So are you gonna do what's right here — or are
     you gonna do what's right?

A long beat. The two brothers stare at each other.

          CUT TO:

INT. GRAND ROOM. EMMIT STUSSY'S HOUSE. EDEN PRAIRIE, MN—DAY

Nikki stands by the bar, surrounded by THREE COUNTRY-CLUB TYPES
in suits. They're vying for her affection.

                         MAN #1
          Last winter I shot a moose.

Ray approaches, scowling, takes her arm.

                         RAY
          Come on.

                         NIKKI
          Bye, boys.

          CUT TO:

EXT. EMMIT STUSSY'S HOUSE. EDEN PRAIRIE, MN—DAY

Ray and Nikki exit. A WAITER stands outside with a tray of
champagne glasses for arriving guests. Nikki takes one. A valet
takes Ray's ticket, runs off. Ahead, we see a COUPLE get into a
Bentley, aided by another valet. In all, there are SIX PEOPLE
waiting for their cars.

                         NIKKI
          Did you get it?

                         RAY
          I need a real drink.

Beat. Nikki raises an eyebrow. Ray may be the tough guy at work,
but this alpha male thing doesn't work on her. She gives him **The
Look**. He sees it, wavers.

                         RAY (CONT'D)
      Here's the — it's — not a good time, he said. But, I'm gonna
      — Don't worry. I'll handle it.

We HEAR the *screeee* of a blown transmission before we see THE
CORVETTE. We see Ray shrink a little at the sound of it.

The valet pulls up, puts the car in park. It bucks roughly, then
stops, dark smoke issuing from the tail pipe. The valet gets
out.

Ray starts to go around to the driver's door—wanting to get this
over with—aware of the eyes on them, the judgment. Nikki stands
there. She's not about to open her own door.

                         NIKKI
      Ray.

He looks over, sees her face.

                         RAY
      Sorry.

Ray hurries over and opens her door. She sits. He closes her in,
then goes back to the driver's door. The valet is holding it
open. Ray climbs in, tries to pull the door closed. The valet
resists, holding it open.

                         VALET
      No tip?

                         RAY
      Yeah, get a real job.

He tugs hard, hurting the valet's hand, slams the door.

           CUT TO:

EXT. ROAD. RURAL MINNESOTA—DUSK

Ray's corvette drives back to St. Cloud, the big city.

           ANGLE ON RAY AND NIKKI

in the front seat, not talking. Ray is quiet, re-fighting old
battles in his head. Nikki sits in the passenger seat, reading a
book—*Contract Bridge* by George S. Gooden. Her bare feet are up
on the dashboard.

           ANGLE ON HER PERFECT TOES

Nails smooth and painted.

                              NIKKI
— so that's when we use the Dentist Coup or play a canapé.
And watch out for the Cuthberts. I don't think that cough a
his is real. And whatever happens, don't let those Swedes
force a trump check again.
                         (beat)
Babe?

                              RAY
What?

                              NIKKI
I'm talking about the Wildcat Regional on Thursday. Top
three mixed pairs, we qualify for the Upper Wisconsin Semi-
Professional next month, which — top three in that and the
sport really opens up for us.

                              RAY
Now, hon — you know yer not s'posed ta leave the state.

                              NIKKI
I know, but couldn't ya — I mean, as my P.O. — isn't there a
form you could sign?

                              RAY
                         (pained)
Well, see — there's a lot a sticky — with the first bein,
technically, we're not supposed ta be — you know — datin.
I'm sayin it's mission critical we keep that a secret — so
when it comes ta signing official forms — I mean, talk about
showin yer cards —

                              NIKKI
What are you sayin?

                              RAY
No, just — as ta the legalities — parolee, parole officer,
et cetera — I mean, we're right on the line here.

                              NIKKI
There's big money ta be won, babe.

                              RAY
I know.

                              NIKKI
I'm not talkin a few regionals. We get ourselves on the map
bridge-wise locally in the next few months and I'm talkin
sponsorship opportunities borderin on six figures. Indian
casinos, Vegas, Norway. Then we don't need ta borrow money
from yer stupid brother or nobody else. Right?

He nods, liking the sound of that, but unsure.

                    NIKKI (CONT'D)
          Baby, look at me.

He looks over.

                    NIKKI (CONT'D)
          We're a team.
                    (he nods)
          Simpatico, to the point of spooky. Like how I always know
          when you're gonna lead with a heart or backwards finesse
          — and you got that putter's instinct for when ta drop the
          Murray Applebaum Discovery Play.

                    RAY
          It's true.

                    NIKKI
          Yer the hand and I'm the glove.

                    RAY
          Yer the bottle and I'm the beer.

                    NIKKI
          Or the beer and the glass in my case.

                    RAY
          Right. But it comes in a —

                    NIKKI
          No, I know.

She takes his hand.

NIKKI (CONT'D)
Simpatico.

                    CUT TO:

          ANGLE ON A SMALL PLASTIC CUP

as it's held in a MAN's hand. A beat. URINE comes down in a
stream and fills the cup.

We are in . . .

INT. BATHROOM. PAROLE BOARD. ST. CLOUD, MN—DAY

Ray stands a couple of steps away from an EX-CON who is peeing
into the cup. This is the glamour of Ray's job.

                    CUT TO:

          ANGLE ON A BUNCH OF BANANAS

A pricing gun comes into frame, prices them.

We are in . . .

INT. RED OWL GROCERY. EDEN VALLEY, MN—DAY

A twelve-year-old boy, NATHAN BURGLE, prices the fruit. In
the background, we see his grandfather, ENNIS, ringing up a
customer.

                    CUT TO:

INT. RAY'S OFFICE. PAROLE BOARD. ST. CLOUD, MN—DAY

Ray sits across from a bearded MENNONITE EX-CON, interviewing
him about his progress since the last meeting. The guy is
clearly making excuses, just going on and on.

                         CON
          — but what could I do? The land was fallow and we needed
          grain.

Ray reaches for his coffee.

          ANGLE ON THE CUP

as it leaves frame, we see a coffee ring left on a file folder.

                    CUT TO:

INT. BATHROOM. PAROLE BOARD. ST. CLOUD, MN—DAY

The Mennonite pisses in a cup.

CLOSE ON RAY

He has to watch.

CUT TO:

INT. RED OWL GROCERY. EDEN VALLEY, MN—DAY

Nathan sits behind the counter playing a game on his phone.
Ennis shelves fifths of liquor on the back wall.

ANGLE ON ENNIS

He looks over, sees Nathan isn't looking, unscrews the cap on a
bottle and takes a swig, then closes it and puts it on the shelf
with the others.

CUT TO:

INT. RAY'S OFFICE. PAROLE BOARD. ST. CLOUD, MN—DAY

A FEMALE EX-CON sits across from Ray, putting on lipstick while
she talks nonstop. She's got her makeup kit out and does
herself up.

> FEMALE CON
> — which, I didn't even know that was illegal, because who
> makes the laws anyway — a person in their own home — on
> their own property — I mean, shorta murder shouldn't ya be
> able ta — ya know — just about anything?

                    CUT TO:

EXT. HALLWAY. PAROLE BOARD. ST. CLOUD, MN—DAY

Ray stands in the hall outside the ladies' room. The door opens
and the ex-con comes out, followed by a FEMALE PAROLE OFFICER. The
ex-con hands Ray her piss roughly, and <u>it spills all over him</u>.

                    ANGLE ON RAY

fuming about his fucking life.

                    ANGLE ON A FORM

A STAMP comes down. REVOKED.

                    ANGLE ON RAY

facing the woman. *How do you like them apples?*

ANGLE ON THE WOMAN

as the FEMALE PAROLE OFFICER takes her by the arm and leads her
out of the office, on her way back to prison.

                    CUT TO:

INT. RED OWL GROCERY. EDEN VALLEY, MN—DAY

Nathan closes the cash register drawer. Ennis is sleeping it
off behind the counter. A CUSTOMER exits through the automatic
doors. Nathan picks up a mop.

                    ANGLE ON THE GLASS DOORS

We see a woman, GLORIA BURGLE (30s), approach in a winter coat
and tuque. She's a practical woman, the one who grabs the fire
extinguisher when the bacon catches fire and everyone else
panics.

She steps up to the automatic doors. THEY DON'T OPEN. She
frowns, steps back, tries again. Nothing. She waves at the
sensors. It's like she's invisible.

                    ANGLE ON NATHAN

He notices, puts the mop down. He walks up to the doors. They
open easily. Gloria enters.

                              GLORIA
          That's weird, huh? You ready?

Nathan nods, puts the mop away. Ennis wakes, sits up wiping his
mouth.

                          GLORIA (CONT'D)
          See ya tonight, Pops?

                              ENNIS
          If macaroni and cheese don't float yer boat, might as well
          stay home.

They exit.

          CUT TO:

EXT. BAR. ST. CLOUD, MN—DAY

Ray's Corvette screeches into the parking lot, parks.

          CLOSE ON RAY

as he gets out, looks at the bar.

          CUT TO:

INT. BAR. ST. CLOUD, MN—DAY

Ray enters, looks around. It's not a nice place. He sees—

          ANGLE ON A MAN

MAURICE LEFAY (40s), sitting in a booth. There are two empty beer
bottles in front of him, and a WAITRESS puts down a fresh one.

Maurice is a stoner, his already dulled intellect hobbled
further by all the greenery he smokes. He's wearing a faded
T-shirt that reads *Russia Is for Lovers*.

          RAY

approaches. Maurice doesn't look up. He's just turning his
silver lighter between the fingers of his right hand, and
tapping it on the table over and over, hypnotized.

                              RAY
          Maurice.
                         (beat, louder)
          Maurice!

                            MAURICE
                         (looks up)
          Huh? Oh. Hey, Ray.

Ray takes a folded piece of paper from his pocket, drops it on the table.

                    RAY
          Ya blew yer piss test, pal.

Maurice unfolds the paper, but he already knows what it says.

                    MAURICE
          Bummer. Look —

                    RAY
          A thing like that — normally that gets ya right away
          revoked, but I thought maybe call him up, see what he has ta
          say.

Maurice studies him. He knows nothing in this life is free.

                    MAURICE
          Yeah. Cool, cool.

Maurice looks around.

                    MAURICE (CONT'D)
          Hey — how come we're meetin in a bar?
                    (off Ray)
          Not in the office, I mean.

Beat. Ray sits. He takes Maurice's beer, tips it back.

                    MAURICE (CONT'D)
          I was drinkin that.

Ray drinks the whole thing. He needed that. He puts down the
bottle.

                    RAY
          Let's cut to the quick here. Yer last stretch was six and a
          half fer breakin inta rich folks' digs, and stealin their
          flat screens.

                    MAURICE
          Allegedly.

                    RAY
          No — moron — how it works is — when they convict ya it turns
          into a fact.

He gestures to the waitress for another beer.

                    RAY (CONT'D)
          Now look — I got a place — turns out — a place that needs
          some robbin. A little robbin. Not wholesale burglary. Just a
          specific — just lookin fer a certain item — and if ya do it —

He takes the paper from Maurice, tears it in half.

                    RAY (CONT'D)
     Let's just say yer little problem goes up in smoke.

Maurice studies him.

                    MAURICE
     What are we talkin about?

                    RAY
                   (big deal)
     A stamp.

                    MAURICE
     Cool, cool. Like a — postage stamp?
                   (beat, off Ray—*yes*)
     Okay. So — I mean, I know I'm the moron, but —

                    RAY
     It's not that kind a stamp, numbnuts. It's got — ya know —
     sentimental value. To me.
                   (beat)
     It's my stamp.

                    MAURICE
     Yer stamp.

                    RAY
     Yeah. But it's — ya know — at someone else's house.
     Temporarily.

                    MAURICE
     Cool. Cool. So — why not just ask fer it back.

Beat. Ray stares at him.

                    RAY
     It's, ya know, complicated. Just — get the damn stamp.

          CUT TO:

INT. EMMIT STUSSY'S HOUSE. EDEN PRAIRIE, MN—NIGHT

Stella is cleaning up after supper. Emmit sits at the dinner
table reading some business papers. The TV is on. MOMMA, the
mother-in-law, sits in her wheelchair being fed by the nurse.

The phone rings. Stella answers.

          ANGLE ON EMMIT

reviewing their financials.

                              STELLA (O.S.)
Hon?

                              EMMIT
What's that, hon?

                              STELLA
I said, Sy's on the phone.

Emmit stands, takes the receiver.

                              EMMIT
What's cookin?

                              SY
Ya need ta come down here.

                              EMMIT
Nine o'clock at night, isn't it?

                              SY
The number. Clicks and buzzers. He came.

                              EMMIT
Who?

                              SY
The fella from the —

                              EMMIT
Ermentraub?

                              SY
No. Different fella. Don't wanna say too much on the phone.
Just — ya better come down here.

The line goes dead.

                              STELLA
Everythin okay?

                              EMMIT
                           (hangs up)
Gotta go to the office, hon.

He grabs his car keys off the ring, opens the back door.

                              STELLA
Hon?

                              EMMIT
What's that?

                              STELLA
          Yer in yer house shoes.

He looks down.

                    ANGLE ON FUZZY HOUSE SHOES

Not the kind of shoes to wear to a business meeting.

                              EMMIT
          Good call.

He goes to change.

          CUT TO:

EXT. EMMIT STUSSY'S HOUSE. EDEN PRAIRIE, MN—NIGHT

Emmit's car pulls out of the driveway. We PAN to the RED BRICK
GATE and find the address.

STUSSY 914 MAIDEN LANE

          CUT TO:

          HEADLIGHTS ON THE OPEN ROAD

as the car moves through the night.

          CUT TO:

INT. MAURICE'S CAR (TRAVELING). RURAL MINNESOTA—NIGHT

          WE START ON A PIECE OF PAPER ON THE CENTER CONSOLE.

Emmit Stussy

914 Maiden Lane

Eden Prairie, Minnesota.

PAN UP to find Maurice driving. He's smoking a joint and seems
to be talking to himself.

                              MAURICE
          You ever think about how they never put the morgue on the
          top floor of a hospital? I notice stuff like that. It's
          always in the basement, with, like, its own elevator.

A VOICE responds through the car's Bluetooth.

                         THERAPIST (O.S.)
          And how does that make you feel?

                         MAURICE
        Huh? No. It's — what I'm sayin is — you asked me how I
        define the person called *me*, and I'm sayin I'm always having
        thoughts. Whatdya — insightful.
                              (smokes)
        For example, where does the president of the United States
        buy clothes? Do they shut down like the whole J.C. Penney,
        just so he can try on a suit?

                         THERAPIST (O.S.)
        There's a tailor. He comes to the White House.

Maurice peers through the windshield. It's getting harder and
harder to see. He waves at the smoke.

                         MAURICE
        Now see, I didn't know that.

                         THERAPIST (O.S.)
        Let's — focus. So when you say your parole officer was mean
        to you before, how did that make you feel?

                         MAURICE
        Ya know, man — just — not good, ya know. I mean, here I am.
        I'm tryin, ya know. A new leaf. Not hurtin anybody. I have,
        but, ya know, not currently. Change and all that — growth.
        So —

A long toke. Maurice waves at the smoke, which gets in his eye.

                         THERAPIST (O.S.)
        Are you getting high?

He starts coughing.

                         MAURICE
        No.

He ROLLS DOWN THE WINDOW to clear the car.

        ANGLE ON THE CAR

from outside, in the rear, SMOKE POURS OUT.

                         THERAPIST (O.S.)
        Maurice?

        INSIDE THE CAR

A strong wind blows in.

ANGLE ON THE PAPER

with the address written on it. It lifts up in the wind, turns a
little circle in mid-air and is then sucked out the window.

Maurice tries to grab it, misses.

                         MAURICE
    Shit.

He swerves, almost crashes, before stopping.

         CUT TO:

EXT. SIDE OF THE ROAD. RURAL MINNESOTA—NIGHT

Pitch-black, except for the car's headlights. Maurice has parked
on the shoulder. We can see him in the beams, searching the
white snow for the white page with the address. From the car we
hear a faint—

                         THERAPIST (O.S.)
    Maurice?

Maurice searches some more, but it's hopeless. He straightens.

                    MAURICE
         Screw it. I remember.

He walks back to the car. We DROP DOWN to find the piece of
paper in the foreground, flapping in the breeze.

              CUT TO:

INT. KITCHEN. ENNIS'S HOUSE. EDEN VALLEY, MN—NIGHT

A small house, basically a geriatric bachelor pad. The kitchen
is small, cluttered. There's a CRAFT TABLE against one wall,
where Ennis builds models.

Ennis sits at the round dining table with his grandson Nathan.
They've eaten dinner. Nathan opens a small BOX. Inside is a
PRESENT from his grandfather.

It's a wood carving of a man standing next to another wooden
figure, who's lying on the ground.

                    NATHAN
         Cool.

                    ENNIS
         Trash is under the sink if you hate it.

                    NATHAN
         No, it's — what is it?

                    ENNIS
         Nothin. Just a dumb thing I made.

Gloria brings over two plates of supermarket angel food cake
with strawberries and Cool Whip.

                    GLORIA
         Somethin special fer the clean plate club.

She puts the dessert in front of the two of them. Ennis pokes at
his, scowling.

                    ENNIS
         Told ya. I don't like strawberries.

Gloria picks up his plate, unfazed.

                    GLORIA
         More for me then.

She sits, digs in.

                         GLORIA (CONT'D)
So, like I said, the thinkin is — absorb the local precinct
into the larger county force.

                         ENNIS
Leaving you jack shit.

                         GLORIA
Language. No, I'd — I'd still be the highest ranking, you
know, local officer — just not —

                         ENNIS
Chief.

                         GLORIA
Right.
                      (to Nathan)
Whatdya got there?

                         NATHAN
Model Grandpa made me.

                         ENNIS
Like I said, it's just a stupid carvin, rememborin the time
we went campin.

Gloria pats his hand. He acts gruff, but she knows Ennis loves
the boy.

                         GLORIA
                      (to Nathan)
So don't forget, yer at yer dad's this weekend. He and Dale
are gonna take ya ta the symphony.

Nathan nods, eating.

                         NATHAN
Is Dale my other dad now?

                         GLORIA
Well, no. I mean, he and yer dad haven't been together that
long. But if they got married —

                         ENNIS
Not legal, is it? Two men.

                         GLORIA
                      (ignoring him)
If they did — well, ya know how Ennis here is my stepfather
— married my mom after Grandpa passed? Well, I guess Dale
would become yer stepfather.
                      (beat)
I think. I honestly don't know how it works.

                              ENNIS
           I can tell ya how it works in the Bible.

Gloria and Nathan exchange a look. She rolls her eyes. Nathan
smiles.

                              GLORIA
           Another beer, Pops?

Ennis nods.

                              ENNIS
           Now yer speakin English.

           CUT TO:

INT. HOTEL BALLROOM. ST. CLOUD, MN—NIGHT

It's the first round of the Wildcat Regional Bridge Tournament.
We are in a hotel ballroom filled with square folding tables,
resting on the kind of loud print pattern carpeting that
implies.

           ANGLE ON DETAILS

From the room:

—A DECK of CARDS is shuffled.

—A TINY PENCIL is sharpened.

—A SWEATER with knitted playing cards.

—A TOOTHPICK is placed between a man's lips.

—A lot of FLANNEL.

—AN ELDERLY WOMAN adjusts her custom gelled SEAT CUSHION.

—BIDDING CARDS laid into plastic trays.

—A COLORFUL (handmade) SCOREBOARD ranking players, names written
in marker by a man in a sport coat and slacks.

—The PLAYERS, most elderly, but some high schoolers and a
contingent of SWEDISH, KOREAN, and FRENCH ringers.

           ANGLE ON NIKKI SWANGO

entering the room in slow motion. She is dressed to kill. Ray
walks beside her in cowboy boots and a western shirt.

                    CUT TO:

LATER

Nikki and Ray sit at a table. Their first opponent is the MAN
with the toothpick. His partner is a FATTER MAN with a ball cap.
They look at Nikki when she sits like she's the setting sun.

                              NIKKI
                            (smiles)
          Hello, boys.

We see she has an effect on them. The cards are dealt, play
begins. They organize their hands. Nikki makes eye contact with
Ray.

                         NIKKI (CONT'D)
          Two clubs.

                            TOOTHPICK
          Three hearts.

Ray analyzes his cards, thinking about Nikki's opening bid.

                              RAY
          Pass.

The bid moves south.

          ANGLE ON RAY

He checks his phone.

          ANGLE ON PHONE

No messages.

                         NIKKI (O.S.)
          Dummy.

Ray looks up.

                         NIKKI (CONT'D)
          You're the dummy.

Beat. Ray gets it. He lays his cards out on the table.

          CUT TO:

EXT. HIGHWAY. RURAL MINNESOTA—NIGHT

Lit by streetlights, Maurice's car approaches camera.

                           MAURICE (O.S.)
          Okay. This is — I got this.

               CUT TO:

INT. MAURICE'S CAR (TRAVELING)—SAME TIME

Maurice leans forward, scanning the road signs as they pass
overhead. He's stoned in a bad way now.

                           MAURICE
          It was, uh, the guy's name was Stussy, on *something Lane*.
          Like *Midnight Lane*.
                              (beat, thinking)
          No. Bingo — *Maiden Lane*.

               CUT TO:

INT. BAR. ST. CLOUD, MN—DAY (FLASHBACK)

We are back in the bar earlier, looking at the piece of paper as
Ray PUSHES IT towards Maurice. It lays on the table next to an
empty beer bottle.

Emmit Stussy

914 Maiden Lane

Eden Prairie, Minnesota.

               CUT TO:

INT. MAURICE'S CAR (TRAVELING)—NIGHT

Maurice scans the road.

                           MAURICE
          And the town was — something biblical, like — Eden —
          village, or Eden —

               ANGLE ON A ROAD SIGN

A highway exit: **Rt. 23, EDEN VALLEY**, 30 miles.

               ANGLE ON MAURICE

He swerves towards the exit.

                           MAURICE (CONT'D)
          Eden Valley. Triple goddamn bingo.

               ANGLE ON THE ROAD SIGN

as the car passes. *EDEN VALLEY.*

                DISSOLVE TO:

INT. BAR. ST. CLOUD, MN—DAY (FLASHBACK)

We ZOOM IN on the piece of paper Ray gave Maurice.

Emmit Stussy

914 Maiden Lane

We PUSH IN until we see the words.

EDEN PRAIRIE.

                CUT TO:

EXT. ENNIS'S HOUSE. EDEN VALLEY, MN—NIGHT

Gloria and Nathan exit the house. Through the open door we see
Ennis asleep in his easy chair, a blanket over him, the TV on.

                        GLORIA
                       (calling)
        Night, Pop.

Mother and son approach her car, which we now see is a POLICE
PROWLER.

                        NATHAN
        Can I run the siren?

                        GLORIA
        Once. On the highway.

The car drives away. The CAMERA TRACKS along the driveway with
it, letting it turn out onto the road and drive away.

Beat. We watch the taillights, then the CAMERA PANS and we find
ourselves looking at ENNIS'S MAILBOX. It reads—

STUSSY.

                CUT TO:

INT. STUSSY LOTS, LTD. ST. CLOUD, MN—NIGHT

The elevator doors open. Emmit steps off. Sy is waiting.

                        SY
        I put him in yer office.

                        EMMIT
        Who?

                              SY
          Didn't get a name. Here from the lender, he said. I told him
          it was late, but he just got off a plane so —

              ANGLE ON EMMIT'S OFFICE

     as seen through the dividing glass. A MAN sits in a guest chair
     across from the desk. Who he is is hard to make out.

              ANGLE ON EMMIT

     He doesn't like this.

              CUT TO:

     INT. EMMIT'S OFFICE. STUSSY LOTS, LTD. ST CLOUD, MN—NIGHT

     Emmit and Sy enter. The man is V. M. VARGA, 50. Also known as
     The Man Who Wasn't There. Emmit goes around to his desk.

                              EMMIT
          Hey there — Emmit Stussy — thanks for — well, honestly, we
          didn't know if our message —

                              VARGA
          You called the number.

                              EMMIT
          Yeah, we, uh —
                         (glances at Sy)
          — like I said, we didn't —

                              SY
          — all you get — when you call —

                              EMMIT
          — clicks and buzzers, which — hard ta leave a —

     Beat. Varga says nothing.

                         EMMIT (CONT'D)
          But — good news. You're here, and we're in the black now,
          Stussy Corp., and — well, your firm was nice enough — Mr.
          Ermentraub — the broker, he, uh, arranged for yer firm ta
          lend us that money last year, and we're happy to say we're
          ready to pay back in full.

     He smiles at the simplicity of it. Varga shrugs.

                              VARGA
          That's okay.

                                    EMMIT
I'm sorry?

                                    VARGA
You keep it.

                                    EMMIT
Keep — it.

Varga nods. Emmit looks at Sy, as if to say *do something*.

                                    SY
I apologize. I didn't catch yer name.

                                    VARGA
I'm V. M. Varga.

                                    SY
And you work for —

                                    VARGA
With Narwal, yes.

                                    SY
Well, now — it's — see, your firm, Narwal — like I said,
last year we borrowed a hefty, uh — sum, and I know you're
not bona fide FDIC, but, I mean, unless you boys do business
differently in — where are you from?

                                    VARGA
                                    (beat)
America.

He doesn't sound American.

                         SY
          Well, in America, normally, when you lend somebody money —

                         EMMIT
          If that were us, he's saying, in your shoes, well, I'd
          expect the money back — with interest — which — we're happy
          to — like I said — we got it. I just need ta know where to
          send the check.

                         SY
          Or a wire transfer, if you —

                         EMMIT
          Exactly. Just give us the digits.

                         VARGA
          Investment.

A beat. *What did he say?*

                         SY
          One more time?

                         VARGA
          You called it a loan. It wasn't a loan. It was an
          investment. We're investors.

                         EMMIT
          Investors.

                         VARGA
          The problem, I think — you're confusing the word *singularity*
          with the word *continuity*.

                         EMMIT
          What?

Varga realizes he's going to have to dumb it down.

                         VARGA
          The word *begin* and the word *end*, are these the same?

                         EMMIT
          No, but —

                         VARGA
          Then why talk about ending something that's only just begun?

Beat. Sy and Emmit try to process this turn.

                         SY
          See — now — the document we signed last year —

                              EMMIT
— when we met with your broker —

                               SY
Mr. Ermentraub.

                              EMMIT
Buck Lewis introduced us. And he said, your broker — we were
very specific about a short-term —

                               SY
— and nowhere in the document did it say anything about —
and believe me, I'm a lawyer, so you know I vetted it very —

                             VARGA
Well — a document is just a piece of paper.

                               SY
A legally binding — actually — a contract.

                             VARGA
To be clear — you had a problem — as you said — last year.
The real estate business, well, this is a bad business. So
you try the normal channels. The banks — but your company is
still failing. So you come to us.

                               SY
For a loan.

                             VARGA
You never thought to ask why we might lend you a million
dollars with no collateral required.

                               SY
See now, we were under the impression —

                              EMMIT
Our fundamentals are strong, our holdings.

                             VARGA
My point is, that was the time for questions, yes? Not this.
                             (beat)
Now, we've taken the last year to study your business.
Properties, cash flow. So we can better disguise our
activities.

Emmit and Sy exchange a look. *Activities?*

                              EMMIT
Look, we just wanna pay the money back and — you know — be
on our way.

VARGA

As I said, the first sum was an investment for you to keep.
All future funds will be run through your front office,
the same as other Stussy income. A few thousand a month.
More or less. I'll get you the specs and instructions for
how to account for the comings and goings in your software.
We already have access to the system, so we can monitor
activity, make sure you're adjusting.

EMMIT

Uh —

Varga stands.

VARGA

It goes without saying — don't mention this to anybody.

He leaves.

      ANGLE ON EMMIT AND SY

What just happened?

                    CUT TO:

EXT. GAS STATION. EDEN VALLEY, MN—NIGHT

A mom-and-pop shop on a small corner lot. Maurice's car pulls
in.

                    CUT TO:

INT. MAURICE'S CAR. EDEN VALLEY, MN—CONTINUOUS

Maurice climbs out. He goes inside. We are in the backseat.
Through the windshield we see Maurice go inside, talk to the
clerk. The TV is on inside.

The clerk produces a PHONE BOOK. Maurice pages through it, finds
something, tears out the page. The CLERK protests. Maurice
ignores him, then exits the store, comes back to the car and
climbs in.

                    MAURICE
     Malta Road. Malta.

He puts the torn phone book page on the center console.

               INSERT ON THE PAGE

We see **E. Stussy, 15 Malta Rd**.

                    CUT TO:

INT. ENNIS'S HOUSE. EDEN VALLEY, MN—NIGHT

Ennis sleeps in his chair in front of the TV. The camera PUSHES
PAST HIM into the kitchen.

We approach the KITCHEN TABLE. There, where Nathan left it, is
the model his grandpa carved him.

                    CUT TO:

INT. GLORIA'S PROWLER (TRAVELING)—NIGHT

Gloria drives Nathan home. He's texting on his phone.

                    GLORIA
     See now, that always makes me feel queer. Readin in the car.
               (beat)
     Whatdya think about that model yer grandpa made ya? Pretty
     sweet, huh? He's a good guy. I know he drinks too much, but
     I think — well, deep down we've all of us got something
     positive inside us, don'tcha think?

As she's talking, Nathan realizes something. He looks around on the seat, the floor. Gloria notices.

                         GLORIA (CONT'D)
          What's goin on?

                         NATHAN
          The model. I left the model.

His search becomes more frantic. Gloria frowns.

                         GLORIA
          Aw, hon. It's late. Swing by in the mornin, maybe? Pick it up?

                         NATHAN
          No. It's — he made it fer me. I hafta —

Nathan seems unreasonably upset. Gloria nods. He's had a lot of change lately and she thinks she should indulge him. She slows the prowler.

                         GLORIA
          Okay then. Lemme flip a b-word.

                    CUT TO:

EXT. ROAD. EDEN VALLEY, MN—NIGHT

The prowler pulls a U-turn, heads back to Ennis's house.

                    CUT TO:

INT. ENNIS'S HOUSE. EDEN VALLEY, MN—NIGHT

          ANGLE ON THE TV

A sci-fi movie. The camera FINDS Ennis, asleep in his chair. A
SCREAM from the movie wakes him. He sits up, looks around. He's
sober now, or at least as close as he ever comes. He gets up,
shuffles into the kitchen.

He sees the model on the table, picks it up. So much for *he
likes it*. Ennis puts it back on the table, goes to the freezer
to find a drink.

Then HEADLIGHTS illuminate the house, turning in, the lights
raking the walls.

They hit ENNIS and he squints, vodka bottle in hand. Who could
that be at this hour?

                    CUT TO:

INT. HOTEL BALLROOM. ST. CLOUD, MN—NIGHT

Ray and Nikki play bridge. They win the game.

                              NIKKI
          We're doin it, babe. All the way.

Beat. Ray's happy—he has a thought.

                              RAY
          I'm gonna — see a man about a boat.

          CUT TO:

INT. HOTEL BAR. ST. CLOUD, MN—NIGHT

Ray goes to the bar, dials his cell phone. It rings.

                              RAY
          Come on. Answer the phone.

                         MAURICE (O.S.)
                         (voice mail)
          Yello.

                              RAY
          Yeah, it's —

                           MAURICE
          Gotcha — I'm not really on the phone right now. I mean, I
          am, but I'm not, which is — when ya think about it — pretty
          trippy. So —
                              (takes a hit)
          — leave a message.

          Beep.

                              RAY
          Maurice, hi. It's yer parole officer. I, uh, wanted ta maybe
          take a pause on that thing we — not do it, I mean — tonight
          — so — gimme a call as soon as you get this.

          He hangs up. Shit. *Where is this guy?* Nikki comes over.

                             NIKKI
          Babe. They're startin the next round.

                              RAY
             Yeah, I'm — ya know —

          Ray pockets his phone.

                             NIKKI
          We got 'em on the run, but hon, ya gotta focus. These big-
          league sponsors aren't just lookin fer flash. It's about
          seein the whole picture. Strategy. Which is my strength, you
          got the steely gaze, but still —

              ANGLE ON RAY

          He's got to make a choice.

                              RAY
             Yer right, hon. I'm — we got this.

          They put their foreheads together.

                             NIKKI
          Yer twice the man your brother is. Now let's go kick ass.

              CUT TO:

          INT. GLORIA'S PROWLER (TRAVELING)—NIGHT

          Gloria drives back towards Ennis's.

                            GLORIA
          When we get there I'll run in, okay? Ya know how Ennis gets
          when ya wake him up.

Suddenly, HEADLIGHTS hit her (on a collision course) and she
SWERVES as ANOTHER CAR races past in the other direction.

                    CUT TO:

EXT. ROAD. EDEN VALLEY, MN—CONTINUOUS

Gloria's prowler SWERVES off the road, manages to stop on the
shoulder without crashing.

                    CUT TO:

INT. GLORIA'S PROWLER—CONTINUOUS

Gloria turns to Nathan.

                         GLORIA
        Okay?

He nods. Her eyes go the rearview.

                         GLORIA (CONT'D)
        He didn't even stop.

             ANGLE ON THE MIRROR

Red taillights are visible in the distance.

             GLORIA

Picks up her handset.

                         GLORIA (CONT'D)
        Hey Donny, come in.

                         DONNY (O.S.)
                       (on the radio)
        Yeah, Chief.

                    GLORIA
        Yeah, I'm on Malta and some fool nearly ran me off the road.

                         DONNY (O.S.)
        Oh yeah?

                    GLORIA
        Yeah, didn't get a license or nothin. Some kinda sedan. Are
        you —

                         DONNY (O.S.)
        Well, I'm at the precinct, ya know, in case we get a 911.

                    GLORIA
        Sure, well, nothin ta do about it, I guess.

                         DONNY (O.S.)
          I could call the county boys.

                         GLORIA
          And say what? Be on the lookout fer a sedan with taillights?

                         DONNY (O.S.)
          Yeah, good point. Just chalk it up ta bad luck, I guess.

                         GLORIA
          Okay then. See ya tomorrow.

               CUT TO:

EXT. ENNIS'S HOUSE. EDEN VALLEY, MN—NIGHT

The PROWLER pulls in. Gloria gets out.

                         GLORIA
          Back in a sec.

She approaches the house. We track with her.

               ANGLE ON THE FRONT DOOR

hanging open.

               ANGLE ON GLORIA

That's odd. She climbs the front steps.

                         GLORIA (CONT'D)
          Ennis?

Nothing. She goes in.

               CUT TO:

INT. ENNIS'S HOUSE. EDEN VALLEY, MN—CONTINUOUS

The TV is still on. Gloria enters the house.

               ANGLE ON ENNIS'S CHAIR

Empty, his blanket on the floor. The TV is still on. But as we
look around we see that the place has been trashed. All the
cabinets and drawers have been flung open. The closet door is
ajar.

               ANGLE ON GLORIA

as she realizes what she's seeing.

GLORIA

    Jeez, I better —

She hesitates. Should she go back to the car, get her gun?

GLORIA (CONT'D)

    Ennis?

She looks around. There is a metal TROPHY on the floor. She
bends, picks it up, then advances holding the trophy aloft as a
weapon.

    ANGLE ON THE KITCHEN

We can see the stove, but the table is hidden by the wall.
Gloria enters frame and we track with her as she enters.

    CUT TO:

INT. KITCHEN. ENNIS'S HOUSE. EDEN VALLEY, MN—CONTINUOUS

As we come through the door we see Ennis is sitting in a chair,
his back to us. He has been DUCT TAPED to the chair.

ANGLE ON GLORIA

seeing him.

                            GLORIA
    Ennis?

She doesn't run to him, but checks the corners of the room,
making sure they're alone.

ANGLE ON THE WOOD CARVING

on the table.

ANGLE ON GLORIA

She sees it, but goes to Ennis.

ANGLE ON ENNIS

as we come around him in profile and REVEAL his face. His head
is tilted back. His eyes are bugged out, face beet red, blood
vessels burst. His NOSE and MOUTH have been GLUED SHUT.

    ANGLE ON GLORIA

Horrified. She can't believe it.

                    NATHAN

appears in the doorway.

                         NATHAN
         Mom?

                         GLORIA
         Outside. Go outside! Now!

Nathan sees Ennis. Fear hits him, but his mother's voice moves
him. He turns and RUNS OUTSIDE.

              CUT TO:

EXT. ENNIS'S HOUSE. EDEN VALLEY, MN—MOMENTS LATER

Gloria gets Nathan in the prowler, hands him a canister of
pepper spray.

                         GLORIA
         Lock the door. Call Donny and tell him ta radio the state
         police. I'm gonna search the rest a the house.

                         NATHAN
         Mom.

                         GLORIA
         I gotta. I'm chief. Like I said, lock the door. Ya see
         anyone, lean on the horn, okay? Anybody tries fer ya, use
         the pepper spray, just like I taught ya.

He nods. She goes to the trunk, gets her shotgun and flashlight,
slams the trunk.

              CUT TO:

INT. ENNIS'S HOUSE. EDEN VALLEY, MN—MOMENTS LATER

Gloria climbs the stairs to the second floor. There is a bulb on
a chain at the landing. She pulls the chain, then heads up the
hall, checking the rooms.

              CUT TO:

INT. LIVING ROOM. ENNIS'S HOUSE—CONTINUOUS

Gloria comes down the stairs. She looks around, goes into the—

              CUT TO:

INT. STUDY. ENNIS'S HOUSE—CONTINUOUS

a small "office," more of a nook, really. It's where Ennis did

his books for the store. All the papers are on the floor. The
desk drawers have been thrown open.

Gloria looks around.

      ANGLE ON A PAINTING

on the wall.

      GLORIA

studies it, then goes over, leans it away from the wall, <u>looking
for a safe</u>, but the wall is blank.

As she STEPS BACK, the FLOORBOARD creaks under her feet. She
kneels, sweeps the paper away, revealing an old throw rug. She
moves back, lifts the rug away, revealing the old wooden planks.

Gloria presses on them with her hand, until she finds the one
that creaks. She tries it. It's loose. She pries it up, then
the one next to it. Peering into the hole, she clicks on her
flashlight.

      ANGLE ON THE HOLE

Inside is what looks like an old metal box about two feet square.

      GLORIA

takes it out. Beat. She opens it.

      ANGLE ON THE BOX

In it are THREE PILES OF SCIENCE FICTION BOOKS, covers facing up. They are paperbacks of a certain type—pulp fantasies with colorful paintings of robots and tight-shirted women on swirling red planets encircled by rings.

      ANGLE ON GLORIA

This is not what she was expecting.

                GLORIA
   Huh.

Gloria picks up one of the books, looks at it.

      ANGLE ON THE BOOK

It's called PLANET WYH. The author's name is THADDEUS MOBLEY.

On the cover, A ROBOT stands over a prone MAN.

      ANGLE ON GLORIA

She PULLS Nathan's CARVING out of her pocket.

      ANGLE ON THE CARVING AND THE BOOK

The carving matches the two figures on the cover.

      ANGLE ON GLORIA

What does it mean?

      CUT TO:

EXT. NIKKI'S APARTMENT. ST. CLOUD, MN—NIGHT

Ray and Nikki approach her front door. Nikki is giddy, jumping around, hugging him. He seems embarrassed by the public display of affection, but can't hide his happiness.

      ANGLE ON RAY AND NIKKI

through the windshield of a car parked across the street—a telltale air freshener hanging from the mirror.

They go inside.

       CUT TO:

INT. LIVING ROOM. NIKKI'S APARTMENT. ST. CLOUD, MN—NIGHT

It's not a fancy place, but well cared for. We are moving
through the living room, hearing the sound of running water
from the BATHROOM. We pass an OLD AIR CONDITIONER stuck in the
window, plywood on either side—but not airtight. A little BREEZE
blows past us as we pass and sways the curtains.

We find the BATHROOM DOOR, half open, and move towards it.

       CUT TO:

INT. BATHROOM. NIKKI'S APARTMENT. ST. CLOUD, MN—NIGHT

Candle lit. Ray and Nikki are in a jacuzzi bubble bath. He's
lying against her. They are both looking at their phones. Beat.
Ray puts his down, looks around.

                            RAY
    This is nice.

Nikki is typing.

<pre>
                              NIKKI
        Huh? Oh, yeah.
                          (puts her phone down)
        Amazing.

    She picks up her wine.

                              NIKKI (CONT'D)
                          (savoring it)
        Third runner-up, Wildcat Regionals. Just posted it on my
        Facebook.

                              RAY
        We played good.

                              NIKKI
        We didn't just play good. That hand I got — ten hearts —
        that doesn't just happen. That's — whatdya call — fate or
        luck.

                              RAY
        Plus my steely gaze striking fear into the hearts of the
        elderly.

                              NIKKI
        I'm prouda you, mister. You really — you focused. It's like
        I said — simpatico.
                          (marvels)
        Third runner-up.

                              RAY
        In the Olympics that's bronze.

                              NIKKI
        Now, see. That's the kinda thinkin that's gonna take us
        straight to the top.

    Just then they hear the SOUND of the apartment DOOR opening and
    closing.

    Ray looks at Nikki. Is she expecting anyone? She shakes her
    head. They hear FOOTSTEPS approaching the half-closed door.

            ANGLE ON THE HALL

    partially obscured by the door.

            ANGLE ON RAY AND NIKKI

    They both lean to try to see around the door.

            ANGLE ON THE DOOR

    A shadow falls on the wall outside. The door swings open,
    revealing:
</pre>

MAURICE. He comes in like it's no big deal that he's broken in and found them naked in the bath. He may not even notice the state they're in.

                    MAURICE
     So, I got it, Ray. I did — but — I won't lie — it didn't go
     smooth.

He goes over to the closed toilet, tears off some sheets of toilet tissue, lays them on top of the seat. He studies the seat, swaying, then, satisfied, he sits.

Nikki looks at him—Maurice is so stoned he may nod off any second—then turns to Ray.

                    NIKKI
     Ray, there's a man in my bathroom.

                    RAY
     That's — let's not jump ta any conclusions.

                    NIKKI
     Are you sayin he's not a man, or he's not in my bathroom?

                    RAY
     I'm sayin — I can explain.

Maurice fumbles out a cigarette, puts it between his lips.

                    MAURICE
     I had ta — there was some actin required — in throwin the
     gas station attendant off my scent, but —

He pats his pockets, looking for his lighter.

                    NIKKI
     There's no smokin in here.

Maurice fumbles with the lighter, can't get the flame to come
out.

                    MAURICE
     And also — if I'm bein honest — I sure hope that fella with
     the stamps wasn't a friend a yers, Ray, cause — well — let's
     just say, when an ex-con threatens ya, demands the goods —
     well, the smart money says cooperate.

This gets Ray's attention.

                    RAY
     What?

Nikki turns to Ray, processing.

                              NIKKI
                       (*What's going on?*)
Ray.

Maurice finally gets the lighter lit. Now he tries to find the
end of his cigarette with the flame.

                             MAURICE
          I mean, I could say nobody got hurt — that it was, ya know,
          effortless — but I'd hate ta end the night by breakin
          another commandment, so —

Ray stands now, grabs a towel from the rack.

                               RAY
          Now — that wasn't part a the — nobody said anything about
          hurtin —

Nikki studies her fiancé.

                              NIKKI
          Ray. Look at me. What did you do?

Ray wraps the towel around himself.

                               RAY
                          (to Nikki)
          Nothing — I just — gimme a second.

Maurice is nodding off on the toilet, the lit cigarette dangling
out of his mouth.

                          RAY (CONT'D)
          Hey. Shitbird. Wake up.

Maurice snaps awake.

                          RAY (CONT'D)
          What did you do?

                             MAURICE
          Nothin — just, what ya asked, drove out ta Eden Valley and
          robbed yer guy — the rich one — though I gotta say, that
          place wasn't exactly a palace.

                               RAY
          Prairie.

                             MAURICE
          Come again?

                               RAY
          Eden <u>Prairie</u>.

Maurice stares at him. Nikki studies Ray.

                    NIKKI
        Ray, did you hire one of yer parolees to steal money from
        yer brother?

                    RAY
        No. I mean, not money. Just — takin back what's mine.
        The stamp. I told ya that. How he bamboozled me out of a
        fortune, and I just — all these years — I let it go, but no
        more. You need a ring and this is our time.

The truth out, he studies her, worried he's ruined everything.

                    NIKKI
        That is so — romantic. Come here.

He leans down. She kisses him. Maurice watches, smokes.

                    MAURICE
        That's sweet. Although — I mean — "brother" — musta been
        from another mother, cause — man was he old.

Ray looks up.

                    RAY
        What are you talkin about?

                    MAURICE
        But hey, what matters is I got what ya asked, and now you
        can — we tear up the piss test and you can —

Maurice pats his shirt pocket, pulls something out, hands it to
Ray, who studies it.

                    MAURICE (CONT'D)
        — I should prolly get outta town fer a while, if I'm bein
        honest, given the level of uncooperation and consequences
        thereof.

        ANGLE ON A BOOK OF STAMPS

The kind you get at the post office.

        ANGLE ON RAY

He's stunned.

                    RAY
        What the shit is this?

                    MAURICE
        It's — whatdya — stamps.

Ray grabs Maurice's shirt, raises his fist.

                         RAY
          What did you do?

Maurice produces a GUN from his jacket pocket, shows it to Ray.
Ray backs off. Nikki covers herself instinctively.

                         MAURICE
          Look. I'm — don't be — puttin yer hands on me — raisin the
          tone a yer voice — not after the night I had, doin what you
          — the risks I took on accounta you. Your needs.

Ray looks at the gun, then at Maurice.

                         RAY
          Emmit Stussy, Eden Prairie. It's a short drive.
                         (off Maurice)
          I wrote it down.

                         MAURICE
          No. You said —
                         (confused)
          — I did what you said. The address on the — Eden Valley. I
          looked it up. And now — I'm outta pocket here, Ray. I got
          — I think I covered my tracks pretty good, but — and look —
          since ya touched me — I'm gonna hafta demand a dollar value.
          Five thousand, which is — more than fair, considerin that
          fella we robbed is prolly dead.

Ray stands stunned, trying to process what's happened.

          ANGLE ON NIKKI

Now that she has the lay of the land, she makes her move.

                         NIKKI
                         (to Maurice)
          What's yer name, handsome?

                         MAURICE
          Well, now, I'm not sure I should tell ya, on accounta I
          gotta think about coverin my tracks here.

                         NIKKI
          Well, darlin, I've seen yer face, and Ray knows yer name,
          so —

He nods. That makes sense.

                         MAURICE
          It's Maurice.

                              NIKKI
          Okay, Maurice, will you hand me a towel, and we can maybe
          discuss this in the living room like civilized people?

Nikki stands, showing herself to him, naked as the day she was
born. Maurice stares at her. Ray does also. Holy shit.

                          NIKKI (CONT'D)
          Ray. The gun, Ray.

Ray snaps out of it.

                              RAY
          Right.

He lunges to grab the gun, but Maurice is faster. He moves out
of Ray's reach, raising the gun.

                            MAURICE
          Hey, that's not — you tricked me.

Nikki faces him, naked and unflinching. Maurice backs out of the
bathroom.

          CUT TO:

INT. LIVING ROOM. NIKKI'S APARTMENT—CONTINUOUS

Maurice continues towards the door.

                            MAURICE
          Ya got — I'm givin ya till tomorrow ta get my money. Five
          thousand. Otherwise, well — maybe I turn ya in to the cops,
          or shoot ya. Or her. Robbin yer own brother. That's just
          low.

He backs away slowly. They watch him go.

The front door SLAMS. Ray turns to Nikki.

                              RAY
          Now, hon. Lemme explain —

But she grabs a ROBE from the back of the door, and RUNS PAST
HIM, wrapping herself up on the move.

                          RAY (CONT'D)
          Hon?

But Nikki doesn't go to the front door. She runs to the kitchen.
Ray grabs another ROBE, follows her.

INT. KITCHEN. NIKKI'S APARTMENT—CONTINUOUS

Nikki heads for the cabinets.

                              NIKKI
          Three floors, ten seconds per floor.

Ray follows, putting on a robe.

                              RAY
          Hon? What are you — ?

Nikki opens a drawer, searching for something, grabs a flathead
screwdriver.

                              NIKKI
          Then cross the front hall, eight seconds.

Ray reaches to comfort her, imagining she's shaken up by the
break-in.

                         NIKKI (CONT'D)
          Not now.

She pushes past him, running to the window with the air
conditioner sticking out of it.

          ANGLE ON THE WINDOW

She jams the screwdriver between the window frame and the
plywood on one side, leaning on it, trying to loosen the board.

                              RAY
          Hon, what are ya —

                              NIKKI
          Quiet. I'm countin.

And she is, under her breath.

                         NIKKI (CONT'D)
          Twenty-one, twenty-two, twenty-three.

          CUT TO:

INT. STAIRS. NIKKI'S APARTMENT BUILDING—SAME TIME

Maurice reaches the second landing. One to go. But his cigarette
has gone out. Shit. He pauses, tries to re-light it, then sees
it's wet from where Ray grabbed for him, so he pulls it out of
his mouth, drops it on the landing, then descends.

          CUT TO:

INT. LIVING ROOM. NIKKI'S APARTMENT—SAME TIME

Nikki pops the board off one side of the window. The air
conditioner sways, but holds. She reaches for the other board.

                         NIKKI
    Forty-two, forty-three.

Behind her, Ray doesn't know what to make of her actions, or
what to do.

                         RAY
    Can you believe this guy? I gave him a simple — even wrote
    down the damn — and now — just my luck. Just my damn luck.

Nikki starts loosening the other side.

                         NIKKI
                    (to the board)
    Forty-four, forty-five.

          CUT TO:

INT. LOBBY. NIKKI'S APARTMENT BUILDING—SAME TIME

Maurice reaches the front door, opens it.

          CUT TO:

INT. LIVING ROOM. NIKKI'S APARTMENT—SAME TIME

          ANGLE ON THE SCREWDRIVER

digging between the window frame and the board. A screw pops,
then another.

                         NIKKI
    Is he out?

                         RAY
    What?

                         NIKKI
    The other window. Do you see him?

Ray goes over, looks out.

          ANGLE ON THE STREET

Beat. Maurice emerges from the front door.

          ANGLE ON RAY

Seeing him, he realizes what she's doing. His eyes widen. He
turns.

                         RAY
    Yeah. He's — he's coming. Hurry.

He goes to help her, leaning on the board. With a final wrench, the board pops free. The air conditioner wobbles.

                CUT TO:

EXT. STREET. ST. CLOUD, MN—SAME TIME

Three stories below, Maurice slows, flicks his lighter. It flares once, twice, then the flame catches and he lights his cigarette. He takes a deep drag, exhales, then starts to walk.

                CUT TO:

INT. LIVING ROOM. NIKKI'S APARTMENT—SAME TIME

           ANGLE ON THE AIR CONDITIONER

It teeters.

           ANGLE ON RAY AND NIKKI

They exchange a look. Then Ray lifts his foot and GIVES THE AC UNIT a little push with his toe.

The window slides up. The air conditioner FALLS. The camera follows it into a second of BLACK—and then—ROTATES FORWARD to find the street below. The camera is the air conditioner now. And it is flipping end over end, heading for Maurice, who's walking straight into its path.

We rotate up the side of the building, finding the black sky (and before that, Nikki's apartment window—Ray's head popping out to watch), then continues our flip.

                CUT TO:

EXT. STREET. ST. CLOUD, MN—SAME TIME

Maurice takes a few steps, his car visible at the corner, and then—BAM!—the air conditioner flattens him (setting off car alarms on the block).

A long beat. Did that just happen?

                        RAY (O.S.)
      Wooo! Did you see that?

                CUT TO:

INT. LIVING ROOM. NIKKI'S APARTMENT—CONTINUOUS

Ray is leaning out the window.

                              RAY
           Did you — oh my God.

Nikki PULLS HIM in.

                             NIKKI
           Get down. Someone'll see.

Ray is hyperventilating. There's no way Maurice survived.

                              RAY
           Right in the — no way he's — I mean, game over. Holy shit.

Nikki grabs the phone from the counter, dials.

                         RAY (CONT'D)
                          (notices)
           What are you —

She holds up a hand, affects a professional actor's level of
hysteria.

                             NIKKI
           Yes. 9-1-1 — it's — there's been an accident. On the
           sidewalk. The air conditioner — my —

She pushes Ray, covers the mouthpiece.

                        NIKKI (CONT'D)
           Get dressed. You gotta go.

                              RAY
           What?

                             NIKKI
                         (into phone)
           Thank God. It's nine-forty Hanover Street. Hurry, please.

She hangs up, all business.

                        NIKKI (CONT'D)
           It was an accident. I've been tryin ta get the landlord to
           take that unit out fer, like, six weeks. That's on record.
           And tonight — I don't know. It musta come loose somehow.

She shoves him.

                        NIKKI (CONT'D)
                          (to Ray)
           Yer his parole officer. You can't be here. I gave a fake
           name when I rented the place. I got ID.

                              RAY
           That's against — babe, it's a violation of yer — probation.

                         NIKKI
          Ray!

                         RAY
                   (snaps out of it)
          Right. Right. Good call.

Ray grabs his pants off a chair (they undressed in a hurry),
pulls them on.

                         NIKKI
          We'll talk about this later.

He grabs his shirt, gets it on, grabs his shoes, stumbles for
the door.

                         RAY
          You are so — sexy.

She smiles, gestures for him to hurry up.

                         NIKKI
                   (into phone)
          Thank you, Officer. Yes, I'll stay on the line.
                   (covers the mouthpiece, to Ray)
          Don't forget the stamps.

He goes to the bathroom, grabs them off the floor.

                         NIKKI (CONT'D)
          Burn 'em, okay?

He nods. She grabs him, kisses him.

                         NIKKI (CONT'D)
          I love you.

                         RAY
          Baby, you have no idea.

She holds up her hand.

                         NIKKI
                   (into phone)
          Yes, I hear the sirens. Thank you.

She waves to Ray. *Go.*

                         NIKKI (CONT'D)
                   (whispers)
          Back stairs.

Beat. He nods, exits.

                    CUT TO:

EXT. NIKKI'S APARTMENT. ST. CLOUD, MN—NIGHT

We are outside the window, watching as Nikki turns and prepares
to face the cops.

As we do, the CAMERA CRANES BACK, showing the other windows of
the building, some dark, some with people going about their
business. A couple of HEADS are sticking out, looking towards
the street, where a crowd has started to gather around the stain
that used to be Maurice.

SIRENS grow in the distance.

                    CUT TO:

EXT. ENNIS'S HOUSE. EDEN VALLEY, MN—NIGHT

The COUNTY POLICE are there now, TWO CARS. A FORENSIC TEAM is
inside the house. Gloria stands by her prowler. Nathan sits in
the open passenger seat of Gloria's prowler.

DONNY comes over.

                    DONNY
          Forensics is done in the kitchen. They wanna bring Ennis
          out.

                    GLORIA
          Maybe wait till his grandson is out a sight, tell 'em.

                    DONNY
          Roger wilco.

He exits as A GRAY LEXUS pulls up. Gloria's ex-husband, RON,
gets out of the passenger seat. His partner, DALE, is driving.
They go to Nathan. Ron hugs his son. He is a lumberjack of a
man, balding, in a flannel coat. Behind him, Dale is a thin man
in a red down vest, who stands nervously.

Gloria comes over.

                    GLORIA
          Take him to Dale's, huh? I don't know how long —

                    RON
          Whatever ya need. Already turned the lights on in his room.

                    NATHAN
          I wanna stay with Mom.

Gloria bends to talk to him.

GLORIA

No, hon. Mommy's gotta work now.

NATHAN

No.

Gloria hugs him for a long moment, then whispers something in
his ear. He listens and, finally, nods. She stands.

GLORIA
(to Ron)
Let's say no school tomorrow, huh?

Ron nods, leads Nathan back to his car. Gloria watches them go.
She doesn't know what to make of this world anymore. As Dale's
car pulls out, she turns and gets to work.

End of Episode 301

EXT. EMMIT'S HOUSE. EDEN PRAIRIE, MN—DAY

It's morning, snowy and cold. As we look at the
Stussy mansion we hear David Bowie's narration of
Peter and the Wolf.

> DAVID BOWIE (V.O.)
> *Each character in the tale is going to be*
> *represented by a different instrument of the*
> *orchestra.*

> CUT TO:

INT. MASTER BEDROOM. EMMIT'S HOUSE. EDEN
PRAIRIE, MN—DAY

EMMIT STUSSY dresses for the day in slacks and
a sport coat.

> DAVID BOWIE (V.O.)
> *For instance, the bird will be played by the flute.*
> *Like this.*

Music plays.

> ANGLE ON A SHOE HORN
as Emmit uses it to step into his loafers.

> ANGLE ON EMMIT
He pushes the button on a <u>rotating tie rack</u> and
watches as the ties go around and around.

Music continues over—

EXT. RAY'S APARTMENT. ST. CLOUD, MN—DAY

Also morning. We PUSH IN on the downstairs door of a shabby low-slung apartment building.

> DAVID BOWIE (V.O.)
> *Here's the duck, played by the oboe.*

Music plays.

CUT TO:

INT. BATHROOM. RAY'S APARTMENT. ST. CLOUD, MN—DAY

RAY STUSSY stands at the bathroom mirror. We get the sense this is a big moment for him. He takes clippers, trims off his mustache. He studies the result, then lathers and uses a razor to shave himself clean.

Music continues over—

CUT TO:

INT. BEDROOM. RAY'S APARTMENT—DAY

Ray, now clean shaven, takes a suit from a dry
cleaning bag. He puts it on. **NIKKI SWANGO**
enters.

> DAVID BOWIE (V.O.)
> *The cat by the clarinet.*

Music plays.

Nikki helps Ray with his tie as the music plays. Then
she grabs a WIG, helps him put it on.

> CLOSE ON RAY
who now looks very much like his brother, Emmit.
He studies himself in the closet mirror, unsure of
how to feel.

CUT TO:

INT. STUSSY LOTS, LTD. ST. CLOUD, MN—DAY

SY FELTZ studies the scale model of a parking lot.

> DAVID BOWIE (V.O.)
> *The bassoon will represent Grandfather.*

Music plays.

Sy reaches down, re-parks one of the cars. Sensing
movement, he looks up, watches as—

> YURI GURKA

gets off the elevator with two coffees.

> DAVID BOWIE (V.O)
> *The blast of the hunters' shotguns played by the
> kettledrums.*

Music plays.

Yuri goes to the entrance to the east wing, knocks.
MEEMO opens the door. Yuri goes in.

> ANGLE ON SY

as he leans slightly in order to see down the hall.

> ANGLE ON THE HALL

As the door closes, we see briefly that a large COPY
MACHINE is running. A COMPUTER ROOM is lit up
behind it.

Music continues over—

CUT TO:

INT. RESTAURANT. ST. CLOUD, MN—DAY

V. M. VARGA sits in a booth. A WAITRESS comes
over carrying plates. She puts a plate of steak and
eggs in front of him, a plate of hot cakes on another.
Pie. A side of bacon. Potatoes. Enough food for three
people.

> DAVID BOWIE (V.O.)
> *The wolf by the French horns.*

Music plays.

> ANGLE ON VARGA

We are looking at him low across the plates as he
studies his feast. WE PUSH TOWARDS him as he
begins to eat, ravenously, like an animal.

Music continues over—

CUT TO:

INT. BATHROOM. RESTAURANT. ST. CLOUD—LATER

We PUSH TOWARDS a STALL. The door is closed.

INSIDE we see Varga take a silk handkerchief from
his pocket. He lays it on the floor in front of the
toilet. He kneels carefully, tucks his tie into his shirt,
between the buttons.

It is a ritual we are witnessing. A controlled loss of
control. A scientific purge.

Then he leans forward and makes himself vomit up
all he has eaten.

Afterwards he wipes his mouth, stands. He picks up
the handkerchief and carefully folds it.

MOMENTS LATER he washes his hands, dries them
and adjusts his tie. He sprays breath spray into his
mouth—one squirt, two.

Music continues over—

CUT TO:

EXT. TWO-LANE ROAD. RURAL MN—DAY

An EDEN VALLEY prowler heads north.

Music continues over—

CUT TO:

INT. POLICE PROWLER (TRAVELING)—DAY

GLORIA BURGLE drives.

> DAVID BOWIE (V.O.)
> *And Peter by the strings.*

Music plays.

Gloria drives, lost in thought on her way to the big
city.

> DAVID BOWIE (V.O.)
> *Are you sitting comfortably? Then I shall begin.*

*Music plays, but this time it's our sweeping Fargo
theme as we—*

CUT TO:

TWO MEN GO TO SEE A RABBI.
They're having an argument they need
him to settle. The rabbi listens as both
men make their arguments. Then he
tells the first man you're right.

But before the man can gloat the rabbi turns to the second man and says you're also right. Overhearing, the rabbi's wife comes into the room and yells at her husband. Both men can't be right. It's impossible. The rabbi turns to her and says *YOU ARE ALSO RIGHT.*

Fargo, Season 3

PARTICLE PHYSICS OR HOW ELECTRONS ARE LIKE PEOPLE. There is a theory in physics that states electrons can be proven to exist only when they are interacting with other electrons. The rest of the time, as they move freely through space, electrons are impossible to observe and therefore *may not exist*. In other words, electrons are real only when they collide with other electrons.

The same can be said, metaphysically, about people, especially **GLORIA BURGLE**. We are most real when we are together, and less real when we are alone. This is the origin of Minnesota Nice in some ways—a small community isolated in a frozen tundra. Their response? An exaggerated sense of friendliness—they are particles bouncing vigorously off each other to form a heightened togetherness as a defense against the alternative, which is ceasing to exist.

And let's be honest, Gloria Burgle is increasingly alone these days. She's losing people, in fact. A year ago, her husband left her for another man, so now she splits custody of her son—one week on, one week off. And to top it off, the only family she had left, her stepfather, has just been killed. As a result, Gloria is an electron floating free in space. And in those moments of isolation, she wonders—*Am I really here?*

INT. WOMEN'S ROOM. PAROLE OFFICE. ST. CLOUD, MN—DAY

Gloria exits the stall, goes to the sink. She waves her hands under the automatic soap dispenser. Nothing happens.

We hear peeing from a stall, then a woman's voice.

> WINNIE (O.S.)
> Oh Lord, my Lord. It's a test. Yer test. And we will rally.

Gloria tries the faucet. Nothing. She waves her hands with more verve.

> GLORIA
> C'mon already.

> WINNIE (O.S.)

> (calling)
> You wouldn't — friend? — you wouldn't have a putter-inner by chance?

Gloria realizes the woman is talking to her.

> GLORIA
> How's that?

> WINNIE (O.S.)
> Or a pad? It's — well, this is not the way things were meant to go, but the Lord must have his — (reasons) — not to get — anyway, if you could find yer way clear to abettin a sister in need. One who was s'posed to be with child, but — apparently — is not.

> GLORIA
> Sorry. I don't have — regulations, you know. We're not meant to carry a purse

and I'm — it's not my — time of the — I could ask the clerk. She might have —

WINNIE (O.S.)
No. It's — don't burden yerself.

We hear the TP roll being rolled out from inside the closed stall, then pants fastening. Gloria waves her hands under the soap and water some more with no result.

The stall door opens. We see WINNIE LOPEZ of the ST. CLOUD POLICE DEPARTMENT. From her strong Minnesota accent you'd never guess she was Latina. Winnie is what we call unfiltered, having none of the Lutheran temperance and reserve that normally defines the region.

She comes out of the stall, hiking up her utility belt.

WINNIE (CONT'D)
Well, what are the odds? A second female in uniform. You said "regulation" and I assumed —

She offers her hand.

WINNIE (CONT'D)
Winnie Lopez, St. Cloud Metro.

Gloria holds up her hands, as if to say you don't want to shake these.

GLORIA
Gloria Burgle, Eden Valley police.

Winnie checks her badge.

WINNIE
And chief to boot.

GLORIA
Fer about thirty-six more hours.

Winnie reaches back, adjusts her pants.

WINNIE
Sorry, I got about a hundred pounds a TP crammed in there.

She puts her hands under the automatic soap dispenser. She gets a nice stream of foam. The faucet goes on.

WINNIE (CONT'D)
I been cranky as a female dog since breakfast. Now I know why. We been tryin — me and Jerry — for months now. Like those old Roadrunner cartoons with the wolf and sheepdog. How they punch a clock ta go to work. Mostly missionary, if I'm bein honest. We used ta spice it up, but these days it's about the shortest distance between two points.

GLORIA
I've — uh —

WINNIE
He'd pop faster from the back, if I'm bein honest, but I think it's important to look each other in the eye when it comes ta makin babies. You got kids?

GLORIA
Uh, one. Nathan. He's twelve.

Winnie waves her hand under the automatic towel dispenser, dries.

WINNIE
That's what Jerry wants. A shortstop. Or maybe a switch hittin third baseman. I got my fingers crossed for a girl.
(throws out the towel)
Well, I better hit it. Here on a 10.30 — leavin the scene of an accident — except the vic don't wanna press charges, turns out, so — you?

GLORIA
Uh, murder.

WINNIE
Jeez.

GLORIA
Yeah.

Beat. Winnie hikes up her utility belt.

WINNIE
Well, happy trails.

She exits. Gloria gives one more attempt to get soap or water to come out. Nothing.

These concepts of physics and philosophy will come to define the third year of *Fargo*. The notions of quantum mechanics, Heisenberg's uncertainty principle, Niels Bohr's quantum leaps, the idea that there are no certainties, only varying levels of probability. You see, just as the paths that electrons take cannot be predicted with full certainty, neither can the paths of men. We can only ever calculate the *probability* of where they will appear. This is also true of the way we tell stories in the *Fargo* universe. There is an element of unpredictability, of randomness that cannot be overstated. Multiple particles on a collision course, but when they will collide and in what order we can never predict for sure. This echo between particle physics and humanity will be explored in great depth this season, both overtly and covertly.

EXT. SPACE—DAY/NIGHT

Stars twinkle in the vast blackness. A SPACESHIP passes through frame, trailing smoke. We FOLLOW IT and discover a green and blue PLANET. The SHIP descends.

      AT GROUND LEVEL

We find the ship, sticking out of the ground. It has crashed.

The CAPTAIN lies beside it, grievously wounded. The ANDROID MINSKY, a robot, stands nearby. It has been designed to be friendly and unintimidating.

           CAPTAIN
          (calls weakly)
Minsky.

           MINSKY
I can help!

           CAPTAIN
I'm dying. I need —

He is racked by coughs. The ROBOT scans him with a light ray, makes some beeping sounds.

> CAPTAIN (CONT'D)
> No. It's too late for me. You must find a way to get word back.
> (coughs)
> Let them know — it wasn't all for nothing.

He dies.

> ANGLE ON MINSKY

Beat. It pokes him. He's dead. Beat.

> MINSKY
> I can help!

We will explore this idea of real and unreal through another character, in some ways the polar opposite of Gloria. Because where Gloria wants to be *more* connected to the world around her, **V. M. VARGA** goes out of his way to remain isolated. He is *The Man Who Doesn't Exist*. He never shakes hands, wouldn't hug his mother (if he had a mother) or engage in physical intimacies of any kind. Varga, a man in his fifties, is a new kind of criminal—international, low profile, borderline invisible. He is a mover of money through electronic channels. And unlike the flashy criminal masterminds of old, Varga flies coach, dresses like Willy Loman, moving between blandly furnished townhouses around the world, under-tipping. He has settled in Minnesota because it is the blandest, safest, most stable and least remarkable place in the world.

Varga, we propose, is the next step in capitalism. Just as the corporation supplanted the family business in season 2, so now does this invisible man (a man without a country)—whose wealth exists in bitcoins and digital transfers, who is everywhere and nowhere at once—supplant the bulky inelegance of the corporate structure. He is capitalism reduced to its purest form, a shark that exists purely to eat, a man who fluctuates between states of existence and nonexistence.

INT. STUDY. EMMIT'S HOUSE. EDEN PRAIRIE, MN—NIGHT

Emmit sits behind his desk. Varga wanders the room, studying things.

> EMMIT
> You think I'm gonna make you a partner? In my firm? You just blew in on the wind Thursday.

He grabs for the phone.

> EMMIT (CONT'D)
> I'm callin Sy.

> VARGA
> And here I thought you were the boss.

Emmit hesitates.

> VARGA (CONT'D)
> In the favelas of Brazil there are six-year-olds with Glocks. They rove in packs, stealing anything they can find. Mexican lowlifes stream into this country, like wolves, eyeing our women and children. In Congo, a family of six lives on ten cents a day. Turn on the TV, what do you see? Boat people, mass migration. You're living in the age of the refugee, my friend.

> EMMIT
> Look, if you don't wanna take yer money back, well — I can't make ya —

> VARGA
> You see it, don't you? Millions of people bought houses they couldn't afford and now they're living on the street. Eighty-five percent of the world's wealth is controlled by one percent of the population. What happens when these people wake up and realize you've got their money?

> EMMIT
> Hey, I just charge for parking.

> VARGA
> You think they're gonna ask questions when they come with pitchforks and torches? You live in a mansion. You drive a ninety-thousand-dollar car.

> EMMIT
> It's a lease, through the company.

VARGA
Look at me. This is a two-hundred-dollar suit. I wear a secondhand tie. I fly coach. Not because I can't afford first class, but because I'm smart. So look at you and look at me, and tell me who's richer?

EMMIT
I feel like this is a trick question.

VARGA
There's an accounting coming, Mr. Stussy. You know I'm right. Mongol hordes descending. What are you doing to insulate yourself? Your family? You think you're rich? You have no idea what rich is. Rich is a fleet of private planes filled with decoys to mask your scent. It's a bunker in Wyoming and another in Gstaad. So that's action item one. The accumulation of wealth. And I mean *wealth*, not money.

EMMIT
What's action item two?

VARGA
To use your wealth to become invisible.

Varga travels with two bodyguards, the Ukrainian-born **YURI**, and **MEEMO**, an Indonesian, both orphans of poverty adopted off the streets, because starving dogs are the most loyal. Like Lorne Malvo, Varga has a fascination with human weakness. It is our own humanity, he believes, our dogged connection to each other, to ideas like love and family, that keeps us from reaching our full potential. Varga sees himself as *more real* because his impact is global. Having a small, local impact on the world—being a good husband, a good father—is the same as having no impact at all in his mind.

in CONVERSATION with Carol Case (Series Costume Design, Seasons 1–3)

NOAH: I remember sending you an email saying, "What if we dress Yuri mostly in sporty stuff like a baseball jacket." You know the things you'd think Americans would wear if you were coming from Eastern Europe with no idea of how Americans dress.

CAROL: We tried having him and Meemo both [in] varsity coats at one point and that didn't work. It worked much better to have them dress differently.

INT. STUSSY LOTS, LTD. ST. CLOUD, MN—DAY

The elevator doors open. SY FELTZ exits, approaches his office. Through the glass he sees V. M. VARGA behind his desk. Varga has his feet up and is examining a framed photo of Sy's wife.

Sy's hackles go up. He—

INT. SY'S OFFICE. STUSSY LOTS, LTD. ST. CLOUD, MN—CONTINUOUS

—storms into his office.

> SY
> What the goddamn hell?

Too late he realizes that YURI and MEEMO are also in the room, flanking him from behind on either side of the door. Sy feels threatened, but he tries to hold the moral high ground.

> ANGLE ON VARGA
> who studies the photo.

> VARGA
> You have a fat wife.

> SY
> Excuse me?

> VARGA
> Which part of what I said is giving you trouble?

> SY
> This is my office.

Varga puts down the framed photo.

> VARGA
> A fat woman is inherently untrustworthy, as she is a sensualist who sees no real difference between a pastrami sandwich and a dick in the mouth.

> SY
> That's — there's no call for that kind of — language.

Varga reaches for a coffee mug that reads "World's Best Dad!" He SLIDES IT across the table towards himself.

> VARGA
> The female Jew is especially vulnerable to the zaftig seduction of the forbidden — being part animal.

Varga stands. He unzips his pants.

> SY
> What are you doing?

Varga holds Sy's eye as he pulls his cock and balls from his pants and dips them inside the mug.

> VARGA
> Do you know what a chicken is?

> SY
> (in shock)
> What?

> VARGA
> A chicken. Do you know what a chicken is?
> (off Sy, stunned)
> A chicken is an egg's way of making another egg.

He repacks his member, then zips up.

> VARGA (CONT'D)
> It's a question of perspective, you see. The chicken sees things one way. The egg another. So let's start again. This isn't your office. Just as your wife wouldn't be your wife if I came to her in the night with a platter of cold cuts.

Varga glances at Yuri, who is instantly at Sy's elbow.

> YURI
> Sit, my friend. You have shock. All is well.

He helps Sy sit down.

> SY
> I just — I'm not — I need a minute to —

Yuri pours water from a pitcher into the tainted mug. Varga has turned to the window and is looking out.

YURI
No problem. No problem.

Yuri offers the mug to Sy.

VARGA
Have a drink. You'll feel better.

Sy recoils.

SY
I'm not — (drinking that) — are you out of
your mind?

Yuri looks at Meemo, who pulls his jacket back
to reveal a sidearm in a holster.

YURI
A nice drink, refreshing.

SY
(sees the gun)
That's — are you threatening me?

Meemo PULLS his 9mm, CHAMBERS A ROUND,
the sound loud in the glass-walled room. Sy
can't believe what's happening. Panicked, he
looks at Yuri.

ANGLE ON YURI

He smiles encouragingly—Sy's best friend—
and offers Sy the mug.

SY
takes it. Slowly, reluctantly, he puts it to his
lips, takes a small sip.

YURI
No.

Yuri tips the mug up from the bottom. Sy has
no choice but to drink.

YURI (CONT'D)
The whole thing.

He forces the water into Sy, some of it spilling
down Sy's shirt. When it's done, Yuri takes
the mug away as Sy stumbles to his feet,
coughing, sputtering.

SY
Jesus.

VARGA
Yuri tells me you spoke to the police
yesterday.

Sy freezes. For the first time he truly realizes
the inescapable danger of his situation.

SY
That's — you can ask them — she came
to me, not about — anything — but there
was a — one of our cars was — some
kind of accident — a fender bender — so,
you know, unconnected to — this —
completely.

Varga sits behind his desk.

VARGA
You may have, during the course of the
day, a strong impulse to act. It's perfectly
normal. A man of your station, forced to
play the cuckold. Resist. Remember, it's a
matter of perspective. What's happening
here is good. You and I are partners
now. Contracts have been signed by the
majordomo himself. So you see, lives are
changing for the better. All you have to
do is review the accounts, write up the
deals, and approve the paperwork. Do
you understand?

SY
I —

Beat. He looks at them, nods.

VARGA
Good. Yuri will show you to your new
office.

Sy turns, stunned.

VARGA (CONT'D)
Don't forget your mug.

Beat. It's not optional. Sy comes over, retrieves
his mug—*World's Best Dad!*—and holding it,
follows Yuri out of the office, Meemo bringing
up the rear.

EMMIT STUSSY, the parking lot king of Minnesota, entered V. M. Varga's orbit when Emmit was at his lowest point. It was the financial crash of 2008. Real estate was in the toilet and Emmit's business was on the verge of collapse. Varga offered him a loan—but instead of a simple payback plan, Varga makes Emmit's company part of a complex money-laundering operation.

Emmit's business partner warned Emmit about taking the money, but Emmit was desperate, so he took the loan (thinking it a onetime transaction) only to now find himself a small but continuing part of Varga's complex operations—a vast network of underhanded interests around the world that turn criminal gains into bland Midwestern profit.

INT. FOYER. EMMIT'S HOUSE—MOMENTS LATER

Emmit opens the front door. Varga is outside, holding his briefcase.

> VARGA
> I feel like maybe we started poorly.

Emmit looks back to make sure no one can hear them.

> EMMIT
> Jesus. It's dinnertime.

Varga sniffs the air.

> VARGA
> Schweinekoteletts.
> (explains)
> Pork chops.

> EMMIT
> And applesauce. But that's not the —

Varga stands.

> VARGA
> Brilliant. We can talk while we eat.

EMMIT
Now that's not — just a goddamn — a step too far is what this is. Comin ta my home.

VARGA
Why do I feel you're not happy we met — when all I want is to make you rich?

EMMIT
Look around, I'm already rich.

VARGA
No. You're not.

CUT TO:
INT. KITCHEN. EMMIT'S HOUSE. EDEN PRAIRIE, MN—NIGHT

Varga sits with Emmit and Momma at the kitchen table. Stella brings over a plate for him.

STELLA
I wish you'd let us sit at the real table. In the dining room.

VARGA
I'll tell you a secret, madam. I was a housemaid's boy, ate three meals a day in kitchens below ground. So, my dear, you're making me feel right at home.

This pleases her. She sits. Varga begins wolfing down his food. He turns to Momma.

VARGA (CONT'D)
And how are you this evening, young lady?

STELLA
That's Momma. The matriarch. But she doesn't talk. Not since the stroke.

VARGA
What a shame. I'm sure she had a lovely speaking voice.

STELLA
(to Emmit)
I wish you'd told me about company.

VARGA
That's my fault, missus. I have a tendency to drop in unannounced, but Emmit

and myself, we have some amazing opportunities ahead of us, and you know how they say *time is money*.

STELLA
Really.

EMMIT
I don't wanna talk business in front of them.

STELLA
Emmit. Don't be rude.
(to Varga)
I don't mean to gossip, but are you — English by any chance?

VARGA
What gave it away?

She laughs. He's charming her.

VARGA (CONT'D)
I like to think of myself as a citizen of the world. London, Manila, Johannesburg, Tokyo, Rome.

STELLA
Have you been all those places?

VARGA
And more, my dear. Which is what I wanted to talk to your husband about. Broadening our partnership — or A-broadening it, if you'll excuse the pun.

STELLA
Partnership?

EMMIT
He's — exaggeratin. We have — some dealin's, more in the realm of finance.

VARGA
You're right. Can't be broadcasting our intentions.
(to Stella)
Your husband, madam, is a consummate businessman. A true professional. I learn something from him every day anew.

He finishes off the meal, takes the briefcase from the floor, lays it across his lap. He unlocks it, pulls out a sheaf of papers.

VARGA (CONT'D)
Now I brought the contracts you asked me to draw up, if you want to review them.

He hands Emmit the sheaf. Emmit looks at them, confused.

VARGA (CONT'D)
(to Stella)
And if I might be so forward, missus, as to ask for the location of your W.C.

STELLA
Our what?

EMMIT
He means the crapper.

STELLA
Emmit!
(to Varga)
It's just down the hall on the right-hand side.

At the same time, Varga makes Emmit into an experiment, pushing him to transcend human emotions like love and empathy and become a true capitalist. Money, he suggests, is both real and unreal. *Where exactly is the money you keep in the bank?* The fact is, the most accurate way to think about money is the way you think of God. An abstract idea, both everywhere and nowhere. We take comfort in the idea that even though we can't see "him" he connects us, makes us real.

Why, asks Varga, is it acceptable to wage war for God and not for the almighty dollar? As Stalin once said, *The death of one man is a tragedy. The death of a million is a statistic.* This is who Varga is, a sophist who uses words to seduce. But deep down he is a man without belief. The true capitalist, after all, bets both for something and against it at the same time.

In Varga's mind, Emmit was his best self when (as a teenager) he tricked his younger brother, Ray, into trading a stamp collection for a Corvette. This was an act of pure capitalism. Varga pushes Emmit (who prides himself on being a family man, who has convinced himself that he is a good brother despite this original sin) to renounce his feelings of shame and regret. *Stop trying to be a good man*, he says, *and be a Great One.*

INT. OFFICE. EMMIT'S HOUSE—NIGHT

Varga sniffs the air.

VARGA (CONT'D)
Why does it smell like an unflushed toilet in here?

EMMIT
We had a — there was an incident.

Varga stops at the photo of the donkey, glass cleaned of graffiti.

VARGA
Is this where you hung it?

EMMIT
What?

VARGA
The stamp. The famed Two Penny Red, U.S. A misprint, if I'm not mistaken. The two was backwards.

EMMIT
How do you —

VARGA
It's very Old Testament really. This feud between you and Raymond.

CUT TO:
INT. BIG RIG. ST. CLOUD, MN—DAY
(FLASHBACK)

Varga sits at his computer. On-screen is Emmit's FACEBOOK page. Likes and dislikes. Family photos. Pictures from the anniversary party.

VARGA (O.S.)
Did you know there are twenty-five chapters in the book of Genesis that refer to the feuds of brothers. Cain and Abel most famously.

ON-SCREEN

We see the family tree, friendly postings, emoticons. We see a SCOWLING PHOTO of RAY, click the link.

VARGA (CONT'D)
Joseph was betrayed by his brothers, and sold into slavery. Don't forget the sons of Issac: *And my brother Esau was a hairy man, but I am a smooth man.*

Varga studies his prey online. We see Ray and his car, a hunting trip with parole buddies. This is what we do now—we display ourselves to friends and strangers alike—like sheep posting their grazing route to make life easier for the wolves.

CUT TO:
INT. STUDY. EMMIT'S HOUSE. EDEN PRAIRIE, MN—NIGHT

Varga faces Emmit.

VARGA
Then not another peep. Corinthians. Leviticus. You'd think all the brothers of history had worked things out — but of course we both know that's not true.

EMMIT
Look, pal. I don't know what you're —
or how — private matters between me
and —

VARGA
I hear things. I hear them because I listen.
I see them because I watch.

Beat. Emmit realizes what he's saying.

VARGA (CONT'D)
Phone calls, emails.

BACK TO THE TRUCK

Varga sits at the table, a cigarette burning,
headphones on. We hear a phone
conversation.

EMMIT (O.S.)
What's cookin?

SY (O.S.)
Ya need ta come down here.

EMMIT (O.S.)
Nine o'clock at night, isn't it?

SY (O.S.)
The number. Clicks and buzzers. He came.

EMMIT (O.S.)
Who?

SY (O.S.)
The fella from the —

EMMIT (O.S.)
Ermentraub?

SY (O.S.)
*No. Different fella. Don't wanna say too
much on the phone. Just — ya better come
down here.*

BACK TO EMMIT'S STUDY

Emmit is horrified.

VARGA
You can't be too careful is my motto. See,
I have big plans for us, Emmit.

Emmit isn't used to this, being prey. He's
always been the wolf. He's past the anger
stage now and on to bargaining, desperation.

EMMIT
Can't I just give the money back?

VARGA
I'm sorry. You're in the pan, my friend.
And you know where you go when you
leave the pan.

EMMIT
The — (pan)?

VARGA
The frying pan. You know where you go
when you leave?

EMMIT
Into the fire?

VARGA
They're coming. Pitchfork peasants
with murder in their eyes. And me, your
guardian angel. Which is why I've been
to Chase this morning. They've agreed to
increase your line of credit by five million
dollars.

EMMIT
How —

VARGA
By acting as your agent. Your partner.

Varga pats the stack of documents on the
desk.

VARGA (CONT'D)
Those are some of the papers you need
to sign. I've studied your books. Action
item one: you're not just in the parking lot
business anymore.

EMMIT
What business am I in?

VARGA
The billionaire business.

Beat. We see the seductiveness of the idea hit
Emmit. To become a *billionaire*.

VARGA (CONT'D)
But first, you need to tell me — is your
brother gonna be a problem?

EMMIT
Ray? No. He's — it's just — a dumb rivalry.

VARGA
And the girl?

EMMIT
I don't — I mean, he's — honestly? — a
loser — so what else could she be?

Beat. Varga thinks about that. Emmit studies
him. One last fear gnaws at him.

SY FELTZ, emmit's right-hand man at Stussy Lots Ltd., is on the other
shoulder, trying to keep Emmit grounded. Emmit is torn, but ultimately
decides that he and Sy need to extricate themselves from Varga's orbit. So
they hatch a plan to sell the company. The trick is to do it in secret. Because if
Varga finds out, he will come for their heads.

INT. WALK IN CLOSET. EMMIT'S HOUSE—
CONTINUOUS

Emmit sits on the floor of the closet, among
his wife's clothes.

SY
Emmit?

EMMIT
She left.

SY
Did you sign partnership papers? Did you
make Varga a partner? In our firm?

EMMIT
I didn't think it was possible. The evil of
this man. A brother. My brother.

SY
He's in my office. He put his schvantz in
the mug Esther gave me. I had to throw it
away.

Emmit stands, comes at Sy.

EMMIT
You said you were gonna fix this. You
swore he'd go away.

SY
Enough about your stupid brother. We're
in trouble here. This is a — enemies are at
the gates. Inside the gates — fornicating
with our cookware.

Emmit studies him with disdain.

EMMIT
What is the point of you?

SY
What?

EMMIT
The point. What is the point of you?
You're supposed to be a fixer. But
nothing's fixed. Everything's broken.

Sy is stunned. The idea that this is all his fault.

EMMIT (CONT'D)
They sent my wife a sex tape.

SY
Why would your wife wanna watch yer
brother have sex?

EMMIT
Not him, dummy. Me. Ray with a wig,
pretendin — and he shaved his mustache,
he and his crook whore. You were
supposed to stop them.

SY
I —

EMMIT
And don't come in here whining about —

(mimicking)
— we're in trouble. Who's the one who
found Ermentraub? The go-between,
which led to Varga. Where was the
diligence? The due diligence?

Sy is on his heels now.

SY
You said — I wanted to — go deeper, but
you said —

EMMIT
Enemies at the gates. Who let 'em in?

SY
I never — You need to — unchain me — if
I was free? — my hands? — I could — yer
brother wouldn't bother us again. That's
fer sure.

EMMIT
It's the Delilah, this — floozy — pushing
him, putting ideas in his head. And now
— they think I'm — my family. Some kinda
— when all I ever did was — and there's,
look at me — I have good inside. A good
person.

SY
Course you do. Think of the children —
the lives you help.

EMMIT
I'm not some — weakling, can't control
his — twenty-five years and never once
did I look at a woman sideways. Sit-downs
with the door open. Professional, always.

SY
You're a model. A role model. I look up to
you. Everyone I know.

EMMIT
Well, you need to fix this. Whatever it
takes.

Beat. Sy considers that.

SY
Shackles off?

EMMIT
And throw away the key.

SCREEN TIME AKA THE END OF MINNESOTA NICE. As we've discussed, we are at our most real when we are together—colliding. What, then, to make of the latest development in human affairs? The virtual community, the social network, the "friends" we collect online. These screen-based interactions promise to bring us closer together, while actually pushing us further apart, making us less real. This is the danger of the modern world. We are replacing real community with online substitutes that trick people into thinking they're connected to more people, when in reality they're less connected to anyone.

At the same time, we will begin to suggest that Minnesota Nice itself is in danger of being destroyed. That what made this isolated community unique, its togetherness, is being eroded by the outside world.

INT. EMMIT'S OFFICE. STUSSY LOTS, LTD.—
CONTINUOUS

Emmit is at his desk, reading the paper. He looks up as Sy enters.

EMMIT STUSSY
Did you see this bullshit in the paper? Some old-timer in the country — they push in his door, tie him up. He runs a general store and some hopped-up junky thinks he takes the register money home.

(reads)
Ennis Stussy. Eighty-two years old.

Beat. *Will he make the connection?* No. He lays the paper down.

                    EMMIT
It's not the Minnesota I grew up in. I'll tell you that.

                    SY
It's a tragedy.

A long beat.

                    EMMIT
Did you — need somethin?

                    SY
Oh. Uh, there's a — may be a problem. Not sure yet. Just, uh —

He looks around warily, then comes in, closes the door.

                    SY (CONT'D)
                    (lowers his voice)
— this Varga fella. I got a call from the Oakbridge lot.

                    EMMIT
The raised one?

                    SY
No. Ground lot under the highway. Doesn't get a lot of traffic.

                    EMMIT
Right. Why'd we buy that one again?

                    SY FELTZ
Sprawl-wise you thought it'd be a good investment long term. Maybe turn it into condos one day.

                    EMMIT
Right. We should talk to Stan Grossman about that. Test the waters.

                    SY
That's — yeah, I'll make a note.
                    (beat)
Anyway, seems there's a big rig parked there now.

                    EMMIT
On the lot?

                    SY
Mmmm-hhmmm.

                    EMMIT
That's against code.

                    SY
Well, okay — there's that too. But more, uh, to the point — what's in it? And I'm a little troubled by the escalation. Money loaned is one thing. But this — a truck full of — well it could be anything. Booze, guns. The kinda demeanor this fella has.

Beat. Emmit has a dawning realization.

                    EMMIT
You think maybe it's —
                    (beat)
— I mean, I don't even wanna say it out loud.

                    SY
Slave girls?

                    EMMIT
What? No. I was gonna say drugs. You think it's slave girls?

                    SY
                    (backpedaling)
No. I mean — I saw this *Frontline* about — they get these girls from possibly Taiwan or the Ukraine and — like an ad in the paper situation — *models wanted* — and then — I mean, somehow they smuggle 'em over here and turn 'em out, as like prostitutes, under you don't even wanna think what conditions.

                    EMMIT
In trucks though?

                    SY
Well, I don't know about the logistics, vis-à-vis workplace, but as you said — some things you don't even wanna say out loud. Which — I mean, he's capable, this Varga fella, don't ya think? Just from the one meeting.

Beat. Emmit nods. This Varga fella is a bad
seed for sure.

> EMMIT
> We should probably drive over there, take
> a look.

> SY
> Or — and this is the other way to go —
> not.
> > (off Emmit)
> See, I'm thinkin about deniability. What
> they call *plausible*. Cause, if we — look, if
> Irv's right and we —
> > (mouths *look*)
> — then we know. Which, in a court a
> law —

> EMMIT
> Got it. Yer — that's — good thinkin.
> > (beat)
> So what do we —

> SY
> I think we gotta wait and see what Irv
> turns up. Then, whatever dirt, we use to
> extricate ourselves overall.

Beat. Emmit sighs.

> EMMIT
> Eighty-two. They tied him to a chair, glued
> his nose and mouth shut.

> SY
> > (shakes his head)
> What's this world comin to?

For example, Gloria's one-room police station is being absorbed by the larger
county force (run by Sheriff **MOE DAMMICK**). This big-city bully, the enemy
of civility, is a man who punches down. For Gloria, who—like all the people of
the region—avoids confrontation at all costs, it will take time and pressure to
build the will to confront her boss.

   This you see, is Gloria's real fight. She is fighting for a vanishing way of life,
the idea that we are stronger together than apart.

INT. BAR. ST. CLOUD, MN—NIGHT

Gloria is drinking at the bar in her civvies. Winnie comes in, also wearing civilian clothes.

> WINNIE
> Reinforcements have arrived.

> GLORIA
> Whiskey or beer?

> WINNIE
> Well — not s'posed ta be drinkin durin ovulation, but at the same time — if I have to stare that thing in the eye one more time sober, I may jump outta window, so —
> > (to the bartender)
> Moscow Mule and make it ornery.

She hangs her jacket on the back of the chair, sits.

> GLORIA
> Still punchin the clock, huh?

> WINNIE
> With all the romance a two lumberjacks choppin wood. Thank god fer KY. So — when ya called — well, can't say I was sorry.

Winnie's drink arrives. She sips it. It's strong.

> WINNIE (CONT'D)
> Hoo-ee. A couple a these, I might just sing that thing a song.

She raises her glass. Gloria raises hers.

> WINNIE (CONT'D)
> To showin up and fightin back.

They clink glasses, drink.

> GLORIA
> Except —
> > (beat)
> — it's over. The good guys lost.

> WINNIE
> Fer the present, but we all know Jesus wins in the end.

> GLORIA
> I'll drink to that.

She does. Beat.

> GLORIA (CONT'D)
> Ya know, before ya got here I was thinkin — see Ennis — my stepfather — he wrote this book. A lotta books actually. Before

he changed his name to the name on a toilet.

WINNIE
The name on a —

GLORIA
Toilet. He was somebody different. Thaddeus Mobley. Outta Spokane. And he wrote, like I said, these space books, made up, I mean — and I read one — *The Planet Wyh* with the H at the end. And it was about this — android, I guess you'd call it — who — his master died and he wandered the universe alone for two million years.

WINNIE
Jeez.

GLORIA
Yeah, and all he could say was — *I can help* — but he couldn't, or at least he never did. But he kept on sayin it. *I can help.* And he kept failin.

WINNIE
Fer two million years.

Gloria nods.

GLORIA
Which is — if ya had ta define it — the way I feel most days.

WINNIE
Come on now.

GLORIA
And the other days — if I'm bein honest — what I feel is — invisible. Or, not invisible, but *unreal*. Does that make sense?

WINNIE
No, ma'am.

GLORIA
Well, there's the fact that automatic doors don't open fer me, see — and the sensors on like the sink or the soap dispenser never sense me. And when I make a phone call — no one can ever hear me. So I got this theory — in private — that I don't

actually exist.

Beat. Winnie studies her, then reaches out with her pointer finger and pokes Gloria. She's clearly real.

GLORIA (CONT'D)
Right.

Beat. They drink for a minute.

WINNIE
I got a whole speech I could make.

GLORIA
Please don't.

WINNIE
But here's what I think you need.

She turns on her stool.

WINNIE (CONT'D)
Stand up.

GLORIA
Why?

WINNIE
I wanna show you somethin.

Gloria stands. Winnie stands.

GLORIA
What?

Winnie steps up and HUGS HER, wraps her arms around Gloria and squeezes. A bear hug. At first Gloria resists, but then she slumps, lets herself be hugged. And then she lifts her arms and hugs Winnie back.

After a long beat, Winnie lets go, steps back.

WINNIE
Okay?

Gloria nods. Maybe she cries a little bit.

WINNIE (CONT'D)
Good. Now better you go ta the ladies', clean yerself up. We got some heavy drinkin ta do and I can't have people thinkin I forced ya.

Gloria nods.

> GLORIA
> Thanks.

> WINNIE
> Please. We got the bond a the uniform.
> Plus I like ya.

> GLORIA
> I like you too.

She goes to the ladies'.

> CUT TO:

INT. BATHROOM. BAR—MOMENTS LATER

Gloria enters. She goes to the sink.

> ANGLE ON THE SINK

The faucet and soap dispenser have automatic
sensors.

> ANGLE ON GLORIA

Just her luck.

> GLORIA
> Great.

She thinks about walking out, but then puts
her hand under the faucet.

> ANGLE ON THE FAUCET

as water pours out, just as it was designed.

> CLOSE UP ON GLORIA

What the heck? She tries the soap dispenser.

> ANGLE ON THE DISPENSER

as soap falls into her hand.

> ANGLE ON THE SINK

as Gloria puts her hands under the stream.

INT. DHS INTERVIEW ROOM. JFK AIRPORT, NEW YORK—DAY

We are BEHIND A MAN, facing the DOOR. There is a CLOCK on the wall beside it. The door opens. Gloria enters. She sits across from the man.

REVEAL: it is V. M. Varga—same sad suit, same tan overcoat (new obviously, but the same). He looks at Gloria without recognition.

> VARGA
> Oh that this was my salvation. A weary traveler, I.

> GLORIA
> Agent Burgle, Department of Homeland Security.

> VARGA
> Ah, the nation-state defending its borders. And me but a simple salesman.

> GLORIA
> Salesman of what, Mr. —

> VARGA
> Rand. Daniel. I sell accounting software.

> GLORIA
> From Brussels. Is that where you live?

> VARGA
> Good lord no. I'm a citizen of the air, madam. Moving, always moving.

She studies him.

> GLORIA
> You don't remember me, do you?

> VARGA
> Surmise.

> (off Gloria)
> Because I haven't greeted you, I don't remember you.

> GLORIA
> Do you?

> VARGA
> We may have met once, in my younger days.

She takes a photograph from a folder, slides it across the table.

ANGLE ON THE PHOTO

It's the surveillance photo from the storage unit elevator, the shot of Varga, vaguely pixelated.

ANGLE ON VARGA

Studying it. If he's intimidated, he doesn't show it.

> VARGA (CONT'D)
> Are you familiar with the Russian saying — *the past is unpredictable?*

> GLORIA
> I'm pretty sure you made that up.

He smiles.

> VARGA
> Possibly. And yet which of us can say with certainty what has occurred — actually occurred — and what is simply, rumor, misinformation, opinion?

> GLORIA
> A photograph is considered proof in a court of law.

VARGA
Photographs can be doctored. One's eyes can be deceived. We see what we believe, not the other way round.

GLORIA
Six people dead — including a state trooper — two hundred million dollars unaccounted for. Those are facts. And you at the heart of the morass. How else am I supposed to see it?

VARGA
(beat)
A man wakes one morning and decides to kill four men over a certain age, all with the same last name.

GLORIA
That didn't happen.

VARGA
And yet if evidence is collected, if confessions are made — if a verdict of guilty is entered in a court of law — then its happening becomes as the rocks and rivers. To argue that it didn't happen is to argue with reality itself.

GLORIA
Did you know Emmit Stussy was murdered? Three months ago. Shot in his own home.

VARGA
(to himself)
Pitchfork peasants.

GLORIA
What?

VARGA
I said, it's a dangerous world for men of standing. Human beings, you see, have no inherent value other than the money they earn. A cat has value, for example, because it provides pleasure to humans. But a deadbeat on welfare? Well, they have negative value. So — ipso facto — Emmit's death is more tragic than the death of a wasteling.

GLORIA
That's — you can't believe that.

VARGA
It's true, whether I believe it or not.

GLORIA
Did you kill him?

VARGA
(amused)
Emmit? From Brussels?

GLORIA
They have phones in Belgium, yeah? Email?
(beat)
Mr. Varga.

VARGA
You're asking if there are phones in Belgium?

Beat. She takes his measure. It's clear he's not going to confess. In fact, he seems to be playing with her. But in her mind Gloria's the one with all the power, and she didn't come all this way to get the run around.

GLORIA
Lemme tell ya what's gonna happen next. Three agents from Homeland Security are gonna put handcuffs on ya and take ya to Rikers, and we're gonna charge ya with felony money laundering and six counts a conspiracy ta commit murder. And then I'm gonna go home ta my son — it's his birthday tomorrow and I promised I'd take him ta the state fair. You ever guess a pig's weight or eat a deep-fried Snickers bar? There's no better way ta spend a Saturday in this, our great American experiment. So while yer eatin mashed potatoes from a box in a dark room, think a me among the amber waves a grain.

Beat. Varga thinks about that. He doesn't seem worried.

VARGA
No.
(leans forward)

That's not what's going to happen next. What's going to happen next is this — in five minutes that door is going to open, and a man you can't argue with is going to tell me I'm free to go. And I will stand from this chair and disappear into the world. So help me God.

                    GLORIA
                  (confident)
         Rikers and Snickers bars. You'll see.

He *tsks*. It's sad really, how hard she's fighting the inevitable.

                    VARGA
         Agent Burgle, Gloria. Trust me. The future is certain, and when it comes you will know without question your place in the world. Until then, we've said all there is to say. Any further debate would be simply wasting our breath — and if there's one thing I can't abide, it's waste. Goodbye.

He sits back, closes his eyes, a man without a care in the world.

                 ANGLE ON GLORIA

She looks at him. Confident in her reality, and yet there is also some doubt.

                 ANGLE ON VARGA

We PUSH on his FACE, the light on it darkening, so that by our closest mark we have echoed Varga's introductory shot.

It's possible that under his breath he's humming Beethoven's *Apassionata*.

                 ANGLE ON GLORIA

We PUSH ON HER as well. The door and clock are visible over her right shoulder. As she studies Varga we PUSH PAST HER and CLOSE ON THE DOOR and the CLOCK.

We move slowly. Any moment now the door will open and one of two things will happen. Varga will be arrested, or he will go free.

But until the door opens, both realities are equally possible. Which you believe will happen—justice or despair—depends on you.

ACCEPTANCE IS THE KEY TO HAPPINESS. In a world where humans and articles obey the same laws, Ray and Emmit are two unstable electrons bound together, volatile, but joined. Each isn't who they are without the other.

Ray and **NIKKI SWANGO** are two weak electrons that bond to make a stronger atom. They are better together than alone.

INT. NIKKI'S APARTMENT. ST. CLOUD, MN—
DAY

Ray lets himself in with a key. THREE GIANT SUITCASES sit by the front door. One is sealed closed with a belt. The window they dropped the air conditioner out of is boarded up.

Nikki stands at the coffee table, where she has four bridge hands dealt out, cards faceup. Nikki circles the table, studying them.

NIKKI
Burt Lurdsman —

RAY
What?

NIKKI
— is the name. His name. The sponsor I told you about. Potential. I'm trying to visualize.

RAY

I, uh — they've got it listed — the initial report — as *accidental*. Maurice. His cause of death. Misadventure by major appliance. Which is, that's good, right?

NIKKI
(focused on the cards)
He's in vacuum cleaners. Invented some kind of — *whatdya* — filter. Out of Bismark. And he's looking for a new team. The Sanduskys got leukemia — one of them, I heard. So he's in the market. Which is — Christmas fer us — potentially.

Ray comes over to her. She's doesn't look up.

RAY
Babe, we gotta — I need you to focus. We're not — we dropped a two-hundred-pound AC on an ex-con — and yeah it looks like the cover-up is workin, but there's a long way to go before we're outta the woods here.

He grabs her shoulders to get her attention. Nikki looks up at him, then frowns, focuses on his face. She sees something she doesn't like, SLAPS HIM.

RAY (CONT'D)
Ow.

Beat. She studies him further, then SLAPS HIM AGAIN.

RAY (CONT'D)
What the hell?

NIKKI
There's somethin wrong with yer chi.

RAY
What's that?

NIKKI
Like yer energy flow.
(studies him, concerned)
Yer all blocked up, babe. We can't have that.

He slumps, dropping whatever façade he's been holding up.

RAY
I'm — I just — I never killed anybody before.

NIKKI
Well, me either. But life's a journey, ya know?

He sits heavily onto the sofa.

RAY
And — I'll be honest — I got some remorse.

NIKKI
Course you do. You're not a heartless killer. You got the soul of a poet.

RAY
I do?

She straddles him on the sofa.

NIKKI
You bet. You're my honey bear.

She runs her hands through his hair, but he can't relax.

RAY
What if they catch us? Ya know what happens to ex–law enforcement in the clink?

NIKKI
They won't catch us. Like you said, it was an accident. And we'll be outta here today. I gave a fake ID to the cops. The apartment's rented under an assumed name. Anybody thinks to follow up and it's just a dead end.

RAY
What about that fella Maurice killed? The other Stussy?

NIKKI
Wasn't he really old?

RAY
So?

NIKKI
Hon, they don't look at those cases as close as the young ones.

RAY
I don't think that's —

NIKKI
Hon. It's just common sense — what with
them bein so close to the grave and all.
Besides, you said yerself, he messed up —
yer man — killed some random geriatric
in the sticks who happened to have the
surname. So even if they wanted ta solve
it, the police, what possible solve is there
— except unfathomable pinheadery?

He studies her, impressed that she can think
so clearly.

RAY
You thought of everything.

She smiles, kisses him.

NIKKI
Thought and action. That's us. The next
Burt Lurdsman Grand National Champions.

They make out a little.

NIKKI (CONT'D)
Don't get any ideas, mister. I'm on my
period.

She plays with the buttons on his shirt.

NIKKI (CONT'D)
Just remember — when the APB fer
Maurice turns up a dead body, you write
Case Closed and file the papers at the
dead letter office.

Beat. He feels better. He grabs her ass.

RAY
Scotty's right. You got a real nutcracker
back there.

She straightens, the mood broken instantly.

NIKKI
Who?

RAY
My boss. We were talkin and —

NIKKI
You talked about my ass with yer boss?

RAY
No. He just — I was usin his computer on
account a vermin ate through my cord,
and he was — he asked if I still had you —
as a con — and I said —

NIKKI
I hate that word. Con. It's so — negative.

She stands, starts collecting the cards from
the table.

RAY
We weren't talkin about yer ass, hon.

She shoves the cards into her purse.

NIKKI
What am I thinkin? We're never gonna
land Burt Lurdsman with yer chi all
blocked like this.

He stands, not knowing how to get her good
mood back—or even clear on what the
problem is.

RAY
Well, okay, how do I unblock it?

NIKKI
We gotta — find some psychic Drano,
or —
(she realizes)
— you know what it is, don't ya? The
blockage? It's yer stupid brother. The
history between you. And how it made
you go crazy and hire a doofus to break
into his house.

RAY
Now, hon. I didn't hire him. I was
blackmailin him.

NIKKI
My point is — this is a blood feud. We
can't be fightin a blood feud while we're
trying to land a big-time sponsor.
(beat, does the math)
We're just gonna hafta do it ourselves.

RAY

Do —

NIKKI

The stamp. Get the stamp back.

RAY

Now hon —

NIKKI

It's either that or make peace with him. Are you willin ta do that? Forgive and forget? Bygones?

ANGLE ON RAY

Beat. It's clear he isn't.

But what is the role of ambition in the life of a particle? What is the role of love? This is the difference between people and electrons. People have a choice as to where they go and what other people they collide with and bond to.

INT. BOWLING ALLEY—NIGHT

Nikki and Wrench limp inside. She zips her warm-up, dirt and leaves in her hair, tries to make herself presentable. They make for a ragged pair.

Wrench is barely upright. Nikki points him to a booth, helps him sit.

ANGLE ON THE BOWLING LANES

We are looking over the empty bar (the "Lebowski shot"). Nikki comes into frame, sits. A BARTENDER comes over (back to us).

BARTENDER

You want shoes?

NIKKI
What?

BARTENDER
Shoes.

NIKKI
No. Just — whiskey. Make it a double. And one fer my friend.

He goes off. Beat. Her breathing slows, the adrenaline of the chase wearing off. We PUSH IN ON HER. Beat. The bartender puts her drink in front of her.

He leaves and we PULL BACK AND TRACK RIGHT to reveal a MAN on the stool next to her.

He is PAUL MARRANE (last seen in Los Angeles in episode 303). He holds up two fingers in a pinching motion.

PAUL MARRANE
(to the bartender)
Just — this much — sherry.

Nikki sips her drink. Paul looks over at her.

PAUL MARRANE (CONT'D)
Tsuris?

She looks at him.

NIKKI
Huh?

PAUL MARRANE
Job sat on his dung heap, covered in boils.

NIKKI
Mister, it's been a long day.

PAUL MARRANE
They're all long. That's the nature of existence. Life is suffering. I think you're beginning to understand that.

She sips her drink.

NIKKI
Amen.

PAUL MARRANE
Can I show you something?

He turns. There is a cardboard box on the bar stool to his left—which we might not see over the bar. He reaches into it and pulls out a KITTEN.

He puts it on the bar between them.

                    NIKKI
Aw.

She picks it up, looks at it. This is exactly what
she needed.

                PAUL MARRANE
Ray is the cat.

                    NIKKI
What?

                PAUL MARRANE
His name. I call him Ray. I know, it's not
really a cat's name, but when I looked at
him that was the name that stuck. But
then this is how it is, I think. Are you
familiar with *Gilgul*? It's Hebrew, a word to
describe how an old soul attaches itself to
a new body.

Nikki puts the cat's face up to hers, looking
into its eyes.

                    NIKKI
Ray?
                    (beat)
Is that you?

The cat looks back, not answering.

                PAUL MARRANE
Unfortunately, some souls cannot find a
body to enter. They become lost. Rabbi
Nachman believed the Jewish victims of
the Massacre of Uman were lost souls.
Seventeen sixty-eight in Ukraine. Untold
thousands killed by the Cossacks, women
and children — their bodies dumped in a
hole and forgotten. When Rabbi Nachman
first visited Uman, he saw the mass
grave and called it a garden. He told his
followers he wanted to be buried there —
the Master of the Field. His soul, he said,
would bind and comfort theirs.
                    (looks around)
Have you been to this place before?

                    NIKKI
The bowling alley?

                PAUL MARRANE
Is that what you see?

His drink arrives. *Cheers.* He sips it.

                PAUL MARRANE (CONT'D)
Hits the spot.
                    (beat)
We all end up here eventually — to be
weighed and judged. As it is now, for you
and your friend. Some thought he should
stay behind, but I convinced them he was
on a better path now.
                    (studies her)
And you —

                    NIKKI
What about me?

                PAUL MARRANE
El nekamot Adonai, El nekamot hofia.

                    NIKKI
I don't —

                PAUL MARRANE
Who will rise for me against the wicked?
Who will take a stand against evildoers?
                    (beat)
Do you need a ride?

                    NIKKI
A —

                PAUL MARRANE
There's a car out front. A green
Volkswagen beetle. This is the universe at
its most ironic. Don't worry. Its sins have
been swept clean. You and your friend
should take it. The keys are under the
mat.

She looks at him, still holding the cat.

                    NIKKI
I — thank you.

                PAUL MARRANE
Don't thank me. Simply deliver a message
when the time comes.

                    NIKKI
A message. To who?

PAUL MARRANE
To the wicked. Tell them — *though thou exalt thyself as the eagle, and though thou set thy nest among the stars, thence will I bring thee down, saith the Lord.*

NIKKI
(trying to get it straight)
Though thou exalt —

She trails off. It's been a long day.

PAUL MARRANE
That's okay. You'll remember.

She stands, still a little dreamy, holding the cat.

PAUL MARRANE (CONT'D)
Ray.
(off her: *what?*)
I'm afraid you'll have to leave the cat.

Beat. She looks the kitten in the eyes again, whispers something to it, then hands it to Paul.

NIKKI
Do me a favor, will ya? When the Gophers play, pour a little beer in a bowl and put it in front of the game.

Paul smiles.

PAUL MARRANE
Lekh lekhah.

Nikki nods.

CUT TO:
EXT. BOWLING ALLEY—DAWN

Nikki and Wrench exit, still limping, but feeling somehow rejuvenated. They cross to a GREEN BEETLE, get in.

The car PULLS AWAY and out of sight. Beat.

THE CAMERA PANS RIGHT and finds YURI as he exits the trees.

CLOSE ON YURI
as he sees the bowling alley, his head bloody.

CUT TO:
INT. BOWLING ALLEY—MOMENTS LATER

The same empty shot of the bar as before. Yuri comes in, sits, addresses the off-screen bartender.

YURI
Napkins.

The bartender enters frame, hands him a stack of cocktail napkins. Yuri holds them to his bleeding ear. We PUSH IN ON HIM.

YURI (CONT'D)
And some Vodka.

Beat. The CAMERA LANDS in a SINGLE. Then the bartender puts the drink in front of Yuri. As before, we PULL OUT AND TRACK RIGHT. As before, there is Paul Marrane.

Yuri sips his vodka, then feels Paul's eyes, looks over. Paul smiles at him.

PAUL MARRANE
Yuri.

Yuri lowers the blood-soaked napkin from his ear.

YURI
Shto takoi?

PAUL MARRANE
You are Yuri Gurka, Cossack of the plains, grandchild of the Wolves Hundred. I have a message for you from Helga Albracht and the Rabbi Nachman.

Yuri blinks at him. He hasn't heard Helga's name in a long time. Then Paul turns and looks straight ahead. Yuri follows his eyes, turns to look.

ANGLE ON A COLD BARREN FIELD

We are CLOSE ON a DARK-HAIRED WOMAN standing amid a crowd of old-world Jews. They are the face of cosmic justice.

A CHRISTMAS SONG begins to play.

The simple electron is its best self simply by being what it is. But people are routinely unsatisfied with who they are and what they have. This is the basis of the tragedy that defines the Stussy brothers. **RAY STUSSY** believes that he has been tricked, that Emmit (in conning him to trade the stamps for the car) has stolen the life he was meant to have.

INT. WEDDING SHOP. ST. CLOUD, MN—DAY

Ray comes out of the dressing room in a tuxedo that is snug on him. He models it for Nikki.

RAY
Whatdya think?

NIKKI
(beat, gently)
A bigger size, don't ya think? Be more comfortable.

He studies himself, nods. The helpful ASSISTANT hovers.

ASSISTANT
We have it in a 44.

NIKKI
We'll try that.

The assistant hurries off. Nikki stands, futzes with Ray's bow tie.

NIKKI (CONT'D)
You're sweatin.

RAY
Just — it's a lotta money — a hundred grand. Are you sure — I mean, maybe if we ask fer less —

NIKKI
Are we worth less? You and me. Our value, I'm sayin. To the world. What makes him rich and us not? Larceny. Your brother stole from you. Your birthright. Like the snake in the garden. And then he built this falsehood. Self-made man my ass.

Ray nods. She makes a lotta sense.

NIKKI (CONT'D)
That business is <u>your</u> business. His mansion is <u>your</u> mansion, on accounta the stamps — what he stole and used to start this empire. What's fair here is complete surrender. We're *compromisin* by asking for a hundred grand. He's gettin off easy.

Ray nods. The assistant comes back with a bigger tuxedo.

ASSISTANT
Here ya go.

Beat. Ray looks at Nikki, then takes the tux and goes back into the dressing room.

ANGLE ON NIKKI
as she studies herself in the mirror, the bride-to-be. Her phone buzzes. She answers it.

NIKKI
You got me.

INTERCUT WITH:
INT. SY'S HUMMER (TRAVELING)—DAY

Sy drives, on the phone.

SY
Congratulations. You're officially the stupidest person alive.

NIKKI
Who is this?

SY
It's Menachem Begin. Who do you think it is? You made a sex tape and gave it straight to the wife.

Beat. Nikki's stomach sinks.

NIKKI
No, we —

SY
You left it on the stoop. Three people live in that house. What did you think was gonna —

Beat. Nikki decides not to play defense.

NIKKI
Tears, were there?

SY
She left and took the mother-in-law. So whatever leverage you think you have —

NIKKI
He's gonna pay.

SY
Fer what? She left.

NIKKI
The way we figure it, that's money owed for start-up fees. Collateral Ray put down as a youth. He's part owner in the enterprise, in other words. And we're not gonna stop till we get what's ours.

SY
(beat)
We should meet. You and me. Hammer out an end to this —

NIKKI
The end is you pay.

SY
She watched the tape, asshole. Asshole. She watched the tape.

NIKKI
So she believes — right now — that her husband slippin dick to a redhead is a true story. Factual. We were askin a hundred grand to keep her from knowing. Now I'm sayin <u>two hundred grand</u> to tell her the other truth.

SY
There is no *other truth*.

NIKKI
You sure about that? We got video evidence, Emmit's screwin his secretary. It's a fact.

SY
It never happened.

NIKKI
That doesn't make it less of a fact. And I'm
sayin, the price of convincin her to the
other truth is two hundred grand.

Beat. Sy struggles to keep control.

SY
Stussy Lot three five zero. One hour.

He hangs up. Nikki pockets her phone,
thinking. Ray comes out of the dressing room.
Nikki turns to him.

NIKKI
Baby. Look at you.

RAY
It's okay?

She slides her arms around him.

NIKKI
It's amazing.

They kiss.

NIKKI (CONT'D)
I gotta do a girl thing. See you at home
later?

RAY
You want me ta — come? Not like I gotta
work.

NIKKI
Yer sweet.

She touches his lips with her finger, exits.

The reality, of course, is that the brothers are fundamentally different people.
Even with the stamps, Ray would never have become the Parking Lot King of
Minnesota, just as without them Emmit would never have become a parole
officer. But it is the nature of Ray to feel gypped, to assign blame to others,
rather than accept it for himself. Just as it is in Emmit's nature to patronize
Ray, to define himself as a self-made man who owes nothing to nobody
(ignoring the fact that he has built his empire on an act of immorality).

INT. RAY'S APARTMENT. ST. CLOUD, MN—
NIGHT

The back door opens. Ray comes in. He goes
into the—

INT. LIVING ROOM. RAY'S APARTMENT. ST.
CLOUD, MN—CONTINUOUS

There on the table is the velvet bag. He grabs
it.

From behind him he HEARS:

EMMIT (O.S.)
You win.

Ray turns. Emmit is sitting in the dark.

EMMIT (CONT'D)
I'm done. Whatever you want, just tell me.

Ray looks around. He's been tricked so many
times he expects a sucker punch.

EMMIT (CONT'D)
I co-signed the mortgage. You think I don't
have the key?

Ray cradles the bag, turning instinctively away
from Emmit.

RAY
I just came fer my money.

Emmit looks at the velvet bag Ray clutches.

EMMIT

A Dalmatian. At the bank. You poured her in the trash. The dog. We got her fer Grace when she was seven. Luverne. Didn't live that long. Car got her. But we'd grown attached.

RAY

I was lookin fer my stamp.

There it is. The ancient struggle.

EMMIT
(beat)

Ya know, I was thinkin about it on the way over. I can't think of a single person that doesn't like me. Except you.

RAY

That's what they say ta yer face.

EMMIT

No, Ray. I'm a fair man. I treat people honestly, help 'em when they're down.

RAY

Them you help.

EMMIT

When have I not helped you, kid? Everything you asked. Co-signin the mortgage, repairs fer the car.

RAY

I'm not less than you. Some child that needs —

EMMIT

Ray, come on. We did this already. We been doin it fer twenty years. Enough.

He reaches next to him, pulls out the framed stamp. He offers it to Ray.

The tragedy that defines *Fargo* in all its forms is one based on self-delusion and an inability to communicate. Jerry Lundegaard could not face the truth of his life, nor could he simply ask for help. Emmit and Ray's feud could be solved if each demanded respect of the other and admitted the truth of who they are, but they can't. And so they are doomed.

ANGLE ON RAY

Here it is, a thing of myth. The journey of his life. He reaches for it, takes it.

ANGLE ON THE STAMP

Framed against black. We can see Ray's reflection in the glass.

EMMIT (CONT'D)
It's finished, okay? Words said in anger. Crimes committed. We've both done things. There's a certain — madness, I think. Brotherhood. Buttons you push in me. That I push in you. Grudges. But I don't want that anymore. All this bad blood. So I'm giving you the stamp.

Beat. We see the sentiment resonate with Ray. He wants this over too. And yet something about what Emmit says gnaws at Ray.

RAY
Well — you're not giving it to me.

EMMIT
No. I am.

It bugs Ray that he has to spell it out.

RAY
You can't gimme what was mine from the start.

Emmit tries to keep the peace.

EMMIT
Okay.

But Ray is getting worked up—the beating Nikki took, a job lost, and now on the run from the law.

RAY
No, that's —

Ray shoves the frame at him, this coveted prize that has become a kind of albatross.

RAY (CONT'D)
Take it.

EMMIT
It's yours.

RAY
I said take it.

But Emmit puts up his hands, like a man surrendering. *I don't want it.*

EMMIT
I don't want it.

RAY
Take the damn stamp.

Ray shoves the frame into Emmit's chest. It hurts.

EMMIT
Stop.

RAY
Take it.

He shoves it at Emmit. But this time Emmit grabs it, shoves it back violently. The frame HITS Ray's chest, FLIPS UP, the GLASS BREAKING.

And in that moment, <u>something happens</u>. As the frame drops, we see BLOOD arc out of Ray's jugular, a piece of glass sticking out of his neck.

Ray, stunned, reaches for his neck, touches the glass.

Emmit stares, frozen in horror.

EMMIT
(weakly)
Don't.

But Ray PULLS OUT THE GLASS. It's like pulling the cork from a bottle. Blood flows out, pours out of him.

Emmit steps back.

EMMIT (CONT'D)
Jesus.

ANGLE ON THE FLOOR

Blood splashes the floor, but Emmit steps out of its reach.

ANGLE ON RAY

The life running out of him. He reaches out for Emmit. *Help me.*

ANGLE ON EMMIT

Terrified, wanting to help, but doing the opposite.

RAY'S MOUTH

Opens and closes like a fish that can't breathe. He drops to his knees. Beat. As Emmit watches, Ray falls forward and lies there,

his body emptying, his breathing becoming shallow, then stopping altogether.

A LONG BEAT

The room settles, becomes still. The CAMERA FINDS EMMIT. He is stuck in place, in shock.

EMMIT (CONT'D)
(quietly)
Ray?

But he doesn't go to Ray. Instead, Emmit forces himself to move, going to the threshold of the living room. He stops and then carefully lifts each foot to check for blood. He doesn't want to leave footprints.

> They are particles who believe they can predict their paths, but who are actually subject to all the same random forces as everyone else.

INT. EMMIT'S CAR (TRAVELING). RURAL, MN—DAY

He stares out at the landscape, lost in thought. Then—

The engine dies, the car slows.

EMMIT
What now?

He steers onto the shoulder, comes to a stop.

CUT TO:
EXT. ROADSIDE. RURAL, MN—CONTINUOUS

Emmit steps out of the car, looks around.

ANGLE ON THE LANDSCAPE

Not a house in sight.

EMMIT
Shit.

EMMIT
takes out his cell phone.

ANGLE ON THE PHONE

No service. It's the last straw.

EMMIT
chucks the phone at the pavement. It smashes. He stamps on it for good measure, taking out all his frustration. In the distance—

A TRUCK
approaches from the same direction Emmit came.

EMMIT
looks up, sees it. He's embarrassed to be caught acting like a crazy person. He waves—*a little help?*

THE TRUCK
pulls in behind the BMW, stops. It's front windshield is tinted.

EMMIT squints at it, some instinct warning him.

The driver door opens. NIKKI SWANGO climbs out. She holds the SAWED-OFF SHOTGUN.

> EMMIT (CONT'D)
> Jesus.

She approaches, the gun half-raised.

> NIKKI
> Are you as low as you can go?

> EMMIT
> What?

> NIKKI
> I asked if ya still feel like you got room ta fall, or whether this is bottom.

Beat. Emmit takes the question seriously.

> EMMIT
> Honestly? If you'd asked me yesterday I'da said I couldn't go lower than locked up in jail — starin at life behind bars or the electric chair — but now here we are today. Lower still.

> NIKKI
> Oh, I been watchin. This Varga fella, he plucked you like a chicken. But he's gone now. So I'm gonna finish the job.

She raises the shotgun. Emmit throws up his hands.

> EMMIT
> Wait, please. I got —

> NIKKI
> What? Kids? People who love you? I don't think that's true anymore. The kind a man who'd poison his best friend, kill his own brother.

> EMMIT
> I didn't — mean to —

> NIKKI
> Oh, ya didn't mean to — see ya later then.

She pretends to turn, then raises the shotgun.

> EMMIT
> At least — let me call my wife.

> NIKKI
> You smashed yer phone.
> (beat)
> He's a kitten now, Ray. In case you were wonderin.

> EMMIT
> He's —

> NIKKI
> I looked in his eyes. My Ray, who never got ta say goodbye. Who you left bleedin on the floor, sadness in his eyes. Yer own brother. What did he ever do except look up ta ya? Ask ta be treated fair?

Beat. Emmit thinks about that.

> EMMIT
> Do it.
> (off her)
> Shoot me. Put me outta my —

She raises the shotgun.

> NIKKI
> (under her breath)
> *Though thou exalt thyself as the eagle — and though thou set thy nest among the stars, thence will I bring thee down, saith the Lord.*

> EMMIT
> What?

> NIKKI
> (louder)

Though thou exalt thyself as the eagle —

ANGLE ON EMMIT
listening. Then he <u>sees something</u> over her shoulder.

          NIKKI (CONT'D)
— and though thou set thy nest among the stars —

ANGLE ON NIKKI

She sees his eyes go past her. It could be a trick, but she can't risk it.

          NIKKI (CONT'D)
— thence will I bring thee down, saith the —

She trails off, glances behind her.

ANGLE ON A POLICE PROWLER
approaching in the distance. Still too far to see what's happening, but getting closer.

ANGLE ON NIKKI

She has a choice to make.

          NIKKI (CONT'D)
Shit.
           (beat)
Get back in yer car. Move!

Emmit opens his car door, gets inside. Nikki hides the sawed-off behind her back, turns to watch the police car approach.

It drives past them, slows, and pulls in <u>ahead of Emmit's car</u>.

ANGLE ON NIKKI

Shit. She keeps her cool, bends slightly and rests the shotgun on the back bumper of Emmit's car, then walks towards the prowler.

THE PROWLER DOOR
opens. OFFICER TERRY CROWLEY steps out. He is a by-the-numbers former Marine, with a wife named Janet and three kids. At night he does those paint-by-number kits to help him relax.

Nikki smiles, makes herself into a beam of white light. Harmless.

          NIKKI (CONT'D)
It's not — we're fine.

          OFFICER CROWLEY
Not a parking lot, folks. The side of the road.

          NIKKI
I know. We were just — it's kind of a long story. But in the end of it, we all go home, so — thanks fer stoppin. It's real Christian of ya.

ANGLE ON CROWLEY

He looks at EMMIT.

ANGLE ON EMMIT

Staring straight ahead, sweating.

ANGLE ON CROWLEY

He can tell something's not right.

          OFFICER CROWLEY
Step away from the car, ma'am.

Beat. Nikki steps back from Emmit's door. Crowley steps forward, raps on the window. Emmit rolls it down.

          EMMIT
Everythin okay, Officer?

          OFFICER CROWLEY
License and registration.

          EMMIT
Of course.

He reaches for the glove box.

          OFFICER CROWLEY
You too, ma'am.

          NIKKI
I've gotta — my purse is in my truck. You want me to —

Emmit hands his license and registration to Crowley.

> EMMIT
> Here ya go.

> OFFICER CROWLEY
> (to Nikki)
> Hold on.

> EMMIT
> It's a lease, registered to the company. But it's my company, so —

Crowley looks at Emmit's papers.

ANGLE ON EMMIT

He glances at Nikki, thinks about saying something.

ANGLE ON NIKKI

She doesn't like how this is playing out. She takes a step backwards, then another.

CROWLEY
looks up, notices.

> OFFICER CROWLEY
> Ma'am — stay put.

> NIKKI
> (another step)
> I'm just — I'll get the license.

She takes another step back. The farther she gets, the bolder Emmit feels.

> EMMIT
> She's —

> OFFICER CROWLEY
> Ma'am — I'm serious.

> EMMIT
> You should — she's got a —

Nikki takes another step. She's almost to the back bumper.

> NIKKI
> This is silly. We're just —

> EMMIT
> — gun.

At the words, Crowley puts a hand on his service revolver, steps away from the car, out into the road, so he can see them both.

> OFFICER CROWLEY
> Sir, get out of the car.

> EMMIT
> No. I'm — she's the one ya should —

Crowley pulls his weapon, points it at Emmit.

> OFFICER CROWLEY
> Outta the car. Now.

Emmit opens the door, puts up his hands, climbs out.

ANGLE ON NIKKI
shuffling back, almost to the rear of the car.

ANGLE ON THE BACK BUMPER

The shotgun resting there.

ANGLE ON NIKKI
weighing the odds, the probabilities.

> OFFICER CROWLEY (CONT'D)
> Ma'am, do not take another step.

ANGLE ON EMMIT

He can feel this going sideways.

> EMMIT
> Listen ta me — she's — I'm harmless.
> She's the — fer Christ sake — shoot her!

ANGLE ON NIKKI

Out of options.

She LUNGES FOR HER WEAPON, as—

CROWLEY turns on her, aiming his service weapon.

> NIKKI
> brings up the shotgun.

ANGLE ON THE SCENE
from across the road (all three cars visible), as the shotgun and pistol fire at the same time. Nikki and the trooper both go down.

A long beat.

CLOSE UP ON EMMIT

He has thrown his hands up to protect himself. We PULL BACK to reveal he is unscathed. He lowers his arms.

ANGLE ON THE TROOPER

dead on the road. We DRIFT ACROSS HIM, FIND NIKKI, her feet towards us, lying on the asphalt. We PUSH IN and find her face. There is a hole in the center of her forehead. Dead, she stares at the sky, unseeing.

ANGLE ON EMMIT

He can't believe it. The shotgun blast should have killed him. How did he escape? It appears his punishment is to bear witness to all the suffering he has caused.

WIDE SHOT OF THE SCENE

As we watch, Emmit climbs into his car. It starts. He drives off.

A TIME-LAPSE SHOT

As we PUSH SLOWLY across the road towards the scene. A PROWLER PULLS IN, then ANOTHER. An AMBULANCE ARRIVES. ANOTHER.

CRIME TAPE IS SET UP. The OFFICER'S BODY is removed on a gurney.

GLORIA'S PROWLER ARRIVES. She gets out, studies the scene.

NIKKI is loaded onto another gurney, loaded into an ambulance. Still we PUSH. The EMERGENCY VEHICLES DRIVE AWAY.

We CLOSE ON GLORIA, alone now, landing in a CLOSE UP. She has solved nothing, helped no one. All she has done is bear witness, like the Android Minsky.

                    GLORIA
          Okay then.

She exits frame.

IN CONVERSATION WITH
MARY ELIZABETH
WINSTEAD

Nikki Swango

NOAH: You and I met for that first season, early on, and it would have been a very different show. But it all worked out for the best, I think.

MARY: Yeah, I know, totally different. I think I was meant for Nikki Swango and was meant to wait.

NOAH: Her name was not yet created but you were born to play her.
   I ran into you at something. I was at this party where I was like, "Why am I at this party?"

MARY: Yeah, they're always like, "It would be good for you to go to this party." Then you end up staying for ten minutes and then leaving. But that was fortuitous that we saw each other. I remember seeing you once before or hearing from you once before when I was on a show. I just remember not being available. I was going to do a cameo or something?

NOAH: Right. In this World War II thing. Weird, fake Ronald Reagan thing for season 2. I'm trying to remember—you got one script or a couple of scripts?

MARY: I got one to begin with and then I got a second one maybe a month later or something. But still well before we went into production.

NOAH: Was the bridge-playing stuff in that first draft you read?

MARY: Yeah, the first draft I read, in terms of Nikki's stuff, stayed the same pretty much.

NOAH: The bridge-playing is really interesting because it wasn't in it originally. You want to show that she's strategist and she's the smart one. And bridge is such a throwback game.

MARY: Yeah, a strategist game.

NOAH: Classic Americana.

MARY: Yeah, it's so perfect for *Fargo*.

NOAH: You and Ewan took lessons, right?

MARY: Yeah, we did. I think we had two lessons or I had one on my own and then one lesson with Ewan McGregor. And then we went and watched one tournament when we first got to Calgary. One of the first things we did there. And you just see that it's so perfect for the *Fargo* world because it is really cutthroat but in a comical way because it's so casual and there's these fold-out plastic chairs and most everyone is over sixty years old.

NOAH: How much do you feel like you knew going into it?

Carol Case *(Series Costume Design, Seasons 1–3)*: It was fun to dress a character like that where the sky is the limit. Other than having to do the action, it was somebody's fantasy really. It was so much fun. And all of her stuff I locally purchased. Most of it wasn't superexpensive high-end fashion stuff. That coat was from the mall.

MARY: I remember we FaceTimed before I read it and you were just preparing me a little bit for the character and the story. I didn't quite know what to expect. As all *Fargo* characters are, she was too complicated to try to fit kind of everything about her into one conversation, especially having not read the script. I think you were trying to make it clear to me that however she seems in the first couple of episodes is not necessarily who she is going to be by the end. And that she is going to go on this really unexpected journey.

NOAH: Did I spoil the Ray demise?

MARY: No, you didn't.

NOAH: It must have been odd. You had those first six hours with Nikki and Ray, and then there was no more Ray, and then very quickly it became a very different show.

MARY: I can't remember when I found out about Ray. I think it was when you, Ewan, and I had dinner and you told us. I really thought the whole show was going to be the Ray and Nikki story and I remember thinking, "What happens to Nikki then?"

NOAH: Yeah, well, she turns out to be the protagonist in the story and in some ways the whole show. She's the underdog. Carrie Coon's character is so steady. But Nikki's the one who gets beaten in a parking lot and ends up on a prison bus.

MARY: I can't say I ever expected the sort of journey she goes on and places she goes to. And how challenging it would be physically.

NOAH: Then we went up there and we made that first hour and it was a lot of you in a Corvette and a little bridge tournament thing and a couple of days in a bathtub basically. And Scoot [McNairy]!

MARY: Yep, that sums up episode one. Scoot was so fantastic. "What-do-ya, stamps" is still one of my favorite lines of anything ever.

NOAH: It's all in the casting right. The writing too, maybe, but the casting goes a long way. And we decided at a certain point that she should be from Chicago I think. Which I think was a really good choice.

MARY: Yeah, it was you who thought of that. At first, I thought, "Oh no, I want a *Fargo* accent." But then once I started working on her, I was having little bit of trouble figuring her out. With the Chicago accent, it suddenly wasn't as difficult anymore.

NOAH: Those hard, flat vowel sounds, they just popped.

MARY: Suddenly, her attitude came alive and it made so much more sense. And I was like, okay, he knows what he's doing—this Noah Hawley.

NOAH: There's some really indelible scenes for me and scenes I wasn't there for the filming of, but love: the dress shop scene, the phone call with Michael Stuhlbarg, and of the other reality.

MARY: I also love that scene because you sort of see her posturing a little bit there. Where she's starting to get a little in over her head and she's going, "Okay, I'm going to take this one step further and I'm going to really go for this." But you see that she's a little unsure if it's really going to work out.

NOAH: That dynamic that is sort of the staple of the story-telling, which is that there are other pieces on the board that she doesn't know about and she's going to collide with. If it was just Emmit versus Ray and it was about getting money out of the factotum lawyer guy, she would get it done, but suddenly who is this now pulling up and suddenly you're in a Siberian gulag with Yuri.

Obviously that beating happens off screen and it was a lot about Michael's reaction to it.

MARY: Oh God, it was so heartbreaking seeing Michael's face.

NOAH: The point of view of the show shifts, and so hopefully, if we do our jobs right, you are rooting for everybody, even David Thewlis at some point or Yuri. So when you put Nikki and Sy together, suddenly you feel empathy for both of them. You thought you were always going to root for her, but maybe . . .

MARY: Right, yeah. How are you going to know where your allegiances are?

NOAH: I think that's part of the fun of the show.

MARY: Well it's definitely part of the fun of playing the characters, to be able to love these people who do terrible things.

NOAH: What was that Ewan experience like? Obviously you try to cast for chemistry, but there is no way of knowing . . .

MARY: With all the seasons, you've been so great at bringing people together who are just really going to click. The whole cast was that way. Everyone was like-minded and similar in our approach to things, and I think Ewan and I were that way from the get-go. We just had so much fun playing these characters.

NOAH: It was fun transforming Ewan into this poor schlep. God was good to him in the height and looks department and to take him to this receding hairline, potbelly place, and yet he's got this impossible girlfriend and this love and she's not playing him. She really loves him.

MARY: And he really became Ray to me. I didn't see the prosthetics and the wig and it was totally just Ray. It was like it was seamless.

NOAH: Then we killed him off and you went a couple of months without being in a scene with Ewan. Until the last scene.

MARY: Then I had to work with Ewan as Emmit. And we both thought it was going to be so weird because we are so used to being Ray and Nikki together. But ultimately, we both loved that scene. I was surprised because I thought it was just going to throw me or something to have to get used to Ewan as Emmit.

NOAH: You were just in a scene with a different guy . . .

MARY: I believed him as Emmit and I had been carrying this hate for this person for this whole season. Wanting to get revenge on this brother and when we did the scene that's just who I saw.

NOAH: And Keith Gordon did such a great job directing that.

MARY: I loved those last couple of episodes. And getting to do that scene with David Thewlis as well was another one of my favorites.

NOAH: The hotel lobby and all the guys in the trench coats. That was a really fun scene to write and I wish I could do it all and I could be there for every moment, but it fills me with such joy to watch the scenes cut together and have trusted the directors to pull it off and to really see it. The brinksmanship. David Thewlis is a master class of nuance.

MARY: The main thing I remember about it was that it was all just so easy. The scripts were so well written, the words are so fun to say, the characters were so fully flushed out and realized, and then you have these actors who are giving you so much to work with and you kind of just have to sit there and just do it. It's so fun.

NOAH: Although the woods scene was not easy, I would imagine.

MARY: No, from a work standpoint, I guess it wasn't always the easiest to do but still so much fun. When are you going to get the opportunity to run through the woods chained to an actor?

NOAH: True. What I was always happy with was defying expectations. The audience thinks that because in season 2 we had Ed and Peggy on the run now we just have Ray and Nikki on the run. And if you think about any brother dying off early, Emmit would be the one. Because it's always the show about the "Lester Nygaard" or "Bill Macy" and it's never the golden boy. That was really unexpected, I think. Then you get into that seventh hour and you grind her down to her lowest point and put her on a prison bus. The audience now is really mad because they think, "Oh, you killed my Ray and now you're sending Nikki to prison and fuck you." And then, no, the beat kicks in and we reveal who Nikki is next to . . .

MARY: It was a great moment. And Nikki in general was a part of subverting expectations, because so many people thought from her initial appearance on the show, "Oh, she's this manipulative person," and I don't think people expected to like her in the end based on this first impression.

NOAH: The femme fatal. And for some reason she's this Chicago parolee but I always heard this New Orleans music for her, so you find that throughout the season of just that joyful sound. But you were out in those woods a lot. I feel like we may still be shooting that eighth hour.

MARY: That was really the longest episodes of television. It went on for weeks and weeks and weeks and the second unit stuff . . .

NOAH: And you weren't dressed for the weather really.

MARY: No. I mean, I did have a lot of layers on and the costume department was amazing in terms of keeping you covered and having heating pads. For the parts we were lying in the snow I'd wear kind of almost like a wetsuit under my sweats. It was intense. I remember reading it and going, "How is this possible to do?"

NOAH: "How are we going to do it in eight days?" The secret is that you do it in fourteen days. And then obviously Russell Harvard is great, but there are challenges to doing scenes at night in the woods with someone who can't hear. You got to get out there and get wet and dirty and climb around.

MARY: I remember in the beginning, there was a few moments of everyone looking at each other going, "Okay, how are we going to make this work?" Because we are all standing there in the middle of the night in the freezing cold weather with this giant action scene and this huge fight where we have to end up decapitating someone. There was this moment of like, "How do we do that?" and then you just start tackling it and doing it and by the end it was so great. Russell and I really bonded through it all. I didn't know sign language, but I picked up a couple things from him. We had to create our own sort of way of communicating. I would help him, especially because he can hear when he has his hearing aid in, but for shooting he had to take it out so when we were shooting he couldn't hear anything. There would be times I would try to tell him something when his face was turned away from me that wouldn't work. So from trial and error we had to find a way to communicate.

NOAH: And then you end up in the bowling alley with a kitten and Ray Wise.

MARY: I love that scene so much!

NOAH: You had no preview of that before you read the script. What was your experience of it?

MARY: I had to read it a couple of times because I didn't know what it meant or what it was supposed to mean. But I came to the conclusion that Nikki and Mr. Wrench had entered some purgatory or state between dying and living. Whatever you want to call it. There was this angelic figure and Ray Wise is the person who gets to decide whether you live or die. And she gets to have this existential kind of moment that she doesn't really question. Just, something

magical happened. She's living and she has this real purpose to go on with. I didn't really know if that was the intention exactly or if there was a clear intension.

NOAH: I felt like it was important to have a sense of cosmic justice to say to the audience, "It's okay; in the end, everyone will get what they deserve." Which is really a Coen brothers' staple, that in the end the past will catch up to you if you live long enough. Mr. Wrench, before he met you, probably would have gone to the hot place. But he's okay because he's on a path with you. But when Yuri walks in it's the cosmic justice of the shtetl.

MARY: Also, those elements are obviously Coen brothers-esque, but it just sort of makes the show feel so epic and having elements that are larger than life. It's just another layer.

NOAH: I think that the rules are whatever you make the rules. I thought with the flying saucer I was going to lose the entire audience. I was amazed that I didn't really lose very many people at all when watching it live and over the next few days of hearing feedback. We created this reality in the show and people just went with it. Here I think the episode was so unusual compared to the other ones. And you were in these woods and there was a sense of killers and animal masks and it just worked out. Then of course the episode is not over and suddenly you're back. And that idea that the last time you see Mr. Wrench and Nikki they get in that car and drive away from the alley. Then they are hidden until the next hour when they take the truck.

MARY: That was so great. The whole episode has a heist-y feel about it [that] was so much fun.

NOAH: I think you know the Swango has becomes an epic poem. The heralds of Nikki Swango. Obviously, she meets her end in a random way.

MARY: Right, yeah, which is—I don't know—sort of perfect. It's again that very Coen brothers–esque sort of Shakespearean-esque thing of so close to getting what she has been going after all this time. And then by happenstance . . .

NOAH: She does; strategically, she does beat everybody. But what you can't strategize about is the randomness of life. That's ultimately the thing that you can't plan for is the thing that gets her. And when you are saying, "This is a true story," those are the things you need.

IN CONVERSATION WITH

CARRIE COON

Gloria Burgle

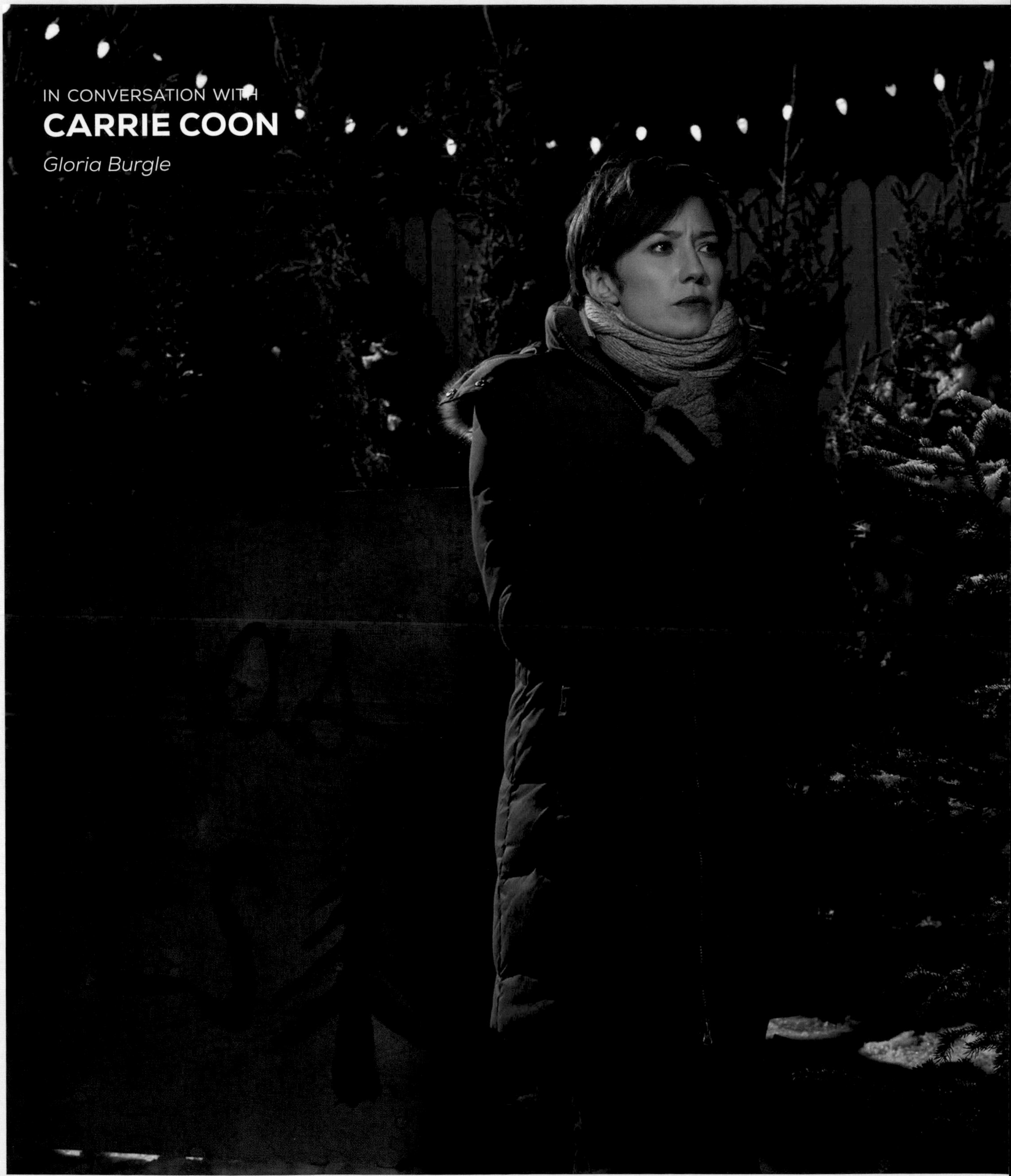

CARRIE: Certainly one of the reasons I said yes to *Fargo* is because of its reputation of having complicated, rounded female character[s]. Which doesn't feel like a cliché to me at all again because it's the identity that the Coen brothers built. Frances McDormand is my John Wayne in so many ways. Which she kind of reprised in *Three Billboards*. It's a legacy that I admire tremendously.

NOAH: And watching Colin Hanks, then Patrick Wilson, and then you go through this awards process, I begin to wonder if it's the uniform that makes it hard to win those things.

CARRIE: I hadn't thought about that. But it makes sense!

NOAH: And it's so funny the clips that they chose at these award shows. Nicole Kidman's crying on the sofa and you're doing this dry procedural beat.

CARRIE: Yeah, so odd! There's nothing flashy about it. And, of course, I was on a show where I did a lot of flashy stuff that no one watched except for critics, but it was really funny and an interesting position to be in.

NOAH: The second year Patrick had a lot of drama to play but certainly for you, between that existential third hour in L.A. and the way the whole show ended, it wasn't this "just the facts, ma'am," or even Frances's level. I mean, in her film she never goes to any of those emotional places because it's not what the film is, but for you, that scene with Winnie in the bar, and with Nikki. All these really big traumatic pieces . . .

CARRIE: They feel very human and grounded. I actually think sometimes TV and film can be very performative and there's a level of indulgence that is asked for. Especially from women. We are expected to cry. I get that direction in a lot of projects: "Can we make it a little more emotional." To me, to play restraint feels more human and more realistic and more resembles the people certainly from that Midwestern *Fargo* ethos.

My people are not emotionally expressive people in Ohio. My family will just sort of stand up a little bit straighter and say, "We'll handle it" if something goes wrong. So, to me, Gloria feels more real than a lot of the things I get asked to play. Which is fun. And restraint is actually a really interesting challenge. Because in some ways it can be really easy to cry. It's something actresses have been doing their whole careers. We have to do it in auditions and we can cry [at] the drop of a pin. But to play against that is so much more interesting. And we had great directors who understood that was what *Fargo* was about and who asked us for that.

NOAH: I know with Jean Smart, who was in the second year and who I'm working with on *Legion*, she did this one scene, and she saw the performance that I chose in the cut, which was not the crying performance. And she challenged me for that choice. But that's the voice of the film and the power of the director or the showrunner. I get to sculpt the performances in post and the trust that you have to put into that, to say "All this great stuff on the cutting room floor. What are you doing to me?"

CARRIE: It's a lesson I had to learn about acting for TV that is so different than theater and so different from film. Film is obviously a lot slower and I feel that there is more calibration of the tone on set while it's happening. But in TV, I had to learn it's about giving a range of choices that then is sculpted out of your control. And I'm grateful for it because it's hard to be objective about your own work anyhow.

NOAH: Then you get to explore it and go, "All right, that was too big, but . . . "

CARRIE: What did I learn and what can I bring into the next take? I remember when I was doing the scene with Winnie in the bar and Keith Gordon, who I've worked with several times on *The Leftovers*, he's a great director, he had us go fully into the most emotional take we could do and then also do the most restrained take we could do and then of course the reality lives somewhere in the middle. Once you have the engine going underneath, it's much easier to then play against the engine, which is much more interesting territory. Most human beings are trying not to cry when they are having these conversations. People don't want to be vulnerable to each other. It's very challenging for them.

I hear about the technology piece more than anything else. People saying, "That happens to me all the time!" My mother always tells me, "Oh, I had a Gloria moment today in the bathroom." It's so funny how connected people felt to that.

NOAH: I know how alienated we are from this technology. In our hotel room last night, my wife took a bath before bed and apparently in those bathtubs there's a dry cycle that comes on. This crazy forced air that's coming out of it. So, we are in bed and the kids are asleep and suddenly this crazy vacuum cleaner noise comes on. So, I go in there, push the button to turn it off, then get back in bed. Then twenty minutes later it comes on again. So, I call down and they say, "Oh, you just have to let it run." First of all, won't it air dry by itself? How is that helping us? By making these devices smarter, we are making ourselves dumber.

A big part of season 3 was how easy it is to change reality and manipulate reality when people stop asking questions and start believing what they want to believe.

CARRIE: Alternative facts are really dangerous and also don't exist.

NOAH: Right. And it was so funny in the writing of this, which I think you and I have talked about before, it was always my goal to explore the opening chyron, "This is a true story" and ask *What the hell does that mean?* And so, all those scenes were in it before we hit this weird election.

CARRIE: Yeah, the world caught up to it strangely.

NOAH: It was always the plan that we would have this Stussy-killing serial killer–like invention. Because it is so patently ridiculous. "Well you've got two dead Stussys, you might as well have a couple more." And then that became as Thewlis said, "If a man pleads guilty and a judge finds it in a court of law, to argue with that is like arguing with reality itself."

CARRIE: Yes, it's so true! And it's terrifying.

NOAH: That scene was your last day, right, you and David?

CARRIE: Yes, it was! And that was a long day. And the thing is there are very few actors I am intimidated by, but David Thewlis is one of them. And it's funny Tracy [Letts, Carrie's husband] jokes that on *The Post* that everybody

was so terrified to be working with Steven Spielberg, Meryl Streep, and Tom Hanks and he was like, "My wife was the only person who wasn't scared."

It's the rare person that can rattle me and David rattles me. I think he's a phenomenal actor. And, of course, all of my nightmares came true. He was word-perfect every take. And was able to play very subtly with the language in the midst of it. I don't think he went up one time. And I found myself feeling insecure and messing up more and not feeling solid on my lines. I pride myself on my preparation—that's pretty much the only control you have in this industry. And I was really nervous and it took me a long time to settle in. I think we ended up shooting it for six hours or something. Poor David—I really wore him out while they were trying to get me there.

NOAH: Hopefully they shot his side first.

CARRIE: I don't think they did. I think he had to support me for hours. And of course, I thought he hated me and wouldn't ever want to work with me again.

NOAH: I don't really think he's capable of that.

CARRIE: I don't think so either. He's really a magnificent person.

NOAH: For someone who plays a lot of villains, he's the least villainous person.

CARRIE: That set was genius too, the way they set it up. It was nice because much like what Ewan and I did with the interrogation scene, what's wonderful about working on *Fargo* is that it is highly verbal and you often get to sit into a scene for a longer time than you do on other shows. And because of the way we were isolated in those rooms, it felt like we were doing a play. It feels like a one-act play. And for me [that] is deeply satisfying because in TV you just don't get that a lot.

NOAH: You had a few scripts? What did you read in the beginning?

CARRIE: I think I had read maybe three to five scripts. It's nice to get a script ahead of time and treat it more like the theater, which is the way I'm used to working.

NOAH: You had asked at a certain point to read the theme document I wrote. Was that helpful for you?

CARRIE: Yeah, I loved it. I always consider myself to be one of those more inside-out preparers. I'm somebody who loves reading. If I was working on a theater show, for example, I would do a lot of research and reading around the thing I was doing. Which is one of the favorite parts about my job, because it invites me to learn about things I don't know about. Having that framework and knowing what your view as the creator of the show is thinking about.

NOAH: Did you show Tracy and go, "Look, this is what real writers do?"

CARRIE: I think I did offer it to him as the pitch document just to say this is the way this is working now. I do make him read a lot of things. Certainly, I make him read a lot of scripts. But he felt the same way as I did. We had seen season 1. We were actually down in Oklahoma settling my mother-in-law's estate. She had died suddenly, we were really depressed, it was the perfect show. It was dark enough, but funny, and that's kind of the space we were all in for a few weeks down there.

NOAH: The most intimidating thing about Billy Bob was that he has an Oscar for screenwriting.

CARRIE: Right, I always forget that.

NOAH: It's not that he's a great actor or any of it. It's that this guy won an Academy Award for writing *Sling Blade*.

CARRIE: That is so funny! That is how they were with Tracy on *The Post*. The writers of *The Post* were just like, "Okay, whatever you want to do, just change it." They were so scared of him, thinking he was judging them all the time. But he knows how hard it is. So, he actually really respects writers and their process.

NOAH: Yeah, he has the ability to just seem effortless.

CARRIE: He's working a lot this year. I'm proud of him.

He's having this weird film career in his fifties, which doesn't usually happen to people. He couldn't get arrested when he was in his twenties out here in L.A.

NOAH: Yeah, I had friends in college where you look at them and you're like, you've got a great face for when you're fifty. You're a character actor.

CARRIE: Yep, that's right. I know I know a lot of women and I'm like just hang in there until you're about thirty-nine. You'll start working.

I wanted to ask you, that scene between Gloria and Winnie, was that something that was sort of inspired by having Olivia in the show or is that something you always intended to happen between them?

NOAH: I'm trying to think, because this year was the least outlined year. The first year I was in the writers' room every day, and we had a 115-page outline and I just wrote that. The second year I was there about 60 percent, so I had about 60 percent of what I could use. And this year I was there about 40 percent and so those last few hours, I knew the big beats and knew, "Okay, this is the one where we create the serial killer." I'd have to look back. But the idea of having these two strong female heroes—originally the idea was that you were this very closed-off person. But Winnie was just an oversharer with a hundred pounds of TP in her drawers, and all that.

CARRIE: I love that meeting. That was one of my favorite scenes. It was a great introduction of a character.

NOAH: And so to reach a point where you finally earned the moment to speak your peace. The whole time, you're like, "I have feelings, I have thoughts, but I'm not going to burden you with them." And you've reached this moment where you're going to show that to her. What I liked is that she said, "There's a whole speech I could make," but she just doesn't make it and instead gives you a hug. And it's nice.

CARRIE: Yeah, that was so nice! It's a sweet scene.

NOAH: So it wasn't one of those landmarks you see way off in the distance. But the closer I got, the more it felt right. Because you know you've lost. And yet I liked her "Jesus always wins in the end" kind of philosophy, which can help to contextualize. It's like, "Oh yeah, they're going to the hot place."

CARRIE: The arc of justice!

EWAN McGREGOR

Emmit and Ray Stussy

Carol Case *(Series Costume Design, Seasons 1–3):* We sort of took the Ray look off some of those country-western singers. That sort of Garth Brooks and the decent western shirt untucked look that you see all over the place. I think it's a common look of men of a certain age that wish they weren't, maybe. I started with that. Emmit was a lot more grays and blues. We kept him a bit more corporate looking. Ray is more in the browns and warmer earth tones.

NOAH: Well, I suppose we have a ski lift to thank for your being in the show, right?

EWAN: Yep, and Nick Grad [co-president of original programming, FX Networks and FX Productions]. I was skiing with my good friend Sasha Alexander and her husband, Edoardo, and our two families. I had never met Nick before, but we were at lunchtime, I guess Sasha is a TV actress and he produced something she was in or knew her. She introduced me to him and we started talking. He asked if I had seen *Fargo*. I said, "No I haven't. People keep telling me it's really good, but I hadn't watched it." He said, "Look, we are doing season 3, and there's two brothers in it. Noah wants them both to be played by the same guy." That I should have a look at seasons 1 and 2 and see what I thought.

NOAH: And then we spoke on the phone once or twice and then I came out, sat down, and sort of walked you through.

EWAN: Yeah, we met at my house and you banged your head on a tree. You remember? You were very embarrassed.

NOAH: I do I remember that. You warned me about it and then I did it. Confidence-inspiring, I'm sure.

EWAN: Doesn't take direction well.

NOAH: Yes, but then I walked you through the story because you probably only read one or two scripts I think?

EWAN: Only one I think. I only read the first one and I signed on only on the power of the first one alone.

NOAH: So I pitched you the arc and that you would lose Ray. I feel like we had that conversation.

EWAN: I don't know that we had that straight on. Maybe you did; of course, you must have done. But I don't think I knew it was going to be so soon.

NOAH: Right, well, it was episode six out of ten, but it felt soon because it went fast.

EWAN: But yes, I had a very bare outline I think. I remember Dearbhla Walsh screwed something up.

NOAH: She just emailed me last night that she won an Irish BAFTA or something for her directing for . . .

EWAN: For our *Fargo*? Good for her. Yeah, she told me when we first had a meeting in my kitchen. She wanted to go through the script. Or no, it was maybe when we were out shooting. She dropped that Widow Goldfarb was in actual fact in on it. And I was like, "Why did you have to tell me?" And, of course, I got the scripts with that in it before we shot the scenes in it anyway. And it wouldn't have mattered, but I felt "Man, I wished I hadn't known that and then I would have been able to play the scene with her not knowing that." You know what I mean.

NOAH: Of course.

EWAN: I tried to reassure myself that had it been a movie, I would have known in advance what was going on. But it was my first experience of that, of not knowing exactly what was going to happen. And the thrill of getting the next episode. I really loved that. It would come in, and as a cast, it's really exciting. You're texting each other, "Fuck, it's here." You might know what's going to happen in it, like I knew Ray was going to die in six, but not the power of what the scene is like.

NOAH: It did seem like if the movie has these archetypes, that you always need to have someone like Marge, and you always need to have someone like Jerry Lundegaard, and you always need to have someone on the real criminal side or even the kind of monstrous side, like Peter Stormare. It

becomes harder to make those archetypes feel original. It felt like Ray is so clearly the hapless loser who is going to be the one who has to make these hard, moral choices, that the moment that we kill him off you go, "Well, no he was the guy. He's the archetype." But no, it's the good-looking brother who has everything who has to live with what he's done. I still think that was the more interesting choice.

EWAN: Oh, for sure. It totally pulled the rug from underneath everyone's feet. I remember when we were watching it weekly, just after six o'clock you'd get emails with people going, "What the fuck?" And honestly, he was so liked on set and by the audience. He was very clearly the crew's favorite. There was no question it was much more on set being Ray, and it was much more fun for the crew when I was Ray. And then when I was Emmit because I had to be in his head a bit more, which was less free.

NOAH: It was hard for me because I loved Ray and Nikki so much. I remember I didn't really want to write episode seven. I didn't enjoy writing it. It was tough. It was sort of the first time that I've ever had that feeling of, "Maybe I did the wrong thing." You know what I mean? Only because I liked them so much.

EWAN: Yeah. It was shocking shooting it. I remember I got really sick. I had a really bad cold and I don't often get sick during a filming of something because I think we have that adrenaline and stuff and you get sick when you've finished something. But it's really odd that when it came to shooting Ray being killed, I just got really badly sick. And I remember it was quite good, because in that scene my voice is so husky as Ray. And then the next day, because we shot Ray that day, and then we came back the following day to shoot Emmit's side of things. And I was in a sort of daze as Emmit because I felt so burly, I just didn't feel well. So, I was sort of cold and shivering and it was perfect for playing that scene.

But I loved it. I loved the scenes when they were together, because it was an incredible experience as an actor to be playing both sides of them. I remember the scenes from both perspectives and it was not odd. I never got confused when I was doing it. My experience of playing the scene as Ray was complete and vice versa. And when I think back to those scenes, like the one out in front of the house in the snow and she's sleeping, I remember it as if I was playing both sides at the same time.

NOAH: That's funny. And then you got to go back and be Ray one more time because we did some additional footage for that episode six.

EWAN: Which totally put me in a way for [*Christopher Robin*] by the way. Every morning I was looking in the mirror with my fucking stupid wig on. Because I then had to keep it really short all through the film. It would have been short for the film in Montreal anyway so it doesn't really matter. It wasn't your fault.

NOAH: No, well, but I seem to remember it being cathartic for you because whatever you ended playing Ray on previously was just some nothing kind of scene.

EWAN: No, I had those lovely scenes with Mary to play, who I was absolutely in love with by that point.

NOAH: Yeah and it needed that opening, she had been beaten in the last episode and you sitting on the stairs while the sun was coming up. Hearing the story from her and getting the gun out of the fridge, or the bullets. And you got your "You betcha."

EWAN: Yeah, that was my favorite one. It was really nice to go back to playing him because I missed him so much, playing him. My experience completely changed after he died because I had less to do. I was like only playing one role. So I ended up having days off and I got back to L.A. more. It was just like doing a normal job suddenly. But also, because of what was happening politically in America with Trump and everything, it was fun to lean into Emmit in that way. He wasn't unenjoyable to play just because Ray was fun, and he was all about being in love. He was a bit clumsy and I always thought quite cool. There's something cool about Ray even besides the bald, fat, and long hair.

NOAH: Other than that.

EWAN: Other than that. But he's right about a lot of things. I liked playing that he was a real dick to people and then you see him with Nikki and he's just like a puppy dog. His whole world is just about this amazing woman, and he can't believe his luck that she's in love with him. But Emmit wasn't unpleasant, but it was fun to lean into that sort of Republican conservatism. It was fun to play that.

NOAH: And those two actors he got to play against also.

EWAN: Oh my God. Fearless [Michael] Stuhlbarg—just amazing. I was lucky all around. I meant it when I got the Golden Globe, it was such a pleasure to work with everyone. There's no Ray without Nikki, it's just all about her and Ray

is all about her. So that wouldn't have happened without Mary. And then with David [Thewlis], listening to him delivering all of that poetry you wrote with him was amazing. I didn't have to act. I was able to be sort of hypnotized by him because Thewlis is such a magician.

NOAH: He thanked me for writing a scene where he ate ice cream on a toilet. He was like, "I never knew this is what I wanted to do in my life, but this scene is my favorite thing." It was a lot of stuff and the roadside—that whole sequence where it was just random luck that the trooper went by and everything. It's beautiful film.

EWAN: Yeah, that car broke down. A mystical breakdown as well, no?

NOAH: No, I feel like she . . .

EWAN: Oh, she did something . . .

NOAH: Right. But then of course I needed you to drive away after, so that's what you did.

EWAN: Yeah, that's what you do. It doesn't have to make sense.

NOAH: In my head *Fargo* is always a tragedy with a happy ending. And here it felt like there was a lot of bittersweet stuff. And for Emmit to go back to his wife and be accepted and have five years go by and you realize he actually made a lot of money and there weren't really consequences for him. But fate caught up with him in the end. But at least he had this beautiful moment before he went, with the pictures on the fridge and everything.

EWAN: Yeah, and then Stuhlbarg's character.

NOAH: Yeah, Sy. I know I felt bad, but I had to do it to him. And then by doing it to him it meant that he wasn't really in the show for the last couple hours. I remember you asked me if I could find a way to give you guys closure with another scene. And I added a hospital scene, but it just didn't feel like it needed to be in the show. I forget, was that Mike Barker directing?

EWAN: It didn't work, did it? And we shot that the day after his father died.

NOAH: Right. Where Michael had to be in the hospital all day. He went on to be in every movie last year.

EWAN: He was in everything! And he was great in all of them.

IN CONVERSATION WITH
DAVID THEWLIS

V. M. Varga

DAVID: I remember I was always asking you, with Varga being so peculiar, whether he was real or not. I remember having suspicions towards the end, towards the last two episodes, that you were going to drop that on us. I mean, possibly his disappearance on the lift, that kind of raised alarm bells. Like, "Oh no, he is going to kill her, he is some kind of shape-shifting spirit." Because you had already done it with Yuri, and with the, I forget his name, the wandering Jew, Paul . . . I want to say Manafort [laughs]. I can't remember the name.

NOAH: Paul Marrane.

DAVID: Oh, Paul Marrane, yeah! You introduced that supernatural element into our series, in the same way you did the UFO element into the second. There's something magical and otherworldly about it. He says several times, "I may not exist." So that was just a few moments where I thought that was maybe the case. But I think I asked you upfront, and you said, "No, he's human, as much as any character played by an actor in a TV series, he's real." And I approached him from a totally real point of view, you know?

NOAH: There's definitely something Faustian about him. He's the demon that shows up to give you everything that you ever wanted, but the price is way too high. There was something to those lines that you had in the last hour about human worth is nothing if you're not earning money, but a cat has value because it gives people pleasure. But people in debt have negative value.

DAVID: Oh, that's right.

NOAH: Just a really dark mind-set about the value of human life.

DAVID: Yeah, and that's what was interesting about playing him, from the first moment when you told me about him when you came to London. Getting my head around him. And then the physical appearance of him where we did the camera tests, and getting the teeth in, and you coming up with the idea of a toothpick. I mean, you just get used to the physicality, right?

What I loved about him most was there was no cliché in him. There's no, "Oh we've seen this before" about him at all. It was a truly—I'd say in my whole career—I'd say the most unique character I've ever played. Without a doubt, nothing comes near. I don't think there's any, in the history of TV or film or book, I've ever seen a character like this, where it's like, "Where the fuck is he coming from? What is his philosophy? And what is he after? And why does he live the way he lives?"

I'm sure—obviously you created him, you wrote him, he's a much clearer character for you, he has to be.

NOAH: I remember sitting down to write that fourth hour, which had the *Peter and the Wolf* introduction, with each character represented by an instrument. And I hadn't planned on it, but I was writing the scene where the waitress brings him all the food, and then I wrote a scene where he was in the bathroom laying out this silk handkerchief on the floor, and then throwing up everything he ate. And I thought, "Oh, that's really interesting, this character . . . "

DAVID: Is that where it came from? I didn't know it came from . . .

NOAH: Exactly. It's just part of the magic of the writing process of . . . you know, he has all this control, and he even has control when he overeats, when he is gluttonous. And so I remember sending you an email, suggesting that he be bulimic, and asking what you thought of it. And you just connected to that idea, and then those awful teeth we had created for you.

DAVID: I loved that, not because it was gimmicky, it never felt like that, it had such a personal connection to me, in terms of something I had come across in my own life. Not just in this, but in a male character—I 've come across it in some women—but it was interesting that I actually knew someone similar to my own age—a man—it's certainly not something not so promulgated amongst men that we get to hear about it. And that particular man that I know also became more useful as well in a way to me, so it was a kind of a nice little bit of serendipity that it reminded me of someone in another way. It's something a little grotesque.

NOAH: The bulimia took this somewhat ethereal character and really grounded him in his body in a way. Where it's like, no matter how elevated our minds may be, our bodies are still these animal bodies with fluids, and as much as we try to transform ourselves into something higher, you know. Everyone's got to shit. So there's something graphic and visceral about that as well.

DAVID: And then into the gums and the blood and the visceral element of his mouth looking like meat, and therefore imagining the smell of his mouth, because it's so, you know . . . I don't think anyone has had such bad teeth in the history of film that's not been a werewolf or a creature. He's got the worst teeth in the history of storytelling! And apart from that, he's also digging metal toothpicks into the gums, I mean that, I just love that, I mean obviously that really struck a chord with everyone.

NOAH: I remember in the next hour, the fifth hour, with the coffee cup, genital scene. That moment where he reveals himself to be an anti-Semite . . .

DAVID: Oh yeah, in the same scene.

NOAH: It's just a shocking, graphic moment. And part of that was because he's a character that's so fun that the audience loves, and he's such an engine of chaos that the audience is having a really good time. So you need to do something to shock them, so that they realize, "No, it's not funny." It's hateful, he's a hateful person on the inside.

DAVID: Especially when your sympathies are so much with Sy at that point, I'd say above everyone at that point. Well, obviously, with Gloria as well. But Sy and Gloria, they still manage to hang on to their dignity at that point.

NOAH: There is something I love, when a story revolves around people being smart and outsmarting each other. And there was something really satisfying about having you be the ultimate strategist, as [a] seemingly indomitable figure of global money. And then here's plucky little Mary, who comes along and outwits you. So there was something so satisfying about writing those last two hours, but certainly that scene of the two of you where you both hide behind trench coats.

DAVID: Yeah, that was fun. No wonder the audience enjoyed it so much, because you don't get to see that kind of beautiful stuff [often], and by then I'm sure they were really rooting for Nikki, and thinking that this is bound to be Varga's downfall. And also of course I love that he survives.

NOAH: It's up to the audience is the thing. "Is he going to get away with it or is Gloria going to win?" is left to the audience. So if you're an optimist, you know . . . I think we're all living through those moments these days of, like, "Is there such a thing as justice anymore? Do facts matter anymore?"

DAVID: That's interesting, because that all started at the beginning, you know, that's what I tell people, I'm still following the story of what's going on in your country so closely. And obviously you'd already started writing about "what is the truth," which is already implicit in Fargo. Is it a true story, is it not a true story, et cetera, et cetera. But you certainly introduced it into my character and made it a major theme. It was all prophetic. A great prophecy, really, because even then in the early days, you couldn't have known what level it's gotten to in the present day. And that's kind of curious given what we're talking about in *Fargo*.

And of course then it went on longer, and the episodes came out, and more episodes delivered. I think it's even more prescient now today, because that sort of seems kind of cute, old, ancient history now, compared to the just tsunami of dishonesty, the story of your country's presidency. I found it fascinating, and it was born, I think, not knowing how to research Varga at the time, and finding myself sat in there in the apartments in Calgary on my days off or my nights off, and I just wasn't able to get much on my cable television, and I just watched a lot of rolling news. And I thought, "Well, I guess this is also fascinating me because it's kind of research. I think Noah's kind of writing about this." Anything written in this era has to be some kind of comment on it, unless it's fantasy or science fiction.

But I felt nothing more so than *Fargo* at that time, and I think it still holds up. And in the future when people see when those episodes were written, when this *Fargo* hit the TV screens, and where America was at that time, it'll always hold water as being a social commentary of that time. And simply in terms of what we're saying about the truth, and what Varga represents as a beacon of a truth, as a demon of the truth, or beyond truth. And what is truth, after all?

NOAH: It's very surreal, because when I set out to figure out what the season was and what the stories would be, it was very much with Kafka in mind and this idea that irony without humor is just violence. And you can't get a more Kafkaesque series of events than what we're living through, and yet there's nothing funny about them. The Russian Cossacks story is my own grandmother's story of fleeing from the Ukraine in 1895 and running from the Cossacks. So all of that stuff was in the story before the election. So it was very eerie to write episodes five through ten, with the introduction of the phrase "alternative facts," et cetera.

DAVID: Yeah, exactly, that happened right as you were doing it.

NOAH: Either you embrace it, and continue to write to it, or you have to decide like, "Is this too topical?" But I just felt like it's the organic nature of the show and I'm just going to follow it through, but certainly the idea that Varga orchestrated this alternate reality in which there is a serial killer of people named Stussy, and found someone to play the part, and confess, and now it's part of the public record, and there's a man in jail, then it's like a fact. And all she has is the truth. It is very unnerving that facts and truth can be different.

DAVID: My daughter's thirteen, and selling the importance of truth and how everything has just turned into chaos when truth is taken away. Because you don't know where you stand, and I just try to stress that to her in all her growing up, and even more so now, for anyone going out into the world. "Why do I have to tell the truth? He's the president and look where he is." And it works, and he's still in power, and it doesn't look like you're going to get him out of it any time soon. No matter what happens with Russia or the porn stars or whatever it may be. He looks like Varga and he's just going to walk away and go, "You can't get me." Because there's always an exit door for him. And any other president before now would have been out a long time ago.

NOAH: Well, Gloria expresses it to her son in that last hour, I think. That there's a violence to realizing the world isn't what you thought it was. And ultimately that is the power that men like Varga have. Yeah, they can physically damage you and kill you, but there's something worse

about undermining every confidence you have in the things that make you feel safe.

I'm trying to think what else. You had that great truck that you lived in.

DAVID: Yeah, I can't pass a truck on the road anymore now without thinking of that. Every time I'm on the motorway or the freeway, and I see a big truck, I'm like, "that feels like home." I was going to say, also talking of Trump, because I don't think it was in the final edit, for whatever reason, but there used to be a picture in there of Kim Jong-un, a little canvas picture on the side of my home. I don't think that made the edit; now I think it was pixelated or Stalin was there or something.

NOAH: Yes. I was asked by lawyers for one of the companies that we made the show for to remove that because I guess they were worried about what happened to Sony happening to them. I thought it was funny that he would have a painting of the "Dear Leader" in his home.

DAVID: And again, even more prescient now. I can imagine Trump has a little picture of him by the bed.

NOAH: Well, look, I've got to get ready and get to set. I want to make a promise to you though, that you won't wander the desert forever. We will find something to do together again. Because I loved every moment.

DAVID: That would be great, mate. And again, there's a new *Fargo* I hear, on the Internet, is that right?

NOAH: There is. We'll probably film it around next winter, the end of next year. I still have to write it all. But you know, I finally have an idea that I think is worthy, and I'll be interested to dive in. You can't do too many, and you can't do them too close together.

BEHIND THE SCENES

SKETCHES BY
CAROL CASE
Series Costume Design, Seasons 1–3

WARREN LITTLEFIELD

Producer

NOAH: We can talk about the origins of *Fargo* a bit, although I feel like people sort of know that story by now. What's perhaps more interesting for us to talk about is what it takes to make the thing every year, that kind of crazy Mac-Gyver-ing that we have to do. And how we ended up on a town that basically made westerns for a budget. A town we instead requests make something epic.

Production-wise, by the second year, we kind of had broken up the work into one producer with the prepping director, and one producer with the shooting director. You tended to be more indoor time than outdoor time, am I right?

WARREN: Yeah, I have pride in researching and recommending to you directors that understand the tone, and get the humor, and then also deliver on the drama. The entire sensibility that you created. While I'm not a stranger to the set, I found that the most rewarding thing, to me, was the strategic planning with the directors, and also of course with Kim Todd. "So how are we going to do this?" Because every single episode that comes from your brain is more than a budget for an FX show that has ever been seen before. So we're ambitious. Particularly when we got to season 2, we were 1979, so every single piece of clothing, every prop, everything in our world was period. And so that just became another level of, "Well, let's see if we can do this."

So I think all of the strategy paid off. Asking: "Will this location serve our needs, what can we do with it, how can we turn it upside down and make it ours?" And I'll use the word 'battle' with our partners. But, as you know, they've been unbelievably there for us, in terms of mounting the vision. Navigating how to get what we needed to bring that vision to life, that's fun for me. I love that process, that war plan, and then going out and being able to execute it. "Yeah, we're going to throw this guy off of the eighth story of a parking structure. Yeah, that seems like fun; yeah, let's do that. And not kill him, even though in the script he will die." That became really a place to live.

Because I think I'm past the point in my life where I'm going to go to a club at night or something—I don't even know if they have them in Calgary—at the end of the day, we know that we're still shooting, and then later on, after we've had a day of scouting, of production planning, of prepping with directors, then that was fun for me, that's when I would show up. I'd wait for the temperature to get significantly below zero, *then* I'd go out and go to set and see how things are going.

NOAH: Right, you don't want to go until it's the worst. I understand.

WARREN: Why make it easy?

NOAH: Famously, in *Wag the Dog*, Dustin Hoffman's character talks about how nobody knows what a producer does. But it has been a real-life lesson for me to learn from you the art of producing. Both the management within the production, the management of the studio and network, our financial partners, the management of the town with agents and lawyers, and scheduling, and then sort of the positioning of the show, publicity-wise. There's a real alchemy to knowing how to put all those pieces together, what battles to fight, when to be the diplomat, when to be the warrior.

WARREN: Thank you, that's quite a compliment. Yeah, I pride myself on that. And I think together, we're a pretty formidable team. Because yes, there are times, where, as you have said with a smile, "You know, he's from New Jersey." And that's where you kind of take a deep breath, you puff up your chest, and you go into battle. And that may be with your partners, that may be about a location, that may be with a director because you know you're headed down a path that you can't get through and you're going to have to make some difficult choices. So I think, as I've often said, management can be with a kick and a hug. And I think both are incredibly important, because we build a family of 250 artists to come together to execute your vision. And they wouldn't be great artists if they didn't have a point of view and they didn't have an agenda to serve. And we need to take the best of their vison and make it into a cohesive one. All that comes back to where you go, "That's what I was hoping to do."

That process is not about hiring terrific, strong, talented people who bring what they bring into their department and to their job, and just letting them go. That's a process where it needs engagement, it needs financial responsibility, or midway through the season, we're out of money. And then the back half of the show would really not look good! And then knowing when we have the ambitions for an episode that opens up and defines who we are for a season, and we're just going to have to go bigger, we're going to have to expand our financial horizons, we're going to break through the budget. We're just going to do more, because that's what it demands to do. The strategizing, the being

in the weeds of those battles, and executing that, it's really, really fun and satisfying when you look at a cut and go, "Yeah, that's working!" Like, that's incredible.

NOAH: Yeah, I think so. And obviously there are ways to get around the big expensive set pieces, because sometimes those are both obligatory and expected, but sometimes you need them, and you have to spend the money to do it.

WARREN: There's Malvo's takedown in "Who Shaves the Barber?" What could've been a four-day shoot of taking down the Kansas City Mob syndicate, taking down that building. That could've been, on a film, a four-day shoot of that entire sequence, and we had a couple of hours. But through the way you conceived it, it became a set piece for season 1, and the way that that was executed was absolutely brilliant. And then the sound design of what happened, as we heard what happened, was actually far more interesting than what we saw. And it was almost like a course in writing and producing. That sequence in season 1 of *Fargo* is something that they study in film school now.

NOAH: Well, that's interesting. And it's the sophistication of what television has become that sound design can now be such an integral part.

WARREN: Yes, of course.

NOAH: And that idea that we stay outside was from the outline stage of that episode, with a diagram in the outline of like, "The camera tracks right, it rises, it says he goes up the stairs, it goes left, he goes up the elevator." The whole story was in there, and then we shot just the parts of it with the guys on the outside, with Key and Peele, and with Billy going into the building. And then one Saturday we sent our VFX editor out there with a still camera and a frozen scissor lift to tile the building.

WARREN: And that particular Saturday was twenty below zero with winds, but the sun was shining, and it was a glorious day for *Fargo*. And lo and behold, spectacular. Ending with the guy being thrown out the plate glass window. I mean, beautiful. Masterful.

NOAH: We're gearing up for season 4 now, and I thought where we are now might be interesting to talk about. "All right, well, we have a script. And we're eight months out, nine months out from prep. What do we do first?"

WARREN: Well, step one is, "Where should this be made?" And of course, in our tour of when we first began with *Fargo*, we considered the Midwest, and realized we would be starting from scratch, that there was no infrastructure whatsoever. So that kind of didn't make sense. And there were really no financial incentives, which made it even tougher. And then we thought, "Well, let's look to the North, to our neighbors to the North." And our trip to Calgary was postponed because Calgary was flooded. Literally, the city was shut down due to massive flooding, and so we continued instead up to . . . where was that location?

NOAH: Winnipeg?

WARREN: Ah yes, "the peg." Which getting to and from made it a scary notion with no actors signed to the series. How would we grab talent from either New York or Los Angeles, and get them out to Winnipeg in the dead of winter? Despite all the incentives that Winnipeg was giving us, that just seemed to not make a lot of sense. And at the end of the day, Calgary provided an alternative. Lots of incentives. As you said, a town that had a lot of pride in the Westerns that they made, and we literally brought them an opportunity to do something they had never done before. And I think our crew really rose to the challenge, they wanted that challenge. And we discovered a lot of really, really talented people, who were wildly excited to not just work in the warm months in Calgary, but to be at work in the dead of winter with us. Truly amazing, and spectacular. So as we look at season 4, we look to America for this very American story, and find the city that best reflects Kansas City in the '50s.

NOAH: And obviously casting becomes a big part of it. We have to look at what are the star roles that will carry over all the hours, what are the big guest roles that might be five or six or seven hours, working our way down to the local gas station clerk, some of whom are my favorite performers in the show.

WARREN: Every single *Fargo* has had local casting that absolutely feels defined, and it allows the audience to just say, "Well, that's real. I'm there, I'm with them." To suspend their disbelief and to absolutely feel like they are in our world.

NOAH: And then I assume once word gets out that we have a script or that we're gearing up to do it again, you start getting phone calls from agents and from actors.

WARREN: It becomes a delightful assault. An assault by every talent agency for actors, where oftentimes they say, "No role is too small. We want to be a part of *Fargo*." And for you, for me, for Rachel Tenner, it's a surge of talent coming

at you. Which is truly wonderful and amazing, and the same is true for directors. That feel, as we first started *Fargo*, we were going for some young, rising, feature star directors, and quickly we understood that they were just intimidated by the Coen name. And despite the fact that we had some very good compliments about your first hour that you had written, they thought it was amazing, they just said, "I can't walk in [the] Coens' shoes."

So the critical decision for us was, "All right, let's not chase rising, young, feature directors." Maybe let's just find someone who understands this sensibility, someone who probably has both comedy and drama on their résumé and is not intimidated by the Coen name and is as excited as you were to take on the mantle and the responsibility of mounting a limited series that's called *Fargo*. And I think Adam Bernstein gave us a really great start in finding where we live. Again, we never turned anyone loose and said, "Yeah, we look forward to seeing the rough cut!" There was a tremendous, tremendous interaction, and engagement, and discussion, hours upon hours. But when it was all said and done, what we got was unique.

I think back to all the doubters who said, "Why would you ever do that? Why would you do that as a series?" And in my life, I have a lot of friends and associates that said, "Hey, you've had some good ideas, you've had some bad ideas, this may be the worst idea you've ever had, to do this! You're going to regret this!" I was like, "You know, possibly. But Noah really, really did a hell of a job, I have a good feeling. We'll see? I guess we're capable of fucking this up, but gosh, so far it feels pretty good!"

NOAH: As I've said, it was such a terrible idea that it was liberating. You figured two people would be watching, and one of them would be hate-watching it. We were very under the radar in a certain way. And obviously in seasons 2 and 3 the radar was very different, and now as we step into this next iteration, it's like childbirth. You try to forget how painful it was to birth the baby, because you have to gear up to do it all over again.

WARREN: Well at the end of season 1, I don't know about you, I got a new tuxedo, and I needed to wear it a lot. And so in a career that I'm very grateful for, for the people I've worked with, the opportunities I've had, it was a rebirth, a chapter for me that became more glorious than anything I had previously done, and wildly, wildly satisfying and exciting to dig down deep and actually produce something. Not just give notes and supervise it and be a suit. But be a snowsuit and make *Fargo* with you.

NOAH: Yeah, it was fun. Let's gear up and do it again.

JOHN LANDGRAF

CEO, FX Network and FX Productions

JOHN: *Fargo* is one of my favorite American films. I think even the idea that one could or should try to make a show based on one of the best American films that's as good as the movie—that's impossible, unheard of. That's not even in the realm of intent. The intent would have been, generally, "How do we take this onetime thing, and translate it into something that we can repeat, episodically, dozens or even hundreds of times, and how do we make it credibly comparable or in the realm of that?"

What was so exhilarating is, first of all, you deconstructed *Fargo* in terms of meaning and intent and technique. And literary technique, and tonal technique. And then you rebuilt it without imitating it, and you wrote something that was *Fargo* and borrowed no single element, not one single element, from the original movie. You had different things that you had created that were serving comparable functions within the story, thematically.

And then you came along and said, "Okay, well, we did that. Now I'm going to do *Fargo* without the fundamental security blanket of the decent, Midwestern female point of view. In fact, there's going to be important women in it, but I'm going to tell where I have a woman in crisis, identity crisis, at the other end of it, who's not *the* villain, but isn't the hero either. And who is a bunch more complicated—and I'm going to now root that crisis in a transformation."

In the third season, essentially what I think you decided is that art has to be honest, it has to respond to the truth as best we understand it in the moment we're living. And the truth right now is that love may prevail, or it may not. And in fact, right now, this notion that the good guys win, is really, really on the ropes. And so you left the ending uncertain or ambiguous. That is a fundamental departure from *Fargo* the movie and from the two prior seasons. And it was very—it's painful for me, on some level, as someone who absolutely loves *Fargo*, loves the movie and the prior two cycles. But it also felt like an honest evolution of understanding that, in fact, if we let things go too haywire, if we don't have any form of law, regulation, if we let money essentially flow without any opposition, and we let it dictate the terms of the world, we're going to find ourselves in a position where even basic truth and decency may not be able to find its way.

NOAH: There's always a moment in *Fargo*, and I don't know if it's literally in the movie, where the worst person in the [show] says, "I'm the victim here." Martin says it, and Kirsten Dunst says it, and certainly Emmit says it. "I'm the

victim here, and all the things I've done are because I'm the victim here." It's the sort of fundamental "up is down," "black is white" illogic that you find in that third year. Even though Gloria knows what reality is, she can't prove it, because the facts have now changed to what society now has "proven" occurred.

I feel like in the end, after she's endured everything, and she's seen everything, she's still sitting in that room going, "You know what I think is going to happen? I think the right thing is going to happen." And there is this certainty to her about it, which I think *is* the happy ending on some level. That she has not become a cynic. So whether that happens or not, whoever walks through the door, I think people should see that as a victory.

JOHN: I think one thing that's interesting to me about *Fargo*, in each cycle, there is a character—a central character—who is fundamentally, spiritually, morally, emotionally healthy. Fundamentally healthy. If anyone was going to turn towards "Hey, I'm the victim here," Carrie's the one. And the fact that she is fundamentally healthy enough to not give up the pursuit of truth, I think it does make her a classic *Fargo* hero.

NOAH: It occurred to me, in thinking about FX, a network born on some level from *The Shield*, a show built around a true antihero, that the first year of *Fargo* arguably fit into that idea. If you looked at Malvo as the sort of driving force, as the antihero. And Lester as hero turned antihero. But then

the second year didn't really fit that model, because the villain was compartmentalized and spread between Mike Milligan and the Gerhardts. And I remember we had a lot of conversations about that second year that it just didn't feel like it was hitting the right notes, or the expected notes, or whatever it was. And I guess I wondered at the time whether that was because on some level, fundamentally, the second year of *Fargo* wasn't really an FX show. That you wouldn't [have] necessarily developed it—if that had been the first year of *Fargo*, would that have been interesting to you?

JOHN: I'll give you an analogy, which is that *The Shield* and *The Wire* came out within months of each other. And at the time, I didn't watch *The Wire*. But I went back and watched it later, and really loved it. And they are in many ways mirror images of each other, in that *The Shield* starts with a central point, which is Vic Mackey. And it tells actually a quite compellingly complicated ecosystemic story that radiates out from the sociopathology of the lead character. And ultimately, there is karmic justice in the world of *The Shield*, which is visited upon that character. Not by any individual, but by the world itself, as it is constructed.

The Wire starts at the spokes of the outer rim of the wheel, and drives back towards the hub. And the hub is not a single individual character; it's the nature of reality itself. And it basically says reality is a manifestation of a complex system which we all play our part in. Once one person exists [in] that part, the system simply deputizes the next person who fills in that role. And so, even though Avon Barksdale's a highly singular character, and a really brilliant piece of writing and acting, Avon Barksdale is not the key to what makes drugs go in Baltimore. Avon Barksdale, he doesn't know it, but he's just a cog in part of a much larger machine, whereas Vic Mackey is a very singular force.

I think fundamentally FX has always been more comfortable with this notion of starting at the hub and spoking outward, as opposed to starting at the wheel and driving inward. And I think the structure of season 2 of *Fargo* is a little bit more like *The Wire*. And also, remember, it took *The Wire* five years to really fully spring the trap on the audience. You wouldn't know from watching season 1 or season 2, or even into season 3, what David Simon's grand design is.

I think the thing with *Fargo* [season 2] was that, first of all, it's very audacious, I think, to try to do something with that many components. And you tell me if this is true: I think you had a sense all along of what you were doing, you believed in it, but you hadn't solved all the narrative and technical challenges that were necessary to do it.

I had, at that point, one really great experience making shows with you. I understood that you were attempting a very, very high-degree-of-difficulty dive. How is it that we were going to have that moment of ignition, where there's a fission or reaction, like it just—boom. Like it just ignited into a thing. And it didn't ignite fully for a long time, and you kept saying, "I know it hasn't. Trust me, I believe it will." And it was thrilling when it did.

NOAH: There's always a lot of ideas that go into the show. The first season was simpler. It really was this idea of Malvo, and civilization, and the animal nature of people. It was really the driving theme of that year. But starting in the second season, the ideas behind the story really exploded. We had the whole Reagan runner, an exploration of that moment in time. We had this idea of "This is the moment in history where all disenfranchised people thought they were going to get a seat at the table," which was represented by Mike Milligan, who is an African American man going, "Why can't I be the boss?" And Jean Smart as the wife going, "Why can't I be the boss?" And even Peggy going, "Why can't I have anything I want, like a man can?" All of those elements went into it, multiple moving pieces, and the fact that the villain had gone from a singular entity to a combination of factors.

JOHN: And don't forget that you were also telling the story of capitalism run amuck in America. And the thing that basically destroyed family business and small enterprise, the conglomerate that basically took over and dispassionately rolled up businesses for scale. You just were happening to tell it through a crime family of multi generations that was losing its purchase.

Fargo as depicted—in the movie and in the first two seasons—is a mythical place to which modernity has not yet come. It's not like they don't have phones or running water. But what they don't have is Internet culture. And we talked about, I think one of the decisions you made really early on is, "Let's do a Fargo that's only a few years in the past," so that it doesn't take place in the literal present, but fundamentally it takes place in the present, and we can't sit there and pretend they don't have the Internet in Minnesota and North Dakota, right?

In season 3, V. M. Varga represents the demonic manifestation of Internet culture. Of the notion of money is just an idea, just symbols that move back and forth. And the notion that therefore all the things that we cherish, the notion of na-

tional borders, the notion of law, the notion of truth, all become debatable in the age of V.M. as a guy who fundamentally doesn't believe in the rule of law, he doesn't believe in truth, he doesn't believe in nations, he doesn't believe in any of that.

NOAH: The idea of greed taken to its final level, divorced of actual physical money, where everything is conceptual. You are who you say you are, and who you need to be in that moment to make that money. He's a predator of a different kind than Malvo, or Mike Milligan, or Dodd, certainly.

JOHN: Including that he doesn't hold a gun. He doesn't beat people. He lives in a symbolic world. And to the extent that that stuff has to be done, it's handled by other people. He's a pure idea.

NOAH: He's able to game everything out, every strategy, every moving piece, but the one thing he doesn't see coming are these Midwestern women, basically, Mary Winstead and Carrie Coon, who somehow managed to just upend everything and turn the tables on him. Because certainly with Mary's character, the one thing that he does not understand is her devotion to this schlub parole office, and why she would seek revenge for this guy. He underestimates her as a strategist, but also just he literally can't comprehend that kind of loyalty.

JOHN: One of my favorite things about season 3, actually, is that we assume that Nikki is—I mean, look, when we meet her, she's a parolee, and seems like a gold-digger on the make, and she's way younger than him, and he's balding, and kind of feels like a loser. He's paunchy, and you kind of assume, on some level, that she's there to get her parole officer on her side. And they kill somebody right away. And then when you discover that, no, actually she really loves him, and she's somebody who ultimately cares about that more than even money. And, by the way, she's capable of matching wits with Varga. She's a really lovely surprise.

NOAH: I talk to writers, and I say, "Look, my goal isn't to make a crime show." There are a lot of things I'm trying to say about these characters, and thematically, et cetera, through the vehicle of a crime show, but I know that in order to do that, it has to be the best crime show on television.

JOHN: But then the question is, how do you take hardboiled fiction, how do you take noir, and turn it into literature? How can it be both? How can it be both a good execution of a compelling genre story, but then also literature on some level?

NOAH: In that first year, we sort of had these moments—the Hasidic family next door to Gus, the woman who takes her clothes off, the meal that Allison Tolman has with this friend of hers who talks about the spiders coming out of her boyfriend's bite on his vacation—there were those sorts of elements where you're like, "Why is this in the story?" And I do think that that fundamental idea, just trying to steer clear of the obvious plot traps, should make something unexpected. The brother, all those elements.

JOHN: Well, they're tall tales. That's the thing. Paul Bunyan isn't a literal character who had a giant, blue ox. There's a mythos, a mythology of the Midwest with these tall tales, and these do connect to that literary genre too, I think.

NOAH: And there's always, in the Coen brothers' work, these elemental figures who kind of blow through these stories, where there's this question of "Are they human or are they some sort of American demon who has always existed?" And that idea with Malvo of "I haven't had a piece like that since the Garden of Eden," or those moments of suggesting that V. M. Varga is a figure who you could see just as easily in 1910 as 2010, they give those stories this universal reach—because the challenges we face and the temptations are not new.

JOHN: And it would be, I think, wildly immodest to suggest that the only enemies or challenges we face are human-made. We face elemental forces too. That's just a reality, and I think that region of the country is harsh. I don't think you'd

live and die in the upper Midwest without understanding that there are elemental forces at work, that are primal, that are above humanity. I think it lends a kind of spiritual modesty to the proceedings when there are elements that are beyond the mechanisms of normal human desire and greed.

NOAH: Well, I don't want to take up too much of your time, but my hope is that we've made something timeless. And that these stories are meant to be watched more than once, and that there are things that you gain from them, cumulatively, from watching them. And what I hoped was true, has proven true, is that there are a lot of people who say to me, "I started with season 2, I started with season 3," and fundamentally, you don't have to watch in any particular order. I remember saying in the pitch, sort of apocryphally, "There could be someone who watches the movie last. 'Oh, this is a really great episode of *Fargo*!'"

JOHN: For me, there was one of my favorite movies called *Fargo*, and now there's four of them. It's just awesome. And it's not the same thing over and over again; you can watch any one of them, or any two of them, or any three of them. They all stand on their own. It's like saying, "Oh, what if we could make more Mozart symphonies? It'd be pretty cool to have around."

NOAH: Yeah, and you just can't repeat yourself, that's why it takes time between them. You don't want to say the same things over and over again. But those elements—that spectrum of good to evil, and human decency and the American experience, and capitalism, and all those things—fundamentally you could make a lot of recipes out of those same ingredients that don't taste the same.

SEASON 4:
A Special Sneak Preview

> OVER BLACK:
>
> We hear --
>
> >   ETHELRIDA (V.O.)
> >   *My history report*, by Ethelrida Pearl Smutny.
>
> MUSIC UP:
>
> >   HARD IN ON:
> >
> >   A CINDER BLOCK WALL
>
> White, non-descript.
>
> We are in --
>
> >   INT. PRINCIPAL'S OFFICE. GROVER CLEVELAND HIGH SCHOOL.
> >   KANSAS CITY, MO - DAY (1950)
>
> A young BIRACIAL GIRL (16) enters frame, as if pushed. This
> is ETHELRIDA PEARL SMUTNY. Her parents (white father, black
> mother) own a mortuary, and so she always smells vaguely of
> formaldehyde. Which, as you would imagine, is not ideal for a
> teenage girl.

It is 1950.

                        ETHELRIDA (V.O.)
            Frederick Douglass, runaway slave, once intoned -- I stand
            before you as a thief and a robber. I stole this head, these
            limbs, this body from my master, and ran off with them.

                REVERSE ON MS. HAGBLOOM

            The Principal's secretary. A heavyset humorless Polish American
            woman. She stares at Ethelrida with disdain.

                        MS. HAGBLOOM
            What'd you do this time?

                ANGLE ON ETHELRIDA

            It's clear she gets dragged to the principal's office a lot.

                        ETHELRIDA
            I been maligned.

                BEHIND HAGBLOOM

            we can see PRINCIPAL CRISCOE through the window of his office.
            He's WHACKING another student's behind with a large paddle.

            Criscoe is a ruddy Irishman with hams for hands. This is how it
            works in the Land of the Free and the Home of the Brave. All of
            us are from somewhere else originally.

                        ETHELRIDA (V.O.)
            My point being, the moment our feet touched American soil we
            were already criminals.

                ANGLE ON PRINCIPAL CRISCOE

            as he comes to his office door, holding the paddle. He's
            sweating, out of breath. He brushes his comb-over into place and
            glowers at Ethelrida, while the beaten student shuffles out,
            crying.

                        PRINCIPAL CRISCOE
            Next.

ACKNOWLEDGMENTS

This series would not have been possible without the faith and support of my family (in size order): Kyle, Guin, and Lev. And thanks to my friends at FX: John Landgraf, Gina Balian, and Eric Schrier. And to Steve Stark and Max Kisby at MGM. Thanks to the producers who worked tirelessly to make the impossible possible: Warren Littlefield, John Cameron, and Kim Todd. Thanks to the actors, who humbled me every day, and the crew, who outworked me. And to Ted Miller, Nancy Etz, John Campisi, Susan Golomb, and Joel McKuin.

And of course to Joel, Ethan, Frances McDormand, Bill Macy, and everyone involved in the making of an American classic.

ABOUT THE AUTHOR

Noah Hawley is an Emmy, Golden Globe, PEN, Critics' Choice, Edgar, and Peabody Award–winning author, screenwriter, and producer. He has published four novels, penned the script for the feature film *Lies and Alibis*, and directed *Lucy in the Sky* starring Natalie Portman. He created, executive produced, and served as showrunner for ABC's *My Generation* and *The Unusuals* and was a writer and producer on the hit series *Bones*. Hawley is currently executive producer, writer, and showrunner on FX's award-winning series *Fargo*, and *Legion* from FX Productions and Marvel Television.